Cost Control of Capital Projects and the Project Cost Management System Requirements

Second Edition

R. Max Wideman, P.Eng
FCSCE., FEIC., FICE., FPMI

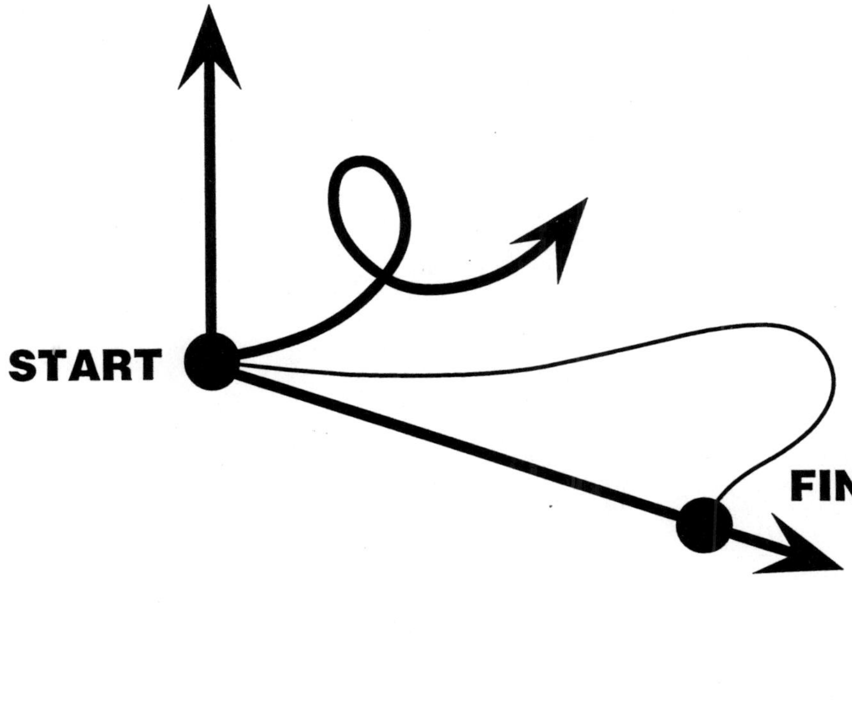

A Handbook for Owners, Architects, Engineers, and all those involved in Project Management of Constructed Facilities

Published by R. Max Wideman
AEW Services
2216 West 21st Avenue
Vancouver, British Columbia, Canada V6L U5
and
BiTech Publishers Ltd.
173 - 11860 Hammersmith Way
Richmond, British Columbia, Canada V7A 5GI

Printed in Canada

First Printing, April 1995
Second Printing, October 1999

Canadian Cataloguing in Publication Data

Wideman, R. Max
Cost control of capital projects and the project cost management system requirements

Includes index.
ISBN 0-921095-35-X

1. Construction industry–Cost control. 2. Building–Cost control. 3. Construction industry–Management. I. Title.

TH435.W52 1995 690'.0681 C95-910389-9

About the Author

R. Max Wideman, P.Eng., is a professional engineer specializing in project management consulting. His experience includes hydroelectric, river, marine, transportation, industrial, institutional, commercial and residential projects. He has also been instrumental in such projects as information systems; social and environmental impact studies; contract, productivity and expropriation claims; and project management audits. He has lectured extensively including Canada, China, Egypt, Iceland, India, Jamaica, Pakistan, the Philippines, Saudi Arabia, the United Kingdom, and the USA.

Mr. Wideman joined the Project Management Institute (PMI), an organization based in Pennsylvania, USA, in 1974 and in 1979 launched the West Coast BC Chapter in British Columbia, Canada. In 1982 he was elected to the International Board of PMI as Vice President Member Services and served as a director for three years. During this time he produced a major upgrade to the Institute's Project Management Body of Knowledge, involving a team of over 80 volunteer members across North America. The report was approved by the PMI Board in 1987.

Mr. Wideman is also author of PMI's Handbooks *A Framework for Project and Program Management Integration* and *Project Risk Management.* In 1985 he was honoured with PMI's Distinguished Contribution to Project Management Award, and in 1986 as PMI Person-of-the-Year. The following year he was elected PMI president, becoming Chairman in 1988. The same year the Association of Professional Engineers and Geoscientists of BC honoured him with their Professional Service Award.

Mr. Wideman is a Fellow of the Canadian Society of Civil Engineering, a Fellow of the Engineering Institute of Canada, a Fellow of the Institution of Civil Engineers (UK) and a Fellow of the Project Management Institute.

The author may be reached at:
AEW Services
2216 West 21st Avenue
Vancouver, BC, Canada
V6L 1J5
Phone/FAX: 604/736-7025
Email: max_wideman@sfu.ca

I have thought that a man of tolerable abilities may work great changes, if he first forms a good plan and makes execution of that same plan his whole study and business.

Benjamin Franklin

Contents

Part 2 Cost Control in the Planning Phases

Part 3 Cost Control in the Producing Phases

Part 4 Practical Application to a Large Construction Project

Appendices

Project Cost Management System - A Definition

The Project Cost Management System (PCMS) is a management tool designed to aid the planning, budgeting, monitoring and control of capital project costs, from concept to commissioning. To the extent that the time value of money has a significant impact on the final cost of a project, the system must also provide for a minimum schedule information input. The PCMS is the central component of any comprehensive project Management Information System.

Preface

Why do capital construction projects turn sour and costs get out of control? It seems largely due to lack of sufficient attention to "thinking the project through," in other words, insufficient planning. Lack of adequate planning is often due to a lack of understanding of the "evolutionary process" of managing a project.

But first, let it be understood that it is impossible to figure out the final cost of a project right from the beginning. It is just as impossible to establish even a reliable estimate of the final cost. At the beginning, sufficient detailed information is simply not available to foresee the future with clarity. Instead, just take one step at a time, each succeeding step with increasing degrees of confidence.

The principles described in this book apply to any size of project.

This is the proper approach to project cost management, indeed, to project management itself. The larger, longer, more complex, or more uncertain the project, the greater should be the number of controlled steps, or stages. With well-defined stages, the principles of effective cost control can be readily applied. This book is organized and based on this concept, the sequential project stages being known as the project life-cycle.

Even so, the chances of satisfactorily arriving at project objectives are slim indeed unless an adequate level of control is exercised. Control, in the project context, implies establishing a plan of what is required, monitoring progress and regularly comparing it with requirements. Most important is the taking of early steps to bring the actual and the plan back into alignment whenever they start to stray apart.

This remarkably simple but powerful idea is typical of any process system with controlling feedback loop. So why do projects get out of control? There are many reasons, but two inherent in the concept outlined above and all too frequently encountered include:

- Lack of sufficient planning in incremental steps to establish what is required
- Lack of ability or willingness to make the required comparisons sufficiently early and to take the necessary corrective action to get the desired result.

The material presented in this book is based on this control-through-life-cycle principle and shows how the pattern changes from planning to producing. The book is intended for both the lay member concerned with project cost control for the first time, as well as the seasoned practitioner seeking to improve performance. It first provides a brief overview of project management control in Part 1. This is followed in Parts 2 and 3 by control in the planning phases and the producing phases respectively. Part 4 describes the practical application of these concepts to a large construction project.

This book's contents provide insights for anyone working with a project team developing and constructing a capital facility.

Central to the control of project cost is a Project Cost Management System (PCMS) to provide the necessary control information to the project's management. The concept of the PCMS is described in Chapter 10, while Appendix A provides a comprehensive computer check list. Other appendices provide additional details including Project Cost Management Techniques in Appendix E and Project Cost Management Terms in Appendix F.

Project management is an exciting world to work in. With sound and effective cost control, it can be very rewarding.

Abbreviations

ACO	Appropriation Change Order
ACWP	Actual Cost of Work Performed
ARR	Appropriation Reconciliation Report
BAC	Budgeted Cost at Completion
BCWP	Budgeted Cost of Work Performed
BCWS	Budgeted Cost of Work Scheduled
CAR	Capital Appropriation Request
CCN	Contemplated Change Notice
CEPR	Commitment/Expenditure Progress Report
CFW	Current Forecast Worksheet
CO	Change Order
CPM	Critical Path Method
CSI	Construction Specifications Institute (Canada)
CV	Cost Variance (at Time Now)
CWIP	Capital Works in Progress
EAC	Estimated Cost at Completion
EFO	Emergency Field Order
ETC	Estimated Cost to Complete
FC	Field Clarification
FFC	Forecast Final Cost (see EAC)
FIS	Financial Information System
FO	Field Order
IDC	Interest During Construction
LOE	Level of Effort
PMIS	Project Management Information System
PCMS	Project Cost Management System
PERT	Project Evaluation and Review Technique
RFQ	Request for Quotation
RFT	Request for Transfer (of funds)
STP	Short Term Plan
SV	Schedule Variance (at Time Now)
SVR	Summary Variance Report
UCI	Uniform Construction Index (U.S.A.)
VAC	Variance at Completion
VM	Value Management
WBS	Work Breakdown Structure

Part 1: Introduction to Project Management Control

CHAPTER 1

A Broader View of Cost Control

1.1 Introduction

A project is a process that, when completed, results in some specific objective or discrete product. A project typically involves an interwoven web of various technical processes that must be coordinated and regulated using project management controls. In case there are any readers who question the need for project control, consider this.

A project is a process resulting in a discrete product.

If a construction project is privately funded but not properly controlled, the money might run out, or the sponsor forced into bankruptcy, before completing the facility. If the project is publicly funded, serious political damage can result from a facility that takes far longer and costs far more than originally advertised. Such projects clutter the landscape. Therefore, project management control must:

- Formulate the project's objectives — and stay with them
- Establish quality and safety standards — and perform within them
- Assess a reasonable completion date — and work toward it
- Figure out realistic project budgets and cash flows — and live within them

In short, the purpose of project control, and cost control in particular, is to give confidence that the organization has the ability to manage the project.

What requires control is planning and management of the work.

So this book is about controlling the costs of capital projects whether those projects are completely new facilities or the upgrading of existing. It provides guidance and recommendations on effective cost management. It does so by outlining the requirements for a Project Cost Management System (PCMS) and the control principles required to support it. Yet the reality is that costs are only a reflection of all the work that must be done on a project. So what requires control is the planning and management of the work.

It is like buying on credit. You cannot save money simply by not paying the bill, though you can and should check the bill to ensure that it is correct. The best opportunity for controlling expenditures comes in deciding what to buy in the first place. Conversely, once work starts the only way to conserve money is in the way the work is done — through productivity and efficiency. There are often significant ways for reducing project costs by improving productivity, so this topic is also discussed.

Once work starts, the only way to conserve money is in the way the work is done.

Once a project gets the go-ahead for implementation, the major part of the cost reflects the options selected during planning and the way they are carried out. Planning and capturing project costs in a way that enables cost control is just one of many vital functions of the project manager and his or her team. Some of these other functions also control the performance of the project. The decision making on the project will largely determine whether costs are really being kept under control.

Therefore, this book would not be complete without at least a brief review of the context of the project cost management function and control issues beyond its realm. These topics will be discussed in the following sections:

In this Chapter:	The Meaning of a "Well-run" Job; Project Boundaries and Resources; Project Life-Cycle;
In Chapter 2	Project Integration Project Processes; and The Makings of Project Success

1.2 The Meaning of a "Well-run" Job

Throughout this book there is a presumption that the job in question is "well run", unless stated otherwise. This needs clarification, as there may be different interpretations of what constitutes a "well-run" job. In the author's view, it means that the whole project runs without interference and without favoring one party over another. Instead, the project is optimized for effectiveness in its planning, and efficiency in its discharge.

A well-run project is one that is optimized for effectiveness in its planning and efficiency in its discharge.

During execution, a well-run job implies that adequate and realistic planning has taken place and the work on site proceeds in a positive cooperative environment. It means that all supporting logistics, such as site services, materials and equipment, match site requirements for the work. This means that optimized crew sizes can maximize their production at least cost all the time. A project that meets requirements and is completed within credible time and cost parameters must surely be perceived as successful. For an owner this would mean that the resulting facility has satisfied the stipulated needs, within reasonable time and cost. For a contractor, it would mean satisfying the owner at a reasonable profit.

Poorly run projects proceed as a voyage of discovery.

In contrast, actual progress on a not-so-well-run project will depart from the plan, or proceed as "a voyage of discovery." The records will reflect lack of understanding of the project's purpose, inadequate planning, or lack of consistent and concerted support. In implementation, there may be wasted labor before sufficient work is available or after the work load has peaked. There may be avoidable rework, lower productivity, higher labor turnover, additional learning costs, added supervision, labor and non-labor related job expenses and overhead, added material storage, handling and wastage, and consequent extended completion.

The author sincerely hopes that the suggestions offered in this book will help to avoid these undesirable features.

1.3 Project Boundaries and Resources

The traditional approach to managing capital projects has focused primarily on getting the project completed on time and within budget. This may have satisfied the accountants but is far from guaranteeing a successful project. The quality and reliability of a truly successful project remain long after the brief euphoria of completing within cost and schedule constraints.

More important are the longer-term perceptions of the project. These days especially, the project manager and the project team need to be very much aware of both the immediate project boundaries and the world

The quality and reliability of a truly successful project remain long after the brief euphoria of completing within cost and schedule.

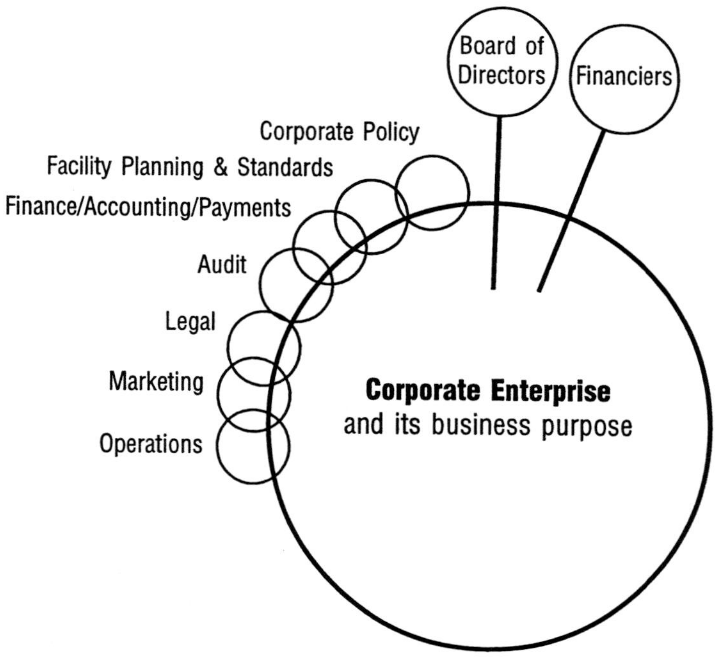

Figure 1-1. Typical Corporate Environment prior to Start of a Facility Project

around it. The "boundaries" discussed in the following sections are the "human" boundaries. To a large extent, the project "content" boundaries, i.e. the project's Scope Statement discussed in Chapter 2, Section 2.1, determine these "human" boundaries.

(a) Within the project's boundaries

The more interfaces, the more complex the environment and the greater the care and effort required to manage the project.

Corporate bodies public and private are responsible for most capital projects. In this setting, boundaries or interfaces are an important part of the project environment. The more interfaces, the more complex the environment and the greater the care and effort required to manage the project. As an example of growth in project complexity, consider the corporation as shown conceptually in Figure 1-1. In Figure 1-2 the same enterprise is at an early project stage when it has identified the need for a project. At this point the project is the responsibility of a sponsor or director and probably a manager working on the concept. The main concerns at this point will be with the project's economic viability and optimizing its financial performance.

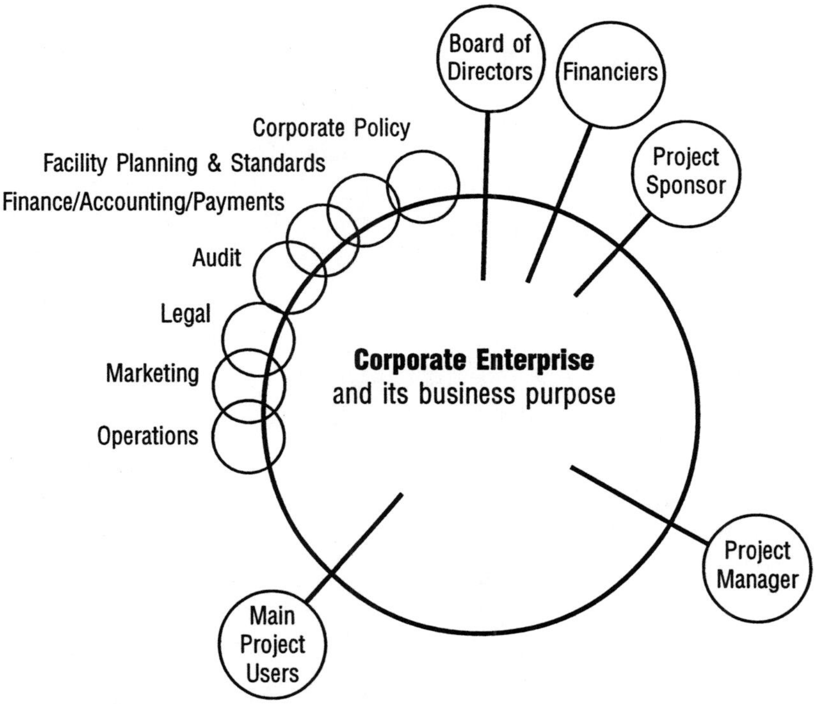

Figure 1-2. Typical Development of a Project

Typically, an enterprise is divided into functional groups who communicate with one another through line or staff relationships. If the enterprise is in the construction business, there may also be a project management functional department. If so, each project will have a project manager assigned for the life of the project. This manager will interface with the

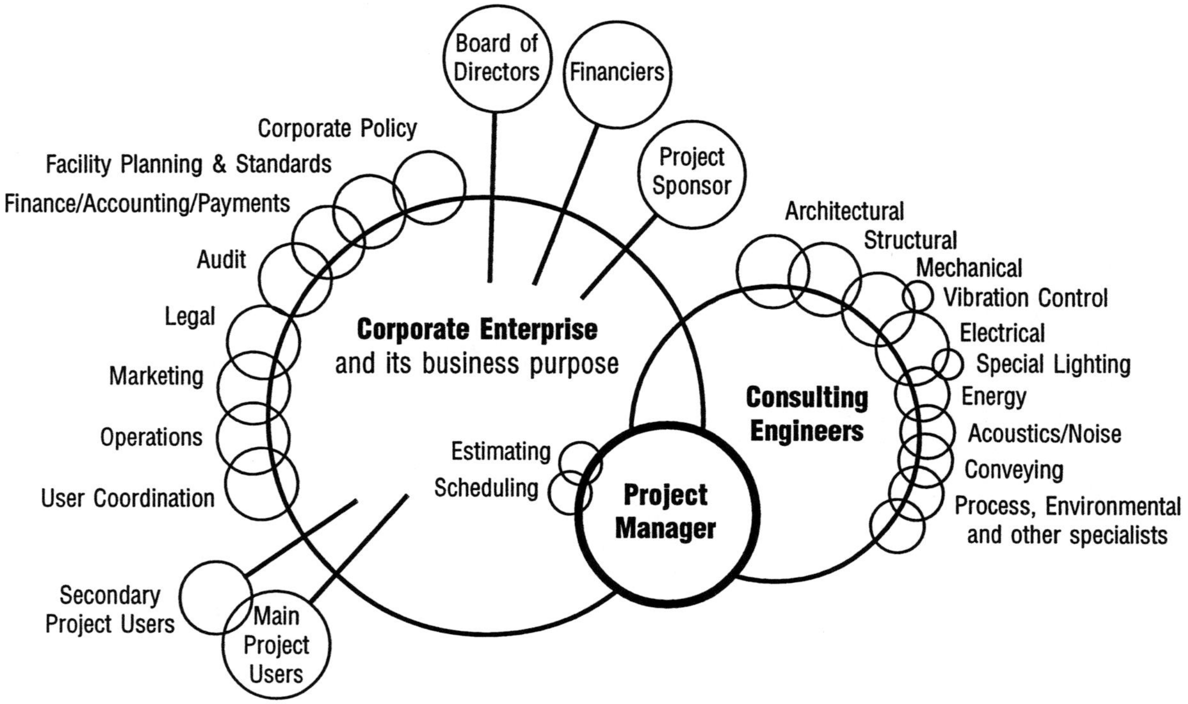

Figure 1-3. Typical Development of a Project Environment - Phase 2: Project Planning

functional groups through formal lines of communication, as well as on an ad hoc and informal basis.

As the project advances, professional consultants will be required and, depending on the type of facility, a large array of expertise may be involved. The project manager may also require assistance with project estimating, scheduling and administration. Figure 1-3 shows these added responsibilities.

It is vital to establish exact boundaries and hence who is responsible for what.

Once the design of the project is developed and approved, it moves into the construction phase. Here, the emphasis shifts to the construction team lead either by one or more general contractors, or a construction manager. Figure 1-4 shows the various skilled trades providing support. At a final stage, the emphasis again returns to the sponsoring enterprise who have to accept, start up and operate the facility.

It will be seen that the group to be managed can become quite large. Almost every party will have some interface with every other. Therefore, it is vital to establish the exact boundaries between each and who is responsible for what. In addition, each person or unit in the group owes allegiance two "bosses", the project manager on the one hand and the "home" department on the other. This relationship is often called a "matrix" structure. It is not easy to manage and requires the project manager to have special skills, the discussion of which is beyond the scope of this book.

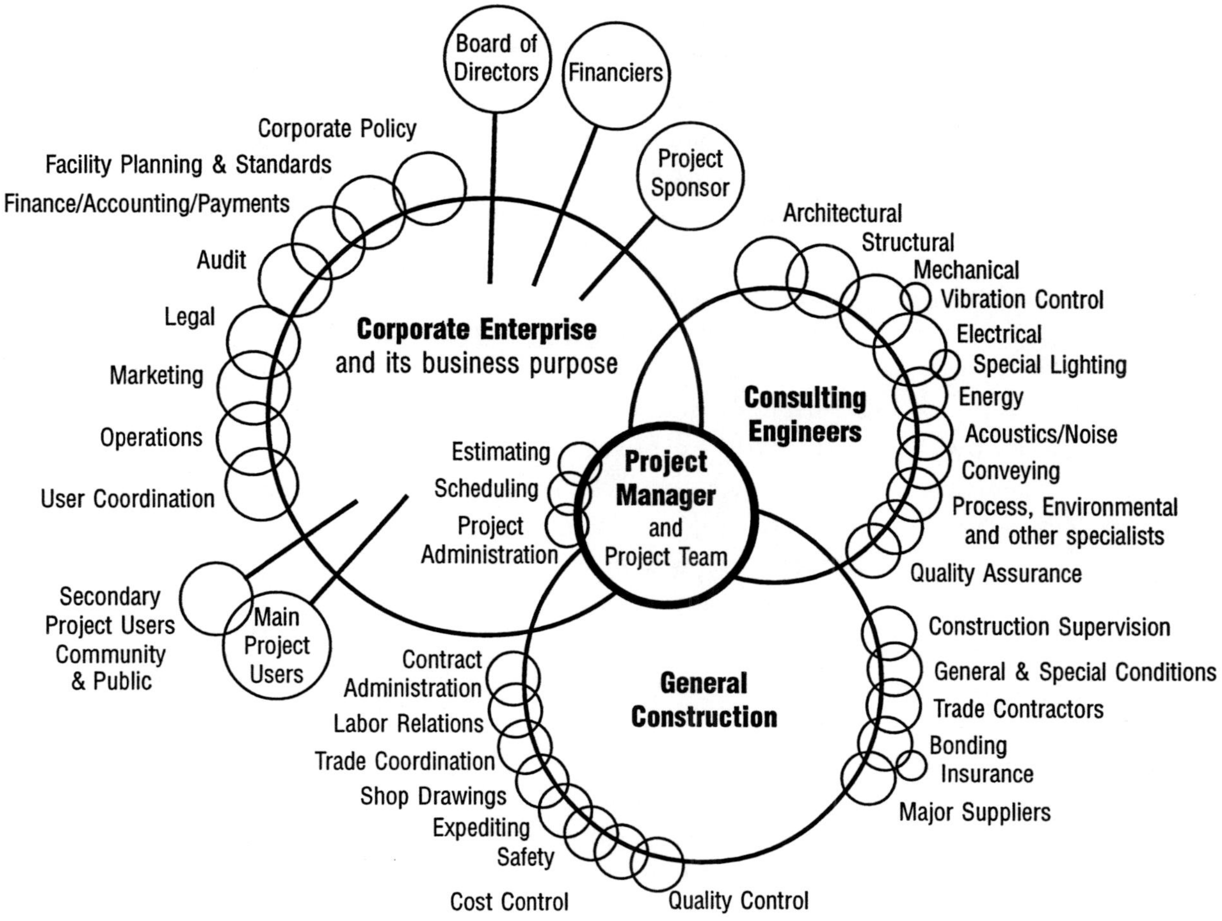

Figure 1-4. Typical Development of a Project Environment - Phase 3: Construction

(b) Beyond the project's boundaries

Events external to a construction project often come as a surprise to the project team and are therefore seen as obstacles to progress. Team members should realize that in all likelihood the project only exists because of a need relating to its environment. Therefore, the team must be ready and willing to be responsive to the world outside.

This requires the project manager to keep track of outside events as well as managing the project. This is particularly true of infra-structure projects, or those with emphasis on development or innovation, or that are subject to increasingly rapid change.

As the project progresses, the outside world constantly reacts. Issues arising are not only discovered as it becomes reality but also have a habit of changing, especially if the project is large and takes several years to complete. This all implies a high degree of uncertainty and risk and requires constant monitoring.

A strategy for dealing with the external environment is discussed more fully in Chapter 18

(c) Project Resources

Major construction projects require the combined efforts of many skilled firms and people specializing in the type of work. The senior management of the responsible enterprise will expect the project manager to conduct all project activities successfully, including design, procurement and construction. To do so, he must clearly state to senior management his resource requirements including such support as estimating, scheduling, accounting and forecasting.

The project manager's success depends heavily on ability to communicate.

On a larger project, he may require other more specialized services such as financial accounting, payroll, systems development, personnel, legal, public relations and property acquisition. Because these services do not normally affect project control decisions, they are usually carried out by independent departments or companies, not directly under the project manager's supervision. So if the project manager is to get the quality of information and service that he needs, he must maintain good relationships with each of these people.

The project manager will also be required to report regularly to the owner, sponsor, or upper management. This level of management will tend to focus on expenditure to date, forecast final cost and the scheduled commencement of an operating cash flow. They will also require a concise summary describing progress, forecast-to-complete, resource requirements and any actions required by them.

Communication is the project manager's major stock-in-trade and the success of his efforts and the decisions taken will depend heavily on the quality of information communicated. The availability of an effective project cost management information system for this purpose is crucial.

1.4 The Project Life-Cycle

There are those who have not had experience of a construction project "in the trenches" so to speak. For them it is difficult to capture the feeling of pressure, stress and ultimate satisfaction of a project well done, that the construction project management process offers. First timers often experience bewilderment at what is happening because, unlike the somewhat steady state of an on-going enterprise, a project has some distinctive characteristics of its own. To be precise, capital undertakings normally have a well defined starting point and well defined "deliverables", which identify the completion of the work. Further, limited resources constrain the work to be done in one way or another and there is an inherent uncertainty and risk associated with project work. These are very typical but distinguishing features and require a special type of management control.

Enter project management as a systematic process for accomplishment. There are many significant differences between enterprise management and project management. For example, the goal of enterprise management is to

The goal of enterprise management is to stay in business — project management's goal is to get finished.

remain in existence, whereas project management phases out after the relatively short lived duration of the project. Operationally, enterprise management focuses primarily on present and past performance, whereas project management is focuses on present performance and preparing for and coordinating future activities. The principle behind project management is very simple – plan before doing. This principle applies at every level from the individual task, through sets of activities, to project stages, to project phases, to the project life-cycle itself.

(a) First Plan, then Produce

Planning and producing are distinctly different activities. The first is an intellectual exercise in which ideas can be tested and adopted or discarded with minimal investment. The latter is largely a manual or mechanical exercise. However, producing does involve a significantly larger expenditure of resources and even more resources if the product is unsatisfactory. In other words, planning is about "doing the right things", i.e. about maximizing effectiveness. Producing is about "doing things right", i.e. about maximizing efficiency.

Therefore, a good motto for the project management team is:

Plan your Work - Work your Plan!

Plan before producing!

This principle is the genesis of the simplest form of project life-cycle consisting of four generic phases, two in "planning" and two in "producing. Figure 1-5 shows the sequence. These four distinct major phases making up the typical life-cycle of a well run project are:

- **Concept** — the idea that will satisfy needs of the enterprise or its opportunities and determine the project's goals and objectives
- **Development** — the conversion of the idea into a plan
- **Implementation** — of the plan
- **Termination** — of the project and transfer to operational mode

You can easily recall these major phases by the letters C-D-E-F, which stand for:

C-onceive D-evelop E-xecute, and F-inish

The importance of solid early conceptual planning in the Concept phase cannot be over emphasized. Conceptual planning is often overlooked in the haste to get into more detail and all the activities involved. Foremost in the conceptual phase is the reaching of agreement on a clear statement of the goals and objectives of the project — the "deliverables". Without establishing this essential basis for the project, there can be little focus in the remainder of the planning for the project.

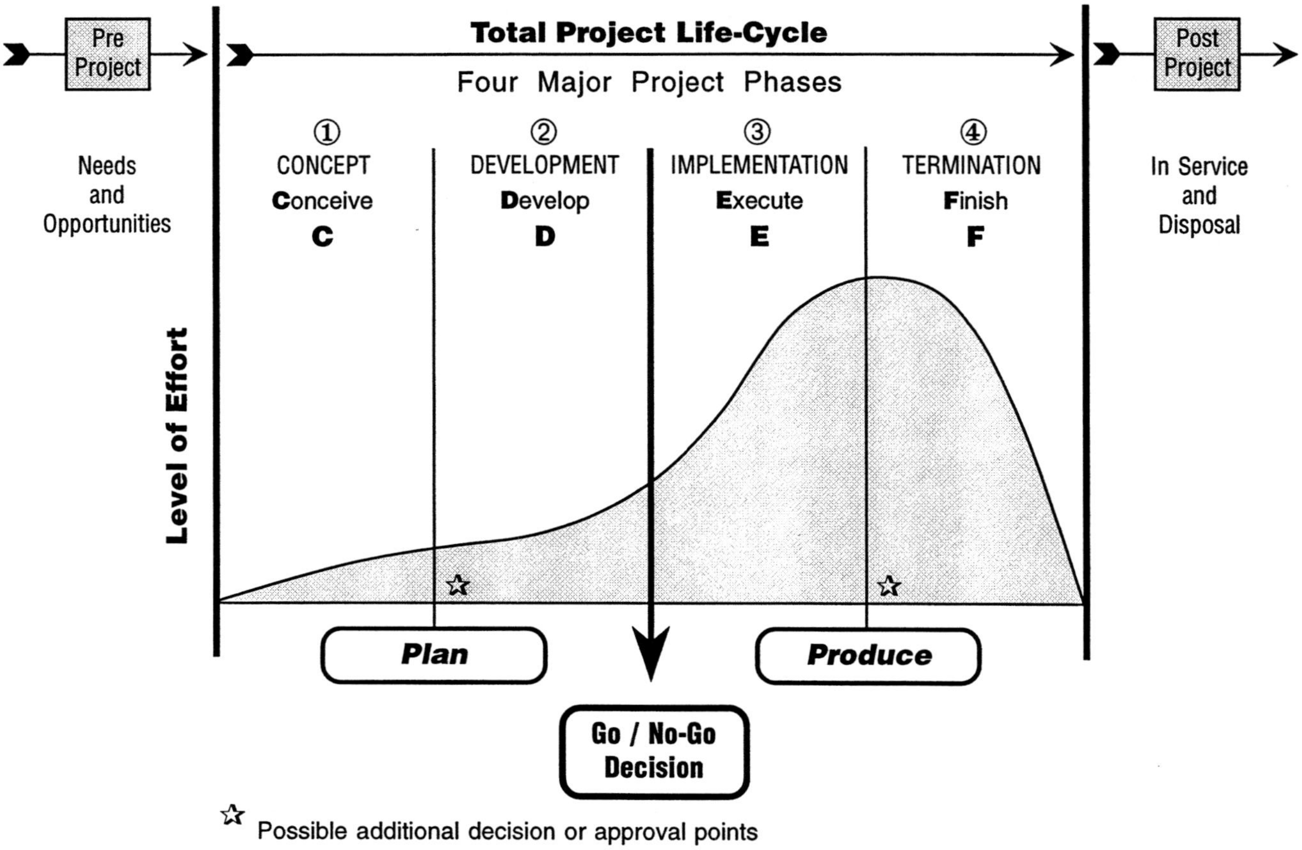

Figure 1-5. The Project Life-Cycle and the Level-of-Effort Curve

Planning in the concept phase is strategic in nature and must respect the environment in which the business operates. Its purpose is to mold functional objectives, operational concepts, financial goals and high-level project planning into useful preliminary documents for scrutiny. The many issues that should be addressed in the conceptual phase, and fed into the Development phase, will have a critical effect on the design, execution, performance and cost control of the resulting facility.

A Work Breakdown divides the work into manageable chunks.

The Development phase expands on the work of the Concept phase. This is the opportunity to break the parts of the project down into "manageable chunks", that is, a "Work Breakdown Structure". A work breakdown structure makes it easier to define the logical sequence and timing of the activities and events to be anticipated in executing the project. With this information, estimates of labor, material and other resources can be prepared enabling the development of cost estimates and budgets.

It will be seen from Figure 1-5 that a "Go/No-Go" decision separates the two planning phases from the two producing phase. The specific output or product of the Development Phase should therefore be a Baseline Plan, often called a Project Brief. This Project Brief, complete with justification, should contain the firm recommendations for an informed Go/No-Go decision. This decision point represents a major Executive Control Point in the project life-cycle.

Once approved, the Project Brief becomes the agreed input for the producing phases and provides the reference baseline for the control of the remainder of the project. Depending on the size and nature of the project, the figure shows how other control points may be established between major phases. Thus, each phase can be treated as a mini-project with its own objectives and constraints — and so it should be, and conducted accordingly.

A Project Brief provides the reference baseline for project control.

The successful conclusion of each phase represents a major milestone. These milestones are really like "gates" between the phase that provide the opportunity to introduce Executive Control Points. Some projects somehow manage to slip through these gates without being in full compliance with project requirements to that point. Inevitably, such projects get recycled back to an earlier phase — to the detriment of the final project cost and schedule, and the project's ultimate success.

(b) The Level-of-Effort Curve

Of special significance is the variation in the level-of-effort (LOE), which is associated with each of these project phases. Figure 1-5 shows this characteristic profile. The LOE curve represents the number of people dedicated to the project on a full or part time basis. In a well run project, this LOE curve is like the outline of a pear sliced down the middle and placed flat face downwards, with the stem at time zero. Compared to the somewhat steady state of the LOE typically associated with managing an enterprise, this LOE profile through the project life-cycle is very different. This is another good reason for adopting project management to run a project.

The level-of-effort represents the number of people on the project.

From Figure 1-5, it will be noted that the number of people involved rises steadily through the first two phases, but increases dramatically in the Execution phase. In this phase, the project typically experiences difficulties with communication and coordination, or shortages of materials and equipment, or other unnecessary delays, and consequent high levels of stress. The success of the execution phase is highly dependent upon the quality of the preparatory planning in the prior development phase.

The Finishing phase is equally dramatic - some might say traumatic. At the peak, there must be a careful balancing act. This is between maintaining full steam ahead to do all the work required, and still being ready to cut the throttle when sufficient work is no longer accessible to maintain full productivity. A major lag in this decision frequently accounts for serious cost overruns. Again, if the original planning has been in anyway inadequate, changes at this point can seriously impact cost, schedule and possibly quality, too.

Failure to follow this simple basic sequence is a failure in managing the project's time dimension.

(c) Typical construction project phase activities

Figure 1-6 shows some of the typical management activities in each phase for building a process plant. Of course, a typical construction project has several sub-phases or stages within each phase. But for our purposes, the four phases shown are generic to any type of project. They serve to underline the vital importance of progressive project concept development and planning to achieve successful project execution and completion.

In construction, the first two phases are often called feasibility and engineering phases, and provide the opportunity to "build the project on paper". The third and fourth phases, which include detailed drawings and

Project Life-Cycle

Plan — Go / No-Go Decision — Produce

	① Conceive	② Develop	③ Execute	④ Finish
Typical Major Tasks	• Gather data • Identify need • Feasibility: - program - process - schematics • Prelim budget • Prelim schedule • Proposed organization • Identify alternatives • Approval to proceed	• Develop: - plan - block diagram - sketches - standards • Further studies • Select equipment • Reconfirm economics • Develop: - WBS - schedule - budget - cash flow - risk plan • Prepare/submit Project Brief • Approval to proceed	• Set up: - work packgs - PERT/CPM - cost plan - organization - controls • Working dwgs & specifications • Design reviews • Order equipt • Issue bids and contracts • Start constructn • Quality control • Forecasting and cost control • Change control • Risk control • Resolve issues • Progress reprts	• Finalize construction • Reviews and acceptances • Train operators • Commission facility • Transfer responsibility • Transfer materials • Reassign team • Settle a/c's • Post project audit • Final report and close records
Organizational Strategies	• Free form • Working committee	• Simple matrix • Task force	• Project team • Strong matrix	• Matrix • Functional
Leadership versus Management Skills	• Visionary • Creative • Conceptualizer • Analytical • Innovative	• Leader • Facilitator • Planner • Integrator • Technically strong	• Team leader • Organizer • Interface manager • People and task oriented • Controller	• Team leader • Trainer • Doer • Technical writer • Compulsion to complete

Creative, artistic, conceptual Right brain → **Systematic, rational Left brain**

Figure 1-6. Evolution of Project Tasks, People and Organization

specifications, encompass the physical building of the project. Of course, the durations of each phase are not all equal. Figure 1-7 shows the more familiar stages of a construction project at its next level of detail and how these relate to the major phases discussed above. The figure shows some typical elapsed times for each major phase as a percentage of total construction time.

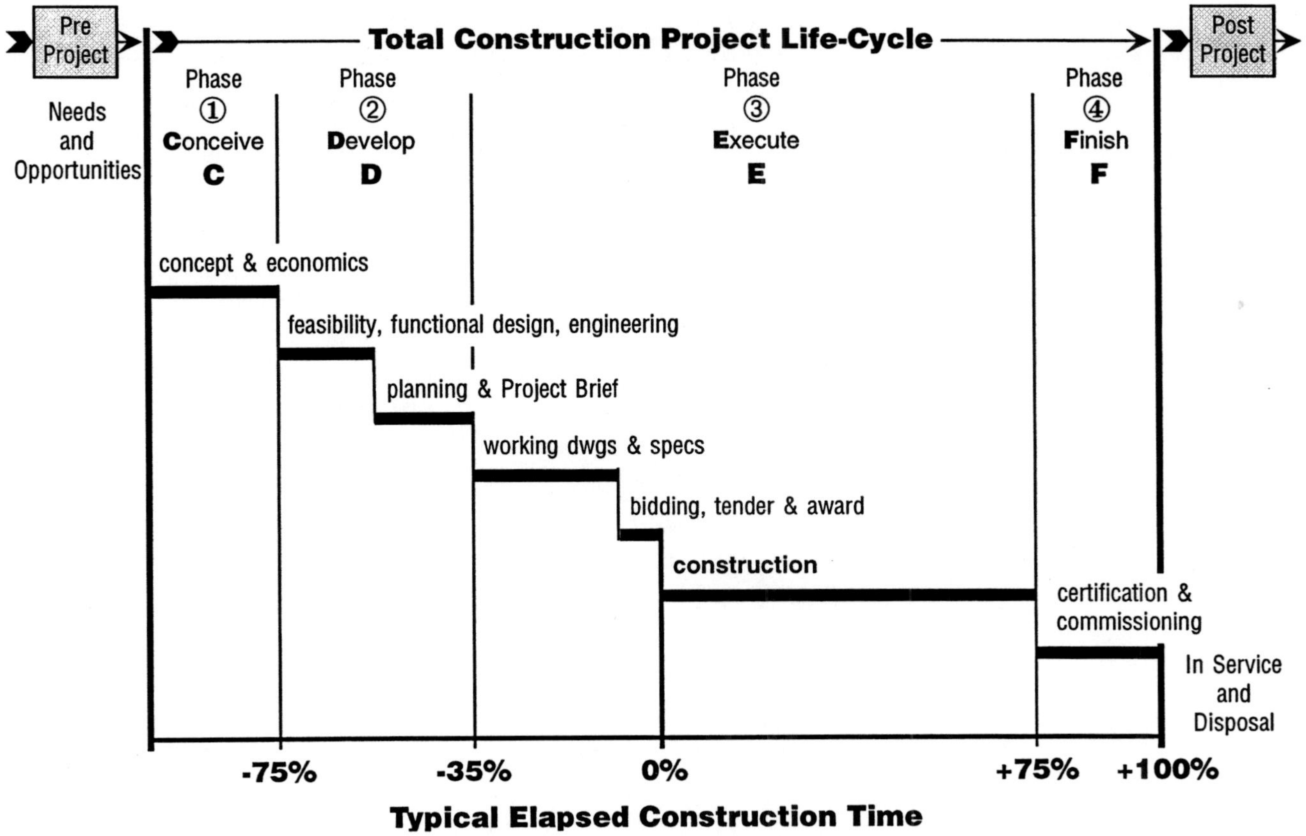

Figure 1-7. Typical Construction Project Master Schedule Bar Chart

In the concepts and economics phase, the organization recognizes its need and conceptualizes its response as a project. Limited sketches, schematics, schedule, budget, and financing proposals are then produced to evaluate and verify the suitability of the proposed solution to meet the need. Other possibilities are also identified. Upon satisfactory completion of these preliminary studies, a proposal should be presented for approval to develop these ideas in terms of economic feasibility (financial) and technical feasibility (functional design and engineering.)

In the Development phase, the sketches and schematics are developed into plans, block diagrams and standards. Equipment is selected and special studies may be conducted concerning specific aspects over which there may be some doubt. The schedule, budget and cash flow are further refined and the economics and justification reconfirmed. The whole result of the efforts of the two planning phases should be consolidated into a Project Brief. The Project Brief is then formally presented to Management with a request for the required funding and any other resources needed. Chapter 7, Section 7.3(a) provides a suggested listing of Project Brief contents.

Decisions taken in this Planning phase are often irreversible and will have a major influence over the shape of things to come. Conversely, mistakes, poor judgment and failure to be decisive in this phase are the main reasons why projects collapse in mid term or otherwise miss their objectives. Impatience, reluctance to spend money or failure to commit adequate planning resources are also common errors. These lead to insufficient attention to thinking the project through with the result that problems have to be faced later. This is often when they are the most difficult and expensive to correct. Therefore, it cannot be over emphasized that the key to project success lies in the quality and extent of early planning.

Failure to commit adequate resources in planning is a common error.

The presentation of the Project Brief and its formal approval and allocation or release of funding represents the Go/No-go decision discussed earlier. This is the most important control point in the life-cycle of any project. Since the major expenditure of effort and funds on the project takes place in the Producing phases, it is vital that management examines the project closely. Management must also take care to ensure that the required information and systems are in place to exercise the required control. Upon approval, the Project Brief becomes the prime source of reference for control of the Execution phase. Cost overruns and failure to meet objectives are almost certain to occur if the project is not based on a clear, unambiguous and well discussed Project Brief.

In the first stage of Execution, a more elaborate organization is set up, working drawings and specifications are prepared and design reviews are conducted to ensure consistency with the Project Brief. Equipment, supplies and construction services are then procured to produce the physical entity. During this time, project management controls and technical controls, involving contract specification, supervision, inspection, quality assurance and performance verification, are all required to ensure a satisfactory final result.

In the second of the producing phases, the Finishing phase, there must be a winding down of the main project effort. Meanwhile, the training of facility operators, the release and transfer of materials and resources, the assembly of project documentation and closing out of contracts, the transfer of responsibility and release of the project team, must all go ahead. This phase requires special attention to ensure that the project does finish when called for and does so in an organized manner.

(d) When to add value

As discussed earlier, the first two major phases of the project life-cycle are largely an intellectual planning exercise in search of the most effective way of meeting the project's identified needs. As such it is typically an iterative process with a relatively small investment of resources. The last two major phases are the Producing phases in which there are significant expenditures of resources on the work required to produce the resulting constructed facility.

Many project stakeholders are incapable of fully visualizing the project until it starts to take shape.

It is not unusual for many project stakeholders to be incapable of fully visualizing the final project until it actually begins to take shape. It is then that they see opportunities to improve the project and propose changes - some much later than others. As we shall see later in this book, changes during construction can have a very disruptive effect and, as the project progresses, the cost can increase out of all proportion to the value of the change. So there is a relationship between the value of a change and its actual cost over time.

Figure 1-8 shows two curves representing this relationship over the project life-cycle. Curve A - Potential to add Value - is clearly highest at the beginning of the concept phase when changes can be made "at the stroke of a pen". As the planning progresses and options and decisions become firm, opportunities decrease and continue to do so with increasing rapidity as the project enters the producing phases. The opportunities tend to level off to zero as the project reaches completion.

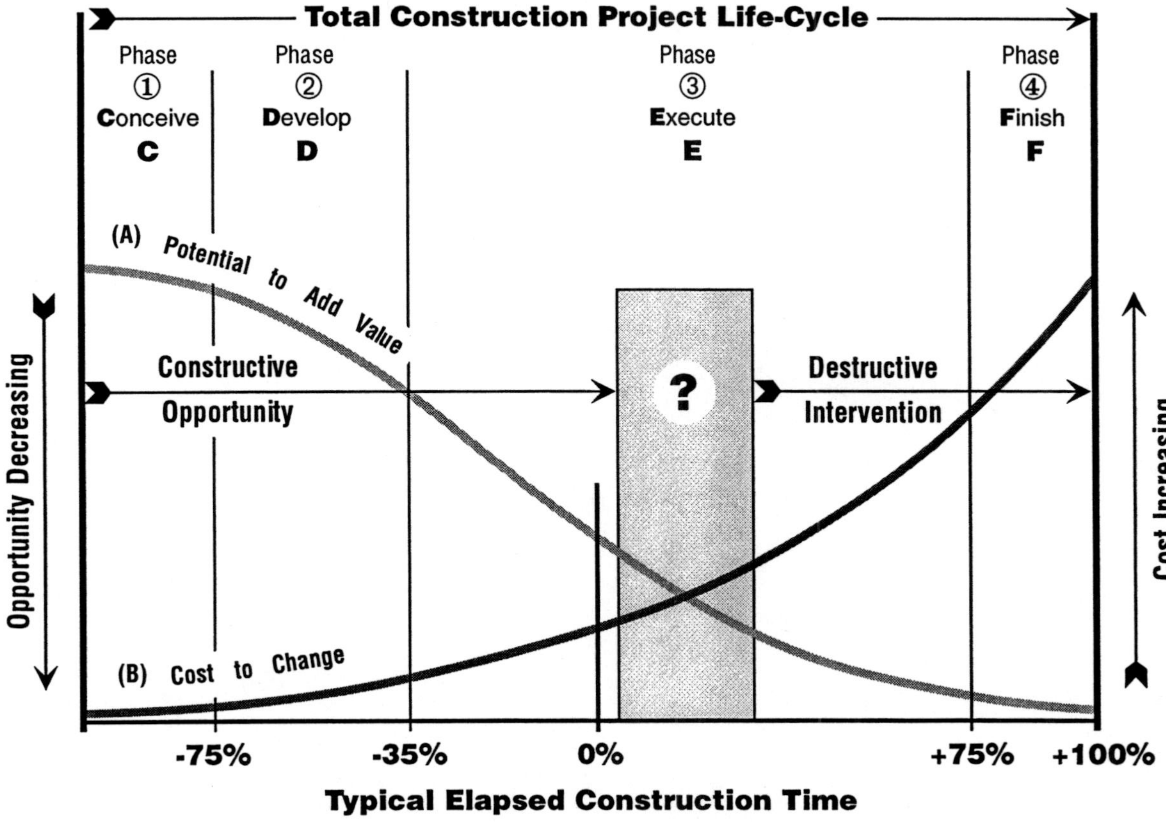

Figure 1-8. Adding Value vs. Cost to Change

Curve B - Cost to Change - represents the cost of making changes either to the scope of the project or to fix things that do not work or are not satisfactory. It will be seen that the Cost-to-Change remains low in the planning phases (where changes are made "on paper") but rises rapidly in the Producing phases (where physical changes may have to be made) reaching a peak at the end of the project. It has been suggested that the cost to make a change or to fix a non-conformance increases by an order of magnitude (ten times) in each succeeding phase. If this is true, a change that costs $10 to modify in the Concept Phase will cost around $100 in the Development Phase, $1000 during early construction and $10,000 by the time the project is being completed.

Changes made too late become destructive intervention — instead of constructive opportunities.

So the question arises, is it worth it? The answer, of course, can only be decided on the merits and timing of the particular change. However, Figure 1-8 does suggest that there is a crossover at some point during the Execution Phase. Beyond this point, changes become "destructive interventions" instead of "constructive opportunities". The implication for cost control is that the project manager must be alert to the changing circumstances of the project, and be ready to resist changes that constitute destructive intervention. This is especially so if they are superficial. The appropriate response in this case is to insist that the owner make any further changes after the project has been completed and handed over.

CHAPTER 2

Harmonizing the Project Effort

2.1 Project Integration

The project manager must have the necessary authority and responsibility for the project throughout its duration.

His or her job is to put it all together — and keep it all together.

The traditional organization is typically set up along functional lines with separate departments for finance, marketing, operations, personnel and so on. These departments act in a staff relationship and often have difficulty in resolving management conflicts because of the need to reach a common consensus. The result is delay and uncertainty, dissipating valuable management effort before giving general direction. If the issue is project related, the outcome may be detrimental to project objectives of scope, quality, time and cost. Therefore, efficient management of a project requires a specifically arranged semi-autonomous organizational structure.

The project management concept that has proved effective and very workable consists of a project team composed of key representatives and headed by a project manager. So, the management of the enterprise can and should assign a single individual as project manager as soon as they launch the project. His or her job is to lead and manage the project. To do so, this person must have the necessary authority and responsibility for the project team and the required resources for the duration of the project.

The project team represents a temporary organizational unit complete with its own formal or informal internal structure, policies, procedures and administrative routine. In this way, all aspects of the project can be coordinated and controlled through a single source until completion.

A project has its own functional management needs that includes the management of the project's scope and quality, human and other resources, as well as time, cost and uncertainty. Depending on the size and nature of the project in question, each of these project functions requires special expertise and training. However, more detailed examination of these functions is beyond the scope of this book. Since each function is an integral part of the whole, careful integration during the planning and execution of the project is essential.

The result should be a well designed and constructed facility that best meets the Owner's combined requirements of function, quality, schedule, and budget. To be successful, the project manager must have the experience and ability to control a large team. Remember, control without experience is worse than experience without control!

2.2 Management Processes

As we saw in Chapter 1, "First Plan, then Produce" was the genesis of the project life-cycle. It also provides the basis for project control. Project control relies on expectations, so the essence of control is to establish what is going to be done and then to see that it is done. Even so, changes inevitably occur because problems arise that have to be solved or changes in external conditions may be impressed on the whole process. Some things that can happen include:

The essence of project control is to establish what will be done and then to see that it is done.

- Some work was overlooked.
- The manner of procurement (contracts) is inappropriate to the degree of definition in the scope of work.
- Team members or the workforce are unable to deliver the required quality.
- Tasks take longer than expected and the work costs more.
- Lines of communication have become blurred or clogged.
- Unexpected events in the outside world (i.e. beyond the project's control) have affected progress or results.
- The time available or original budget was clearly inadequate.

So anyone who finishes a project without having had to revise the plan, and do it several times, is either a genius, very lucky, dishonest, or simply didn't bother to track what happened.

Figure 2-1 shows a conceptual model of project management control. Note how planned and actual data are fed into the control process and immediately compared and analyzed. Depending on the findings, the options are to implement action as planned, modify the action and monitor the effects of the modification, and/or replan. Revision of the project Master Plan should only be entertained after all other options have been considered.

POETS can help!

Control may be more formally defined as corrective action applied to achieve a required outcome having monitored performance and identified a deviation from plan. It is project management's responsibility to apply this process of control continuously, as the project progresses through the successive stages of its project life-cycle.

The project management and control process can be remembered simplistically by the acronym "POETS". As shown in Figure 2-2, POETS stands for Plan, Organize, Execute, Track and Steer. To emphasize the importance yet simplicity of this control process, each of these activities is described as follows.

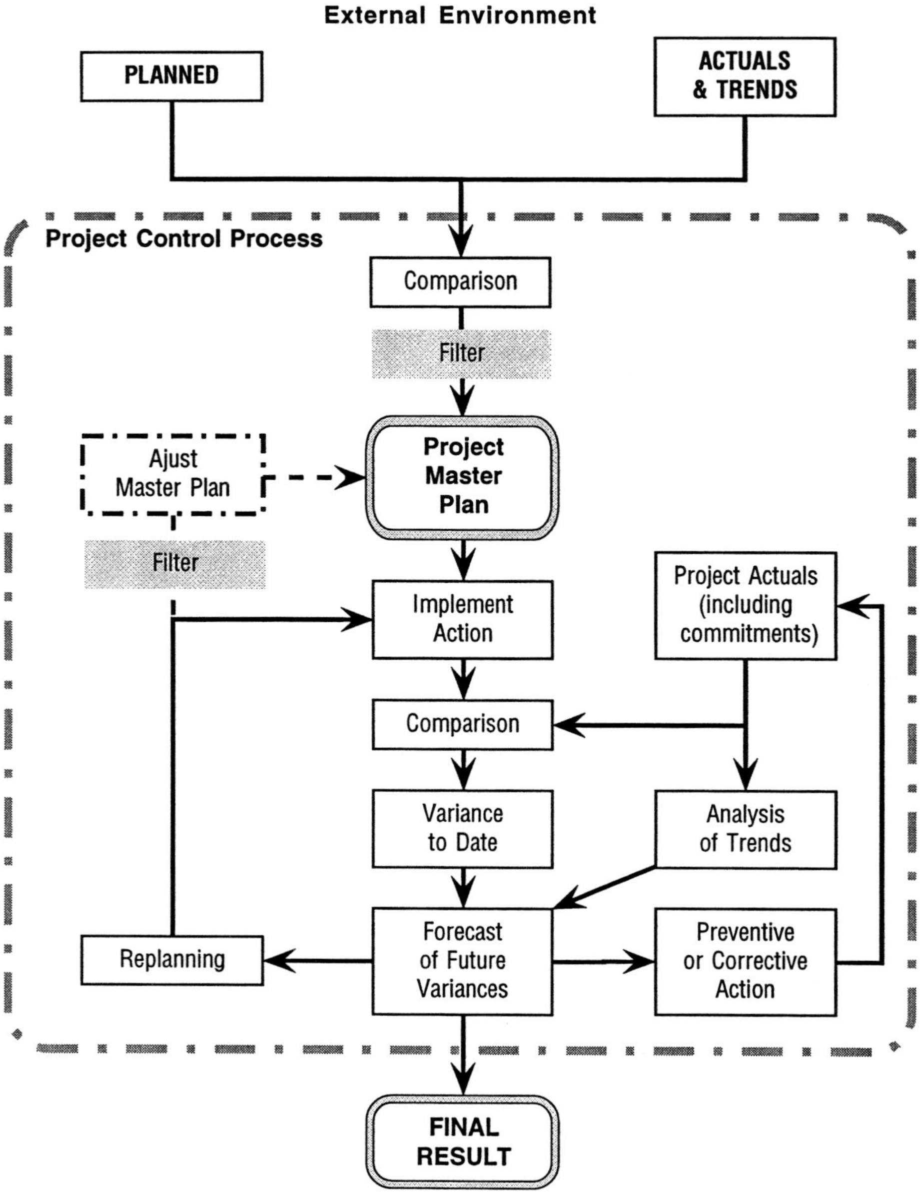

Figure 2-1. A Conceptual Project Management Control Model

(a) Plan

The first step is to plan the project with respect to its total scope (i.e. its required outputs, components or deliverables); quality standards; time and cost objectives. What precisely is to be required? Why? To what standard? If it is a new facility, what is its purpose or what is the process within the facility? How is the job to be done? Why should it be done one way rather than another? Indeed, why should it be done at all? Where is it to be built?

How to track and steer a project:

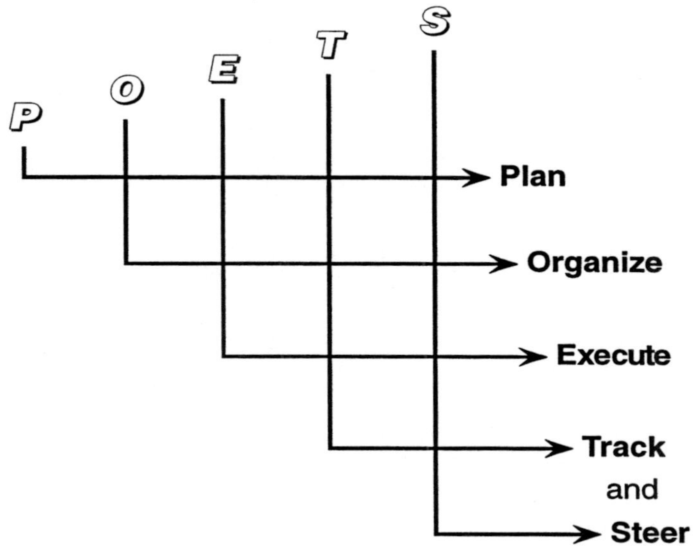

Effective project direction requires team agreement on
What is going to be done
— and then seeing that it ***is*** done

Figure 2-2. POETS help Project Management

Who will design and construct it? How long will it take? What resources will be required in terms of labor, materials and equipment? What risks are involved? What strategies are required to deal with unplanned occurrences? How much will it cost?

There must be a clear destribution of authority, responsibility and accountability.

(b) Organize

The second basic step is really an extension of the planning process. A careful examination of the major activities required to carry out the project must be made to establish an appropriate project management team organization. There must be a clear definition of who will have the authority, responsibility and accountability to execute each major project activity (e.g. planning, estimating, design, procurement, construction and supervision). This may involve assembling resources and obtaining commitments from people from other departments, or otherwise not immediately within the span of project control. If work is to be done by outside consultants and contractors, firms must be selected and contracts established. In each case, the designated party must be given a clear definition of the scope, quality, timing and cost targets associated with their responsibility.

(c) Execute

This is the "production" process over which effective control is to be exercised. However, the methods for executing the Plan are critical to achieving a successful project. The project manager and members of the team must understand the needs of human beings, their individual strengths and weaknesses, and therefore how to meld them into a dynamic and productive working group.

(d) Track

Only monitor the major and critical items in any detail.

This means regular tracking or monitoring, analyzing, forecasting, and reporting in comparison to the approved Plan (as the reference standard). Tracking and analysis of the status must be conducted during the work to provide a basis for timely corrective action when needed. What should be tracked? Here is a general list:

- Work-to-date compared to the plan
- The rate at which work is being completed
- The quality of the work being completed
- The commitment and cooperation of the team and workforce
- The attitudes and morale of the people on the project and the stakeholders associated with it
- The estimated cost at completion (i.e. commitments and expenditures plus estimated cost to complete) compared to plan

To increase the responsiveness of this process, only monitor the major and critical items in any detail, and do this in the simplest way possible. Following analysis, bring any significant deviations from the Plan to the project team's attention. Also, high-light any potential problems in the project status report.

(e) Steer

Very elaborate and complex control tools are not necessarily needed.

Steering involves taking corrective action. Management's options in responding to a significant deviation are either to reallocate resources or modify the original Plan. If this involves any of the original project objectives, obtain the project sponsor's prior approval. The latter alternative should only be undertaken after exploring all other means and this course appears unavoidable. From this it will be seen that without an effective Plan, there will be no basis for comparison, no satisfactory determination of deviation, and therefore no basis for corrective action.

Figure 2-3 illustrates a more detailed view of the control cycle. For control to be effective, the controls themselves must be carefully planned. Yet very elaborate and complex control tools are not necessarily needed.

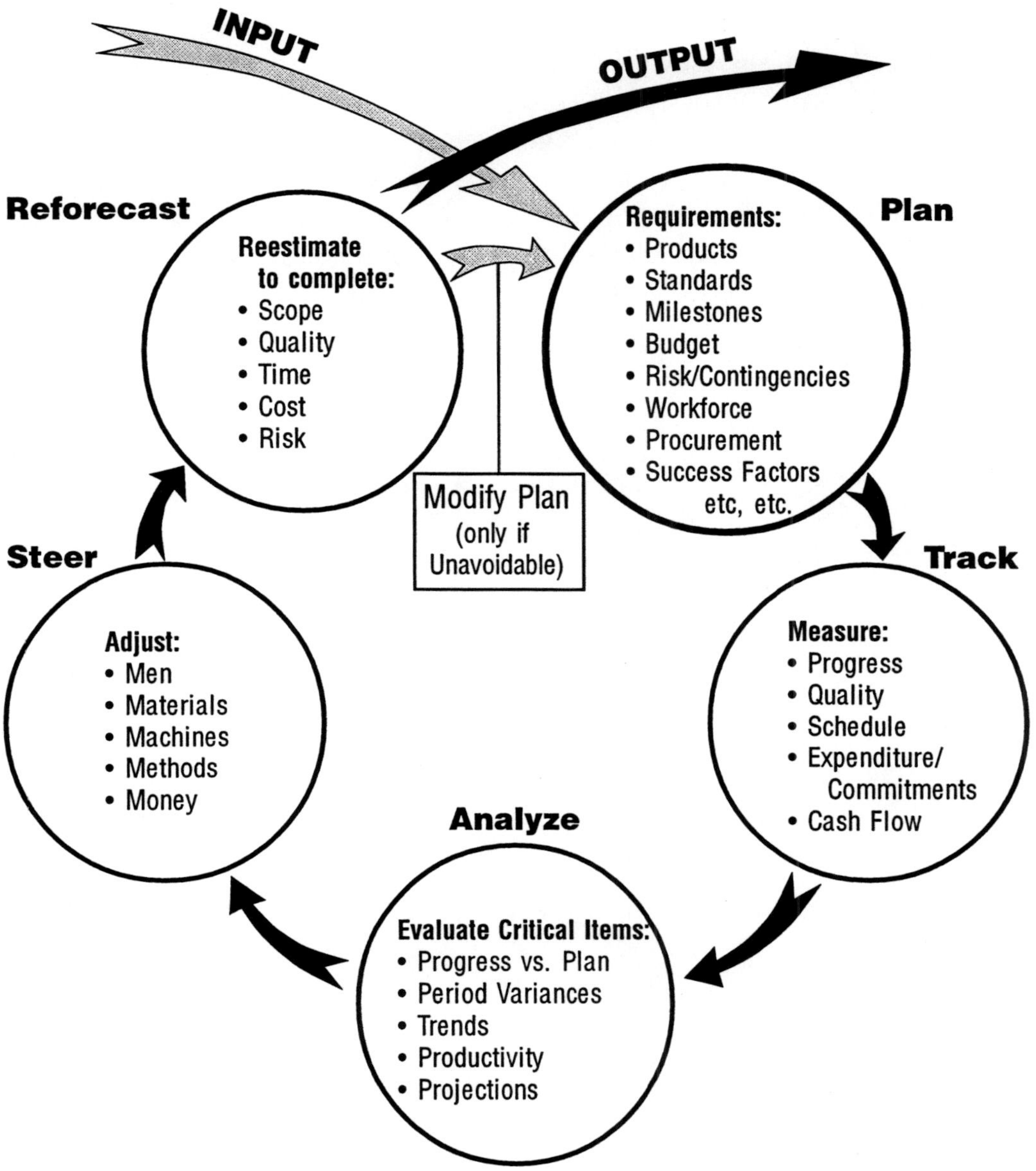

Figure 2-3. The Project Control Cycle

They should be adequate only to assure compliance with the project plan. In other words, they must be responsive to the project situation and enable a control action as early as possible following deviation.

To work efficiently, effective channels of communication must be established early.

The original Plan must provide the basic information for this control process. The development of a Work Breakdown Structure, discussed in Chapter 5, breaks the total project down into a number of divisions, or Work Packages. The Work Packages provide the necessary visibility and control. They should be sufficient to permit reasonable estimates of the time and cost for the scope and quality of each.

For this project control process to work efficiently, effective channels of communication must be established early. Otherwise, trade-off decisions and approvals, together with the required corrective actions, may not be carried out sufficiently rapidly to give the intended result.

There are three separate elements consisting of the management functions of scope, quality, time, cost, risk, people, procurement and communications; the control process; and the project life-cycle, discussed in the previous chapter. These elements form a relationship that may be viewed as three dimensional. Figure 2-4 shows this dynamic function-process-time connection. It is both universal and unique to all project work.

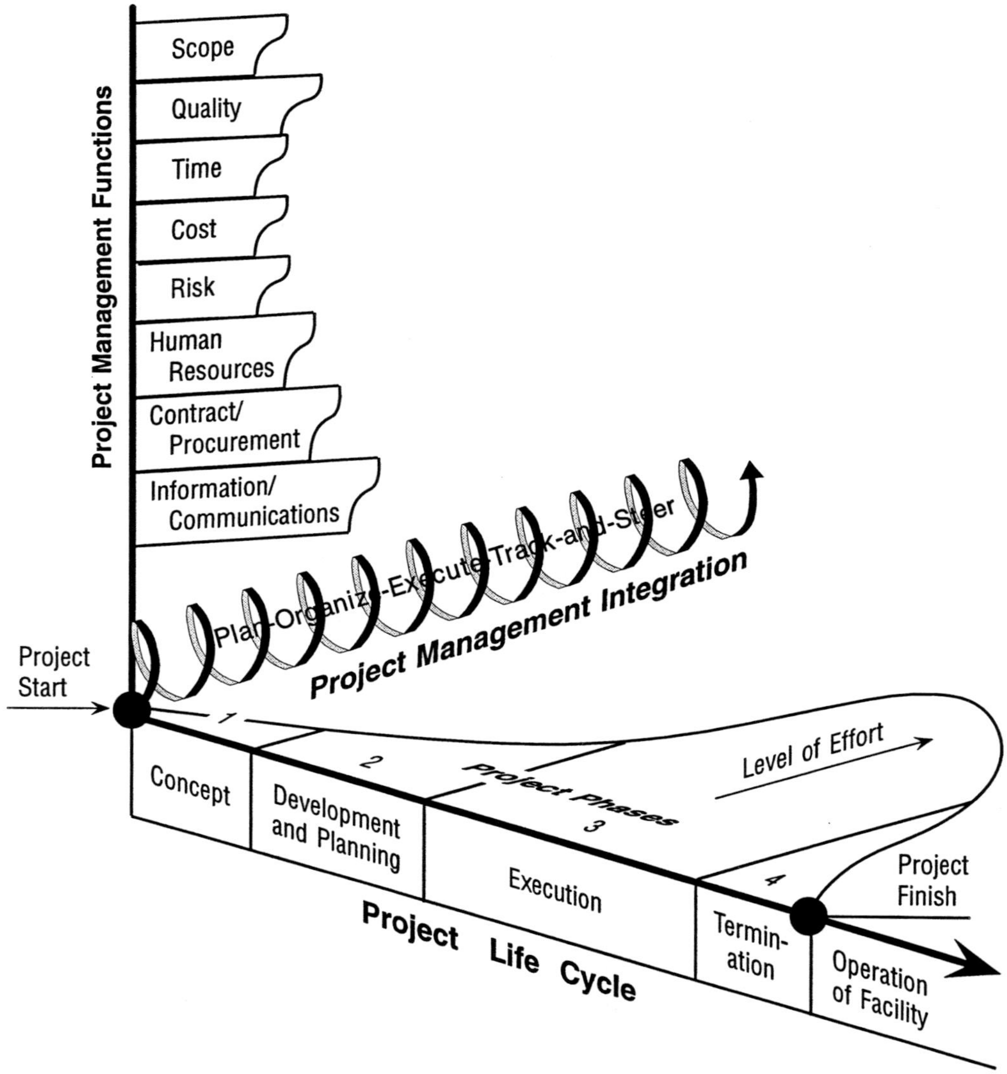

The diagram shows the three dimensions to the project process. These relationships make project management both universal and unique to all project work.

Figure 2-4. The Function-Process-Time Relationship in Project Management

2.3 The Makings of Project Success

It is now generally recognized that a successful project is not simply meeting objectives of scope, quality, time and cost, though obviously these play major parts. Success is a difficult notion at best and depends on whose point of view. It is the perception that matters, and it is the perception of the stakeholders, especially the users or customers, that are the most important in this perception. Anything that can be done to improve this perception should improve the "success" of the project. Chapter 18 discusses some possibilities.

There are a number of aspects to project management that make a profound contribution such as:

- Responsibilities of the project's Executive
- Conducting the project
- Project leadership

(a) Responsibilities of the Executive

Only the organization's Executive can provide an optimum internal environment for managing the project.

In setting up a project, the Executive of the sponsoring organization has a vital role to play in facilitating its success. Only the organization's Executive can provide an optimum internal environment for managing the project. To do so, it should ensure or insist that the following elements are in place.

Project Goal — The Executive must establish a clear goal for the project, as well as its priority position.

Executive Support — The Executive must then support the project goal and project management concept by appointing a project manager and following up with active sponsorship and control.

Competence — The project manager and team members assigned to the project must be competent. Other functional personnel assigned to the project from time to time must also be competent.

Project Team — The project manager should have a say in the assembly of the project team. This helps considerably in obtaining individual personal commitment, support and required quality of service.

External Authority - The project manager must be seen as the authoritative agent in dealing with outside parties, and be the responsible and single formal contact with them.

Internal Authority — The project manager must have the necessary managerial authority within his home organization to ensure resources are available in response to project requirements.

Project Manager Involved in All Major Decisions — No major technical, cost, schedule, or performance decisions should be permitted without the project manager's knowledge and preferably participation as well.

Commitment Authority — The project manager must have both the responsibility and authority to control the commitment of resources, including funds, within prescribed procedures and limits. The results of these decisions must be both accountable and visible.

Management Information Systems — Effective project management information and control systems must be in place, if necessary supported by outside observation, scheduling and estimating resources.

The project sponsor has a continuing role to play.

Having set up the project, the Executive or sponsor has a continuing role to play in:

- The formal management of the project scope
- Championing the project and its team
- Approving the project plan, schedule and budget at consecutive stages
- Ensuring sustained buy-in
- Ensuring timely availability of resources, and
- Ensuring that the project will realize the intended benefits.

While these items do not necessarily guarantee project success, their absence will certainly make success more difficult to attain.

(b) Conducting the Project

Project information expands rapidly as the project progresses.

As noted in the previous chapter, every project has a life-cycle. It begins with initiation of the Concept phase and ends with the transfer of the completed facility to operational status. At the beginning of a project there is only limited information, but as the project progresses this information expands rapidly becoming more definitive through each successive phase. Even at the outset, the rudiments of scope, quality, time and cost can be identified in response to the need for the project. This provides the basis for each ensuing step. Thus, the information developed in the planning phases provide the basis for the Execution phase. The three broad areas that then require control are the working drawings and tender documents; the procurement of contracts, supplies and services for construction; and the supervision of manufacturing, delivery and on-site construction activities.

Even on small projects, how well the project is managed can outweigh the consequences of technical decisions.

As projects become larger or more complex, effective and efficient management becomes correspondingly more significant. Even on small projects, the consequences of management decisions and how well the project is managed can outweigh the consequences of corresponding technical decisions. The tighter the schedule and cost constraints, the more is the need for good management. In the end, the test of effective project management is the degree to which the project's objectives have been met, to the satisfaction of the stakeholders. So, key requirements for managing successful projects include:

- Establishing in the first place a sound business case for the project and defining a set of uncompromising goals
- Assembling a capable and motivated team with appropriate skills
- A competent leader and communicator with an organization that can plan effectively and can execute efficiently
- The use of proven contemporary project management theory and practice in conducting the use of project resources

(c) Project leadership

Over the years, leadership has been the subject of much writing and research and there are many and diverse views on what makes a leader. Recently, the debate has become more intense because the image of a powerful and autocratic personality directing operations is no longer consistent with modern management thinking. Indeed, today's workforce is less and less inclined to respond to such a personality. This is no less true on construction projects.

The characteristics required of the project leader change considerably during the course of the project.

Project leadership may simply be viewed as the ability to attract a skilled group of willing and committed followers towards the goals of the project. From this standpoint, followership is every bit as important as leadership and a willingness by the followers to accept delegation is essential to the project. The leader is expected to delegate through the transfer of authority and responsibility. In return, the followers must be expected to shoulder their share of the burden with reliability and accountability.

Interestingly, the characteristics required of the leader change considerably through the life of the project. At the outset in the planning phases, "visioning", flushing out the "customer's needs", "intelligence gathering", developing a "compelling reason" for the project and its "governance strategy" are all-important. The evolution of the project concept and technical requirements may also require several iterations and reruns. The purpose of these phases, is to optimize the effectiveness of the project. This requires patient leadership and an open mind.

The real work of the project, task execution, gets done in the producing phases. Here, the purpose is to satisfy the customer(s) by conducting the project through to its intended destination under typical project constraints. In this, efficiency and productivity are all-important if the quality standards and the time and cost limitations of the project are to be met. "Getting the message out" is the first step in establishing project control and skilled administration is needed as much as leadership.

It will be observed that information, or intelligence gathering, takes priority in the planning phases but communicating, or getting the message out, takes priority in the producing phases. These intercommunication skills are pivotal to the project management process.

Intercommunication skills are pivotal to the project management process.

From a cost stand point, perhaps the best way of looking at it is to ensure that the project has the necessary skilled "stewardship" throughout its life. This requires a willingness to be accountable for the well-being of the project organization while placing service towards the goals of the project above self-interest. The vehicle for this complex task is a comprehensive project information system.

(d) Knowledge and abilities of the Project Manager

The project manager must have established credentials and experience commensurate with the size and type of project. As a minimum, the project manager should have a knowledge and understanding of the following:

- A demonstrated knowledge of project management in terms of planning, budgeting, directing, controlling and communicating
- An appreciation of project management tools and techniques such as Work Breakdown Structures, scheduling, and scope and cost control
- An adequate knowledge of the technical environment of the project
- An understanding of the owner/sponsor's organizational environment
- An awareness and appreciation of the socio-economic environment of the project

Ideally, the project manager should have the following attributes:

- Willingness to accept responsibility for the success or failure of the project
- Ability to lead through both formal and informal authority in a matrix environment
- Ability to organize and coordinate, especially specialists with superior knowledge
- Understanding and ability to deal with conflicts that inevitably arise

- Ability to harmonize between diverging or opposing technical views
- Ability to foster positive problem solving and negotiation without compromising project objectives
- Ability to assess project status and act accordingly
- Ability to cope with risk
- Ability to handle stress
- Mature judgment
- Ability to win support by effective listening as well as proclaiming project objectives

(e) Summary of requirements for success

So what are the important issues that are most likely to contribute to project success? Here is a suggested list. While satisfying every one will not necessarily guarantee a successful project, the absence of any one may well result in a project that does not reach its full potential.

The vehicle for this complex task is a comprehensive project information system.

- Objectives that contribute to the larger goals of the organization
- Commitment to the project management methodology
- Adaptation of the methods to the requirements of the project
- A complete project plan with a high caliber control estimate and associated schedule understood by all the stakeholders
- A skilled project team lead by an able project manager who all agree on the project objectives
- Clear authority and responsibility for the project manager to carry out the project
- Willingness of the team to change and adapt as the project advances
- Tracking methods that encompass physical measurements, effective trending analyses and reliable cost and schedule forecasts. Methods that result in regular communications on status and results, but minimize the need for excessive meetings and reports.

The chapters that follow focus on a project cost management system designed to satisfy the needs of the project manager, the project team and all other management levels.

Part 2: Cost Control in the Planning Phases

CHAPTER 3

Establishing the Project Scope

3.1 Developing a Project Scope Statement

People who do not know what they want should not be disappointed with what they get — but they always are.

Of all the project management functions listed in Chapter 2, inability to control project scope satisfactorily is probably the most frequent cause of project difficulties, disappointment — and cost over run. Almost as frequently, this can be traced back to an inadequate statement of project scope. Therefore, disappointment with the project can be avoided to a considerable extent by developing a sound Project Scope Statement. The purpose of the Project Scope Statement is to crystallize the intent and establish expectations upon which the success of the project can be built. It must describe the project and reflect its goals and objectives.

Not everyone is familiar with the word "scope", however. According to Webster, it means "ultimate design or purpose". For a construction project, scope simply means the facilities that will flow from the work on the project and any other products including their required physical and functional characteristics. The scope of a project should be set out in an unambiguous scope statement for all to see, understand and follow.

The purpose of the Concept Phase is to get convergence by determined iteration. The purpose of the Development Phase is to refine the details so that the project can be properly planned and detailed.

Writing a good set of requirements, a good Scope Statement, is not an easy task. It depends on having and understanding a good clear set of goals and objectives for the project. These in turn must reflect the organization's needs in the best possible way. Stating the goals is one thing. Agreeing on them is quite another and is perhaps one of the most difficult aspects of successful project management.

Too often, "people go off in all directions" and fail to give sufficient attention to the "front-end". This leads to later frustrations and delays, reevaluations, or even rework. The purpose of the Concept Phase described in Chapter 1, Section 1.4 is to eliminate this divergence and get convergence by a process of determined iteration.

The purpose in the Development Phase is to refine the details of the Project Scope so that the project can be properly planned and detailed for construction following Capital Appropriation approval. It should not be taken as an opportunity to augment the scope with "nice-to-haves" that go beyond the intent of the original scope concept. Such additions represent "scope drift", add to the cost of the project and may result in the project no longer being viable or achievable within the cost constraints.

3.2 Scope Statement and Scope of Work Not the Same

A "Scope Statement" is different from "Scope of Work", though it is closely related. Again according to Webster, "work" refers to "exertion, task, or performance". Therefore, a Scope of Work is typically a narrative description of the work to be performed along the way to achieve the project output. It describes the work contained in the project process, but is not necessarily specific about the amount of work to be done.

"Scope of Work" describes the work to be performed. "Scope Statement" describes the project's deliverables.

The Scope Statement, on the other hand, describes the project's deliverables. The project's deliverables are the physical items or measurable outputs identified as the product or end results of the project when completed. Deliverables are always measurable because they can be observed or counted in some way. It is the Scope Statement that determines the amount of work to be done, and redone if it is not correct the first time. Simultaneously it ensures that only enough work is done to satisfy the project's requirements which is the basis for "scope control".

Besides end item deliverables, intermediate deliverables may be required as stepping stones to the end deliverables. For example, in many construction projects, intermediate facilities such as temporary access, road diversions, coffer dams for foundation construction, and so on, are required to conduct the rest of the work. When significant, these should also be included in the Project Scope Statement. A Scope Statement is essential for maintaining control, especially because of the rapidly increasing cost of making changes as the project progresses.

Any subsequent requirements or changes should be documented by a "scope change" with appropriate review and adjustments in the cost and schedule. If the project is in the producing phases, the change should be documented by a change order as discussed in Chapter 13, Section 13.4. It is the scope statement that determines the project's "boundaries" discussed in Chapter 1, Section 1.3.

3.3 Criteria for a Good Project Scope Statement

A good project Scope Statement should be:

Specific — Being specific is not necessarily being detailed. It should be possible to understand what is to be done without unnecessary constraint in the manner of doing it. Selecting the best approach belongs to the planning Development Phase.

Realistic — There is no point in undertaking a project that is not viable with the resources available, because any effort spent on it will be wasted. That does not stop it being very challenging. The more challenging the project, the more important is the planning of it and the consideration of the risks involved.

Measurable — A project is complete only when the Scope (deliverables) have been delivered. If the scope is not measurable, including measures of performance, the project could be never ending.

If no one has responsibility, it will not get done. If no end date is set, it will not get finished.

Agreed upon — It is very important for the principal stakeholders in the project, especially its sponsor(s), to be agreed on its scope. Otherwise, the team conducting the project will receive conflicting messages along the way, resulting in confusion and demoralization. Such a project is unlikely to achieve its full potential and level of success.

Often a good Scope Statement will be preceded by an introduction providing a background to the project, the reasons for its selection and the opportunities and inherent assumptions involved. This helps to give a much better understanding of the project requirements contained in the scope statement.

Responsible and Time Specific — In addition to the four criteria listed above, responsibility for the project and the time for its delivery should be identified. If no one has responsibility, no one will get on with it, and if the time is not stated, there will be no sense of urgency and it will not get done.

The completeness of a good scope statement can be tested by three questions. Once planned, can you:

1. Estimate it?
2. Schedule it?
3. Measure its quality attributes, characteristics, performance?

3.4 Scope, Quality, Time and Cost: The Tetrad Trade-off

As discussed in Chapter 2, the purpose of project management is to achieve objectives as defined by the parameters of scope, quality, time and cost, and with the general perception of a successful project. However, as every project manager knows from experience, the objectives of scope, quality, time and cost are very much interrelated and not necessarily mutually compatible. Indeed, project circumstances often prevail in which the objective of any one function may not be feasible within the constraints

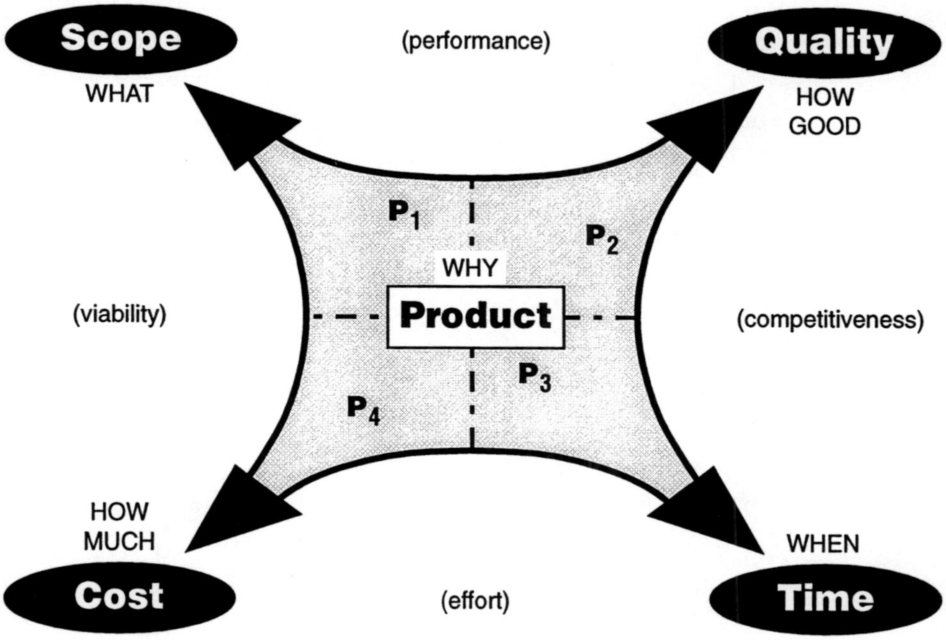

The four objectives (or constraints) of Scope, Quality, Time and Cost are separate but inter-related variables. P1 through P4 represent projects with differing priorities tending towards one or other of these variables.

Figure 3-1. The Tetrad Trade-Off: A Matter of Balance

represented by the others. This is especially true when considerations of risk and uncertainty are included.

Most projects by their nature lean more towards one constraint than any other. Therefore, while managing the project process, the project team must choose options and make decisions accordingly. This balancing act may be characterized as the "Tetrad Trade-off" and represented graphically as shown in Figure 3-1.

Any of the four corners of the Tetrad may be the primary project priority.

In the diagram, P1, P2, P3 and P4 are four different types of project. Project P1, for instance, has scope as its priority and is therefore in the scope emphasis quadrant. Good examples include research and development (R & D) or defense projects. Such projects tend to be less certain in terms of quality and very uncertain in time and cost.

More often, the scope is quite well defined but the emphasis is on quality as represented by P2. Examples include new high-end commercial office or residential construction, or heavy-duty public infra-structure projects where durability and public safety are key concerns. Conversely, P3 is in the time emphasis quadrant such as meeting the opening day deadline of a national exposition, or completing a facility to house the opening night of a theater production. Or, again, the emphasis may be largely on cost such as units in a low-cost housing development for sale or transfer to a local authority.

The inexperienced project manager should be cautioned that a project's priority emphasis may also shift during its life-cycle. For example, a project that is scope-quality oriented at the outset may well shift towards cost-time near the end of its life-cycle. An illustration of this might be a project that, having experienced cost overruns, is running out of project financing.

Conversely, a cost-schedule oriented project may have a tendency to move towards scope-quality. An illustration of this might be the construction of a residential development that needs to be moved "up market" because of a sudden glut of accommodation at the lower end. This kind of shift is difficult to do in retrospect and emphasizes the importance of sound project planning and development from the beginning.

The inter-connection between the four variables of scope, quality, time and cost may be likened to stretching a rubber sheet. There is only so much rubber — and you can only stretch it so far!

Managing the Tetrad Trade-off with skill and understanding is a very important part of managing a project. In practice, rarely does the project manager have the luxury of a project that has equally balanced constraints so that he can accomplish all four, or conversely, has any one of them that has unlimited bounds!

Interestingly, the figure shows how the pairing of the project objectives has significance in the eyes of the marketplace. The combination of scope and cost determines the viability of the project's product. The combination of time and cost represents the amount of effort to produce it. Scope and quality together represent its performance and the coupling of timing and quality, to a large extent, determines the project's competitiveness.

Such combinations represent significant measures of internal project success.

3.5 Developing Project Scope within Cost

Once the project has an agreed and properly established initial Scope Statement, the next step is to develop this into a viable technical and management execution plan. Developing the Project Scope in this way does not imply change. It means progressive expansion of detail.

From a technical stand point, this may require careful selection amongst the available alternatives, and possibly undertaking feasibility studies to decide the merits of competing options. Many technical and management decisions will be involved. During this process it is vital to maintain congruence with the Project Scope Statement as the basis of reference and so avoid "scope drift" as noted earlier. This responsibility also means keeping a constant eye on the concurrent development of an acceptable budget and schedule within the requirements of scope and quality.

It is very important to watch for Scope drift — and resist it!

Acceptance at appropriate stages of development are vital steps in the elaboration of the project scope, especially before starting detailed design work. This means assembling the complete project scope as Work Packages discussed in Chapter 5 and presenting them for approval. The work packages should be submitted to the respective representatives of the user groups for review and "sign off" confirming that the package meets their respective requirements.

The intent is that these preliminary designs become "frozen" as the basis for the detailed design work. The users should understand: "speak now or forever hold your peace!" Simultaneously, the packages should be submitted for "sign off" to the designers and those responsible for implementation to confirm that the content of each Work Package really is complete.

The results of these technical and management efforts during the Development Phase will eventually be accumulated into the project's Brief, as discussed in Chapter 7. During construction or commissioning, items may still surface that either do not work as intended or have been missed altogether. These result in changes to contracts, though not necessarily to the scope intent. Chapter 13 discusses how to manage cost changes. The flow diagram in Figures 3-2 and 3-3 show a simplified sequence reflecting the designers' technical role in maintaining project cost control through the stages of the typical project life-cycle. Note particularly, the inputs to, and outputs from, the designers' activities and how they affect project cost control.

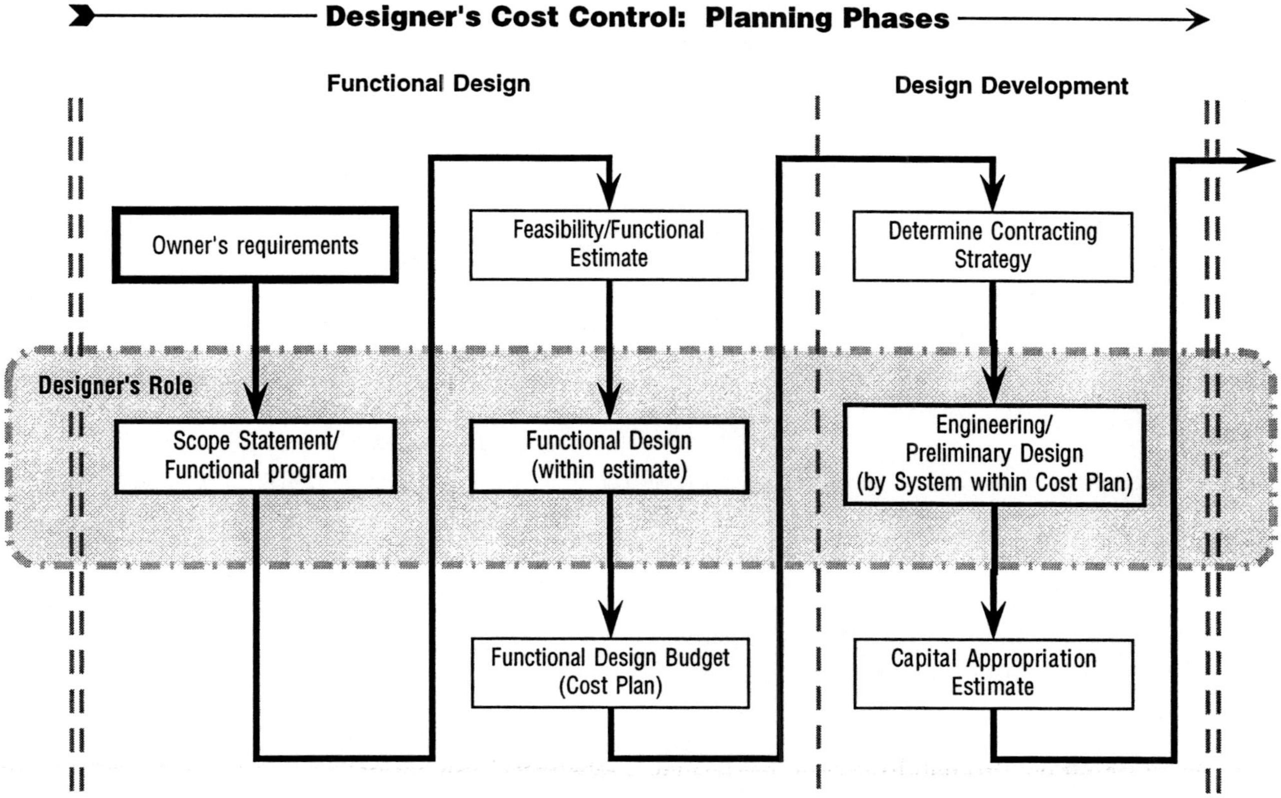

Figure 3-2. The Designers' Role in Cost Control - Information Flow in the Planning Phases

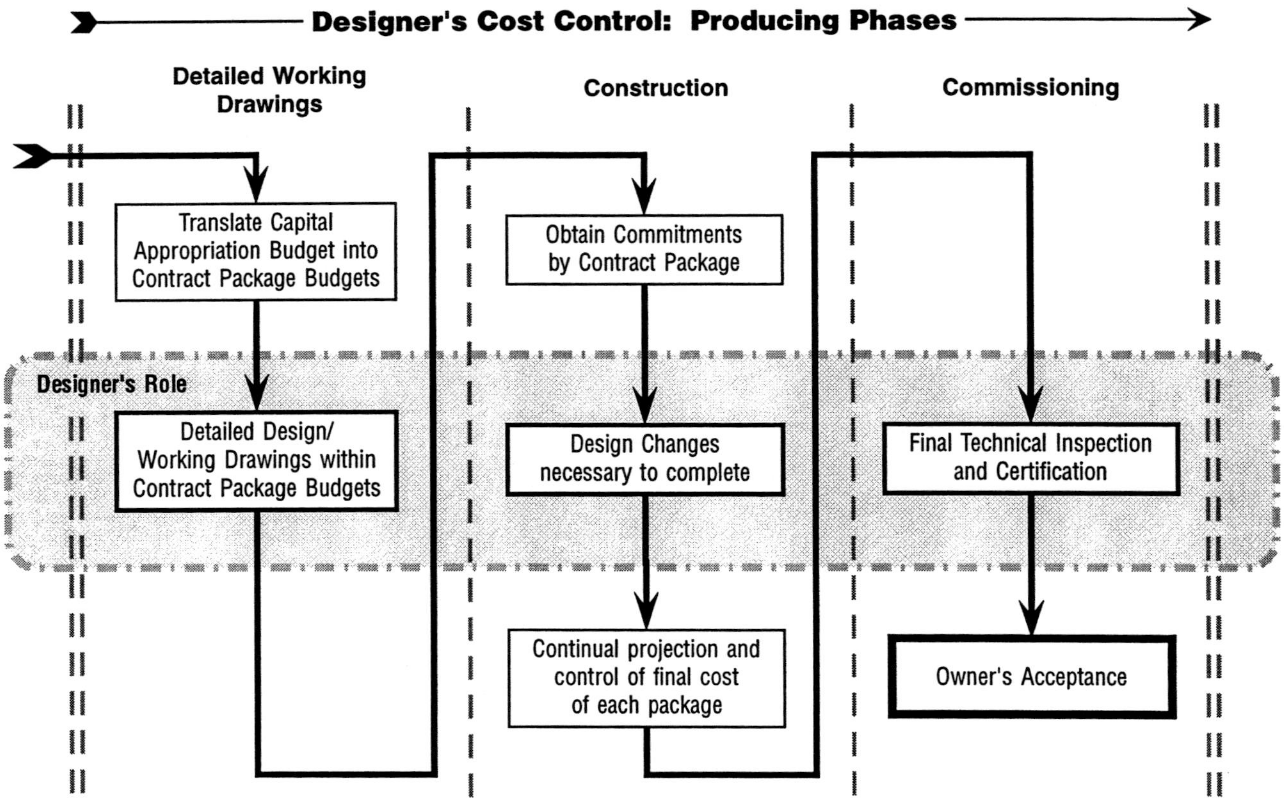

Figure 3-3. The Designers' Role in Cost Control - Information Flow in the Producing Phases

3.6 Value Management

An important technique that is available for keeping the cost of the project scope in line is Value Management. This technique provides a systematic approach to imposing scope performance, and a way of bringing estimated costs into line with budgets and ensuring that they remain in line. It differs radically from simple cost cutting based on smaller quantities or cheaper materials.

VM involves objective analysis of the essential functions, and selecting optimum value.

Value Management (VM) focuses on functionally acceptable substitution. VM may be defined as "A systematic and creative effort to ensure that product and performance are provided at the lowest total cost, consistent with project objectives. It involves an objective analysis of the essential functions and engineering of the major units, items or tasks within the project." It is a means for selecting optimum value consistent with project objectives.

Traditional design practice typically results in the various architectural and engineering disciplines developing their individual sets of plans and specifications. Separately, they meet the project design criteria and all codes and requirements of the various authorities having jurisdiction in their given areas. Unfortunately, with compartmentalized sub-agreements, each design professional tends to elaborate on its own requirements and then reviews and modifies these requirements almost in isolation. Since each discipline understandably prescribes maximum performance and safety factors, unilateral decisions may result. These can have the collective effect of modifying the original project criteria and standards.

These undesirable conditions result in a project that is not necessarily the most economical or acceptable in terms of its original project objectives and end use. Effective decisions in arriving at lowest total cost, especially including operation and maintenance of the resulting facility, require a team approach by people knowledgeable in the respective areas.

Effective decision making requires a team approach.

VM gives focus for this team approach through a series of creative workshops. In these workshops a group of experienced people, some of whom are involved in the project and others who are not, imaginatively examine the project, or selected parts of it. Since it is essential to involve senior staff in these workshops, the VM effort itself must be optimized. In other words, the effort must concentrate on those areas that will yield the greatest benefits.

A cataloguing of the contents and parameters of the Project Scope Statement, or its derivative documents such as a Design Brief, should identify the most fruitful areas to examine. An information base or "cost model" is then developed from historical data. Comparison of this cost model to the current project estimate should identify areas of major cost, which could benefit from closer study.

An objective, cost oriented, VM coordinator then mounts an organized effort to obtain optimum value for every dollar spent in each selected area. Unit or system functions are carefully analyzed. Anything that adds cost to an item without adding to its function, is modified or eliminated. All expenditures relating to supply, construction, maintenance, operation and replacement should be considered during this process.

The questions to ask in a VM workshop are:

- What is it?
- What does it do?
- Do we really need it?
- What must it do (primary and secondary functions)?
- What does it cost?
- What would do the same job?
- At what cost?

Sometimes, the alternatives are even better.

Armed with up-to-date technical information on materials and methods, a creative session is then held to develop alternate solutions for the specific function. Feasible alternatives are analyzed to permit a selection offering the most cost effectiveness. This may require making weighted evaluations involving trade-offs of both economic and non-economic factors.

1. Information

Objectives: - Provide an information base or "Cost Model"
- Select areas for detailed study

Questions: - What is it?
- What must it do?
- What must it cost?
- What is it worth?

Technique: - Functional Analysis
- Cost-worth concept
- Graphics
- Cost and energy modeling

2. Speculation

Objectives: - Generate alternatives for meeting requirements
Questions: - What else will perform the required function
Technique: - Creative thinking process (brainstorming)

3. Analysis

Objectives: - Evaluate and select best cost saving alternatives

Questions: - What will alternatives cost?
- Will the alternatives meet the required functions?
- Which proposals have the greatest cost savings?

Technique: - Life-cycle costing
- Weighted constraints evaluation
- Idea ratings

4. Proposal

Objectives: - Present best alternatives to the decision maker
Question: - How best to present proposals?

Technique: - Narrative reports
- Schematic overlays
- Graphics

5. Final Report

Objectives: - Define and quantify results
Questions: - What was actually implemented?
Technique: - Standardized comparative reporting

Figure 3-4. The Five Steps in a Value Management Workshop

The final step is to document and sell the results to the respective decision makers. This involves obtaining directives for their adoption into the project, and making corresponding adjustments to estimates and budgets.

Three progressive VM workshops are recommended.

For ease of reference, Figure 3-4 sets out these five successive steps. For effective cost control, Figure 4-1, Chapter 4, shows a minimum of three VM workshops at progressive stages of the project. Conduct the first VM work shop early enough in developing the concept to precede any economic feasibility studies. As the diagram illustrates, this represents the best opportunity to influence costs, without necessarily detracting from project objectives of scope and quality.

Conduct the second VM study just before seeking approval of the Project Brief and authority for project implementation. This should tighten up the terms of reference and provide clear directions to be passed on to the design teams as soon as the go-ahead is received.

Conduct the third VM study when the working drawings and specifications are 50% to 60% complete. At this point the detailed design is sufficiently advanced to identify design trends, yet it is early enough to make corrections with minimum interruption. It will encourage standardization and simplified solutions to design problems. When properly conducted, this three stage VM approach will ensure that the project is kept on course. It will also emphasize the importance of being value conscious to all those concerned with the project.

To some, Value Management is an interference with the design process. This perception is aggravated by the reality that not all disciplines advance simultaneously. For example, logical dependencies in building work require that architectural design leads the parade, followed by structural, mechanical and electrical, in that order. So electrical design may be only 15% advanced when architectural work has reached, say, 60%. The situation is similar in process engineering projects.

The early application of VM accelerates design because it clarifies design scope.

Experience shows that early application of VM actually accelerates design because it helps to clarify design scope. It also saves time in avoiding misdirected design efforts on false starts, and reduces time loss by early warning of any design-to-budget limit being exceeded.

The cost of VM reviews may range from 0.1 to 0.5% of project costs, yet may result in savings of 10% or more. A pay-off of up to 100 times the VM cost is not uncommon in specific instances. Unfortunately, the benefits of VM do not show up in traditional accounting records, and so the cost of the VM effort must be justified by careful documentation. At the same time, a very positive and strictly factual attitude must be maintained in the documentation, to provide comfort to the participants, and avoid bruising professional dignity.

CHAPTER 4

Planning for High Level Cost Control

4.1 Project Cost Control and Construction Cost Control

In Chapter 1, we explored the changes that take place in the management of a project when it moves from the planning phases into the producing phases. In a corresponding way, there will be changes in the way of controlling cost.

In the planning phases, the project is built on paper.

In the planning phases, the project is "built on paper" and the cost of the project needs to be managed on two levels. At the lower level, there are the costs of the planning process itself that should be only a small fraction of the final total cost of the project. Typically, for a construction project these are hourly and incidental costs incurred directly by the owner or sponsor using in-house resources, or short term consulting paid on an hourly and expense basis. The collection of in-house hourly costs especially may require the introduction of special systems to record the necessary data. On a large project these costs are significant and should be managed as a project-within-a-project using the techniques described in this book.

The objective is to collect and track these costs and this has three benefits. First, it provides control over this component of the total project cost. Second, it is an opportunity to test and refine the organization's project cost control system and, third, it gets the newly assembled project team familiar with cost control discipline. Bear in mind that the planning phases of a project are essentially iterative. So cost control must be flexible enough to encourage creativity to the benefit of the project's ultimate effectiveness and success.

The major project costs are incurred in the producing phases.

The major project costs are incurred in the producing phases, when the project is being built in reality. In these phases the owner or sponsor typically manages the constructed costs by entering into a series of legal commitments such as service agreements, general contracts or trade contracts. There will still be direct costs to collect, but the contracts will form most of the total project cost. The objective of the cost control process by the owner is to maintain costs within approved budgets, especially the cost of changes beyond the approved project scope. The exception to this situation is the organization that is itself in the business of direct construction, that is, acting as its own contractor.

The objectives are somewhat different from the perspective of those performing the contracts. Their objectives are to make a reasonable profit while doing the work. They have their own direct and indirect costs to keep in line with the respective components of their total contract price.

Part B of this book discusses Cost Control in the Producing Phase.

4.2 Project Cost Management through the Project Life-Cycle

At each stage in the development and execution of a capital project, costs must be collected and reported in a fashion and framework that enables good technical and management decisions to be made. Two simple principles must be clearly understood:

- Only future costs can be controlled.
- There must be a standard of comparison.

(a) Only future costs can be controlled

Since only future costs can be controlled, the primary focus must be on the future.

Because only future costs can be changed, the primary focus must be on forecasting the future and not on historical reporting. It follows that the ability to influence the final costs constructively progressively diminishes as the project advances through each successive stage. Indeed, the ability to influence cost drops rapidly as the project concept evolves and key requirements are confirmed. Figure 4-1 shows this graphically. Note that the greatest opportunity to influence the final project cost is at the beginning of the project life-cycle. This is when the optimum size of the facility is being set for the most cost-effective use. This also implies looking at future operating costs because, from the owner's point of view, these will play a much larger part in the financial health of the organization.

Economic analysis enables these future costs to be examined in terms of "present value". This in turn requires many assumptions such as:

- Intended facility operating life
- Allowance for terminal disposal
- Cost of money
- Rates of equipment obsolescence, and
- Projected rates of inflation for various resources such as labor, materials and energy.

Since the curve represents the ability to influence the economic value of the facility, the curve may show further benefit to the facility by continuing to drop somewhat after project completion. This is because it is usually

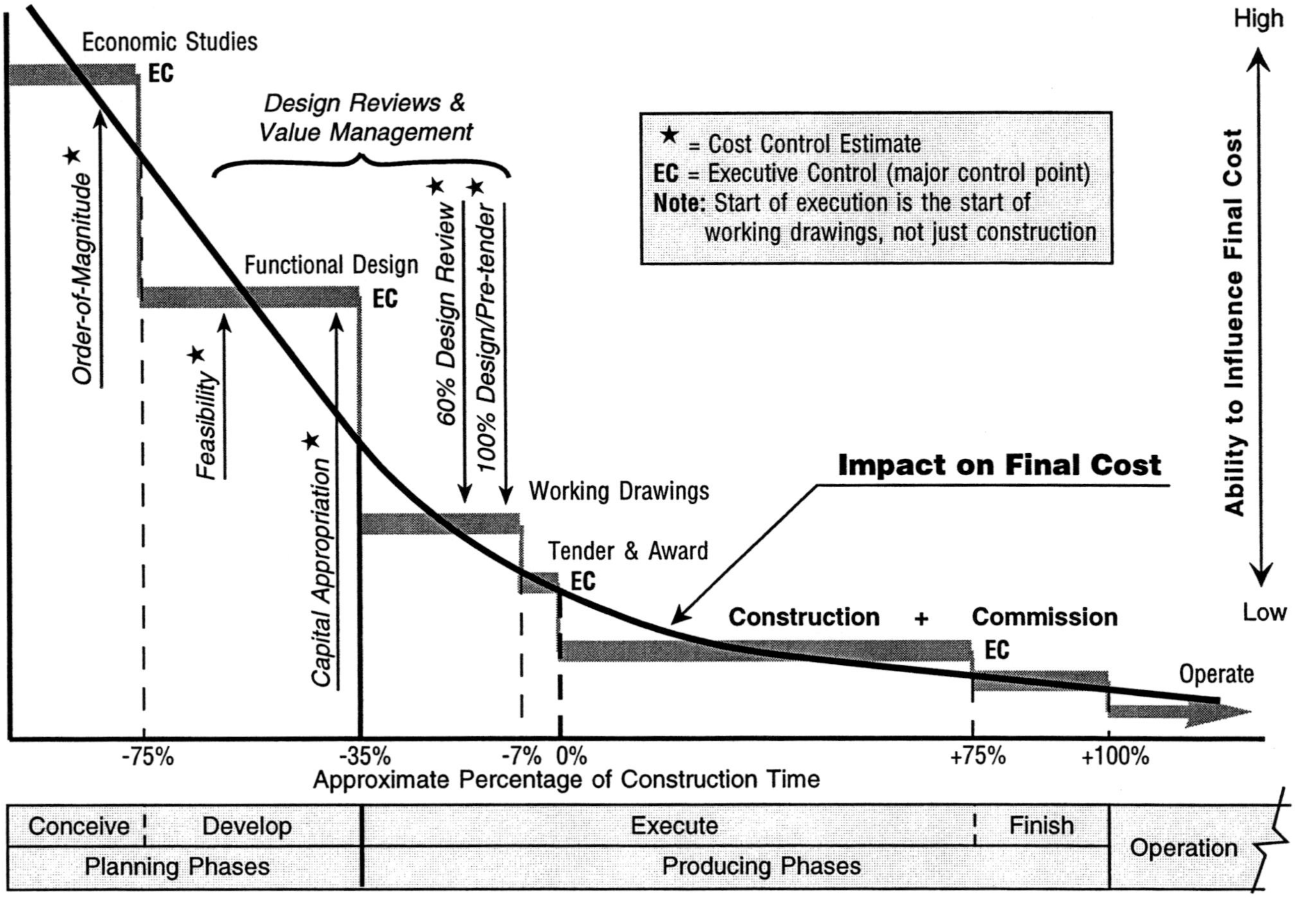

Figure 4-1. Ability to Influence Final Cost of Construction in Progressive Phases

possible to find ways to increase production during the life of a facility by improved operational procedures.

During the design of a facility and the working drawings stages, choices must be made that optimize the relation between facility cost and the requirements expressed in the scope documents. During these stages, and even during construction, pressure to escalate requirements will often come from the facility's users. There is a natural tendency to overstate requirements, or impose design standards higher than those required for the effective operation of the facility. After all, if they are not paying the bill, why not?

The users will make the point that it is cheaper to add enhancements during design, or even during construction, than it is after completing the facility and it is operational. This is not necessarily true because frequent changes can be very disruptive to the project schedule and add hidden costs. Therefore, the project manager must be continually on guard against such tendencies. The merits of any suggested changes should be carefully evaluated, if necessary by Value Management as described in Chapter 2. If guidance is lacking in the project scope documents, the standard of comparison should be the current level of construction and operating costs for similar facilities.

(b) There must be a standard of comparison

Simultaneous evolution of the cost estimate during the Planning Phases will help to maintain the reference baseline.

To provide a standard of comparison, there must be a reference baseline. This baseline can be difficult to maintain during the Planning Phases, because the project plan itself is going through an iterative process of development. Even so, a significant degree of continuity can be maintained by simultaneous evolution of the cost estimate. This will help decisions at each stage. During the Producing Phases the baseline is the approved project budget, the Capital Appropriation.

Scope definitions and cost estimates that become the reference standard for each following stage should be prepared during each preceding stage. As the project information is developed and refined, it becomes possible to draw up successive estimates with increasing degrees of confidence. Figure 4-2 shows this progression and suggests accuracies for typical grades of estimate, at progressive stages of the project.

For ease of reference, the positive and negative ranges of variance in final cost are plotted to positive and negative ratio scales about a center line representing the most probable final cost. The scales are different because

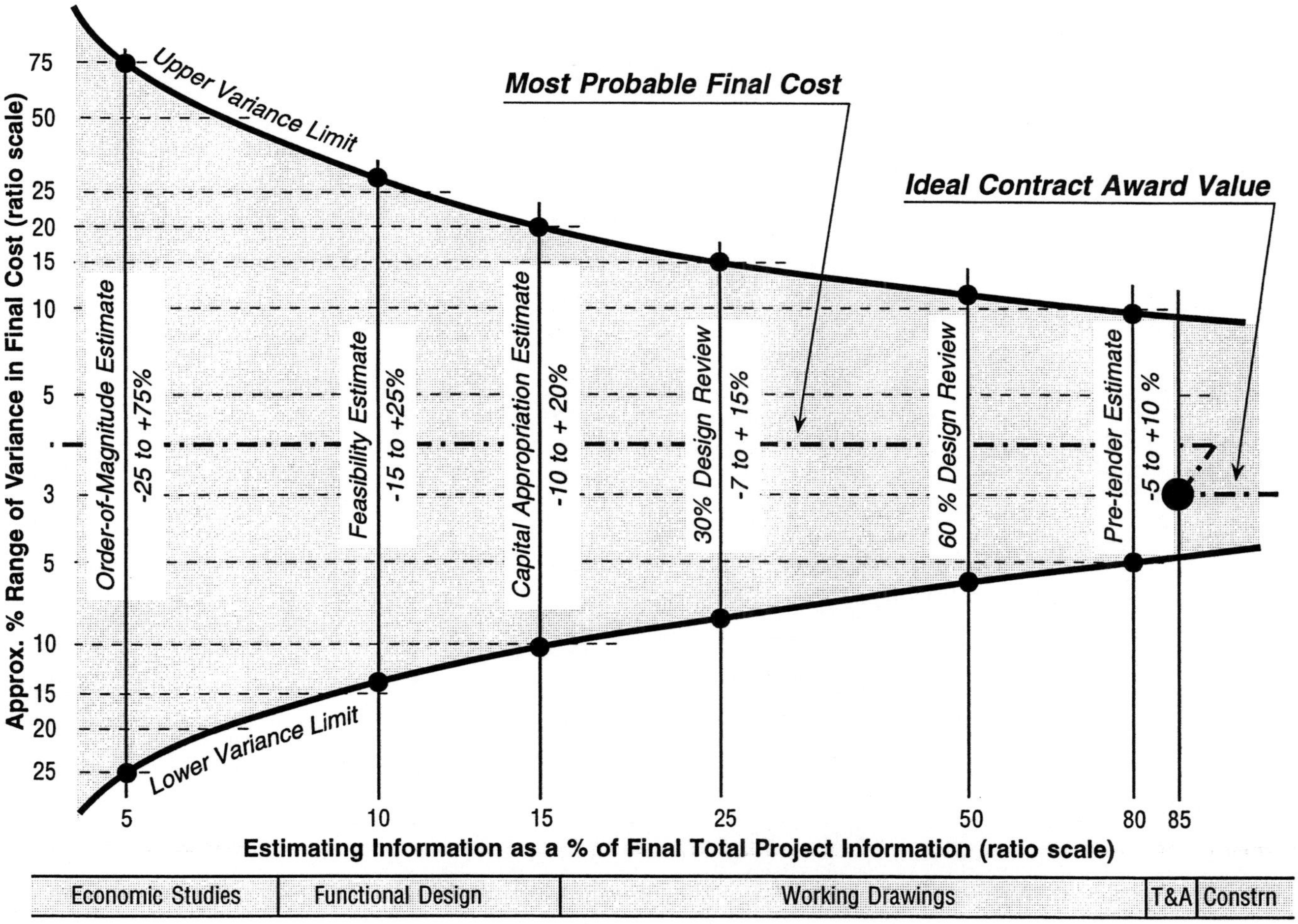

Figure 4-2. The Estimating Accuracy Trumpet

there is much more likely to be an increased cost than a reduced one. This may be due to a lack of information, or because of items overlooked. The horizontal scale, which represents the amount of quality information available, is also plotted to a ratio scale.

Also shown, is an ideal contract award value somewhat below the most probable final cost. This would provide for some final settlement of outstanding matters. Of course, the chart assumes good quality information about each stage, and a competent level of cost control. The typical shape of the curves representing the upper and lower limits of variance in the diagram suggest the name "Estimate Accuracy Trumpet".

All estimates are approximations based on the best information available at the time.

(c) **Suggested grades of estimate**

There are probably as many methods of estimating project construction costs and levels of accuracy for capital cost estimates as there are estimators. Each method no doubt has its appropriate applications and limitations. The point to emphasize is that all estimates are approximations based on the best information, experience and judgment available at the time of estimating. Indeed, even the final reported cost figures on completed projects can differ in detail from "true" costs. This is simply because judgment is required in the distribution and allocation of some costs even while the project is in progress.

Cost control during the early stages of a project need some semblance of order. For this purpose, Figure 4-2 shows five progressive grades of estimate ranging from "Order of Magnitude" to "Pre-tender Estimate". All of them represent the estimated final cost at completion. The names are generally associated with the stage in the project life-cycle in which they are prepared, although these may vary in different organizations depending on the purpose of the estimate and size of project. Figure 4-3 shows their general relationship to the project life-cycle. They are defined as follows.

An Order-of-Magnitude Estimate is no more than an educated guess.

Concept, Conceptual or **Order-of-Magnitude Estimate**

This estimate represents an "educated guess", sometimes called a "guesstimate". It is based on a comprehensive statement of requirements in "mission" terms and an outline solution. It is arrived at by comparison with costs on previous projects in simple global terms. It is strictly limited to an indication of final cost and completion date only. Even so, if several possible alternatives are estimated on the same basis, then it should be sufficient for making a preliminary selection amongst competing projects or between different approaches.

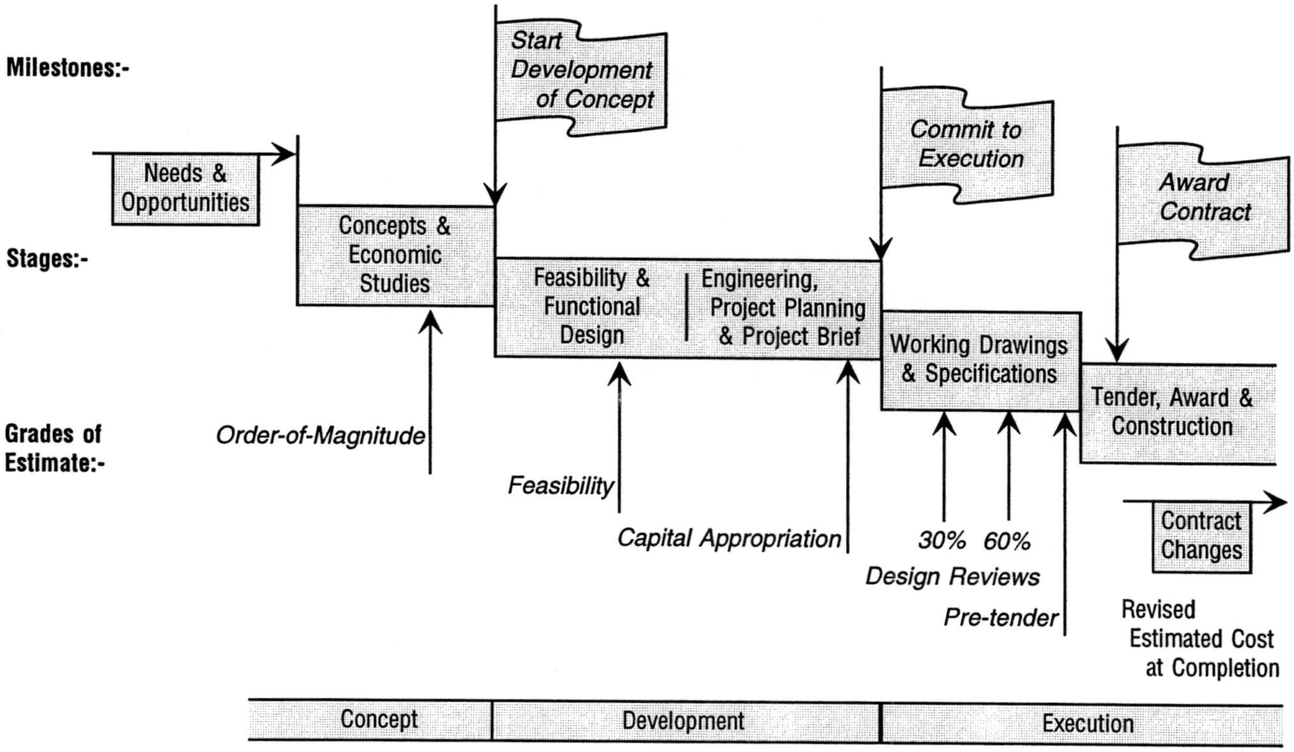

Figure 4-3. The Evolution of Construction Project Estimates

Functional Design, Preliminary Engineering or **Feasibility Estimate**

A Feasibility Estimate should be sufficient for making the correct investment decision.

This estimate of final project cost is based on completion of all preliminary work necessary for starting the engineering design, including knowledge of site conditions sufficient to identify site related risks. It should be sufficient for making the correct investment decision. It is determined "top down" by using "parametric costing" or "experience curves" applied to the project's major components and systems, approximate quantities as available, and design notes. Parametric costing or experience curves are derived from the historic costs of similar components and systems, information that may be available from trade literature and similar sources. Considerable understanding of the content of the values presented and experience in translating the data to the project in question is necessary for reasonable confidence in the results.

Design Control, Cost Plan, Project Cost or **Capital Appropriation Estimate**

The purpose of this estimate is to define the scope of the project, establish a realistic target budget, schedule and cost plan for control during the detailed design, working drawings and specifications stage. It should also make possible a good cash flow projection for evaluating the project's rate of return. It will also provide a basis for cost control procedures during the execution of the work.

This estimate is based on completed engineering design, including the required site data, such that detailed working drawings, specification and contract documents can be prepared. The basis includes definition of the major systems and sub-systems of the equipment or facility, outline specifications, preliminary drawings and models, as appropriate. It is determined partly on parametric costing and as much as possible on developed elemental unit costing. It has the advantage of much more specific information and timing relating to the actual project.

The Capital Appropriation Estimate provides a reference baseline for control during the producing phases.

Figure 4-4 shows a typical elemental unit costing worksheet for a building project. Figure 4-4A shows an example of this cost model planning sheet prepared for a proposed hotel construction project. Note how the worksheet provides for entering Actuals or current Estimated at Completion values for purposes of comparison and project cost tracking.

(%) **Design Review Estimates**

These are estimates prepared at progressive percentage completion of the various working drawings and specifications. They are really "check" estimates to ensure that working details are developed in general accordance with the original project intent. Their methodology ranges between that for the Capital Appropriation and the Pre-tender Estimate that follows. As mechanical/electrical designs typically lag behind architectural/structural designs, these estimates typically contain quantitative estimates for the latter but parametric estimates for the former in varying degrees.

Definitive, Detailed Take-off or **Pre-tender Estimate**

This estimate is based on completed working drawing specifications and contract conditions, including methodology and design of any special requirements such as temporary works. It requires a detailed take-off of all quantities for the work and the application of appropriate pricing to all contract pay items. Because of the level of detail, it is called a "bottom up" estimate. It is conducted from essentially the same position as a contractor preparing a competing tender. While the work involved is significant, preparing a pre-tender estimate has two major benefits. It enables reconsideration of the design before committing heavy construction expenditures and it provides a basis for comparison and analysis of submitted tenders.

A Pre-Tender Estimate provides a basis for comparison and analysis of submitted tenders.

Essential requirements for any grade of estimate include:

- A reliable project definition or scope description (consistent with the stage of the project)
- Systematic procedures and documentation for recording the work-up of the estimate, and

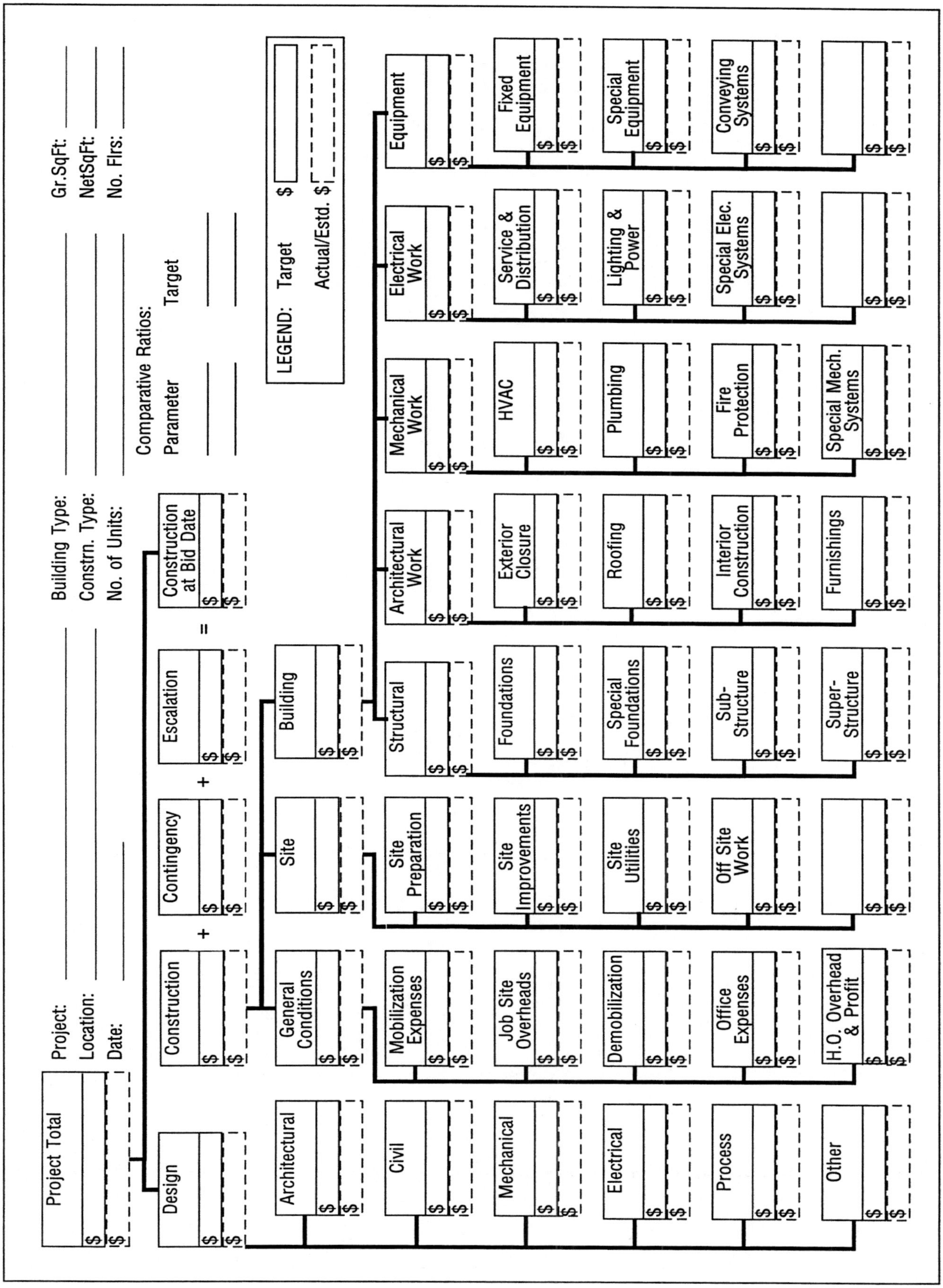

Figure 4-4. Typical Building Project Cost Model

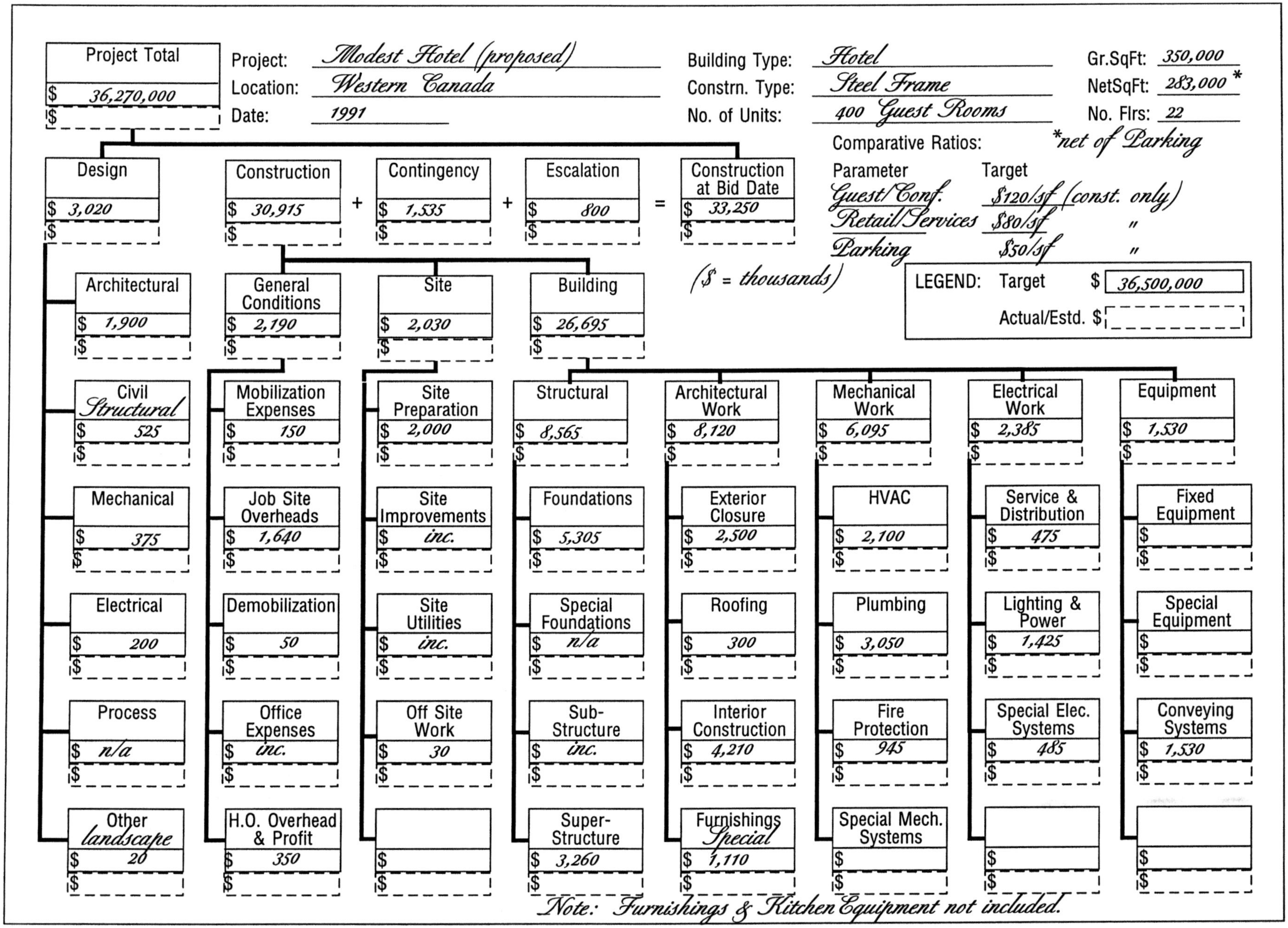

Figure 4-4A. Building Project Cost Model Example

- A database of relevant and reliable "normalized" estimating information.

Normalized means that actual historic cost data has been adjusted to remove any untypical conditions that skewed the originally recorded cost. All estimates should be prepared in a standard format, whether by element

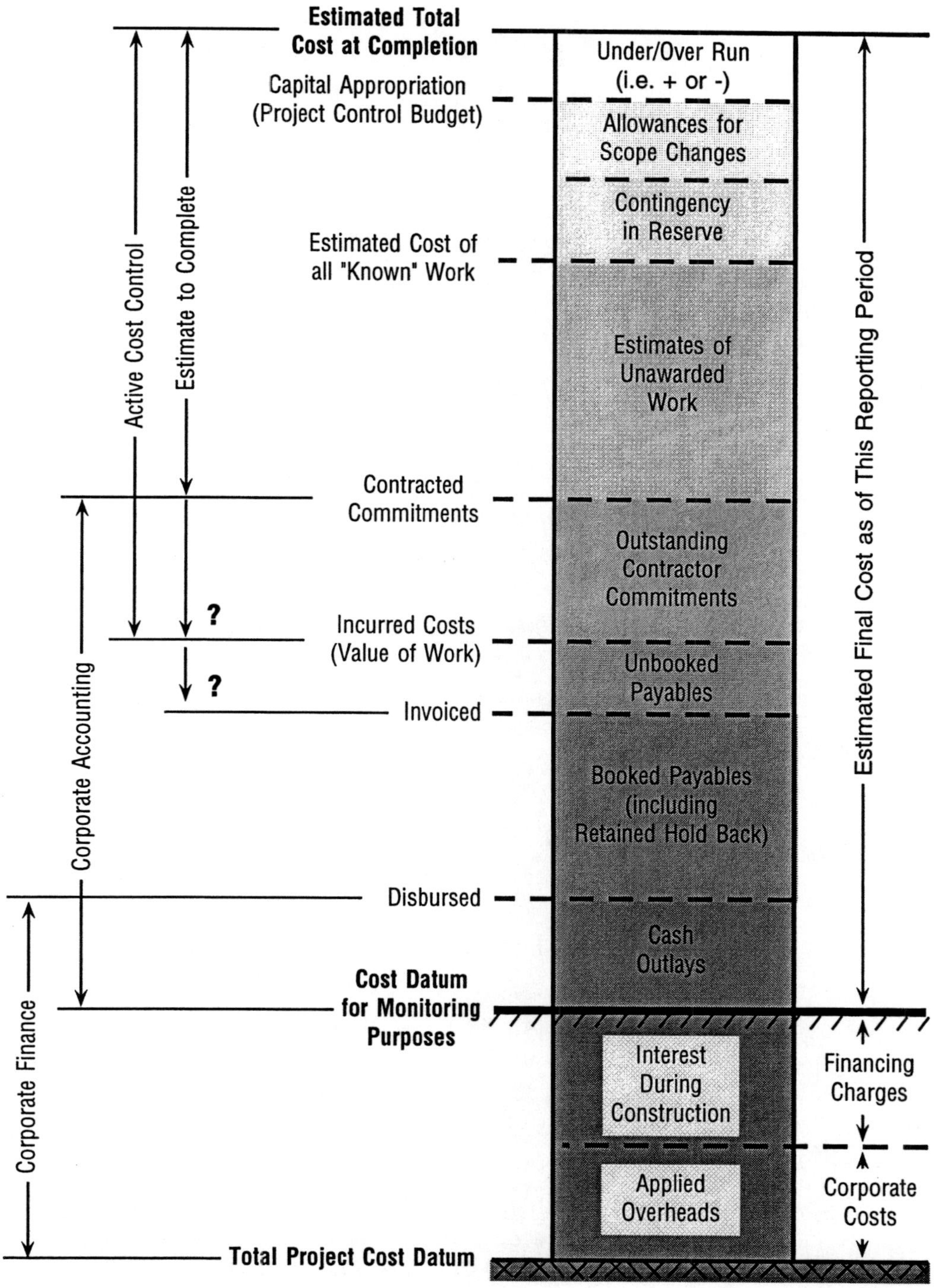

Figure 4-5. A Comparison of Cost Control, Accounting and Finance Domains

or trade, and contain an introduction sheet stating the methodology, basis, data used, assumptions made, and any exclusions.

(d) Financial control not suited to project cost control

It is important that the function of project cost control, that is, project financial accounting and forecasting, is not confused with the parent organization's corporate finance and accounting function. Certainly, the two are closely related. Fiscal accounting provides expense information for project cost control while project accounting provides allocation information for the general ledger. However, Figure 4-5, A Comparison of Cost Control, Accounting and Finance Domains shows that there are major differences.

Only future costs can be controlled.

The perspective of an organization's financial and accounting control system is entirely historical and on a fiscal year basis with conventional accrual accounting. The figure shows the extent to which it covers project costs. In contrast, as noted earlier, only future costs can be controlled so that project cost control must focus on the make up of the estimated total cost at completion. This involves an accurate knowledge of the incurred cost to date and confident estimating of all unawarded work together with an assessment of outstanding contingency and allowances. This requires a sound knowledge of project management, access to technical knowledge and a solid understanding of the project.

Two items that typically are difficult for the project manager to control are Interest During Construction and overhead costs applied by the home office. That is why these are shown "below the surface". Chapter 12, Section 12.1 discusses difficulties associated with reliably estimating cost-to-complete.

In addition, the time span for project accounting is not the fiscal year but on a project-to-date basis and projects typically cross fiscal year boundaries. Costs are also reported as an expense on an incurred rather than an accrued basis. So a financial information system alone does not provide the kind of reporting that is required for project management purposes. To demonstrate this, consider the numbers shown in the table in Figure 4-6.

A project has a budget of $800,000. Scheduled progress to date is 25%, although only 20% has been done — $160,000 worth. The actual cost-to-date is $180,000. A financial control report might simply compare the cost-to-date with the budget-to-date and reflect a $20,000 under run. However, a project cost control report will compare the cost-to-date with the value earned that happens to show up as a $20,000 over run. More importantly, the estimated-at-completion based on current performance shows that the final project over run is now being projected as $100,000. This is a very different state of affairs compared to a $20,000 under run!

Example Project

The following simple example shows how financial cost accounting can fall short of requirements for tracking, managing and controlling project costs.

Project Status: Scheduled progress to date		25%	
Actual progress to date		20%	
Financial Control			
Total budget		$800,000	
Committed to date		$250,000	
Budget to date	(@ 25% completion)	$200,000	
Cost to date (including accruals)		$180,000	
	Apparent Under Run	-$20,000	-10.0%
Project Control			
Budget to date	(@ 25% completion)	$200,000	
Budgeted cost of work performed	(@20% completion)	$160,000	
Cost to date (including accruals)		$180,000	
	Actual Over Run	+$20,000	+12.5%
Estimated Cost at Completion:			
Cost to date (including accruals)		$180,000	
Estimated cost of remaining work based on current performance	80% x $180,000 / 20%	$720,000	
Hence Current Estimated Cost at Completion		$900,000	
Original Total Budget		$800,000	
	Hence Expected Total Overrun	$100,000	+12.5%
Apparent under run based on Financial Controls		-$20,000	
Total discrepancy between the two methods		$120,000	+15.0%

Figure 4-6. The Pitfalls of Financial Project Cost Accounting

4.3 Project Cost Categories: Classes and Types

Cost Classes refer to subdivisions of the project scope. Cost Types refer to the type of entry in the accounting sequence.

Decisions made during the concept phase effectively set the scope of work for the project. The developing project scope description and preliminary design must be frequently checked against the originally agreed requirements to avoid unauthorized "scope drifting" as noted in Chapter 2. Similarly, and as far as possible, successive types of estimate should be developed using a consistent frame of reference so that direct comparisons can be made with earlier estimates. Herein lies an essential element of effective cost management and control.

A project has two broad categories of costs. For convenience, they are called "Classes" and "Types". The term Cost Class refers to project content, that is, subdivisions of the total project scope. Each has dollar values assigned in the estimate or budget breakdown.

The term Cost Type, on the other hand, refers to the type of cost occurring at various stages in the cost management process. Cost Types describe whether the amount is predicted or authorized to occur in the future; whether it is legally committed; or whether it is a past expenditure.

(a) Cost Classes and the Work Breakdown Structure

The formulation of a cost control system begins with breaking it down into logical and manageable pieces. This is necessary for estimating the various components of the project and producing the progressive series of estimates discussed in the previous Section. It also helps to understand the project and how best to manage it.

A WBS breaks the project's scope down into manageable chunks.

The breakdown should be done systematically and, if the breakdown is based on the project's Scope Statement, the result would be called a Project Breakdown Structure. Alternatively, if the project's Scope of Work is used, the result is a Work Breakdown Structure. As discussed in Chapter 3, Section 3.1, the Scope Statement and the Scope of Work are not the same, though closely aligned. The "breakdown" technique is a very flexible one and in practice frequently encompasses some aspects of each approach. Whichever approach is adopted, the term most frequently used is Work Breakdown Structure (WBS), which is what we will use from now on.

The breakdown process works its way through major areas or cost centers, to discipline or function, and on through trade or activity to component or task. The lowest developed level of the WBS is called a "work package". The work package should be defined in terms of work content or deliverables, estimated cost and duration, and is usually identified with a single responsibility unit within the project group.

Conversely, several work packages may form a "contract" package for commitment purposes. Several contract packages may represent a "major area", and the sum of these will form the total project. It follows that the WBS must be compatible with any planned contractual arrangements. In practice, the two are often planned side by side. Chapter 5 describes the WBS technique in greater detail.

A Work Package is the chunk at the lowest level of any particular leg of the WBS.

Once the project is broken down into cost classes to the work package level, each of these must be assigned a numerical identifier for purposes of data collection and automated reporting. These then become "accounts" in the cost system. To provide for logical identifiers, a Master Code Structure (MCS) must be developed to match and suit the WBS. The WBS and its MCS identifiers are built progressively through the planning phases of the project. By the time the Project Brief is being prepared, they should be well established.

As noted previously, the Project Brief is the source document for exercising control in the producing phases. It will contain a project budget submitted for financial approval based on the WBS-MCS structure. Therefore, it is essential that this WBS-MCS structure, and the consequent approved project funding, reflects the manner in which actual costs will be collected. The latter may be greatly influenced by the procurement strategy adopted for the project. In any case, close alignment will simplify the comparison between actual costs and latest forecasts versus budgeted items necessary for effective project control. Chapter 11 describes a suitable Master Code Structure.

There are other classes of cost on project work, of course, but these are used for specialized purposes and not for progress reporting. In preparing estimates, for example, unit costs are assigned to individual labor, material and equipment components. Contract change costs may be classified by origin - see Chapter 13, Section 13.3. In the corporate books of account, costs may be classified according to the type of source document that supports the expenditure. Examples include supplier and contractor invoices, payroll costs based on time sheets, travel and expense vouchers, material costs based on warehouse withdrawal reports, and so on.

It should be emphasized that none of these other cost classes should find their way into the project reporting system used for project management control. On the contrary, the Work Breakdown Structure and its Master Coding should be specifically designed for the project cost control function. All other accounting structures should be rigorously avoided, as a matter of principle.

Both the Work Breakdown Structure and the Master Code Structure should be specifically designed for project control.

(b) Cost Types and the Management Report

Cost Types refer to cost accounting entries at various stages in the cost management process. The following headings describe the various Cost Types that will normally be encountered in capital project cost management reports.

Appropriation - authorized levels of total value for the scope of work represented in the project's cost classes. Though often used, refrain from using the unqualified term "budget". This will avoid confusion with the organization's fiscal accounting. The "project budget" of a long construction project may encompass several "fiscal" budgets.

Commitment - the value of a contract or other legal obligation usually documented by officially signed purchase orders, formal contracts and service agreements.

Expenditure - actual value of goods and services received to date, generally vouched for by a source document such as a supplier invoice. It may also be called "actual cost" and is the type of cost also entered in the corporate books of account. The previous cost types do not typically appear in the books of account, although they may be quoted in executive management reports.

Forecast - predicted levels of future costs arrived at by estimating and judgment.

Estimated Final Cost - the combination of commitments plus forecast costs yet to be committed.

Essentially, all project cost management reports are some form of presentation of cost classes cross tabulated with cost types at a specific reporting date.

It will be seen that any given entry in a cost class will flow through the above series of cost types as it gets updated over time. Therefore, for the system to work reliably, the precise point in the process at which a sum becomes committed, or expended, must be clearly defined by the organization's accounting policies and procedures. For example: is a sum committed when a contract receives a handshake, a letter of intent is issued, contract documents are exchanged, or the signed contract is returned?

Similarly, is a sum expended when the work is done, invoiced for, a cheque issued, or the cheque drawn down? Details though they may be, lack of clear accounting policies frequently lead to errors and omissions in forecasting and therefore lack of reliability in the Estimated Final Costs. Chapter 12, Section 12.1 explores these issues further.

CHAPTER 5

The Work Breakdown and Master Code Structures

5.1 The WBS-MCS Concept

The foundation for the process of tracking and steering a project is a firm baseline plan. This plan must be defined in terms of scope, quality, time and cost each on a compatible basis and in units that can be readily handled. As outlined in Chapter 2, the essential components of this control system, especially for controlling cost, are:

Essential components of a control system.

1. A plan - a statement of what is to happen.
2. Observations - measurements of what is happening.
3. Comparisons - between expectations and actual.
4. Corrections - actions designed to redirect what is happening back to what should happen.
5. Updates - of forecast and plan as appropriate

This simple but powerful idea establishes some important requirements

The tighter the restraints, the tighter the control required.

- The plan must be expressed in terms that can be measured during implementation, otherwise it will not be possible to draw the required comparisons;
- Observations during implementation must be consistent with elements of the plan, and vice versa, to make the required comparisons;
- Observations and the comparative results must be made sufficiently frequently and rapidly to provide the opportunity to take corrective action while time and resources remain.

It follows that the tighter the restraints imposed on a project, the tighter the control required, the more frequent must be the measurements, and therefore the greater the effort required in this process.

The control process described typically involves large amounts of data, even on small projects. Manual processing is a chore and is no longer acceptable considering the power of computers and software now available to almost everyone. However, very large projects with a requirement for a high degree of integration may require main-frame machines. Data processing in this way requires the coding of every element of relevant information. When entering data according to its cost type, as discussed in Chapter 4, it is then automatically assigned for processing to its proper cost class.

The WBS must reflect the way actual costs will be collected. It is an essential communication tool.

Chapter 4 emphasized that the Work Breakdown Structure developed in the planning phases must reflect the way actual costs will be collected in the producing phases. Similarly, the coding structure used for entering the actual data must match the work breakdown adopted for the planning and approval of the project. Otherwise, the automated data processing will not deliver the information needed for project management control. It cannot be emphasized too strongly that the Master Code Structure (MCS) must match the Work Breakdown Structure (WBS) exactly, and vice versa.

The application of a WBS-MCS framework goes beyond direct data processing. It can also provide the basis for a complete project management information system and, as such, is an essential communication tool. Special attention must be paid to the make-up of both the WBS and the MCS.

There are many ways of subdividing the scope of a project. For example, the following are all commonly used:

- Geographic regions, construction areas or "battery limits"
- Major chronological time phases
- Structural or process components, engineering systems or devices, including intermediate deliverables
- Areas of responsibility, such as
  - External vendors, suppliers or construction contracts
  - Functional or technological disciplines, trades or services

Often it is necessary to incorporate several different criteria to form an effective WBS for a particular project, and different categories may be applied at different levels and in different sequences.

5.2 Developing the Work Breakdown Structure

(a) What the WBS is and does

The Work Breakdown Structure (WBS) is one of the most important and powerful techniques available for managing a project. As its name implies, it involves a level-by-level hierarchical segregation of the project components or deliverables into a logical and organized set of elements.

The result is an inverted tree-like structure with the name of the project at the top and the deliverables at the ends of the branches at the bottom.

The WBS can be more formally defined as "A product-oriented family tree of elements that completely organizes, defines and graphically displays the components, software, services and data to be produced, and the work to be done, to attain the specified project outcome." To use the WBS, break down the scope of the project into manageable work elements and subsystems each with clearly assigned responsibilities, logically scheduled tasks and corresponding cost estimates. These manageable elements at the ends of each branch are called "Work Packages".

Each element of the WBS must have clearly assigned responsibilities.

Thus, work packages are created to make the project easier to manage. From a cost control stand point, the question should be asked at each level of the WBS: "What costs are included and how will they really be collected?" The answers to this question very often give a good indication of whether further segregation is required. In this way, the complete WBS is made up of different types of discrete work packages. Section 5.3 discusses work packages in more detail.

In practical terms, the WBS provides the means for communication, and integrating and monitoring all activities on the project. Therefore, it must:

1. Establish an information structure for describing the project in its entirety.
2. Represent the planning of the project, phase by phase.
3. Reflect the procurement strategy during the various phases of the project's life-cycle.
4. Separate sequential and parallel activities assigned to different organizations or groups who will schedule, measure, and control their own performances.
5. Serve as an effective means of communication to integrate objectives and activities of all the internal and external organizations involved in the project, and
6. Provide a meaningful structure for reporting the status of cost and schedule to the project team and other stakeholders.

Record the information associated with each WBS element in a WBS Dictionary.

The information associated with each element of a work breakdown structure can be considerable. This can be captured in a "WBS dictionary", especially useful on larger projects. The WBS dictionary is a record that describes each element of the work breakdown structure in detailed narrative form. It typically includes the element's products, work content, unique master code identifier, cost and schedule data and any other pertinent information. Such a dictionary helps considerably in ensuring the correct and uniform collection, reporting, recording and understanding of project data.

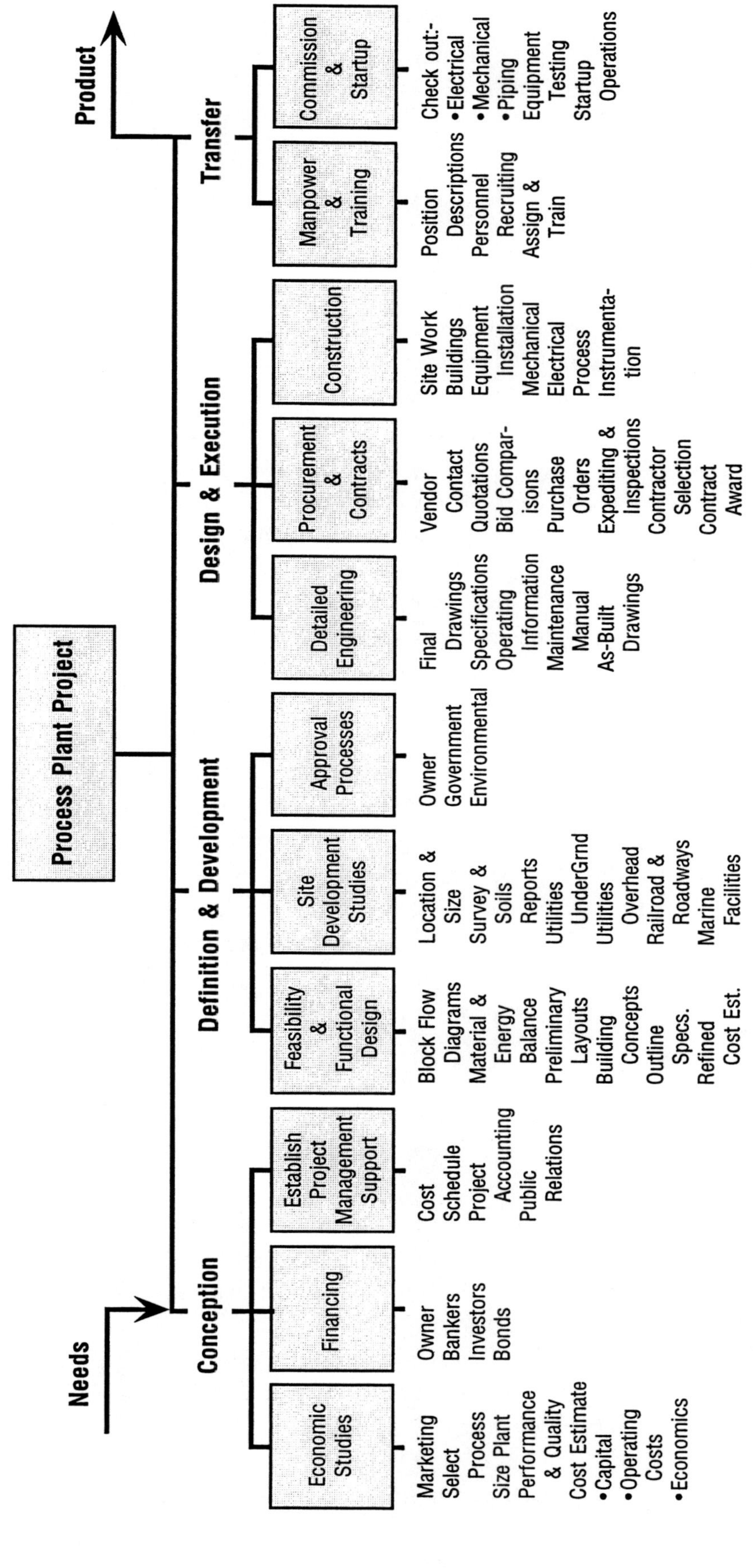

Figure 5-1. Work Breakdown Structure for the Design and Construction of a Process Plant

Figure 5-1 shows a WBS for the design and construction of a process plant. Note how major groupings are arranged sequentially reflecting the project life-cycle. Then each group represents a typical area of responsibility. Within each group there are sets of activities that lead to deliverables, activities that may proceed sequentially or in parallel as appropriate.

(b) What the MCS is and does

The Master Code Structure (MCS) is simply a consistent framework for assigning alpha-numeric labels to the components of a work breakdown structure. Each component is labeled as a unique item reflecting its position in the WBS hierarchical structure.

The sixteen division US Universal Construction Index (UCI) or the Masterformat system developed jointly between Construction Specifications Canada and the US are examples of hierarchical numerical identifiers. The titles distinguish component work at various levels in the make up of a construction project. While these systems are excellent for establishing databases of specification clauses, for which they were designed, they are not necessarily suited to the process of managing a construction project. This is because they tend to be too comprehensive and therefore too complex. They are also entirely numeric. The introduction of alpha identifiers that have meaning can help considerably in the correct coding of input data and therefore improve the reliability and integrity of the whole system.

Organizations responsible for many similar projects, frequently try to standardize at least the upper levels of their Master Code. The use of a consistent MCS across several projects greatly assists the storage and retrieval of historical information for estimating, project comparisons, decisions and control purposes. At its lower levels, the Master Code is usually customized to reflect the particular features and design of the project, and the implementation strategy to be employed.

The WBS-MCS combination should be applied to the project at the earliest possible time during its planning.

It is preferable for the WBS-MCS combination to be applied at the earliest possible point in the planning phases. As the project Scope Statement is developed into the project plan through these phases, so scope definitions can be expanded through successive levels of detail in the coding structure.

The benefits of applying the Master Code concept have been well summarized by W. E. Allen in a paper given to the Project Management Institute in 1973[1]. From his experience on a $140 million multi-building construction program, he concluded:

"With early implementation, the Master Code provides numerous advantages in administering and managing the project.

The Code will:

- Promote communications in all forms through the project;

- Impose a discipline on engineers and architects in organizing and producing detailed drawings and specifications;
- Permit progressive development of cost estimates, time schedules and scopes of work for contract package elements, regardless of their status relative to one another;
- Prevent the proliferation of numbering schemes in the project, and the resulting need for interpretation and cross referencing;
- Minimize the work load in administering contracts in the post-award period;
- Provide a common reference, which facilitates the use of computer systems for cost/time reporting and control.

A Master Code is a key element in effective project control.

The Master Code is the key to establishing an effective project control system, on the large construction project." It might be added that it is the key to control on any size of project.

In summary, for the MCS to be effective it requires:

- Early implementation
- Flexibility and expandability
- Universal application
- Simplicity, and
- Capability of summation.

Chapter 11, The Master Code Structure, gives details of how to structure the Master Code Identifier.

(c) Simple steps to a work breakdown structure

The work breakdown structure must be designed to answer two questions:

1. What has to be done to achieve all the objectives and deliverables of the project?
2. How will these things be accomplished?

Ten steps to a WBS.

Here are ten suggested steps for developing a work breakdown plan that answers these questions.

1. If it is appropriate, or the project is large enough, separate its scope into geographical regions.
2. Separate these major elements according to typical project phases and/or stages.
3. Further separate these elements into intermediate or final deliverables. In practice, the separation into phases and stages may

have done that already. In effect, these elements represent high-level work packages.

4. Separate the resulting elements into structural or process components, engineering systems or devices.
5. Finally, separate these elements into deliverables that can be associated with distinctive types of people or resources. These are the work packages required for planning purposes.
6. Assign titles and MCS identifiers to each work package such that each is discrete and self-evident, and such that all the elements are integrated into a total system with a beginning and an end. Since work packages result in deliverables, they should be represented by nouns, not verbs, and to be discrete these nouns must be specific and not general.
7. Reduce the work packages to a series of tasks having quantifiable inputs, outputs and identifiable points of progress, such that each task can be sequenced, network scheduled, cost estimated and monitored as independent units. Unlike the descriptions of the work packages, tasks can best be described by action verbs. Each task should have one person accountable for all coordination and completion. If these conditions can be met, the work package in question is probably sound.
8. Display the WBS on a time sequenced project basis in a format that best conveys the information to the project team. Suggested formats are either graphically like a family tree, or in a word-processed outline form.
9. The process of segregation and representation should start early in the planning phases. It should continue until each work package is reduced to a manageable level of detail appropriate to the phase or stage of the project and consistent with the project's length, complexity and manageability. This process of segregation will likely be an evolutionary process as the project advances through its planning phases.
10. Always ensure that the completion of all the work packages identified will attain the project's total objectives and deliverables. This is essential to ensure that there are no "crises of omission" during the producing phases of the project.

How long are the branches of this family-tree-like structure, how far do you go along each branch? Until the size and complexity of the element at the end of each branch is manageable! On a small project there may be only a couple of levels of breakdown. On a large project, it may be four and on a very large or long project possibly even more.

If the segregation is done rationally, the size of the manageable element will depend on the type of work and the number and size of tasks it contains. As a result, not all branches will be the same length. Should they all be the same length? Certainly not, but the ends of all the branches must encompass the entire project.

The resulting structure should also look like a well-proportioned pyramid. If it is too flat, check to see if any of the items could be gathered under a common heading at the next higher level. Conversely, if it is too steep, check to see if greater segregation is required. Where several groups of elements contain similar relationships, make sure that they are laid out the same way each time, or even marked for repetition, for simplicity.

If the WBS does not look like a well-proportioned pyramid, then there is something wrong!

The next two sections discuss how to establish different types of discrete work package and rules for ensuring their integrity. Chapter 11 describes the Master Code Structure in detail.

(d) Testing your WBS

How can you tell if you have made a good WBS? What tests can you apply to make sure that your WBS is sound? R. E. Kelley suggests that you should test for correctness, completeness and duplication.[2]

1. In testing for correctness: Are there any element titles that are verbs or actions, instead of nouns? Are there any titles that are unclear or non-specific that could cause confusion?
2. In testing for completeness: Are all the categories of end-results or deliverables included? Have any been left out? Are they all logically arranged in their respective branches? Would a different logical arrangement make the structure better? Are all the items in each branch complete?
3. In testing for duplication: Are there any identical items in different parts of the structure? Is there any overlap of the work involved?

Let the project team develop a WBS that satisfies them — and the rules!

Because a good WBS is so important to the success of a project, the final test is to ask an independent party to examine the result and give their opinion and recommendations. There is no one single ideal solution to a WBS, but the WBS can benefit from synergistic input from the whole project team, and constructive suggestions from outsiders.

5.3 The Work Package

The purpose of a work package is to describe the work to be done by the organizational unit responsible for doing it. Work package is a general term used to describe a subdivision of the whole project and symbolizes a specific grouping of work activities.

It represents the sub-division of the project scope at the lowest developed level of a particular branch of the WBS. As the project life-cycle progresses and planning becomes more detailed, it may be necessary to further subdivide an existing work package. This pushes the work package to a still lower level.

It should be emphasized that the work package does not represent a level in the WBS, and it is a mistake to establish all work packages at the same level. This forces them to be all at some lowest common level and requires the insertion of intermediate unoccupied "dummy" levels on many branches. This leads to unnecessary complexity and confusion in reading and using the structure, especially in the early stages of the project before the structure is fully developed. Today's computers can handle work packages at different levels on separate branches.

It is a mistake to insist that all work packages must be at the same lowest level of a WBS.

In practice, all work packages fall into one of three different categories:

1. Discrete tasks that have a specific objective, end result or output. These normally cover 60-75% of the total work in the project.
2. Apportioned-effort tasks that can be directly related and apportioned to discrete tasks. Examples include quality control or inspection. These tasks are required to support the discrete tasks, and therefore their schedule and budget can be related to the discrete tasks.
3. Level-of-effort tasks that do have product performance standards instead of discrete end results. These consist mainly of the overhead accounts such as management, administration, liaison, coordination, etc. These tasks are characterized by relatively level, time-phased budgets and are not time-limited like the discrete tasks.

5.4 Work Package Rules

As noted earlier, the work package (WP) serves as a vehicle for monitoring and reporting progress, cost and schedule. To be effective for planning and controlling the work, each work package should conform to the following set of rules:

Rule 1. **A WP must represent a unit of work at a level where work is performed** i.e. it should be identified with a work location and an organizational unit.

Rule 2. **A WP must be clearly distinguishable from all other WPs.** That is, a component, system or other discrete deliverable.

Rule 3. **A WP should have scheduled start and finishing dates.** Where a WP is unavoidably long, interim milestones should be identified representative of physical or other observable accomplishments to facilitate measurement of progress.

Rule 4. **A WP should have a budget,** or an assigned value in terms of dollars or work hours.

Rule 5. **A WP's size and duration should be limited to relatively short spans of time.** This will minimize the effort and errors in evaluating work-in-progress.

Rule 6. **A WP's interfaces must be clearly defined.** That is, it must integrate with all other work packages and schedules.

Rule 7. **A WP must represent a level at which actual costs can be collected or assigned.** That is, the WP must be assignable to a single organizational entity.

It must be recognized that during the evolution of project planning, work packages will be affected by the degree of maturity of work definition at any particular time. For example:

- Work packages in the concept stage are based upon preliminary sketches and information. Estimates of time and cost are most likely based on historical data, experience and judgment, rather than detailed "take off" estimates. The scope of these work packages may be large, and the duration quite long.
- When the Project Brief is presented for approval to begin working drawings, work packages will be based upon the final scope of work. The estimates and schedules will be correspondingly firmer providing for better control.
- Before actual construction commences, work packages should be based on a firm design, a firm schedule, firm budgets, and a firm procurement strategy. Such work packages should be identified at least two to six months before performing the work. They should only be revised with the approval of the project manager, normally because of a change order.

A WBS should not be broken down too early or to too great an extent. If some work packages are too small, unnecessary administrative effort and management time will be wasted and the purpose of the WBS as an information vehicle may be defeated. This suggests some additional rules governing work packages.

On smaller projects, the following "test of reasonableness" for determining the minimum size of package is suggested:

Rule 8. **A work package should at least be large enough to be a scope of work that could be competitively bid and contracted for by itself.** In other words, a contract that is sensible in the eyes of the industry, trade or service involved.

On larger multi-million dollar projects in the producing phases, the following rules of thumb are suggested:

Rule 9a. **Design work packages should not be less than, say, 300 man-hours and 2 months duration and not more than 1000 hours and six months duration.**

Rule 9b. For construction work packages, a minimum value of, say, 0.1% of total construction cost is recommended.

During the procurement stage of the project, market conditions or other circumstances may require a revision of the project execution strategy. For example, several work packages may be reassembled into a contract package for procurement purposes. Within such a contract, the identity of the individual work packages should be maintained to help with progress assessment, payment and control. To maintain the integrity of the WBS, the following further rule must be applied:

Rule 10. The same work must NOT appear in more than one contract.

If work of a similar nature is likely to appear in more than one contract package, the respective parts should be clearly identified, and separately defined and coded. In construction, this situation often arises in the unavoidable making good of the work of earlier trades following the work of subsequent trades.

Chapter 11 describes details of an associated Master Code Structure.

5.5 Benefits of a Work Breakdown Structure

The previous sections show that a coded Work Breakdown structure is central to communicating the entire project management process. Benefits of the WBS can be summarized as follows:

- Project mandate definition — links project objectives to the means of doing them
- Scope definition — enables the separation of distinct intermediate and end item deliverables
- Scope of work — enables the parceling into work packages of similar or associated work contained in the project
- Responsibility allocation — helps organize the work so that responsibility can be delegated to appropriate groups
- Plan update and revision — enables the progressive evolution of the project plan
- Estimating — helps determine the cost of the project so that it can be budgeted and tracked
- Scheduling — helps identify logical activity sequencing for estimating the project time dimension
- Risk assessment — enables systematic analysis of areas of project risk
- Contract administration — facilitates the contract procurement process, tracking of contract progress and progress payments

- Work Authorization — Where warranted or adopted, enables systematic work release and a higher level of control
- Performance measurement — when required, establishes project progress on an earned value basis
- Accounting — enables the accumulation of cost information in a consistent and useful manner
- Reporting — provides a consistent basis for data collection, analysis and reporting of project progress

References

[1] Allen, W. E. 1973. The Master Code: Its Application on the Large Construction Project. Seminar/Symposium Proceedings, The Project Management Institute, Upper Darby, PA, p678.

[2] Kelley, R. M. 1988. (Adapted from) Planning Techniques. Kelley Communication Development, Kettering, OH. p58.

CHAPTER 6

Developing a Budget for Appropriation Approval

6.1 What is a Budget?

According to the New Webster Dictionary, a budget is "A little sack, with its contents." How appropriate! In business usage, a budget is a plan expressed in monetary terms that covers a specified period, usually one year.[1]

A budget for a construction project, however, is somewhat different. A construction project budget is a financial plan for producing a complete constructed entity. While this project budget is time related, it is not tied to a fixed period, such as one year. It may be more or less than one year and, in any case, the duration is subject to the uncertainties inherent in any constructed work. For a project that exceeds one year, fiscal controls of the organization may require annual allocations or releases, but the total project budget will still represent the completed project.

A cost estimate reflects the estimated cost of the scope of work. A budget should be an achievable target for controlling costs.

(a) Project Estimate and Appropriation Budget not the same

A project cost estimate should be a reflection of the most likely cost of the identified scope of work based on the best available information at the time. Typically, an estimate prepared for appropriation purposes will

- Avoid unwarranted detail
- Arrive at costs by whatever means makes the most sense in estimating at the time, and hence will
- Follow the physical delineation of the project by
    - Discrete area such as a component facility or similar end-item
    - System
    - Major unit of equipment
- Identify those items which may later be considered as part of the "project cost" but not currently included such as allowances for training, commissioning and other charges as discussed below.

A project budget, on the other hand, should represent an achievable target with reasonable limits for the entire project within which cost control can be exercised with some flexibility. Therefore, an Appropriation Budget will be based on the project estimate but should also

- Include a concise description of the project's scope
- Summarize the philosophy and parameters used in preparing the budget, especially including the method of procurement
- Facilitate the breakdown of project procurement, i.e. by
  - contractor, supplier or department
  - type of labor, equipment or material
- Facilitate control of expenditure as commitments are made
- Provide only necessary detail
- Group and regroup where too much detail would actually hinder control
- Identify and include various additional items as described below.

Direct costs are measurable work. Indirect costs are added "on top".

The requirements for people, resources and time to do the work provide the basis for the cost estimate. To the extent possible, the work should be stated in some form of measurable quantities. These items represent the primary or direct costs. In general terms, direct costs are those that can be associated at source with work directly contributing to the physical completion of some part of the permanent facility. To these costs must be added indirect costs.

Indirect costs are those that contribute to the project as a whole, but cannot be identified directly with specific end-items. These include such items as:

- Construction management supervisory services and related subsistence and expenses
- Temporary construction facilities; other site services such as safety, supplies, small tools and clean-up
- Mobilize and demobilize site activities
- Head office overheads such as project management, communications, secretarial and accounting support, travel and expenses, taxes, freight, and project insurance, and
- Mark-up or profit if applicable.

These items for the most part are typically assessed as percentage add-ons. Some of them are "site indirects" and since they are incurred on site are usually included as part of the "direct constructed cost". The details of the estimate must be specific about what is included and what is not. Care must also be taken to avoid "double counting", e.g. using unit rates applied to measurable quantities that already include some of these components.

Capital Project Estimating
Some Typical Percentage On-Costs for Building Projects

Phase	Description	Approx. % Range (a)	Typical (say) (b)	$10 million Turnkey Project Example (b)
C	• Scope, economics,	1.0 - 2.5	1.5	1.25
	• Owner's associated cost	0.5 - 1.5	1	0.75
D	• Functional design, feasibility, permits, Project Brief	2.0 - 3.5	3	2
	• Owner's associated cost	1 - 2	3	2
E&F	• Construction cost estimate (direct and indirect on "most-likely basis")	100)	) **100. %**	**100. %**
	• Construction contingency (incl.)	10 - 15)		
	• Detailed design, working drawings and tender docs.	7 - 12	9	9
	• Designers' supervision and inspection, or "fast-track" construction management	3 - 7	4	4
	• Project management, incl. cost and schedule control	3 - 5	4	3
	• Owner's project responsibility	1 - 2	1.5	2
	• Interest During construction	25 - 40	33	**(c)**
		155 - 190	160	124 + **(c)**

Ref. Notes:
(a) Based on the construction cost estimate equal to 100%
(b) Based on actual construction of 100% by a general contractor
(c) Calculate based on actual prevailing interest rate over planned schedule

1. Construction cost includes all "contractor's costs", e.g. detailed site investigations, contractor's own supervision, material testing and inspection, etc.
2. Percentages are generally lower the larger the project, but higher the more complex, or the tighter the construction budget, schedule or performance (quality) control required.
3. Percentages are generally higher for "fast-track" projects but the base cost of trade contractors only is lower because the cost of the general contractor's supervision gets transferred to the cost of construction management.
4. The percentages shown represent construction technology which is reasonably well established, i.e. not "high-tech".

Figure 6-1. Typical Building Project On-Costs

Allowances are added on top again.

Lastly, to the total of the project estimate described above must be added "Allowances". As discussed in Chapters 7 and 13, these may include such prudent allowances as Contingency, Inflation, Interest-During-Construction (to cover the cost of project financing), potential Scope Changes, Recruiting and Training of Operating Personnel, the cost of initial stocks of Spares and Miscellaneous operating materials, and so on. In other words, the Capital Appropriation should cover all the costs up to the time the facility generates a reasonable cash flow (or other appropriate usage criteria). Indirects and allowances add considerably to the direct cost estimate.

The table in Figure 6-1 shows some typical percentage on-costs to be added to a base estimate of constructed cost for some typical building projects. The sum of the figures in the first column of the table shows that a construction project capital appropriation must be very different from just the estimate of constructed cost. It may be nearly double even before adding costs for training and start-up. Each entry is a percentage to be added directly to the base figure of 100% (i.e. the items are not compounded).

The construction industry is very flexible, so there are many ways of conducting a construction project.

Very few reliable "actual cost" figures covering these items are generally available for direct comparison because responsibilities can be divided in many different ways between the various parties. The construction industry is very flexible and there is a broad range of possibilities for organizing the management of a construction project.

For example, an owner's costs may only reflect payroll costs and not include the cost of overheads that an independent firm must include. Cost and schedule tracking, or quality inspection and control, may be placed in the hands of the owner, consultant, or general contractor. Financing may be included in a developer's costs, and so on. So there is no standard way for maintaining actual cost records and a uniform definition of content for comparison is difficult to establish.

Be careful when making comparisons of percentage on-costs published in the literature. Such costs are not always clearly reported. For example, are they percentages of the total cost, of the base cost, or even a compounding of the base cost plus each lower percentage in the hierarchy?

(b) Aiming for a Capital Appropriation

Detailed design and working drawings are expensive, and therefore part of a project's producing phases.

If the construction project is being conducted through the project lifecycle as advocated in this book, then a major go/no-go decision point will be reached at the end of the planning phases. This decision will determine whether or not to proceed with the project and incur the costs involved. It should be reemphasized that the detailed working drawings stage of the project represents significant time and effort (cost). Therefore, this go/no-go decision should be taken before the working drawings stage of the project.

This go/no-go decision will be based in part on the budget requirements for the project. In effect, a "go" decision by the sponsor or senior management will provide authority to proceed with the project. The source of this funding may be internal, out of on-going cash flow, or by borrowing through external financial institutions. Whatever the source, the organization has committed to set aside the required funds, usually in a specific amount. This amount is often called an "appropriation". To avoid confusion with the fiscal connotations of the single word "budget", it is much better to refer to "Project Budget", "Appropriation Budget", or just "Capital Appropriation".

At this point in the project life-cycle a fair amount of information about the project will have been generated, though only a fraction of the total information accumulated by the time the project is finished. The information thus far will not be complete and it will not be detailed. Therefore, the proposed capital appropriation presented to senior management for go/no-go decision, sometimes called a Capital Appropriation Request (CAR), will be derived from estimates based on the best available information.

6.2 Information Sources for an Appropriation Budget

The following represent a typical set of corporate information sources for building up a construction project budget to be contained in a Capital Appropriation Request.

- Economic Analysis
- Estimating
- Project Cost Management System
- Financial Information System
- Other Cost Information sources

The PCMS is the major cost control instrument in the producing phases.

Figure 6-2 shows how these sources relate conceptually. Information inputs and outputs flow to and from each of the four main processing systems, as well as between them. Note their sequential arrangement and how information flows in both directions. The systems also increase in size and detail as the project progresses through its life-cycle .

If properly constructed, the Project Cost Management System (PCMS) eventually becomes the major cost control instrument in the producing phases of the project. Chapter 10 describes the PCMS in greater detail. Brief observations on the other related systems follow in chronological order of project development.

(a) Economic Feasibility Analysis

Responsibility for future financial planning and economic analysis usually rests with the Finance Department. Comparative economic studies of macro scale opportunities and "what-if" scenarios are developed for senior management consideration. These studies highlight and rank the needs of the organization and so identify potential projects. They play a major role in the concept phase of a capital project. Some of the most important and far reaching decisions affecting the project are made at this time.

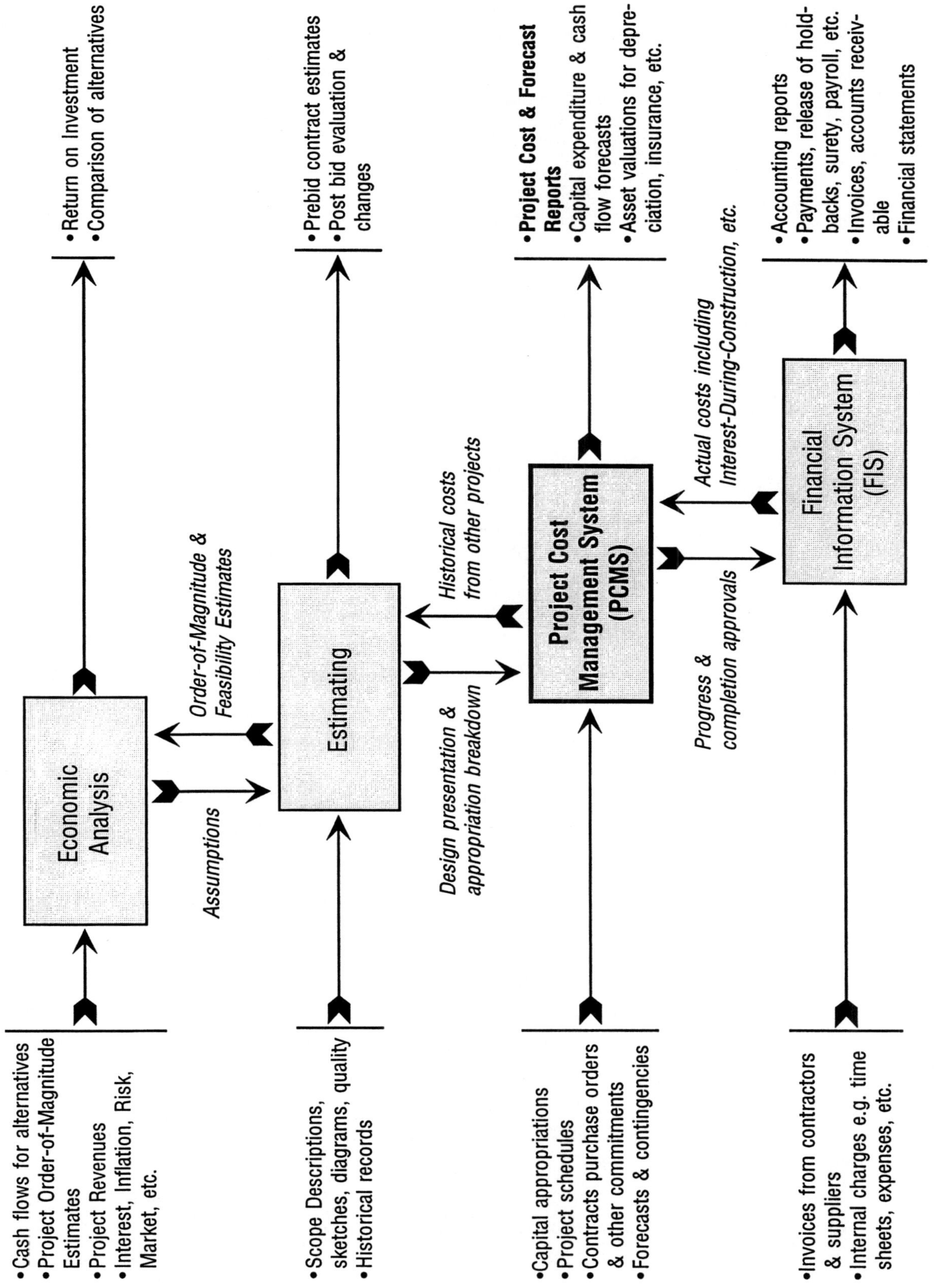

Figure 6-2. Information Flow and Interactions between Project Cost Information Systems

The basis of comparison between competing projects is usually some investment criteria, or investment alternative, portrayed as a series of cash flows on a future time scale. Such criteria include net present value, internal rate of return, payback period, or some combination of each. Competitive advantage and indirect benefits such as tax position, employment levels, diversification and attraction of other business opportunities will also be considered. Still, the process is essentially an analytical tool, and does not capture and store historical data.

During the functional design stage of the project, the process may be further applied for the assessment of design alternatives on a microscale. Therefore, policies, formulas, discount factors, and assumptions about the future, should be carefully documented in the concept phase for subsequent review and application.

(b) Estimating

For the owner or sponsor developing a project plan, the primary purpose of this effort is to prepare estimates with increasing degrees of confidence as the project planning advances. The increased confidence comes from the increased information available. Figure 4-2, Chapter 4, reflects this as a narrowing range of variance. Estimates typically range from order-of-magnitude, for economic analysis purposes, to pre- and post-tender estimates, for actual commitment decisions.

Never give an estimate as a single value. Either give it as a range or state its accuracy.

Estimating is perhaps the most encouraging source of information for preparing appropriation budgets, but great care must be exercised when discussing estimates. All estimates are projections into the future and, as such, cover a range of possibilities. This range depends on the quality and extent of the available information and associated project risks. It is tempting, especially for those accustomed to dealing with historic and therefore explicit numbers, to characterize an estimate as a single value. This is highly unwise.

Figure 4-2 showed that the upper limit of an order-of-magnitude estimate may be at least double its lower limit. Even an estimate for capital appropriation may have an upper limit some 30% higher than its lower limit. Some managers look askance at such ranges. The fact is, you cannot estimate what you do not know, and the unknowns inevitably cost more, not less. The correct message is to ensure solid planning for the project and effective control during its implementation.

After Capital Appropriation approval, control over the detailed design process is exercised by conducting design review estimates at successive stages of the preparation of working drawings. This is essential to avoid scope drift as discussed in Chapter 3. Once the working drawings, specifications and all related documentation have been completed, a pre-tender estimate is prepared to ensure that the estimated final cost of the project is still within bounds.

Pre-tender estimates are also used to provide a basis for comparison of tenders. This sometimes leads to a search for omissions in the lowest tender, or change in contract arrangements or content if prices are too high. Subsequently, post-tender estimates, usually involving the designer, are used to compare scope, where alternatives are presented to improve the facility, or to save money by introducing a design change. In each case, a clear and thorough knowledge of the project scope is required. Consequently, estimates must be developed along the same cost class lines as those used for cost management in the subsequent stage. For reliable estimating, historical costs must be captured and reduced to convenient reference data in terms of unit costs, or percentage mark-ups.

As more reliable information becomes available, the method of estimating changes from "top down" to "bottom up".

During the project life-cycle, the whole basis of estimating changes. The initial order-of-magnitude estimate is developed using a "top down" approach by analyzing the historical costs of similar projects elsewhere. These historical costs are usually saved as consolidated cost per unit of facility space, production capacity, and so on. Some adjustment will be necessary to recognize potential differences such as scale, local construction productivity, transportation distances, exchange rates and inflation. Be careful that the coverage of consolidated historical costs are appropriate and neither omit some costs nor double count them. For example: Do the units being used include all or only some of the costs listed in Section 6.1(a)?

When sufficiently detailed information is available later in the project life-cycle, estimates will be developed "bottom up". This is done by applying reliable unit prices to detailed quantities and requirements taken from the working drawings and specifications. To these must be added specific mark-ups, or add-ons, to cover taxes, contractor's overhead and profit (including financing the contractor's negative cash flow due to holdback or retention money), engineering fees, management overhead, Interest During Construction, and so on. Current trends in operating and maintenance costs must also be monitored for purposes of facility life-cycle costing and economic evaluation once the facility is operational.

Estimates made between the two extremes of necessity tend to be a mix of both approaches. It is this significant shift in estimating approach during the project life-cycle that allows the Appropriation Budget to be elaborated with increasing confidence. The progressive disintegration of the earlier estimates leads to increasing numbers of cost class entries. These require careful monitoring to ensure that effective scope and cost control is being maintained.

(c) Project Cost Management System

The best source of information for estimating is a history of construction by the performing organization. To do this, the organization must establish an effective system for tracking and capturing project costs for future reference. In this book we call it a Project Cost Management System (PCMS).

A PCMS may be defined as a project management tool designed to aid the planning, budgeting, monitoring and controlling of capital project costs from concept to completion. However, project time has a cost associated with it and consequently extended project duration can have a significant affect on the final project cost. Therefore, the PCMS should be able to handle at least simple schedule input. If the PCMS is to be a comprehensive project management information system, then it should also be structured to collect the historic information from previous projects. Chapter 10 describes the PCMS in greater detail.

(d) Financial Information System

The Financial Information System (FIS) is a major responsibility area in any organization. It means the entire set of financial systems normally under the direction of the corporate controller. The FIS is usually run by the accounting and treasury functions and includes payroll, accounts payable, invoicing and accounts receivable, etc.

A Financial Information System, on its own, is unsuitable for controlling project costs.

In simplistic terms, the purpose of the FIS is to take a series of "snap shots" of the financial state of the enterprise at regular intervals. Each snap shot is designed to show the organization's state of health and progress made since the previous "snap shot". Therefore, the structure of its data is in financial accounting terms. That is, the code of accounts must satisfy generally accepted accounting principles, tax regulations, and the requirements of the balance sheet and income statements published in the annual report.

The mode of operation is entirely fiscal and comparisons and data transfers are related to fixed reporting periods. The FIS outlook is historical and its principal functions are data storage and retrieval with little or no data manipulation and analysis. In addition, the payroll system is structured by individual employee name and the accounts receivable and payable systems are structured by client and supplier name. For these reasons, the FIS is rarely a source of very useful information for Appropriation Budgeting without a considerable amount of data manipulation. Even then, the results may be suspect if there are doubts whether all the relevant information has been properly extracted.

For example, cost data for a particular cost class is frequently spread over several accounting periods. Some commitments or charges, such as holdbacks, final payments or even claim settlements may not appear until several accounting periods later. If the expenditure in a cost class runs over the financial year-end, the actual cost data may be even more difficult to extract. This is because corporate books are typically closed at year-end and a new set of accounts opened sometimes with different names. Here, the author has found that reliable and comprehensive information can only be obtained by scanning a complete listing of the FIS entries over an extended period — a long and tedious task.

(e) Other cost information sources

Expenditure Histories from Previous Projects — If the previous projects are those of the organization, this is probably the best source of estimating information assuming the required cost data is available. This is because that data represents the quality of management and performance of the same organization. However, to be useful it does require keeping good records at the time of doing the work. It also requires making sure that the data is converted into suitable estimating information for future use, complete with notes on special circumstances and other pertinent factors. The best records are those that you keep yourself!

Historical component costs can be scaled.

Differences in the size, details, or timing of the reference project are less significant as these aspects are more readily adjusted. For example, many project components can be scaled up or down based on the concept of historical relationships. This empirical approach is known as Parametric Modeling or Parametric Estimating. The concept suggests that costs of many components vary as a function of their size or capacity according to a power law.

For example:

$$\mathrm{Cost}_2/\mathrm{Cost}_1 = (\mathrm{Capacity}_2/\mathrm{Capacity}_1)^N$$

where N is between 0.6 and 0.7. This relationship is useful in extrapolating data from other projects where there are known costs that can be easily extracted. Ideally, the required estimating information should be available from a PCMS introduced on an earlier project. Always be sure that the data used is in fact comparable.

Advice from Outside Vendors — Advice can be sought from outside vendors, suppliers or contractors for specific tasks. This may only be effective if a fair amount of detail is known about the work. Besides, vendors can be reluctant to give more than a "ball-park" figure, if they give anything at all, because their answer might be used by a competitor.

Beware of "ball-park" estimates from vendors!

More likely, the figure will be "padded", or will not cover the complete scope required, to allow for possible future negotiation. After all, seeking this kind of information is like asking for free consulting advice — you get what you pay for! The only reliable cost information from this source is firm competitive pricing in response to demonstrably sincere tender invitations. Not much help for project budgeting purposes.

Expert Advice and Assistance — Beware of casual responses because the expert lacks self interest in the outcome. It is better to employ a professional estimating company for a fee so that their reputation is on the line. Their sources are typically their own recent pricing experience together with commercially available databases. Their advantage is in knowing how to use the data. It is unlikely that the pricing will be "aggressive" (i.e. as low as possible), however, because the company will look much better if the actual cost comes in lower, than if it comes in even only slightly higher.

A careful examination of an estimate from a professional estimating company can provide a valuable insight.

It is also likely that an experienced estimating company will uncover most uncertainties or risks that should be considered. They will also provide details wherever they have had to make informed assumptions. Allowances for these items all help to put the resulting estimate on the high side. A careful study by senior management of the make-up of the estimating company's figures can be a valuable exercise in understanding.

Team Estimating Sessions - Cost estimates of particularly uncertain or contentious items can be arrived at by conducting estimating sessions in small teams of those with previous relevant experience or knowledge. Generally, the approach is to flush out the work to be done, separate it into meaningful components and "guestimate" optimistic, most likely and pessimistic values. From this range of values, some agreed value would be adopted for budgeting purposes. Such an approach is similar to the "PERT" technique for time estimating.

Standard Unit Pricing Guidelines - Sources for unit pricing include vendors brochures and price lists. This source is commonly limited to off-the-shelf items that are currently in stock and does not usually cover work in the field. Work that is done internally by the sponsoring organization may be covered by a schedule of unit prices. This avoids the difficulty of extracting discrete "actual cost" information that is submerged in the FIS system, as discussed earlier.

Standard Percentage On-costs - These represent standard internal management overheads and profit if appropriate. The organization usually set these levels as a matter of internal policy but they may vary according to the project, the client involved or the organization's current financial status.

References

[1] Anthony, R. N., & Reece, J. S. 1975. Management Accounting, Richard D. Irwin Inc. Illinois. p317.

CHAPTER 7

Issues Concerning Capital Appropriation

7.1 Special Points to Note about Capital Appropriation

Several points should be noted about developing a Capital Appropriation project budget and the philosophy underlying the Capital Appropriation process.

(a) Capital Appropriation includes entire project

The Capital Appropriation should include the entire cost of the project and what the appropriation covers should be clearly described in the Project Brief.

A capital project should include all costs associated with the project.

- It should cover all the work described in the scope documents.
- It should be clear on how much of the start-up costs, such as operator recruiting, training, trial runs, prototypes, provision of spare parts, etc. are included.
- It should include all indirect costs such as proportionate corporate overheads, in-house expenses, insurance, etc.
- A contingency allowance should be recognized and, on projects longer than one year, cost escalation should be provided for.
- It should also recognize the value of all assets consumed, such as land, space, permanently reassigned equipment and sponsor supplied materials, etc.
- The cost of interim financing (project financing) including start-up and bridging finance should be included.

In other words, the project appropriation should account for all those direct and indirect amounts that, but for the project, the organization would not otherwise incur.

(b) Budgets that are unrealistic serve no useful purpose

A capital project requires significant discretionary expenditure. Playing games with the budget is not in the best interests of the sponsoring organization.

Capital projects represent significant discretionary expenditures by the parent organization. However, their benefits may not always be clear cut, there may be competing projects with similar levels of benefit, or there may be significant associated risks involved. Strong positions may develop between proponents and opponents so that the project may become a "political" issue. If this happens, the project budget itself may become an issue and be compromised just to get the project approved. Such "games" are not in the best long term interests of the parent organization. The inevitable result will be unpleasant surprises and finger pointing.

Management may still be concerned that the Capital Appropriation Request is too "fat", and that unnecessary money will be spent simply because it has been approved. If this is the case, then a better approach is to approve a somewhat lesser amount with the clear understanding that the difference is being held as a corporate contingency. Either way, budgets are intended to be management control tools. Budgets are based on estimates, but project budgets that are deliberately unrealistic serve no useful control purpose.

(c) Why estimates go awry

Estimates sometimes go awry, especially those prepared internally, because:

The scope of the project is unclear — Undefined objectives and unclear scope, or unrealistic expectations in terms of schedule and cost is evident, or there is unwillingness to invest sufficient effort in developing the required information. This results in inadequately detailed work plans with corresponding vagueness in the resulting estimate and an excessive number of subsequent scope changes. Or there is a lack of comparable historic data and the estimate is naive.

Size and complexity are ignored — Unprecedented size or new technology increase uncertainty in start-up and operating difficulties. Also, complexity is not the same in all data. Twenty-five single storey homes are not the same as twenty-five homes in a single high-rise. If size and complexity are ignored, the project management organization may not be up to the task.

Lack of trust and candor — managers play games with budgets in response to corporate attitudes because they know that they will not get what they ask for. They therefore ask for more, but get cut down even more than expected. Alternatively, they have a personal interest in getting a project launched and put in for a low budget despite the consequences.

Either represents premeditated stupidity! The classic case is probably the Channel Tunnel between England and France. According to reports, early estimates intended for proposal documents to the British and French governments were reworked to unrealistic levels at the insistence of bank officials. The subsequent result was a political furor over alleged delays and cost increases.[1]

The economic or corporate climate changes — the consequence is a change in project priorities and necessary resources are no longer available, or available when required. Such changes in direction may be driven by:

- Inflation
- Labor unrest
- Changes in corporate priorities
- Top management personnel
- In the market for the project's product, or
- The arrival of new opportunities.

Environmental conditions change — construction constraints become more rigorous, public opinions harden against use of the proposed technology, or waste becomes more difficult to dispose of.

A key person leaves — possibly because of promotion, transfer, sickness, or to join another employer. The effect is to leave the project missing a key resource, or requiring a possibly higher-priced replacement.

Focus on the wrong cost items — easy-to-estimate cost items typically get very close attention, while hard-to-estimate items get insufficient attention. It is the latter that often have the most uncertainty and risk attached, which is why they are hard to estimate. People take the easy way out. Alternatively, no reconciliation is possible because the manner of estimating is different from the manner of cost collection.

The "learning curve" is overlooked — the learning curve (see Chapter 15) is not considered when scheduling resources, or when permitting interruptions to the flow of work. This oversight is often because functional managers do not have learning curves in the normal course of their departmental work.

Outside supplier costs increase — outside supplier or material costs, which have not been secured on a fixed price basis, may increase during the project. A project delayed in starting is particularly vulnerable.

Waste and spoilage not factored in — waste and spoilage may be higher for items that are untypical and cannot be used elsewhere. Alternatively, on projects that are untypical a higher level of rework is encountered.

Communication fails — the assumptions and details of the estimate are not adequately communicated to those working on the project. So that what happens bears little or no relation to the make up of the estimate or, conversely, the estimate bears no relation to what is really intended. Examples include:

- The actual work packages bear little relationship to the planned work packages
- Activities start out of their natural or logical sequence
- Management policies on reporting and control are inadequate or are ignored, or
- The reporting system is unresponsive to project management requirements.

If a project is not based on full project cost accounting, it is not possible to tell if it is truly viable.

Finally, beware of unjustified accuracy — irrelevant decimal places, fractions and small change in the make up of an estimate can give the impression of unwarranted precision. An estimate is just that, an estimate. A single bottom line total figure is especially misleading because it represents a range of probabilities, as noted in Chapter 6, Section 6.2 (b). As Aristotle said: "It is the mark of an educated mind to rest satisfied with the degree of precision that the nature of the subject admits, and not to seek exactness where only an approximation is possible."

(d) When the project is not viable

Starting with an (inadequate) budget and then figuring out how to spend it is a poor way to manage a project.

The project may not be viable based on a full accounting as described earlier. Under these circumstances, some managements set a lesser budget and approve the project only on this basis. This allows the project team to proceed into the producing phases but with an inadequate amount of funding. Starting with a budget and then figuring out how to spend it is a poor approach to project management. Such projects are headed for trouble. The project should either be scrapped outright before wasting any more time and resources on it, or funding should be approved only to recycle the project through the planning phases to develop a form that is viable.

(e) Capital Appropriation does not authorize spending

The Capital Appropriation does not necessarily authorize the expenditure of hard cash. There may be subsidiary financial control processes in place that will govern the timing and specific amounts that can be committed, and only then for a particular part of the project. Examples include the advanced ordering of long-lead items of equipment, entering into agreements and contracts for services, project management and so on. The Capital Appropriation itself may be staged, commencing only with preparation of the working drawings. This would enable senior management to "revisit the project budget" when significantly more information is available.

7.2 Schedule Control and Cash Flow

Controlling the project schedule is just as important as controlling the project costs

As reflected by the Rules recommended in the previous Chapter, work packages are very much schedule related. Indeed, the costs of almost all work packages are directly affected by their duration. Therefore, for effective cost control in the producing phases, the time/cost relationship must be identified, and schedule control exercised in a similar way. This requires a schedule that integrates network logic and the project's work breakdown structure, preferably down to the work package level. With this information, progress and cost can be monitored and cost and schedule variances investigated early enough to allow corrective measures to be taken with a minimum of adverse impact.

When each work package is budgeted and scheduled, summation on the time scale provides a cash flow profile. Chapter 14 shows this cash flow profile that provides valuable information for the project team. It also provides vital information for the company controller to ensure that funds are available when needed. Expenditure profiles corresponding to early and late activity starts can also be generated to form a possible cash flow envelope. Actual expenditures, when plotted against the same background data, will then provide extremely useful trend information in support of estimates-to-complete and cost and schedule variance analyses.

Just as project estimating evolves towards a capital appropriation through the planning phases, so also should the scheduling for the project. A broad brush schedule will appear during the conceptual phase. This should evolve into a high level summary schedule, one which increases in confidence as more becomes known about the project. Increasing detail enables the scheduling of the work packages. Conversely, the sum of the work package schedules should obviously roll up into the Master Schedule.

The project team may resequence the work at their discretion, but revision of the Master Schedule should be the subject of a formal review.

A good Master Schedule should show major events or "milestones" at given points in time. When the time comes, recording actual project progress on this Master Schedule will give a rapid visual picture of the total project status compared to the original plan. But what if work is resequenced, for purposes of tactical advantage? Or what if the difference between actual progress and the Master Schedule become so large that the comparison becomes meaningless?

Resequencing of the work should be at the discretion of the project team. If work is resequenced, it should be possible to reflect this at the detailed level without requiring changes to the Master Schedule. If the comparison between actual progress and the Master Schedule become so disparate as to be meaningless, senior management or the project sponsor should call for a formal reprogramming of the whole project. Policies should be established as part of the project plan that this will not take place without following a formal Master Schedule control procedure. Otherwise there will be no control over the schedule. Without control over the schedule, a significant element of control over the project cost will also be lost.

Thus, schedule control should be exercised by ensuring that no change is made to the Master Schedule and its Key Milestone dates unless the following conditions are met:

1. **The target schedule and the current schedule become so far apart that recovery is impossible and target objectives become meaningless.**

2. **A formal reprogramming of the entire project or major portion of it is undertaken.**

3. **Such changes, and their associated cost implications, are recognized and approved by top management, the sponsor, and the funding agency.**

7.3 Executive Control Points and the Project Brief

(a) Executive control points at major milestones

The major milestones discussed in the previous section should suggest control points at which senior management or "executive" approval should be required in the life of the project. These "Executive Control Points", sometimes called "Gates", should be built into the project as a matter of policy and become established as part of project funding approvals. Depending on the size of the project, these Executive Control Points can be designed to give top management the opportunity to give or withhold approval to proceed from one stage to the next.

Executive Control Points at Major Milestone points serve multiple purposes.

Executive Control Points serve a dual purpose. From top management's point of view, they provide the opportunity to exercise a high level of control over the shape and timing of the project. Top management can ensure that the project is developing in a manner consistent with their objectives. Or, if their objectives have changed due say to business circumstances, the project can be modified with minimum upset.

From the project manager's point of view, the Executive Control Points provide him with a mandate to drive the project through to the conclusion of the ensuing stage. It is an opportunity to ensure that top management has confidence in the project and that it is proceeding in the right direction. It follows that both parties must take the time to do their "homework".

In this way, a mutually high "level of comfort" is established that should lead to a sound working relationship. Without such a relationship, direction of the project will inevitably become loose and uncertain, and the opportunity for satisfactory control will be lost. In other words, the essential purpose of this disciplined effort is to establish the best possible level of early information and decision making. In this way, subsequent changes and consequent delays during construction can be held to a minimum.

Choose the number of Executive Control Points carefully.

The number of Executive Control Points should be chosen carefully. Too few give insufficient control to senior management. Too many may hinder the project unnecessarily, especially as there is usually a hiatus while waiting for approval. More Executive Control Points will be appropriate for a larger project, or one that is particularly risky to the organization, than a smaller one or one that is straight forward.

It has been suggested that the cost of making a change increases tenfold with each succeeding phase, because of the amount of work already completed. Figure 7-1 illustrates some obvious points at which to exercise high level control.

As described in Chapter 1, the most important control point in the whole life of a construction project is the go/no-go decision required to

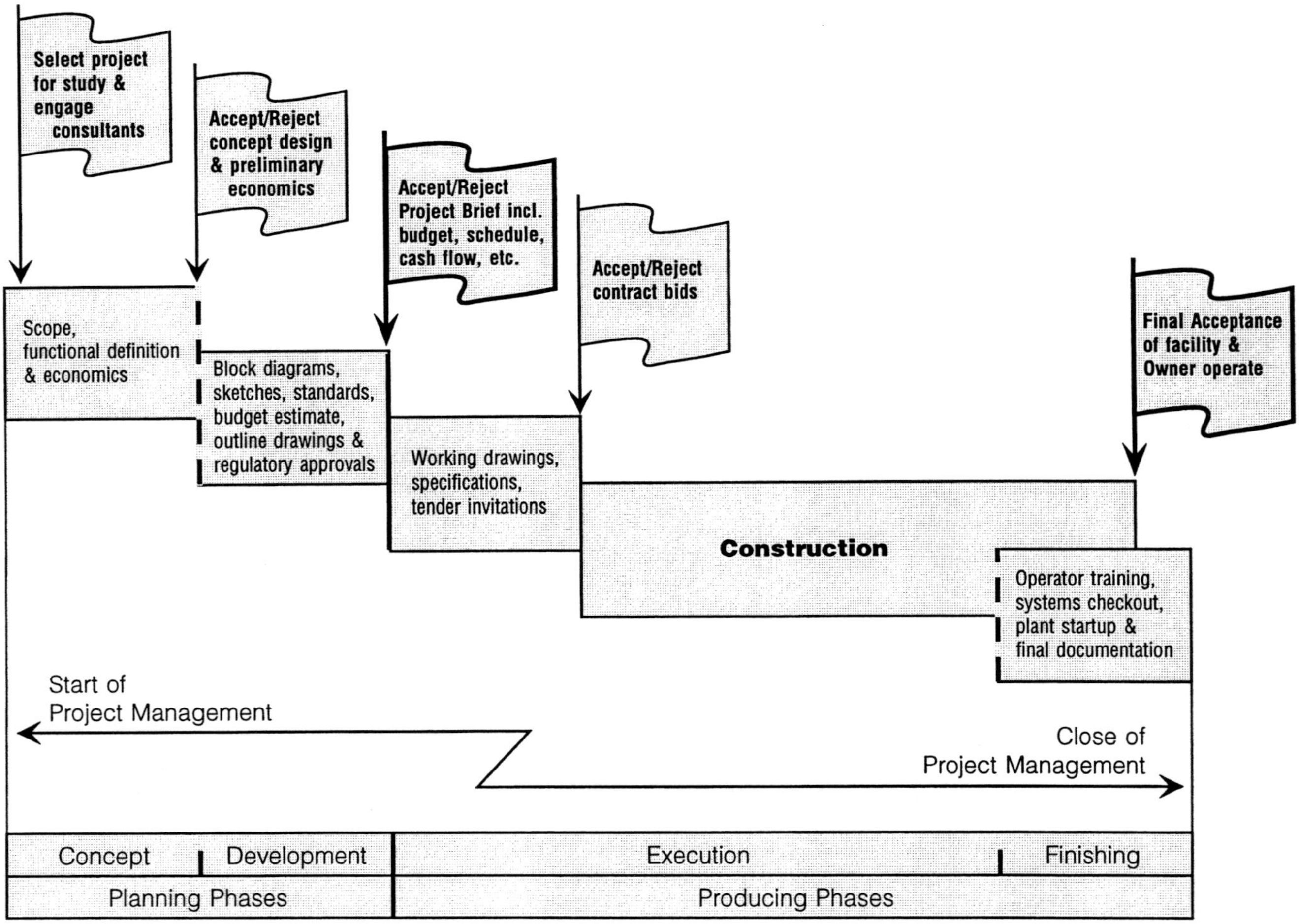

Figure 7-1. Construction Project Executive Control Points

progress from the planning phases into the producing phases. The latter call for heavy financial commitments to carry through with design and construction and a much higher level of effort, supervision and control. If the procurement strategy is to construct under a single lump sum, fixed price contract, then there is a further opportunity to hold back if tenders are not acceptable, but only after completing all the detailed design work.

As described earlier in this chapter, approval of a project Capital Appropriation Request triggers release of funds for these phases. In order for management to make an informed decision, the necessary background information must be sound and well documented as described in the next sub-section.

(b) Project Brief provides full description of the implementation plan

The purpose of a Project Brief is to provide a full description of the project implementation plan in support of a Capital Appropriation Request (CAR). The document should be designed to enable the owner or sponsor to take an informed and confident decision over the commitment of corporate funds for the project. It should be based on the most cost effective means for bringing the facility into reality. It should not be self-serving such as the occupation of in-house resources or the use of unqualified outside services, or even justification for project management.

A good Project Brief should become the project's working bible — and be used as such.

A good Project Brief should at least include:

- An introduction or executive summary
- A general statement of business aims and objectives associated with the project
- A statement of project scope
- The economic and technical approach adopted
- Justification, alternatives, areas of uncertainty and risk
- Regulatory approvals and requirements
- Preliminary design sketches, block diagrams, standards
- Project Master Schedule
- Procurement Plan
- Project estimate and proposed capital appropriation request
- Other resources required from the sponsoring organization e.g. land, space, staff, etc.
- Financial statement and economic projections
- Cash flow projection
- Quality, schedule and cost controls
- Project team organization

It is useful for the Project Brief to contain a short summary of the aims and objectives associated with the project as suggested above. This gives the reader some background and a better understanding for the subsequent material. Even so, it is not appropriate for the Project Brief to be used to justify the original need for the project. This decision, and its documentation, should have been part of the organization's needs assessment and project selection process, or part of a development proposal, at the start of the project planning phases. Therefore, it is not appropriate for the Project Brief to include:

- An analysis of "operational" alternatives
- Facility operating and maintenance costs
- Facility revenue projections

What the Project Brief should be used for.

If the corporate approval process is an extended one, any counter proposals, changes or decisions that are made during this time should be included as an appendix to the final version of the Project Brief. In this way, the final Project Brief document in the approved CAR becomes the prime source of reference for the producing phases of the project. This document then provides a firm basis for:

- Detailed planning and control of project implementation
- Evaluation and approval of subsequent changes
- Evaluation or audit of the project management process during implementation
- Post project assessment and part of the historic record

References

[1] News. 1994. Construction Today, Thomas Telford House, London, May. p5.

CHAPTER 8

Project Risk and Uncertainty

8.1 Avoiding Unnecessary Project Risks

Projects are launched to take advantage of opportunities. For a project to be viable, the expected value resulting from a favorable probability of gain must be higher than that for the consequences and probability of loss. But opportunities are associated with uncertainties and uncertainties have risks attached. Therefore, the risks associated with a project must receive careful examination. They must also be considered in the context of the organization's willingness or aversion to taking risks.

With careful planning and good management some inherent risks in the project management process can be much reduced or virtually eliminated. Steps towards this goal include:

A viable project is one in which the probability of gain is higher than the probable consequences of loss.

- Thorough and realistic appraisal of the project concept, and hence the ability to solidify the project scope definition, through the planning phases
- Observing good project management planning practices, including genuine and realistic estimating of time and cost for defined scope and quality requirements
- Identifying key uncertainties and risks associated with the project in clear concise terms
- Openly examining these risks and identifying ways of mitigation, and/or making due contingency allowances where the scope of work is uncertain
- Preparing contingent action plans and work-arounds
- Verifying quality and constructability of designs
- Developing sound procurement strategies, including contract documents, designed to optimize performance, supported by an appropriate organizational structure and distribution of responsibility

- Ensuring that contract wording contains a clear statement of intent, definition of scope, equitable allocation of responsibility and terms for handling changes and disputes
- Carefully examining contract documents to identify general clarity, potential sources of misunderstanding, and potential areas of risk
- Avoiding incompatibility of, or personality conflicts between, contractual representatives
- Assigning specific responsibility for risk in a way that motivates by recognizing that risk and reward go together
- Seeking innovative but practical solutions to offset potential risk areas through risk management

Benefits of risk management include:

- Objective examination of the project management process
- Proper accounting for risks and uncertainties
- Increased confidence in investment and management decisions following a thorough analysis of the data
- Contingency planning permits controlled and predetermined responses to risks that happen, thus avoiding expensive "fire fighting" reactive modes
- The project team is made aware of appropriate responses without undue delay
- Risks and responses can be documented as a historic record for future reference

The only time a contingency plan is needed — is when one does not exist!
Murphy's Law

Some of the following risk management details are more applicable to large complex projects. However, the principles involved are applicable to any size of project. Assessing project risks and devising steps to accommodate, mitigate or avoid them is another vital part of project cost control.

8.2 Issues Relating to Risks and Uncertainties

(a) Inherent value and recorded cost

The work of a project has an inherent value.

When the scope of a project has been defined and developed in sufficient detail, there is an inherent value associated with the extent of work required to produce the intended entity. However, the actual recorded cost by the end of the project may be influenced by many factors along the way. Such factors include:

- Occurrence of unpredicted risks
- Realization of some predicted risks
- Cost of resulting changes made on the project
- Impact on the cost of implementation of schedule changes or delays

- Management of contingency allowances to offset the impact of these changes
- Attempts to bring costs into line with budgets by improving scope performance (e.g. by value management)
- Impact of inflation on the cash flow, over the period of implementation (i.e. the as-spent money value)
- Impact of delays on the interest-during-construction payments

Much has been written on the uncertainty of project work, particularly of large construction projects spanning several years and subject to political and inflationary changes. Such uncertainties are frequently dealt with in terms of probability and risk, and very sophisticated analyses may result. As described in Chapter 4, the accuracy and credibility of the final project cost estimate improve rapidly with the amount of reliable and detailed information available.

Thus, the earlier it is in the project life-cycle, the less information is available, and the higher the potential risk of error in estimating the cost of implementation. During the economic studies and feasibility analyses conducted in the concept phase, this can be evaluated by developing a series of scenarios. These scenarios incorporate various probabilities that cause various projected results. In this way, the sensitivity to various probabilities may be assessed and management's direction determined accordingly.

Uncertainty diminshes as the project evolves — but never entirely disappears.

As we have seen, uncertainty diminishes as the project evolves. But it is never entirely eliminated until the project has been completed and all costs have been collected and brought to final account. Even then, it should be noted, there may be "latent defects" in the resulting facility. Such defects do not surface until sometime later, but since they can generally be traced to a quality failure, rectification forms part of the project cost.

(b) How much contingency for how much risk?

Prudent cost management requires that part of the project's capital appropriation should be identified as a contingency allowance. This contingency allowance should be structured to cover at least the more probable outstanding risks or uncertainties. This immediately causes some difficult management decisions.

Too large a contingency encourages "gold plating" — too little, quality cutting.

The size of the contingency allowance may vary with the project size, type, duration, location and so on. Typically, it is based on past experience and current judgment. But if the contingency allowance is set too high it may encourage non-essential embellishments ("gold plating"), conceal sloppy financial management, or cause the project to be uneconomic and aborted at the outset. If the contingency allowance is too low, management of the project may become too rigid and either the projected financial outcome of the project is unrealistic or the performance outcome is unsatisfactory.

Some risks may be offset by insurance and bonding. This course also requires careful consideration, positive action, and due allowance in the budget. In effect, part of the contingency allowance is transferred to a cost class (line item) by transferring the risk to others.

Still other risks may be transferred to the contractor(s) by suitable contract wording. Yet, this often results in higher contract pricing, or subsequent claims to cover losses, or both. In general, only those risks that are under the control of the contractor and properly in the contractor's domain, should be written into the contract. To do otherwise is both inequitable and uneconomic.

Transferring unjustified risk to a contractor is both unfair and uneconomic.

The question is, how should management arrive at a satisfactory level of contingency allowance for effective project cost management? This issue should be confronted positively by carefully listing the more dominant project uncertainties and assembling them into related groups. They can then be more readily recognized and the contingency allowance managed more effectively. Table 8-1 gives a listing of some typical project risks.

At the time of capital appropriation approval for project implementation, several categories of project uncertainty should be recognized and managed as recommended. These are:

1. Major unpredictable risks
2. Lower order risks and uncertainties associated with the scope of work
3. Inflation and Interest During Construction

These are described in the following sections and Chapter 13 discusses the distribution of standard allowances for uncertainties associated with the work.

8.3 Assessing Project Risks

(a) Major unpredictable risks

Major unpredictable risks include those that are entirely unforeseen and some that are probably inevitable but their magnitude cannot be predicted. These include such items as:

- The indirect effects of strikes and working to rule by other than those working on the project
- Very severe weather
- Unforeseen major legislative changes (including design, fire, and safety codes, court action awards, etc.)
- Fluctuations in exchange rates
- Political policy changes (reversal and turmoil)
- National disasters, and so on.

A) In Project Concept
- Unclear concept and project objectives
- Unfamiliar field of activity
- Uncertain technology
- Lack of market understanding
- Lack of economic and financial viability
- Lack of attention to funding sources
- Inappropriate facility selection and design
- Unsuitable location

B) During Planning
- Inadequate project planning
- Failure to assess project risks
- Failure to provide for contingencies
- Contingencies & allowances not separated
- Inadequate field data
- Inadequate design or critical design flaw
- Unsound capital cost estimate

C) Environmental Conditions
- Adverse impact on physical environment
- Unstable political system
- Inadequate local infrastructure
- Lack of acceptance within social fabric
- Changes in social responsibilities
- Lack of support by local industry
- Regulatory intervention in:
  - Environmental protection
  - Site location and requirements
  - Design standards
  - Construction standards
  - Health and safety standards
  - Local, national or international content
  - Legal interpretation
  - Supply of raw materials
  - Pricing
  - Taxation

D) Organizational
- Unwieldy multinational consortium
- Joint venture partner mismatch
- Uncooperative foreign participant
- Unsatisfactory sponsor sharing, split or sourcing
- Unsatisfactory commercial arrangements
- Inappropriate project organization
- Sponsorship or senior staff changes
- Insufficient project support
- Untrained project management team
- Captive or uncooperative engineering team
- Unmotivated participants
- Limited local resources or skills
- Poor project performance

E) During Execution
- Inadequate execution planning
- Precipitous project initiation
- Changes in sponsor/client/users' organization
- Changes in sponsor/client/users' expectations
- Changed conditions in project's technical aspects
- Delays due to:
  - Political approvals
  - Regulatory approvals
  - Design inadequacies
  - Lack of coordination
  - Unforeseen site conditions
  - Material shortages
  - Labour shortage
  - Labour stoppage or "work to rule"
  - Late funding, payment, deliveries
  - Accidents, sabotage or terrorism
  - Unusually severe weather
- Owner/operator scope changes
- Lack of understanding how all the parts fit together
- Contractual disputes
- Failure to complete contract

F) Control Difficulties
- Lack of communication and direction
- Lack of feedback on progress, problems or solutions
- Lack of commitment to succeed
- Unrealistic objectives of Scope, Quality, Time & Cost
- Inability to control Scope, Quality, Time & Cost
- Cost overruns due to
  - Schedule delays
  - Contracting and procurement methods
  - Salary and wage negotiations
  - Inexperienced workforce
  - Lower-than-expected productivity
  - Contractor claims and court action awards
  - Inflation, increased cost of labor, materials

G) During Start-Up and Operation
- Lack of start-up planning
- Hand-over and start-up difficulties
- Unanticipated technical hurdles
- Inadequate operator training
- Excessive operating costs
- Insufficient revenue stream

H) Market Conditions
- Precipitous market pursuit
- Missed "window of opportunity"
- Inadequate or intermittent energy supply
- Intermittent material supply
- Fluctuating raw material cost
- Changes in exchange rates
- Customer/user rejection
- Limited exporter capability
- Limited local experience
- Limited marketing capability
- Ineffective marketing or sales effort
- Failure in market demand
- Default on purchasing or trading agreements

Figure 8-1. Table of Project Risks (National and International)

These are risks that cannot be insured against and so must be assumed by the organization. These risks should not be allowed for in the project's cost control budget if only because it would not be possible to arrive at a sensible allowance. Instead, they should be recognized at the highest management level, where top management must decide whether of not they are comfortable with the risks in question.

Major unpredictable risks should be the responsibility of the sponsoring organization.

Depending on the size of the project and the severity of the occurrence, any of the risks described could conceivably undermine the financial stability of the sponsoring organization. Therefore, funds to fit the required remedial action would have to be sought from top management. Top management would thus have an opportunity to reassess the situation after the event, and either decide to provide the necessary additional funding, or modify, postpone, or abort the project altogether.

(b) Assessing lower order risk and uncertainty contingency

Lower order risks and uncertainties, typically mean those associated directly with the identified scope of work for the project. This should be the true meaning of "contingency". Contingency should not be taken to mean an allowance for things that would be nice to have if we can afford it! Such "nice-to-haves", if they are to be included, should be covered by separately identified allowances.

Don't use contingency for "nice-to-haves". They belong under Allowances.

Some risks and uncertainties will stem from the possibilities of regulatory intervention and similar unforeseeable events. Others may stem from physical or social changes occurring during the remainder of the project and that adversely affect the final cost. Such uncertainties should be covered by a separate "Unforeseen Allowance", but only if considered prudent. Since the uncertainties in question may or may not occur, this allowance may or may not be spent.

A simple practical way of identifying and dealing with lower order project risks, uncertainties and even opportunities is to hold a team brainstorming session devoted to this purpose. The process is straightforward and effective, helps people think creatively without feeling inhibited or being criticized by others and indirectly helps to build a pro-active team spirit. To avoid getting swamped in too much detail, focus is limited to the "vital few" by invoking Pareto's Law of Distribution, or the "80/20 Rule", see Figure 8-2.

Vilfredo Pareto, by the way, was a 19th Century Italian sociologist and economist who studied the distribution of wealth. He conjectured that the distribution of incomes, however equal or unequal, can always be described by a particular mathematical formula. This highly generalized empirical relationship postulates that the few (about 20% of the wealthy) control the majority (about 80%). This "80/20" idea has been applied to many areas where there are a large number of items with a particular type of distribution. For example, a cost effective approach to project cost management

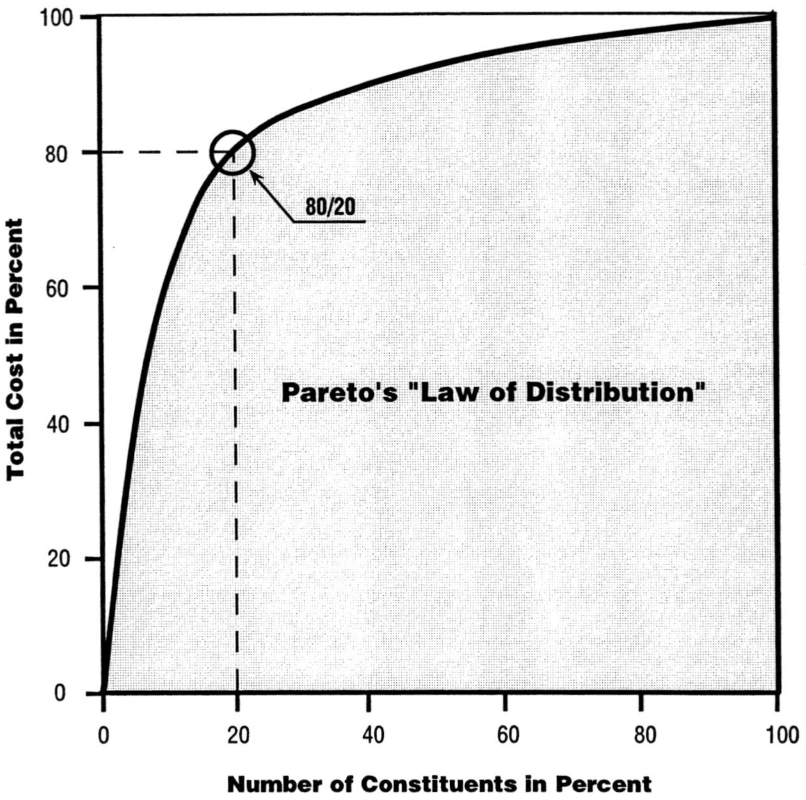

Figure 8-2. The 80/20 Rule

would be to keep your eye on those 20% of cost classes that account for 80% of the total costs on the project.

Similarly, by identifying and preparing for the top 20% of possible risk concerns, it should be possible to capture the "vital few" that are most likely to influence the project in a significant way. The steps in the process are as follows:

Assemble a list of possible risks and focus on the "vital few".

1. Assemble a group of five to ten people who have knowledge and experience in the various aspects of the project.
2. Brainstorm all the things that could go wrong. Use the Risk Wheel shown in Figure 8-3 to stimulate ideas. List each item as a single line statement. This should produce a long inventory of possibilities.
3. Now identify the top 20% that appear to have the greatest impact and probability on the project's cost and schedule and relist them in approximately descending order of significance.
4. Conduct a "What if" analysis on the worst item.
5. Develop a plan to avoid, solve or reduce the problem.
6. Better still, how could the situation be turned to advantage?
7. If the response is to make some provision in the contingency allowance, then also take a majority opinion on the probability of occur-

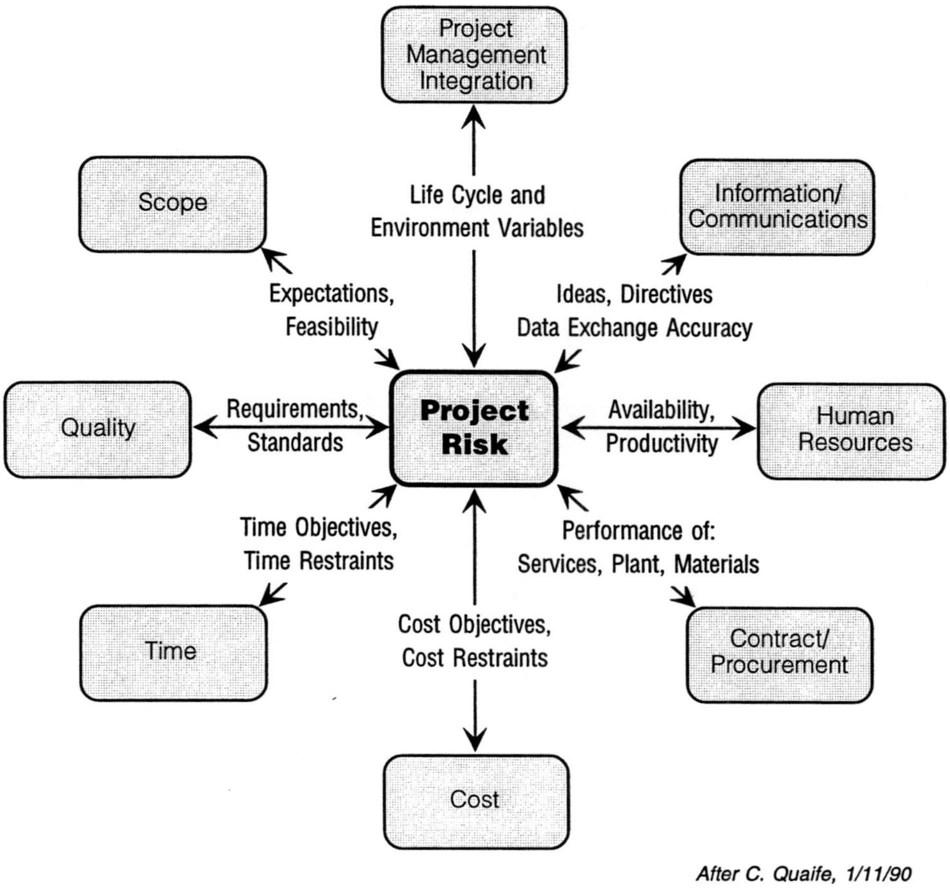

Use this diagram as a memory trigger and to integrate risk identification with other project management functions

Figure 8-3. The Risk Wheel

rence. The item can then be included in the tabular layout suggested in the next section.

8. Repeat steps 4 through 7 on the other items until the "top 20% list" of worst items has been accounted for.
9. Factor appropriate steps into the plans for the project.

If the top 20% of risks are not self-evident, calculate and select by "criterion" value.

Identifying the top 20% risk concerns is not as easy as it sounds, especially for a long list of items. Also, people have difficulty in thinking in terms of percentage probabilities. A good approach to this problem is to grade the severity of each item by consensus according to the following:

5 Catastrophic
4 Severe
3 Medium
2 Moderate
1 Insignificant

Then similarly determine the probabilities of each as follows:

5 Highly probable (90% probability)
4 Moderately probable (70%)
3 Possible (50%)
2 Unlikely (30%)
1 Highly unlikely (10%)

Having assigned two numbers to each risk concern, multiply them together to give a criterion value. This produces a 15-point scale between 1 and 25. It should now be easy to pick out the required top 20%.

By adopting this simple general approach, the chances are that you will be sufficiently prepared with enough flexibility to tackle most situations that are likely to arise.

(c) Simple risk contingency calculation

A simple calculation to arrive at an allowance to cover the consequences of lower order risks can be determined by using the tabular layout shown in Figure 8-4. Identify each risk event, and assess its probability of occurrence and its estimated impact on time and cost. The total allowance is then the sum of the estimates times their respective probabilities.

Description of Risk Event	Probability of Occurrence	Estimated Delay as Consequence (Time at Stake)	Schedule Allowance (Days)	Estimated Cost of Consequence (Cost at Stake)	Budget Allowance
Risk Event #1	Probability P_1	Critical Delay D_1	$P_1 \times D_1$	Cost C_1	$P_1 \times C_1$
Risk Event #2	Probability P_2	Critical Delay D_2	$P_2 \times D_2$	Cost C_2	$P_2 \times C_2$
etc.	etc.	etc.		etc.	
			Σ P x D		Σ P x C
			Estimated Cost of Schedule Overrun: (where $\$_t$ = cost of daily overheads)		Σ PxDx$\$_t$
			Total Value of Risk Allowances:		**$???**

Figure 8-4. Simple Risk Allowance Estimating Sheet

The exercise itself may well identify higher-than-reasonable risks requiring a more specific focus. Such higher risks must obviously be brought to senior management's attention for appropriate action. Depending on the resolution and the controllability of the particular risk, it may be necessary for project management to establish a disclaimer regarding the consequences.

In summary, effective risk and contingency management require a positive and systematic approach. By doing so as the project progresses, changes in the status of the allowances, and therefore the trends in the final cost at completion, will be very good indicators of the health of the project. Also, adverse trends will be brought to light more readily and can be reported to those who can influence the course of future events in the interests of the project's ultimate success.

Regular risk and contingency management provide a good indication of a project's health.

(d) Formal Cost Risk Assessment

Cost risks arise from variations in both cost and time and, as shown in the simple calculation in the previous section, they need to be taken together. Most estimators would probably agree that cost and schedule estimates are more likely to be overrun than underrun. Therefore, on larger, more uncertain or more contentious projects, it may be desirable to undertake formal risk assessments on both cost and time estimates for the project.

For example, the determination of an appropriate contingency allowance may be based on setting a specific low level of probability of overrunning the total budget. If this is the case, not only should expected values be determined for each item but also the cumulative distribution of risk should be derived for the whole cost-schedule system.

Formal risk assessment on a large and risky project can be invaluable in designing the project's management plan.

This can be done by a modern quantitative risk assessment combining distributions in a network. Such an approach also avoids the pitfall of computing the risk only on the critical path. The risk associated with a near-critical, or even a clearly non-critical path can be much higher than that on the critical path if the values on those other paths are far more uncertain.

The benefits of a quantitative risk assessment can be considerable. It can

- Force the collection of necessary and valuable information for the project
- Provide a better understanding and awareness of the business environment and the risks involved
- Specifically identify the major factors that are likely to impact the final results
- Quantify the probable impacts of these factors individually and collectively

- Enable efforts to mitigate or avoid these factors
- Improve project planning
- Reduce the likelihood of "unpleasant surprises" and enable prompt response
- Justify the project's Capital Appropriation Request

Formal cost-schedule risk assessments should be conducted by those knowledgeable in the methodology.

8.4 The Effect of Time on Cost Information

Network scheduling and bar-charting are important parts of project planning, required to establish an orderly sequence of project activities. They are not strictly sources of cost information. However, money has a time value resulting from interest on borrowings and from inflation. So the project schedule provides an important component in estimating the total cost of the project.

Many attempts have been made to establish a fully integrated cost and schedule computerized program, some with more success than others. The idea of this automation is very appealing and most scheduling software programs offer a useful cost component. However, the manner of scheduling activities for purposes of tracking schedule and the manner of allocating costs for purposes of cost control, though similar, are rarely entirely compatible at the detail level. Therefore, any direct schedule/cost interface between the schedule network and the cost and financial control systems should allow the networks to be developed independently of cost control or financial and accounting considerations. Conversely, the latter should not be completely dependent on the former, otherwise the whole process may become inoperable due to opposing system requirements.

Time costs money, but tracking time and cost together rarely works because of incompatibility at the detailed level.

Notwithstanding these reservations, it is useful to have some automation of this interface. This permits approved schedule refinements to update such forecasts as the disbursement, fiscal budget projection, long range cash flow, escalation provision requirement and IDC charges. A simple bar chart schedule derived from the Master Schedule should suffice for this purpose, if it is reliable and representative.

To ensure reasonable stability of cost information that is time sensitive, the Master Schedule should provide high level control. This Master Schedule should be developed and maintained to show only major activities and key milestone events as discussed in Chapter 7. Chapter 7, Section 7.2 discusses policy and procedural conditions under which changes to this Master Schedule may be made. General progress and its influence on cost can then be reliably measured against this Master Schedule.

8.5 Adjusting for Inflation

Recent years have seen periods of substantial levels of inflation and significant fluctuations year by year. Any project in which design and construction extend beyond a year must take inflation into account. The problem is that the value of cost classes in the capital appropriation will be fixed at the time of approval. The associated actual expenditures, on the other hand, will be incurred much later when the value of that money has changed. Even if the rate of inflation could be predetermined with certainty, the incurred cost of each scheduled activity may still vary according to when it actually takes place.

Where project implementation does not exceed, say, a couple of years, the simplest course is to provide an allowance for inflation in the budget and then make appropriate transfers. Policy regarding such transfers should be included in the Project Brief, possibly based on actual changes in related cost, to provide effective control. Where construction is to be undertaken under a single fixed price contract, the contractor usually assumes responsibility for managing inflation, and a budget allowance for inflation should not be necessary.

The contractor, on the other hand, is saddled with the problem of managing inflation. However, the contractor preparing a firm price bid for work covering several years can at least plan when work activity expenditures will occur. The contractor's best approach is to prepare its estimate based on current costs of labor, material and equipment prices and make separate adjustments for inflation. This way, if the projections should be changed or the project delayed, it will be possible to make corrections to the calculation of the inflation allowance only, without having to rework the entire estimate.

When the duration of a project covers many years, the approach of providing an allowance becomes unsatisfactory. This is because the cumulative effect of inflation becomes an item of major significance in the project budget. The complexity of past and future transfers also make it difficult to assess the true status of the project.

If inflation is all pervasive, only the figures change — not the inherent value.

If it is assumed that inflation is all pervasive then it affects the whole economic environment. In that case it has an effect only on the numerical value of the budget figures, and not the inherent value. It depends how the project is to be financed. Economic studies for the project are conducted in terms of "present value", that is, future cash flows are adjusted for the time value of money and assumed inflation. In a reverse manner, the project budget is constructed according to which years the expenditure of the various cost classes will to take place. In this way, the numerical values of the various cost classes of the budget incorporate projected inflation at the time of completion of that cost class.

If this approach is adopted, it is usual to exercise meaningful cost control by striking a limited fiscal budget each year based on the latest inflationary expectations. The actual total project cost status at any time will then reflect the actual inflation since the original capital appropriation was approved and the projected inflation to the time of project completion.

This requires maintaining a close connection between the project scheduling system and the project costing system to identify when the costs were, or will be, incurred. Computerized project cost management system programs are now available that successfully integrate cost and schedule to the extent necessary. They also accommodate multiple inflation indices and permit cost to budget comparisons. These comparisons may be in terms of either the original appropriation value, current value, or the projected value of money at the time of project completion.

Don't let inflation confuse budgetary control on long-duration projects.

Here a word of caution is necessary. A cost incurred this year can be deflated for comparison with last year's budget figures. Alternatively, the budget can be inflated to make comparison in this year's money values. Theoretically, both can be further inflated, for comparison in next year's money values, alongside all the other entries occurring next year. This last approach, however, is not correct. Not only does it lead to a much higher set of figures for the project, but the final figures themselves would not reconcile with the company's books of account. Nor would this approach take into account interest-during-construction discussed in the next section.

To maintain the integrity of the entries in the Project Cost Management System, all entries in Project Cost Reports should be shown as original amounts. Any adjustments for inflation should then be shown as a separate line item, preferably at an intermediate summary level.

8.6 Interest During Construction

Interest-During-Construction (IDC) is sometimes called Allowance for Funds Used During Construction (AFUDC). It represents charges against the project on account of the monies invested in it prior to commissioning the facility and capitalization of total project expenditures. Alternatively, it is the cost of borrowing the money required to meet project expenditures as the project advances to completion. IDC is part of the amount to be capitalized when the project goes into revenue service. The rate of interest charged depends on the source of funds, including internal and external sources, and the rate itself may vary during the life of the project due to money market conditions.

Even if a project is financed out of current revenue, the money spent still has a "lost opportunity" cost.

Even if the project is financed entirely out of current revenues, there is still a lost opportunity cost attaching to the funds consumed in the project. Here it is the amount that could otherwise have been earned by investing the money being spent on the project and should therefore still be included in the project's total estimated cost. Either way, this item can be a significant portion of the total project cost, often as high as 10 to 20% or more, depending on interest rates and project duration. In any case, interest rates do tend to track the rates of inflation.

With this understanding, we can return to our computerized project cost management system, with its capacity to adjust for inflation. When a cost is incurred, both the actual cost and its associated budget amount must be frozen for all future projections. At this point the amount becomes firm and inflation is no longer an issue. Instead, interest charges on the amount start to become payable. Therefore, instead of forward inflating, IDC starts to take over and the final total cost for the project, including IDC, will agree with the organization's books of account. This final total of all costs captured in this way will also represent the real cost of the project in terms of money value at the time of project completion.

Money not yet spent attracts inflation, but money spent attracts interest charges. Spending switches entries from one to the other.

Interest, as a cost class, is sometimes overlooked in the budget breakdown established for project cost control purposes. This may be because it is seen as an overhead or indirect charge. This is a mistake. Including IDC as an active part of project cost control ensures that appropriate focus is given to the time value of money. It emphasizes the consequences of late decisions, or the possible benefits of incurring additional costs required to accelerate activities on the critical path to completion.

IDC is normally cut off and capitalized at the time the facility is started up and commences revenue cash flow. After this, interest payments on borrowed capital become part of the operating expense. Because IDC accumulates as a direct result of project expenditures, and is proportional to time, it puts an increasingly heavy premium on the value of time as the project nears completion. Towards the end of a project it often becomes the justification for crash programs-to-complete with heavy overtime working and obvious labor cost overruns.

Therefore, IDC should be a clearly identified cost class in the Project Cost Management System code of accounts. This will ensure that, if properly orchestrated, such last minute crash programs can still be properly justified as an overall project cost saving.

CHAPTER 9

Contracting Strategy and Risk Allocation

9.1 Contracting Strategy

Selecting the style of organization for executing a construction project is an important part of its planning. The style selected will have a considerable affect on the project's realization and how costs can be controlled.

The work involved in the different phases and stages of a project may be the subject of different agreements or contracts. For example, in the project development phase, social, environmental, market and technical studies may be procured from different specialists. Even a separate risk analysis study may be commissioned for a large or critical project. In subsequent stages detailed specification, design and supervision or quality control and expediting may be the subject of separate specialized packages, and so on.

More contracts mean more coordination requiring more careful project management.

The greater the number of separate packages under separate and discrete responsibilities, the greater the amount of coordination required and the greater the resulting risk. Therefore, early in the development of the project, the project owner or sponsor must develop a suitable contracting strategy and establish an organizational structure consistent with the intended project objectives. The structure selected must reflect the proper division of responsibility for these various components in terms of scope, quality, time and cost, including appropriate delegation of project management responsibility. The strategy must also recognize the need for management coordination and integration of the various contracts over time by making corresponding provisions in each service agreement.

There are many different ways of structuring a project to suit differing objectives and circumstances. Different structures assign risk in different ways. Perhaps the most significant issue is the total distribution of responsibility for project risk as reflected by:

- The ways in which management responsibility is structured
- How it is delegated, and

- How it is incorporated into the various service agreements and contracts

9.2 Traditional versus Fast-track Construction

In the "traditional" approach to construction, the entire facility design would be completed, followed by competitive contract tendering, followed by awarding a single contract to a general contractor on a fixed price basis. The major activities in the producing phases of the project are entirely sequential. This approach will probably result in the least constructed cost but will also take the longest to build.

If early completion is an owner's primary consideration, a process of phased construction or "fast-tracking" can be adopted. In this, there is deliberate overlapping of design work, tendering and construction. This enables the earlier construction activities, such as site clearing, excavation and foundation construction, to commence long before the entire design of the facility has been completed. This can be done by direct coordination of the design disciplines and the corresponding construction trades involved.

Traditional versus Fast-track construction is a tradeoff between time and cost-risk.

This approach requires special "Construction Management" expertise in the construction process if coordination of all the various parties is to be effective. Construction Management has been defined as: "A process of professional management applied to a construction project from implementation to completion for purposes of controlling quality, time and cost to the client's satisfaction."

It follows that the "fast-track" nature of this process is considerably more risky than the traditional approach, requires tighter and more direct control, and requires more supervisory staff. The optimum saving of time in the producing phases is probably about 25% to 30%. Attempts to save more than this only results in a subsequent increase in design changes, added rework, and loss of morale and productivity. This is especially so if it is due to slippage in early detailed design decisions. In extreme cases, the consequence is simply increased cost at no saving of time, or the time may even be extended.

From these brief comments it will be seen that selection of an appropriate type of procurement strategy for the particular project is crucial. The forms of contract selected must also match the strategy adopted, and a large variety of contracts have been written in attempts to match given situations. Ideally, the form of contract should match the project's particular emphasis, whether scope, quality, time or cost as discussed in Chapter 3, Section 3.4, and allocate responsibility and risk accordingly. Having determined the execution strategy, the selection of the right form of contract requires:

- The identification of specific risks
- Determination of how these risks should be shared between the parties, and

- The inclusion of clear legal language in the construction contract documents that puts this into effect.

Finding the most cost-effective and equitable sharing of risk is a challenging task. Standard contract (or purchase order) documents prepared by various levels of government, organizations that undertake a lot of procurement, or standard model documents prepared by construction associations are typically used. Specific allocations of risk are intrinsic in such standard forms, but the principles behind the allocations are rarely stated[1]. Such intrinsic allocation of risk may or may not be appropriate to the project's execution strategy.

9.3 Some Suggested Risk Sharing Principles

Various authors have suggested principles governing the allocation of risk between the parties to a contract.[2] First, it is necessary to identify the various risks associated with the selected procurement strategy. Then, base contract selection or formulation on the answers to the following questions:

Risk allocation and the selected contracting strategy must be in harmony.

- Which party is the source of the particular risk and therefore best able to control the events that could lead to it happening in the first place?
- Which party can best manage the risk, if it occurs?
- Is it or is it not preferable for the client to retain an involvement in the management of the risk in question?
- If the risk is such that it cannot be controlled, which party can or should carry the risk?
- Will the cost incurred or premium charged by the recipient of the risk be reasonable and cost-effective?
- If the risk occurs, can the recipient sustain its consequences?
- Or will it simply lead to the possibility of other risks of a different nature being transferred back (e.g. slow down or collapse of the project effort through demoralization or bankruptcy)?

It is essential that the party that may be the cause of the risk, and therefore best able to manage it, shall also be responsible for its consequences. To do otherwise is not only patently unfair, but is an open invitation to costly disputes and litigation. It is strongly recommended that a systematic approach is adopted to project risk identification, analysis and equitable allocation, and its distribution clearly expressed in the wording of the contracts. If this means departing from standard contract forms, so be it. Good contracts are very much to the benefit of the total project and accordingly are cost-effective.

9.4 Types of Contract

A contract is a legal act in exchange for a legal consideration.

Different authorities define the term "contract" in different ways. Also, the "law of contract" depends on the jurisdiction in which the facility is being constructed, and this may vary considerably. However, two requirements appear to be immutable — in return for a legal act there must be legal consideration. The legal consideration is the mechanism for payment that should be responsive to the risk conditions.

In construction projects, contracts are many and various, being first identified by the type of work and then by the method of reimbursement. Examples of types of work follow.

Types of work

- On-site construction by a General Contractor
- Construction Management through Trade Contractors
- Supply only of materials or equipment
- Installation only
- Services only
- Combination of any of the above

These different types of contract range from fully cost reimbursable to fixed price lump sum for the identified work. For example:

Method of reimbursement

- Actual cost plus various types of fee
- Target price, or fixed price plus an incentive
- Unit prices applied to remeasured quantities
- Fixed price (lump sum)
- Combinations of the above on different parts of the project

Match the contract to the extent of information available — and hence the risk involved.

The type of contract should be matched to how much is known about the work to be done. Work that is essentially undefined and/or cannot be scheduled is obviously highly uncertain, is therefore risky, and is unlikely to proceed except on some form of cost reimbursable basis. Work that is fully described, that can proceed without interruption and be reliably scheduled and estimated, can be tendered and awarded on a fixed price basis.

Figure 9-1 shows the relationship between different types of contract and the allocation of risk. If the contract and its payment terms are properly matched to the situation, then it will also reflect the degree of uncertainty or risk. So it follows that one of the most significant differences between the various forms of contract is the way in which risks are handled and paid for. As shown in the Figure, contracts range from those that are cost-based to those that are price-based.

In cost-based contracts all costs actually incurred in the performance of the contract are reimbursed. In addition, a fee is paid to cover profit and

any associated costs and overheads that are not defined as reimbursable. It follows from this arrangement that most risks are paid for by the owner and covered by the agreed upon fee, unless specified otherwise. This corresponds to the CPPF type contract shown in Figure 9-1. Unfortunately, this type of contract does nothing to encourage efficient working, indeed it discourages it, and trust between owner and contractor is a key element. The CPFF contract is something of an improvement, since the fee is fixed and the more the work costs, the less is the effective markup received by the contractor. Even so, the owner's direction of the work must be efficient and as agreed.

In cost-plus contracts, the risk of overrun is with the Owner. In fixed-price contracts, it is with the Contractor.

Firm Fixed Price contracts are at the other end of the scale. With an FFP contract, the owner and contractor agree that specified deliverables will be produced for an agreed price (i.e. a total lump sum payment). In such contracts payment covers all costs, overheads and profit and the contractor includes in the price(s) all necessary contingencies for risks specified and/or implied. To a slightly lesser extent, price-based contracts include unit price contracts where the risk of variation in individual quantities is covered by remeasurement.

Priced based contracts have the distinctive merit that they can be put out to competitive bidding. This is a system in which a contractor offers to perform a specified amount of work for a given fixed price. Offering the work to competitive market forces enables the selection of best value to the project and hence is very beneficial in terms of cost control. For the system to work properly, the contractor must be able to estimate the amount of

Scope of Work Information	very little		partial		almost complete
Risk and Uncertainty	high		moderate		low
Type of Probability	subjective				objective
Types of Contract	**CPPF**	**CPFF**	**CPIF**	**FPPI**	**FFP**
Consequent Risk Allocation	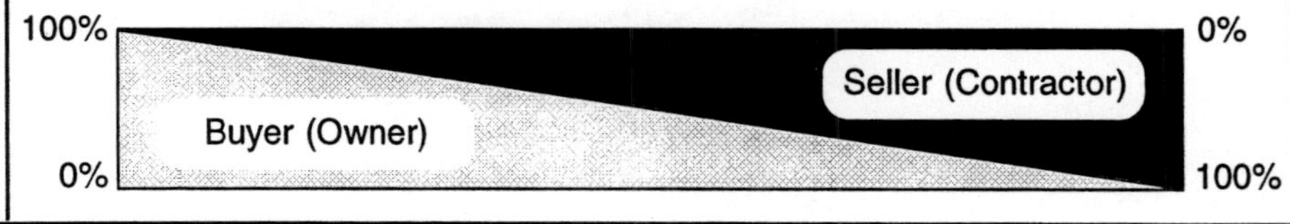				

Note: Contract Types ranked according to degree of Contractor's Incentive

CPPF - Cost Plus **Percentage Fee**
CPFF - Cost Plus **Fixed Fee**
CPIF - Cost Plus **Incentive Fee**
FPPI - Fixed Price **Plus Incentive**
FFP - **Firm** Fixed Price

Figure 9-1. Different Types of Contract and the Allocation of Risk

work required, generally by taking off physical quantities and applying unit prices. Even so, the work involved in the quality of many deliverables cannot be estimated unless the extent of required activities that go into them is made clear. This is why a complete design showing physical dimensions, content and clear unambiguous specifications are required.

An Owner who interferes with the management of the work on a fixed-price contract is asking for trouble.

In this way, the contractor can establish the cost with a good degree of reliability. However, pricing is partly a function of past experience and partly of an assessment of the productivity that can be achieved in the particular circumstances. Not only must the amount of work be known, but also knowing its consistency and continuity is crucial. It follows that firm price work must be under the control of the contractor at all times and interference of any kind must be strictly avoided in order to protect the contractor's profit margin.

It will be seen that the more that risk is assumed by the contractor, the less the contractor is willing to allow the owner to interfere with the work. As a corollary, the more risk assumed by the owner, the more the owner can get directly involved in the organization and management of the work and, if disposed, make changes along the way. Thus, under cost-plus there can be a high degree of flexibility. In fixed-price contracts, management and organization of the work must be in the hands of the contractor with rigid procedures for making changes.

9.5 Selecting the Construction Contract

At first glance, it might be supposed that the cost-plus approach is the ideal form of contract. In practice, it is the subject of very detailed and accurate cost and progress record keeping that even then may be the subject of independent audit and dispute. Perhaps more important is the lack of incentive to control cost and schedule by those directly doing the work. To meet these objections, and arrayed between, are a variety of cost-plus-incentive types of contract.

Cost-plus contracts lack incentive to control costs.

Figure 9-2 shows three projects with different degrees of scope definition but each with the same expected value. The respective curves show the ranges of probability of achieving the realistic cost estimate represented by 100%. The range of uncertainty in each case, suggests the appropriate type of contract.

The table shown in Figure 9-3 shows the impact of different issues on four different types of general contract from the owner's perspective[3]. It also shows how the different types of contract allocate responsibility for the cost of the risk events. Note how responsibility shifts from one party to the other according to the terms of payment.

As noted earlier, more than a single contract will be required if any form of construction management is adopted for the project. There will be a series of contracts that may run consecutively or concurrently and, typically, these will be trade contracts rather than general contracts. Though

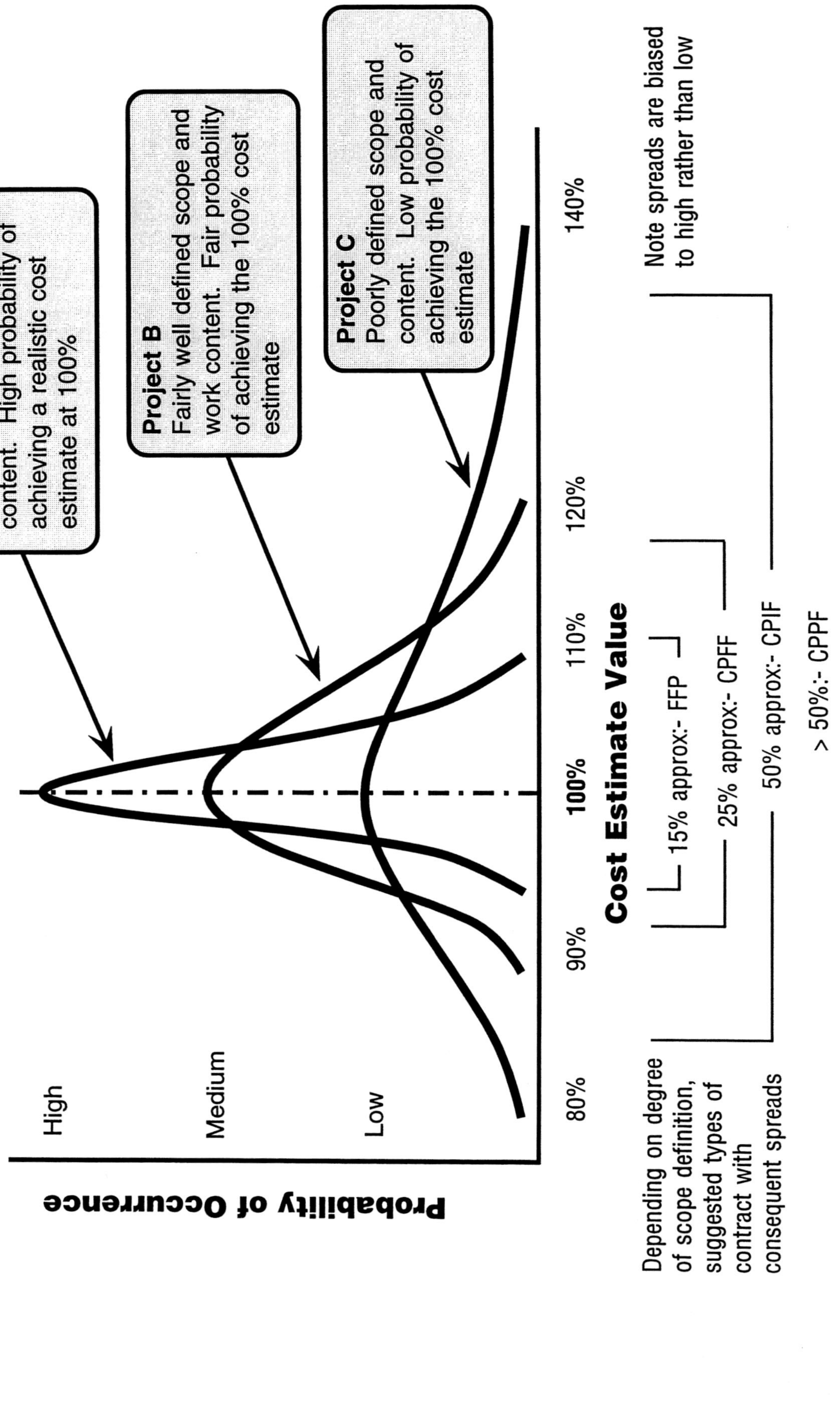

Figure 9-2. Relation between Scope Definition, Risk and Contract Selection

the wording will be different, the same principles apply but a high degree of coordination will be required that will be the responsibility of the owner or sponsor. The ability to exercise this responsibility must therefore be written into each contract.

With multiple contracts, responsibility for construction management must be written into every contract.

Important considerations in the formulation of contract packages under construction management include:

- Nature of the work (Industry practices or degree of specialization.)
- Optimizing size and content (Too large and good smaller contractors may be excluded. Too small and competent large contractors may not be interested.)
- Optimization of effort and resources (Must avoid duplication.)
- Local conditions (The affects of local support and infrastructure on costs.)
- Schedule constraints (Network logic.)
- Availability of funding (Owner's cash flow.)

As noted earlier, the larger the number of contracts, the greater the effort required in contractual coordination, the higher the risk of problems arising and the greater the probability of consequent claims.

9.6 A Question of Attitudes

In describing successful projects, many authors reflect on the enthusiasm and cooperative team spirit that they enjoyed on the project. It is not only the correct selection of the organizational structure and forms of contract that determine whether or not project objectives are successfully achieved. It is also the attitudes of the parties involved. Even so , an effective structure and good contract wording can go a long way to establish good relations, because these avoid the frustrations generated by inappropriate structures and contracts.

Good contracts provide for an equitable distribution of risk.

Obviously, this includes an equitable distribution of risk and the means for handling it in the event that it arises. Suggested characteristics of good contract risk conditions include[4]:

- Clear definitions of risk and their assignment
- Positive incentives linked to risk assignment
- Flexibility for different assignments of different risks between the parties
- Strong emphasis on planning and good management practices designed to avoid unnecessary risks in the first place

Handling project risks in the manner described may require a departure from traditional forms of contract. However, if the result is to avoid or reduce the number of contract disputes, and the costs of dispute settlement,

Issue	Type of Contract			
	Lump Sum	**Unit Price**	**Target Cost**	**Cost Reimbursible**
Financial objectives of owner and contractor:	Different but reasonably independent	Different and in potential conflict	Considerable harmony. Reduction of actual cost is a common objective provided cost remains within the incentive region	Both based on actual cost but in potential conflict
Contractor's involvement in design:	Excluded if competitive price based on full design and specifications	Usually excluded	Contractor encouraged to contribute ideas for reducing cost	Contractor may be appointed for design input prior to execution
Owner's involvement in management of execution:	Excluded	Virtually excluded	Possible through joint planning	Should be active involvement
Claims resolution:	Very difficult, no basis for $$ evaluation	Difficult, only limited basis for $$ evaluation	Potentially easy, based on actual costs. Contract needs careful drafting	Unnecessary except for fee adjustment. Usually relatively easy
Forecast final cost at time of bid:	Known, except for unknown claims and changes	Uncertain, depending on quantity variations and unknown claims and changes	Uncertain. Target cost usually increased by changes, but effective joint management and efficient working can reduce final cost below an original realistic budget	Unknown
Payment for cost of risk events:	Depending on contract terms, undisclosed contingency, if any, is in contractor's bid. Otherwise by claim and negotiation	Depending on contract terms, undisclosed contingency, if any, is in contractor's bid. Otherwise by claim and negotiation	Owner pays actual cost of dealing with risks as they occur, and target is adjusted accordingly	Owner pays actual costs

After R. W. Hayes et al, Risk Management in Engineering & Construction, Special SERC Report, London, 1986

Figure 9-3. Risk Implications of Different Contracts from a Client's Perspective

then the respective managements will have more time to spend on the real issue, that of creating a successful project.

References

1 R. W. Hayes et al. 1986. Risk Management in Engineering Construction, Special SERC Report by the Project Management Group, UMIST, Thomas Telford Ltd., London, December.

2 *Ibid.* p26. Other authors include D. B. Ashley, C. E. Porter, N. M. L. Barnes , J. G. Perry and P. A. Thompson, p30. See also Contract Risk Allocation and Cost Effectiveness, CII Publication 5-3, Austin, Texas, November 1988.

3 After R. W. Hayes et al. 1986. Risk Management in Engineering Construction, Special SERC Report by the Project Management Group, UMIST, Thomas Telford Ltd., London, December. p29.

4 *Ibid.* p28

Part 3: Cost Control in the Producing Phases

CHAPTER 10

The Project Cost Management System

10.1 From Appropriation to Control Baseline

Make sure the project team has access to, and fully understands, the Project Brief.

Once the Capital Appropriation for the producing phases of the project has been approved, the work begins in earnest! Project Management's first step is to examine the Capital Appropriation Approval documentation for any special conditions that may have been added as part of the approval process. The second step is to make sure that the team fully understands all the project requirements and the background information contained in the Project Brief. This is especially necessary if there has been a change in project management responsibility.

The third step is to examine the make-up of the Capital Appropriation itself. The objective is to make sure the document includes all the items in a way that is suitable for project cost control purposes. If this is not so, a tactical rearrangement of the necessary items should be developed and agreed with the project sponsor, and corporate controller. If not already in existence, the fourth step is to put in place a complete Project Cost Management System.

10.2 Project Cost Management in the Producing Phases

Convert the Capital Appropriation into a working baseline — with team agreement.

Upon acceptance and approval of the Project Brief, the corresponding Capital Appropriation becomes the basis for the allocation of capital for design and construction of the project. From the perspective of cost control, it should be noted that the project's estimate reflects the sum of the most probable costs of each element. The Capital Appropriation, on the other hand, should provide an envelope that includes the total estimate with allowances for contingencies and inflation.

There is, therefore, a conversion process involved, which may require examining the varying estimating accuracies and uncertainties attaching to each project element or cost class. A realistic Appropriation breakdown, based on the project estimate in the Project Brief, must be established, and agreed, by the project team.

As discussed in Chapter 8, contingency sums, often determined by experience, provide for estimating and design errors, or for design and scope changes that may become necessary to make the facility work satisfactorily. Allowances may also be included for possible owner required scope changes but unspecified contingencies should be avoided.

Thus, provision is made for specified risks. Each should be abstracted, separately identified and related expenditures become subject to specific authorization. These entries should not be regarded as "slush" funds to be drawn on at will by any members of the project team.

The Project Brief itself becomes the "working bible" for the detailed design. Armed with an approved Project Brief and an agreed appropriation breakdown, the project manager can then coordinate and direct a design and construction team that is the most suitable for the particular project. The detailed design process of preparing working drawings and specifications can now begin in earnest.

Two thirds of all project information will be generated during the working drawings stage.

It has been estimated that this relatively short detailing stage generates over two thirds of the total project information. This dramatic "explosion" of information is shown graphically in Figure 10-1. Because the information generated will decide the exact details of the project — and its cost — the preparation of the working drawings and specifications must become the focus for intensive project cost management.

There are several paramount notions to effective cost control during this stage. Management should:

1. Provide a target cost for the designer to work to. A cost plan that allocates the capital appropriation to work packages provides such a target.
2. Motivate the designer to make cost effective design decisions by having him participate in cost management activities. The designer should take part in the cost reviews and reforecasts for the packages he is working on. Having the designers themselves responsible for forecast preparation produces even better results.
3. Maintain vigilance for unauthorized scope changes. Additions to scope are often introduced under the guise of normal design development. Owner-user inspired changes and "gold plating" by the designer both contribute to this tendency for the work to grow unnecessarily.
4. Arrange for review of drawings at progressive stages of completion such as 30%, 60% and 100%. This allows bringing the design "back on track" without unnecessary wheel spinning. It may also provide a forewarning of additional coordination required or of difficulties to be anticipated later in the project.
5. Involve a construction manager or similarly experienced person from (say) the 30% design point so that the design reflects constructability. Designs which cannot be built in an efficient

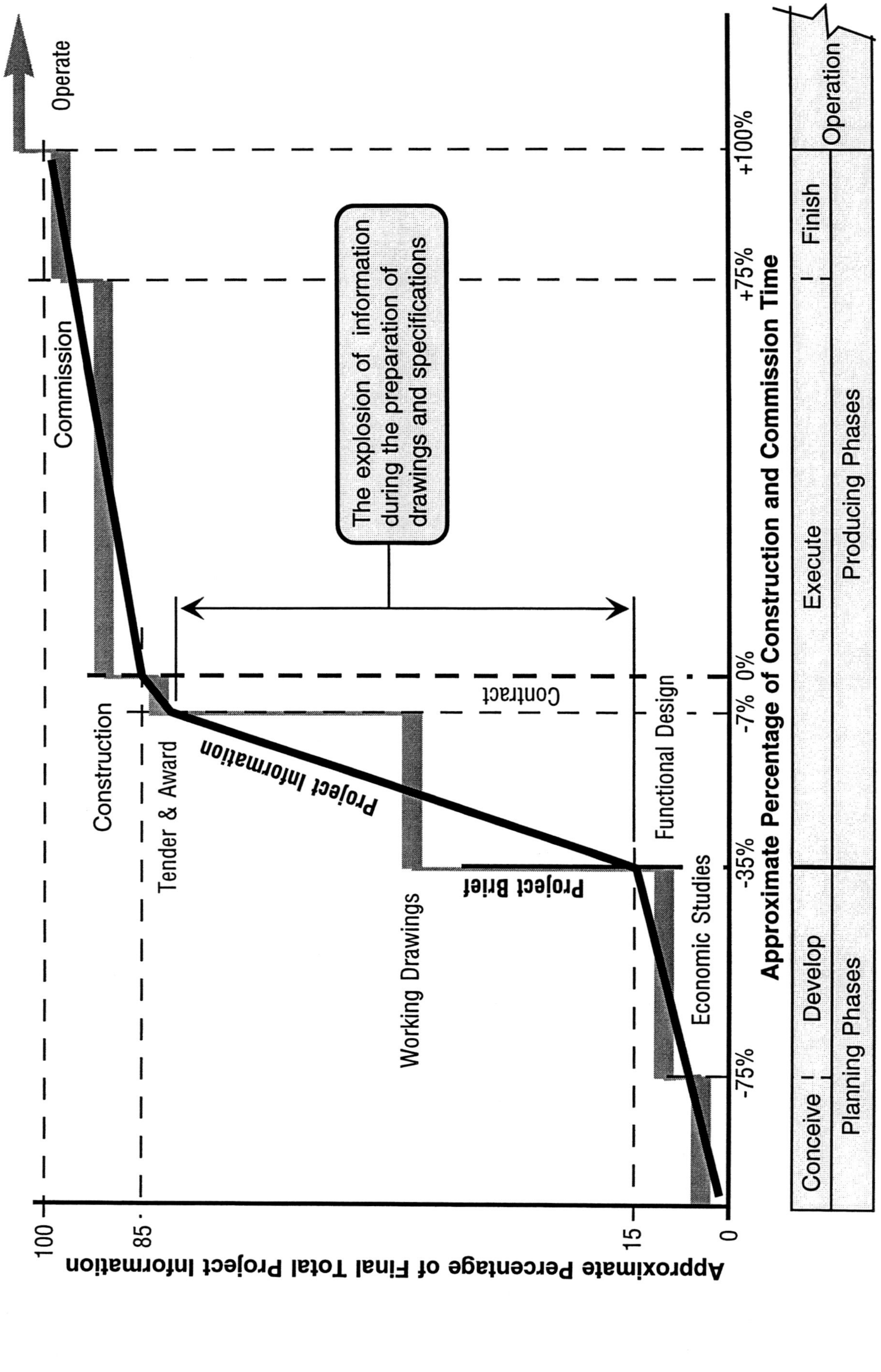

Figure 10-1. The Information Explosion

manner may contribute to subsequent claims for extras as well as costing more than necessary in the first place.

6. Ensure the design is indeed complete and realistic at 100%. Incomplete engineering and design omissions are often the major reasons for delays and poor cost performance. Omissions have to be dealt with on an ad hoc basis when they surface during construction. "Force account" work and prices negotiated under duress for correcting them will be costly.
7. Do not overlook the specifications. Review them for quality level and avoid ambiguities. Avoid naming proprietary products without the option of offering competing alternatives.

Procurement is an important part of cost control, but it can be affected by market conditions.

When working drawings and specifications are complete, the next focus for cost management is the procurement process. Procurement is an important part of cost control. It may take many forms from general contract to trade contracts, and lump sum to cost plus as discussed in Chapter 9.

The extent of market activity at the time of tender invitation can have a significant influence over bid prices, and therefore on project cost. However, the assembly of work packages into well defined Contract Packages and the collection of corresponding Appropriation amounts provides an immediate standard of reference for comparing bids. Management can then decide whether to commit, change the design, or change the form of contract.

In the construction stage, the cost management task becomes one of ensuring that field changes are minimal and progress is not impeded by delayed access, decisions or approvals, which would otherwise cause contractor claims for extras. A contractor should be required, under the terms of its contract, to give notification of potential claims as soon as identified. This enables corrective or avoidance action to be taken with minimum cost impact.

Early or late purchasing should be a matter of deliberate and justified policy only.

One of the most frustrating aspects for a contractor is schedule delay. In this respect the aims of the owner and contractor may be diametrically opposed. The owner may wish to delay specific heavy expenditures to reduce the interest during construction (IDC) component of the project cost. The contractor, on the other hand, will want to secure such items before price increases take effect, both to reduce uncertainty and to improve its cash flow and profitability.

Where there is a long construction period, there is nothing wrong with deliberately delaying a major expenditure to save IDC as a matter of policy. Still, the downside risk of cost escalation and the potential for delay claims must be clearly recognized. Consequently, early purchasing may be equally justifiable.

10.3 System Outline

(a) System description

The following description outlines a Project Cost Management System (PCMS) suited to managing a project from an owner or sponsor's perspective. Figure 10-2 shows a schematic arrangement of the system during project execution. Note how the PCMS is more than just project cost accounting. It is an information processing and communication system.

The PCMS means the entire complex of forms, procedures, processing steps and reports designed to capture and release information concerning the status of a project's future capital cost. The PCMS differs significantly from the financial code or chart of accounts in the traditional corporate Financial Information System (FIS) as noted in Chapter 4, Section 4.2(d). In the FIS, an account is a permanent repository for the collection of various types of historic cost. The purpose of each FIS account determines its type, such as paying particular bills, recording payroll payments and deductions, classifying asset purchases, and so on. This is why the FIS does not suit project management's purpose.

A Financial Information System is no substitute for a Project Cost Management System.

In addition, unlike the corporate FIS, the PCMS essentially ignores calendar time as a criterion. Instead, it focuses on final project cost and the staged components that lead up to that end figure. In other words, the thrust of the reporting function of the system is less on the actual and historical and more on the future.

Reporting dates and periods between reports may vary according to the project, the stage it is in, and project management requirements. Unscheduled reports may also be called for from time to time to satisfy emergency cost reviews. If the PCMS is just an add-on it may only get second priority to FIS demands. If these requirements happen to coincide with typical FIS month end activity, or especially year end congestion, PCMS reports may be considerably delayed.

This is yet another reason for the PCMS to be separate from the FIS. The PCMS needs to be an almost independent system. Nevertheless, it will likely have to meet certain corporate FIS requirements to enable reconciliation and so maintain its credibility.

The PCMS should be run independently, but subject to FIS standards and data input.

To serve project management, the emphasis must be on future costs because only these are still responsive to management control. So the PCMS must be able to handle both "hard" historic or committed costs and "soft" forecast or expected costs. The team should be responsible for specifying, maintaining and updating the data in the system, even though corporate systems are often the responsibility of the finance department. This is to ensure that it serves the needs of the project team and their project management operations. If the organization has more than one project on the system then each project team should be able to use the system independently.

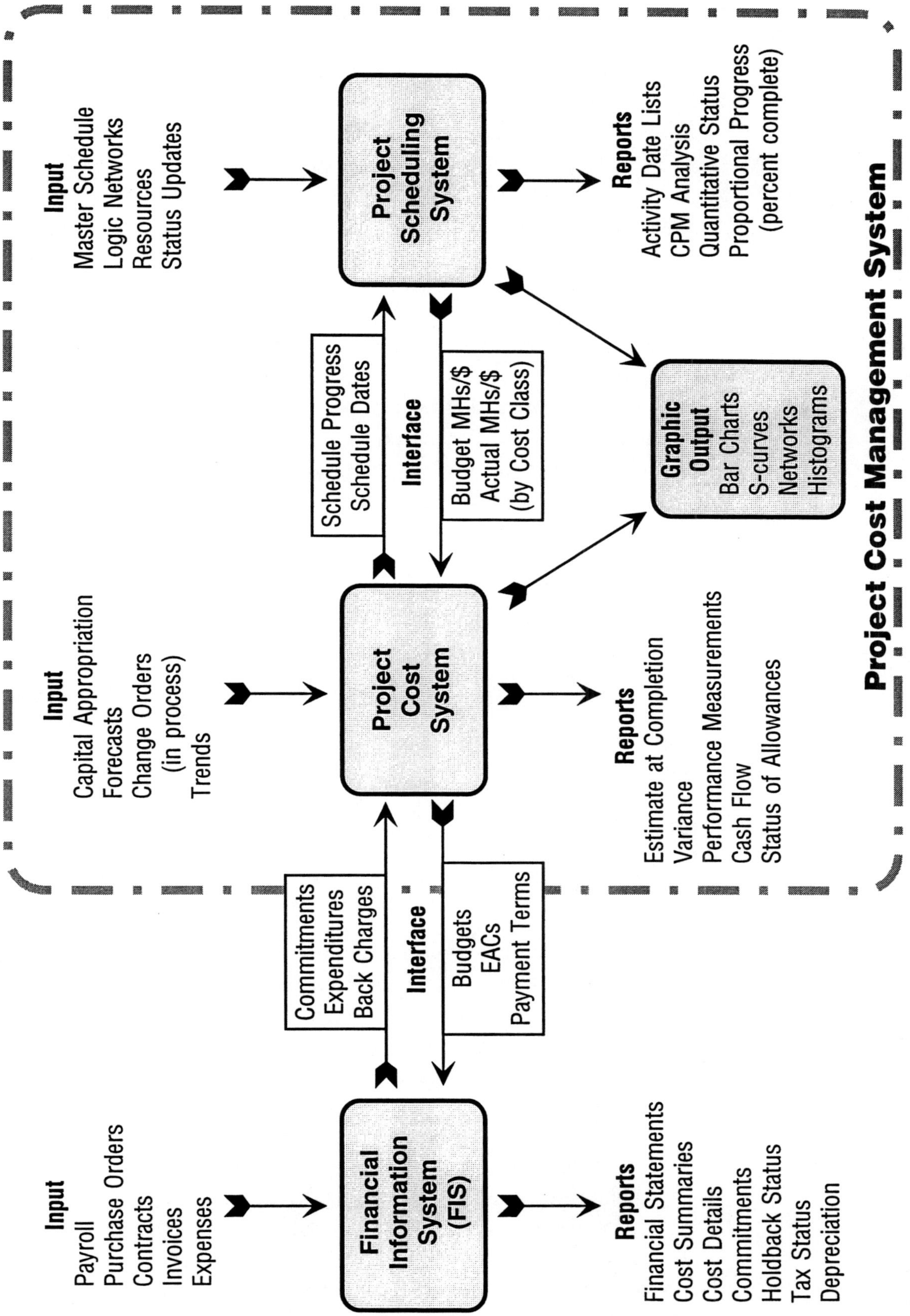

Figure 10-2. Schematic Arrangement of Project Cost Management during Project Execution

The system may be installed and operated by the owner's organization, or the responsibility may be delegated, by contract, to a competent project management firm. Either way, it must be designed to maintain records and prepare reports that will be effective in helping the project team to reach decisions in managing the project. Figure 10-3 shows the extensive influence of the PCMS database through its functional linkages.

(b) System processes

The principal processes involved in the PCMS are data capture, storage, retrieval, and a certain amount of computation and data analysis. Figure 10-4 shows the process schematically. From this figure, it will be seen that cost control of the project is managed at the level of the project's total estimated final cost which is made up of commitments and projections. The status of the project is determined by comparing the project's total estimated final cost, i.e. at completion, to the approved capital appropriation. The difference gives the currently estimated variance as of the reporting date. A comparison of successive variances shows whether a trend is improving or deteriorating.

A busy project manager always finds time to examine the trend in period variance.

For the busy project manager, perhaps the most significant piece of information reflecting the health of the project is the change or trend in period variance . Note that this highest level of project managment is based on commitments and not on actual costs incurred. From a legal stand point, signed contracts, agreements, purchase orders and the like for specified amounts are "firm" costs. According to the FIS, however, they are soft costs until the amounts are invoiced and paid.

If the project is to be managed by commitments and projections, then what is the purpose of also including actual costs? There are several reasons why the project team must keep a close watch on actual expenditures at the next level of detail.

1. On firm price commitments, actual payments must not exceed the committed amount without some documented adjustment. Conversely, payments that fall short must be investigated to find out whether all obligations have been fulfilled.
2. Some commitments may not be firm price but subject to requirements, or subject to measurement of final quantities. Corresponding adjustments must then be made in the PCMS records.
3. Where direct labor is employed, either internally or externally, prior commitments are not possible and actual payroll costs must be tracked together with anticipated future payroll costs.

As explained in Chapter 4, Section 4.3, entries may be thought of in terms of cost classes (work breakdown elements) and cost types (appropriations, commitments, expenditures and forecasts). These are entered or

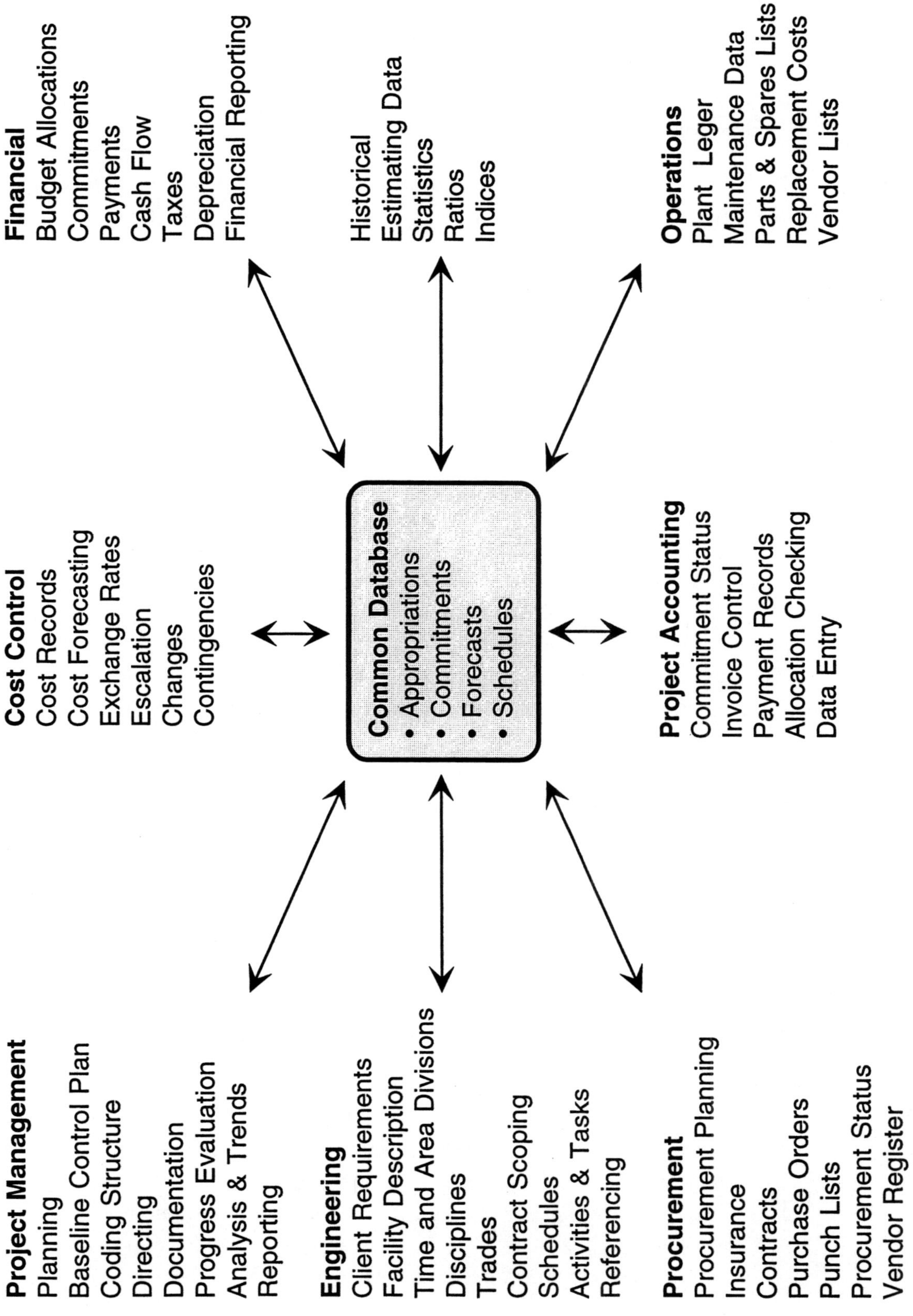

Figure 10-3. Functional Linkages with the PCMS Database

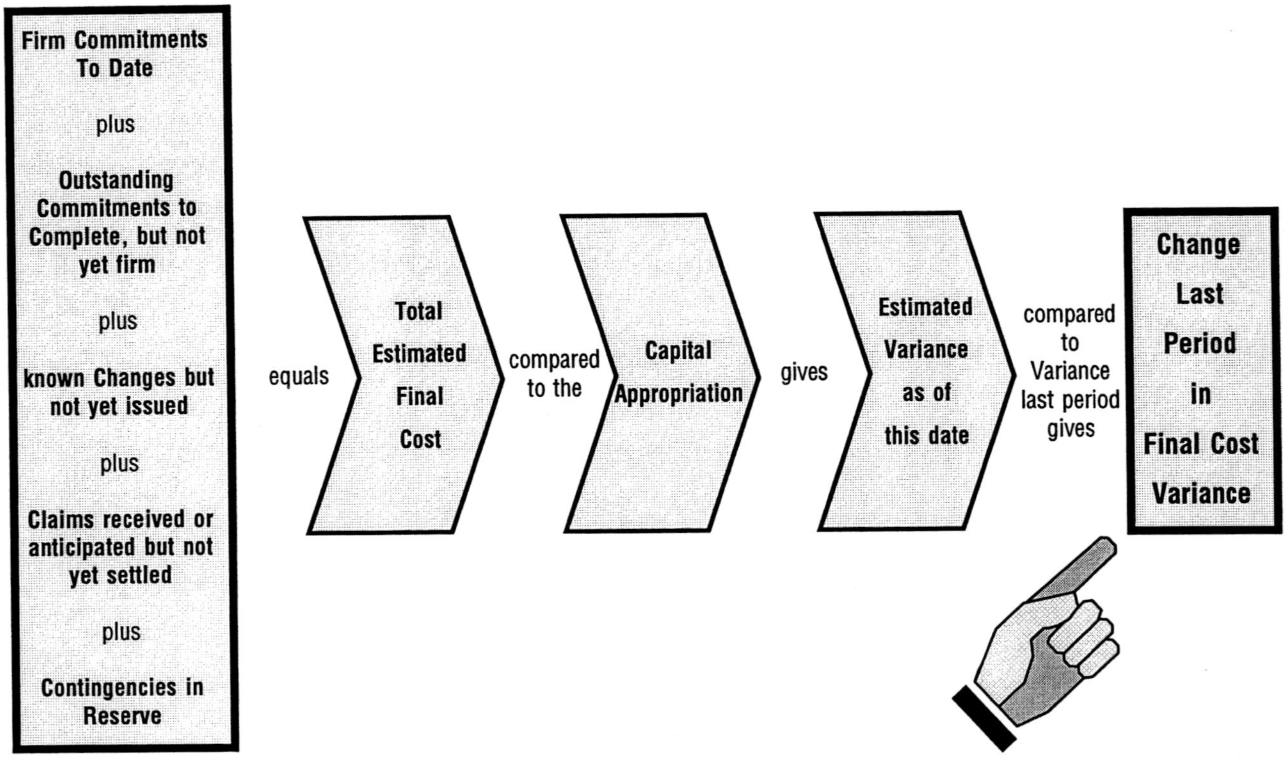

Figure 10-4. Keeping Your Eye on Variances in the Final Cost

updated throughout the life of the project. The record of actual expenditures at any given time should correspond to the Capital-Works-in-Progress account in the corporate books of account.

At the conclusion of the project, the record becomes supporting information for such corporate purposes as capitalization, depreciation, tax assessment, property records, future projects, and so on. The PCMS provides a project management audit trail from the asset accounts back to source documents, such as contracts, tenders and the Project Brief.

10.4 Responsibility for the Project Cost and Estimating Function

Because the financial functions in an organization are well established, they often also service project requirements. The principal outputs of the FIS are the financial and management accounting reports. In these, only the asset category "Capital Works in Progress" (CWIP) captures expenditures on a fixed asset not yet capitalized. The CWIP reflects the sum of expenditures for the project, or projects, to the report date only.

As outlined in Chapter 4, the PCMS reporting requirements and structure are different from those of the FIS code of accounts. Therefore, the project cost report becomes a subsidiary ledger of the CWIP. The appropriate structure of the CWIP itself is one account only for each project in progress.

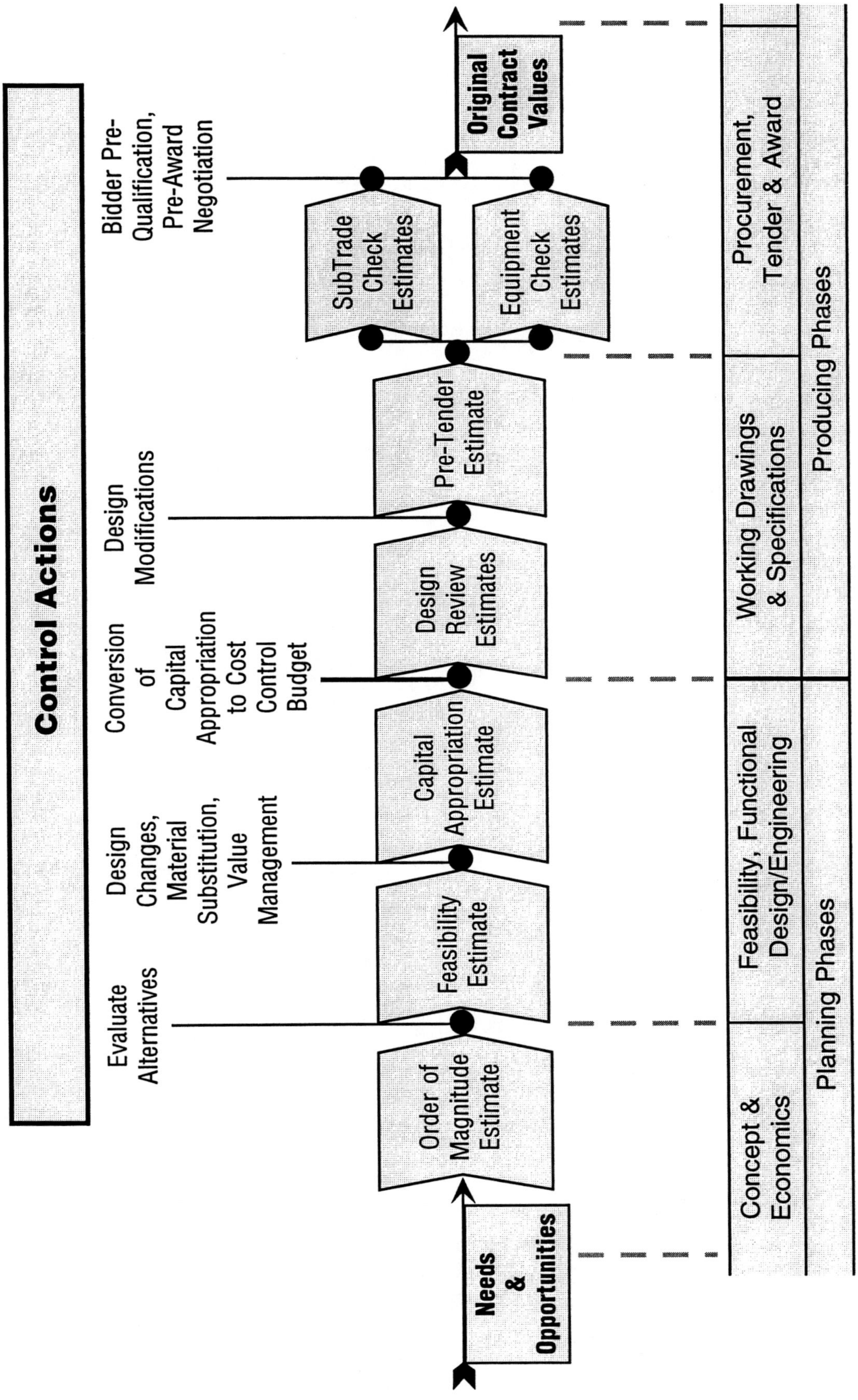

Figure 10-5a. The Project Life Cycle from the Perspective of Cost Control

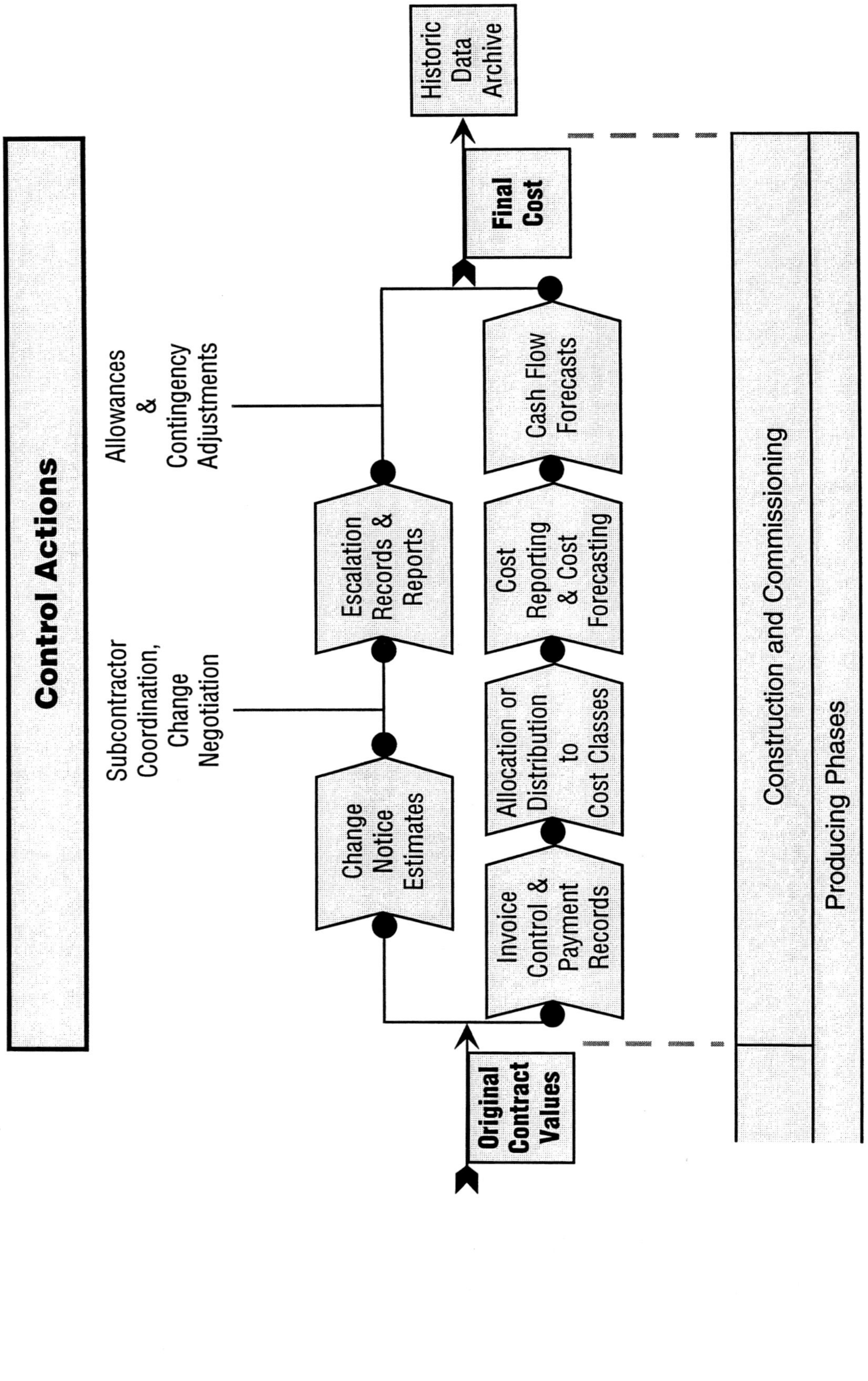

Figure 10-5b. The Project Life Cycle from the Perspective of Cost Control (cont.)

It will be seen that the inclusion of a large project, or even several projects, in the financial system imposes a considerable extra burden on the controller or chief accountant. Such items as the accounting for collection and release of sureties, bid bonds, back charges and holdback releases, require special accounts within the subsidiary ledger, and specific procedures conducted by experienced personnel.

To be effective, the project team must also have status reports on these special accounts, often on demand, as part of the job of assessing contractor performance in the field. When the organization has multiple projects, the project management group may also need to examine the FIS records of an individual supplier or contractor to find out their volume of business and total indebtedness. Such information on a contractor's position is of special interest at time of pre-bid qualification, or before awarding additional work, or if there is a default on another project.

An independently run PCMS helps to avoid overloading the Finance Department.

Thus, a major capital project, or several smaller capital projects, represents a substantial increase in work load and a significant shift in priorities for the Finance Department. For the benefit of all, it is much better to establish a separate project cost and estimating function to manage the Project Cost Management System. It should therefore be the responsibility of a project controller, project estimator, project cost engineer, project accountant or similarly qualified person with responsibility for maintaining the PCMS. This person may be responsible to the corporate controller, and use the same real-cost data sources, but the manner of accounting and reporting to the project team will be quite different.

In extreme cases of very large projects and correspondingly high risk, it may be desirable to establish a completely separate company to account for and take financial responsibility for the project.

10.5 Other Responsibilities of the Project Cost and Estimating Function

In the planning phases, the main responsibility of a project cost and estimating function is to prepare successive capital cost estimates as project planning progresses. These lead up to the basis for the Capital Appropriation Request as described in earlier chapters. As the project moves into the producing phases, the work of the function changes to one of cost reporting and cost forecasting. In this context, some of the responsibilities of the project cost and estimating function may be listed as follows.

- Maintaining the Master Coding System
- Estimates for equipment, materials and services required to complete the project to give an estimated final cost at completion
- Invoice control and payment records
- Allocation or distribution to cost classes and data entry
- Actuals vs. project budget comparisons, variance reports

- Cost evaluations, comparisons of tenders, bids and special critical items
- Cost evaluations of materials, equipment and services
- Cost reports, cost data, progress trends, S-curves and histograms
- Change notice estimates and control
- Analysis and solution of cost problems.
- Escalation, interest and exchange rate trends and statistics
- Status of Capital Appropriation allowances and contingency reserves
- Cash flow forecasts
- Archive of records of costs and estimates

Controlling cost is the responsibility of the whole team — and there are many opportunities for doing so, throughout the project life cycle.

The authority and responsibility for making changes should rest only with project management as the official representative of the owner. However, control over the level of costs incurred rests with all functions, project management, design and engineering, procurement, and construction supervision, each having responsibility over their assigned areas. In other words, it is a total project team responsibility. Figures 10-5a and 10-5b show the numerous opportunities for cost control actions through the planning and producing phases respectively of the project life cycle. The sequence shown represents well-established construction industry practice.

CHAPTER 11

The Master Code Structure

11.1 How the Master Code Works

The Master Code Structure serves as a project code of accounts.

The essence of the Project Cost Management System (PCMS) is the subdivision of the total scope of a project into a systematic hierarchy. The subdivisions identify finite work packages, each with a well defined scope, budget and schedule, established expressly to facilitate management and control of the project. This results in a pyramid like structure.

The Master Code assigns symbols to the elements of this structure and labels each component as a unique item. By reflecting this hierarchy, cost data can be sub-totaled or "rolled up" to any level in the PCMS for summary presentation. In effect, the Master Code Structure (MCS) for a project's PCMS serves as the code of accounts for the project.

The integrity of the Project Cost Management System depends on the correct coding of data, and the correct coding of data can be very time consuming and prone to error. Therefore, the MCS must be workable, meaningful and efficient. The coding should be self-evident, logical and limited to the minimum number of entry digits to improve the accuracy of coding data as far as possible. Every additional coding digit increases the probability of an entry error — and loss of integrity of the whole system!

11.2 Structuring the Code Identifier

(a) Keep it simple – and friendly!

Create a user-friendly code — Data Entry people will appreciate it!

Many complicated forms of identifier have been tried. Many have digits and/or letters in the system serving entirely different and separate purposes. Such systems require every user to be instructed on the structure and to memorize the individual codes. If the identifier is long and complex, and especially if it appears to lack any obvious logic, the probability and frequency of error increases beyond all reason. Such systems quickly lose credibility and fall into disrepute. Loss of a reliable information base can be very damaging to the project management image.

Projects typically involve significant numbers of people working in various locations or different parts of the project organization. Since they also generally work with large volumes of data, optimum simplicity is highly desirable. So a simple hierarchical (roll up or cascade) structure, consisting of a core of five to seven digits, is strongly recommended.

Make the Master Code the universal reference system on the project.

This core code should also be used as the common information vehicle for all aspects of the project. Thus, it will not only be used for designating cost and schedule elements of the MCS, but also used as the reference system for contracts, specifications, project manuals and the like. Supplementary characters may be added to identify resources, such as labor and materials, and to represent drawing numbers, part numbers and so on.

The core coding of a particular project's MCS can be confined to five to seven digits. If the organization has multiple projects, the preceding project identifier may require, say, another four digits. When supplementary characters and numbers are added to identify drawings or part numbers etc., the total referencing number still results in 10 to 14 characters. Supplementary derivative codes and identifiers are discussed in the next Section.

(b) Description of levels in the system

Figure 11-1 shows the MCS and a Work Breakdown Structure (WBS) pyramid designed to suit many different types of construction project. Note how the WBS starts at the top with the total project and first divides into major geographical regions or major time phases. This is the first level of breakdown. The next level introduces disciplines or trade groupings. The level below this generally corresponds to specific trades as reflected in the US UCI divisions, or the Canadian CSI Masterformat Broadscope categories. The fourth level shows Narrowscope items.

Design the details of the MCS to suit the particular project.

It is worth examining the content at each MCS level shown in Figure 11-1 in greater detail. Each level is described below although different projects may require different emphasis and some swapping of content may be required between adjacent levels. A Work Package may be identified at any of these levels, according to the project team's strategy and requirements for managing the project.

Level 0 — identifies different projects.

Level 1 — can be used for segregating major geographical areas of the project such as those contained by "battery limits" or into major independent systems. It can also be used to separate out major system wide responsibilities or cost centers such as the organization's overheads, various internal soft costs, or other non-construction related costs also identified in level 2.

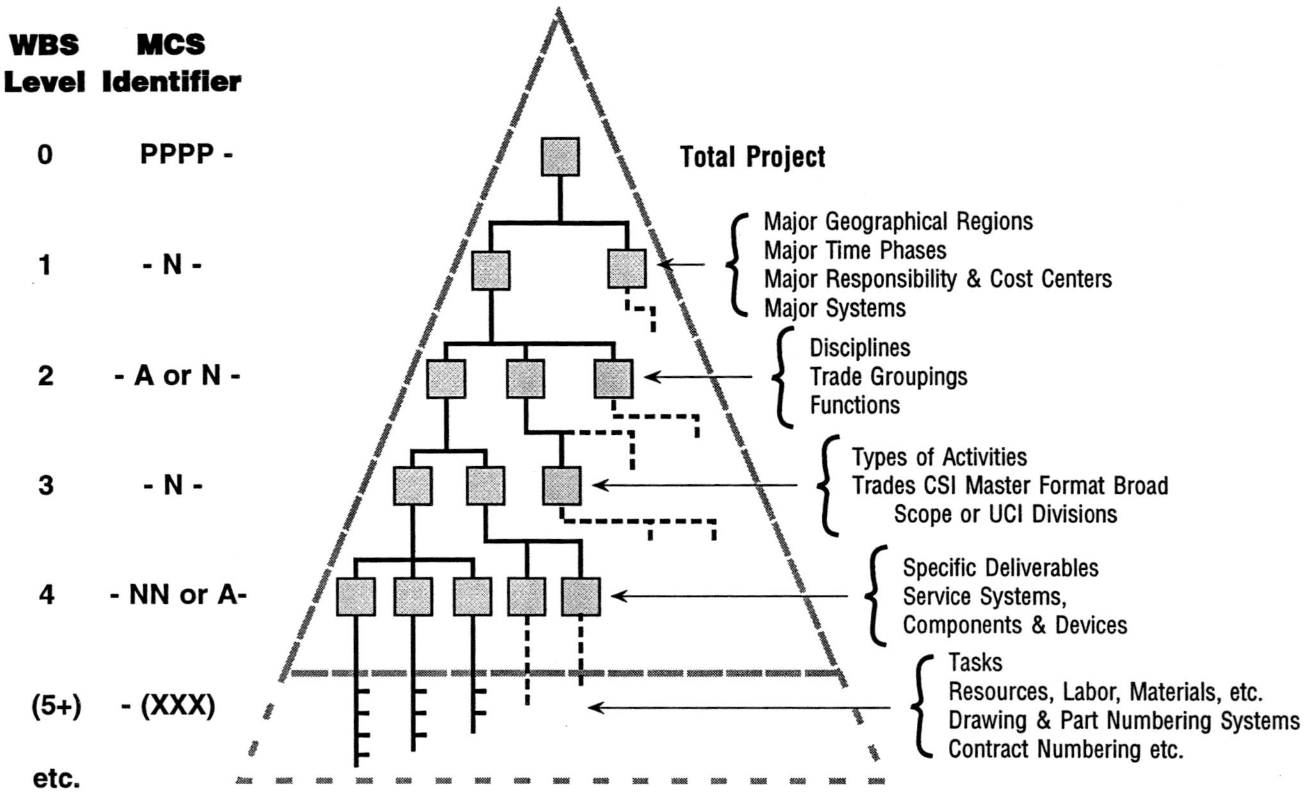

Notes: (5+) = Optional additional levels, usual only on very large projects
(XXX) = Identifiers used for referencing only. Not part of cost allocation code.

Figure 11-1. The Master Code Structure and Work Breakdown Structure

Separation of the project into its major time phases such as feasibility, regulatory application or design and construction should also be done at this level.

Level 2 — separates the work according to discipline or recognized trade groupings, such as general conditions, site works, structural, mechanical, process, architectural and so on. Under overheads in level 1, level 2 may break out packages for, say, internal soft costs, financing, consulting fees, land purchase etc. It may also be expedient to include, within this grouping, reserves for contingency or allowances for unidentified scope changes.

Level 3 — takes the process a step further, and identifies individual trades (equivalent to the Canadian Construction Specifications Institute (CSI) Masterformat Broadscope Divisions or the US Uniform Construction Index (UCI) 16 Division format). Within the overhead area, the "disciplines" mentioned in level 2 above might subdivide respectively into head office overhead, division or departmental overheads (including in-house project management), insurance, legal, construction related permits, public relations etc.; financing debt charges, interest, fees and associated legal; individual consulting fees, including project and construction management; prime cost of land and various associated taxes, permits, fees, charges and survey etc.

Level 4 — generally identifies most of the project's physical work packages if the higher level segregation has been followed as above. These work packages should be separately identified by the name of the resulting deliverable because of the work of the various major trades of level 3. This could include temporary and permanent site works, the structural system, the various mechanical systems, power and communication systems, and so on.

It should be noted that for day to day scheduling purposes, several tasks will be required to make up the level 4 work packages. These are equivalent to level 5 of the WBS. However, these tasks may generally be too small to be included in the cost reporting structure. The four level MCS structure can generally fit the cost reporting requirements comfortably, even on the largest projects. Indications to the contrary on any particular project could suggest inadequate separation at level 1 of the WBS.

Use four levels of the WBS for cost reporting, the fifth level for special referencing.

It should also be noted that not all the work packages in the structure are at the same level. This is because some of the level 1 elements break down into different types of subject matter. Where this occurs, be careful in designing reports at these lower levels to ensure that any work packages ending at a higher level are not omitted. To prevent this, the reporting software system must be designed to search and jump up to the next highest level where data is captured.

Another beneficial feature is the suppression of lines containing zero information, and the omission of all levels of subtotals that are identical with the previous line because there is only a one-line entry to sub-total. For the project team, there is nothing so depressing as receiving voluminous reports containing strings of zeros and rows of subtotals that are identical with the line above.

(c) Application and examples of element identifiers

The left of Figure 11-1 shows the make-up of the element identifier. Note how an alpha identifier is suggested at level 2. Such a character could be the first letter of the trade or function that it represents, barring duplication. This greatly helps memory recall. The alpha character at this point in the total identifier also helps to break up a long sequence of digits. This makes the identifier easier to read, avoids the necessity of inserting added separators such as a comma or period, and so reduces the likelihood of entry error.

As each new element is added, it is given a unique number according to the structure. If the element is subsequently abandoned, its unique number can be deleted without disrupting the numbering system. However, deleted numbers should never be reused. Preserving deleted numbers provides an audit trail and an accurate history of the project.

Never reassign a used code number to another element — It will confuse the audit trail.

Figure 11-2 shows how the MCS enables the rolling up of totals into each higher level or, conversely, the cascading breakdown of subtotals. In this way, cost reports can be called for at any level according to the requirements and responsibilities of the report user.

As a practical example, consider the coding structure used by construction management on an international airport reconstruction project. The standard MCS chosen for this project is in the form PPPP-n-a-nn-nnnn as shown in Figure 11-3. Suppose the project is number 9876, the baggage handling system design has just been completed and approved, and the documents handed over to the Procurement Manager for action. His first task is to number the package. Since the work is part of the Departure Level of the main building facility, project management has allocated the package to the General Building Contractor.

Numbering the package is now straight forward. The Procurement Manager gives it the number 9876-2-B-04. The missing last four digits of the generic number will be used later by the Scheduling Department as the detailed schedule is developed in conjunction with the general and trade contractors concerned.

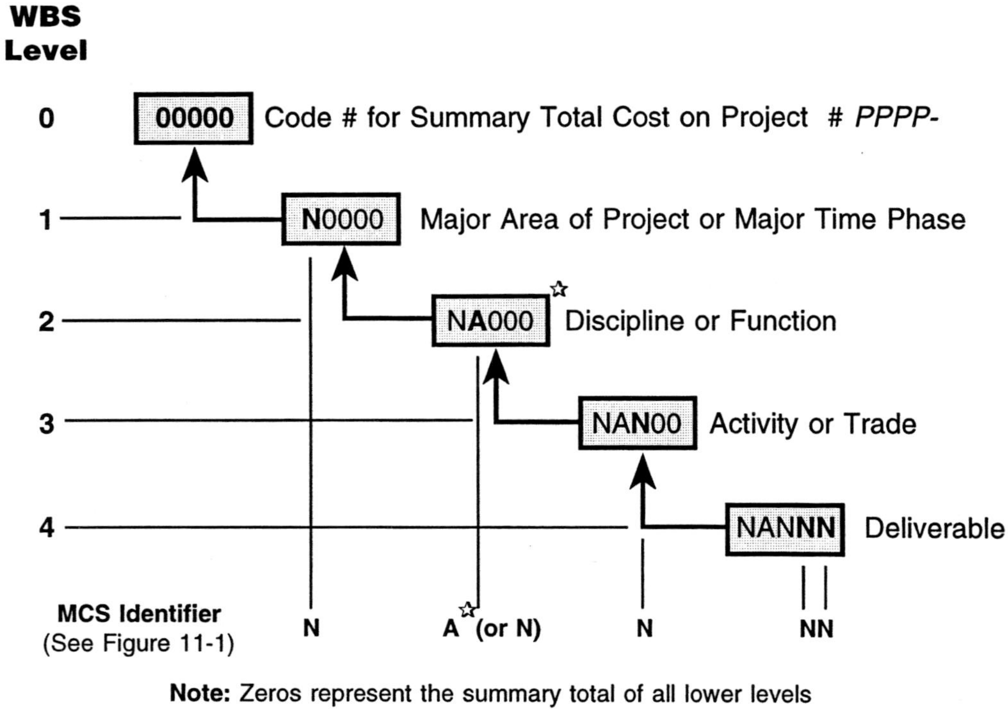

Figure 11-2. The Master Code Cascade/Rollup Numbering System

This example shows the simplicity and flexibility of the system even in use on a major complex project. Figures 11-4a and 11-4b show another example of an MCS which was developed for a multiple building project environment such as a real estate owner or developer. On smaller projects, development of the WBS down to level 3 should be sufficient for identifying the various work packages and their deliverables.

On smaller projects, use fewer breakdown levels.

In the first step for establishing a project's procurement strategy, the design discipline and construction trade packages need to be identified. The second step is to define the scope of individual contracts that may encompass one or more of these work packages.

If consulting services are separated according to discipline, these would be let at level 3. Examples include structural, civil, mechanical, electrical, instrumentation, process, acoustical, architectural, estimating, scheduling, surveying, inspection and management consultants. But if this approach is adopted instead of appointing a single engineering or architectural consultant, make sure who is going to be responsible for coordinating all the design work. It is then essential to identify in every legal agreement who will be responsible for the complete general technical and administrative coordination of the individual subconsultant efforts. This is to avoid serious problems and conflicts in the construction stages.

Separate consulting contracts impose a heavier responsibility and administrative burden on the procuring authority. However, experience shows that there may be considerable benefits in a more cost effective design because of shorter more direct lines of communication during the design stage. Specialist consultants also sometimes prefer to be paid directly by the project owner.

For efficient contract administration and better pricing, the work of a construction contract package should be continuous through the project's schedule. It should also be of sufficient magnitude to attract competitive offers. Incorporating several work packages into a contract package imposes some special requirements on contract administration. For example, the identity of the individual work packages should be retained in the contract document and the contractor should be required to reflect the package identifiers in its progress billings.

Contracts for work that is not continuous add to the cost. Create two or more contracts instead.

For cost plus contracts, a separate package should be created within the project overhead area to capture the contractor's fee. Pre-purchase by the owner of major equipment items having long delivery would also be identified at level 3. A separate contract package should be established for each equipment item, or group of items, purchased from a single supplier.

If construction management, and not a single general contractor, is the project's procurement strategy then trade contracts might be let at level 3 or level 4 depending on the nature of the work or content. If the contract package includes several related specialist trades, it would be let at level 3, while the individual trades that it contains are tracked at level 4. As an example, plumbing, heating, and ventilation typically all come under

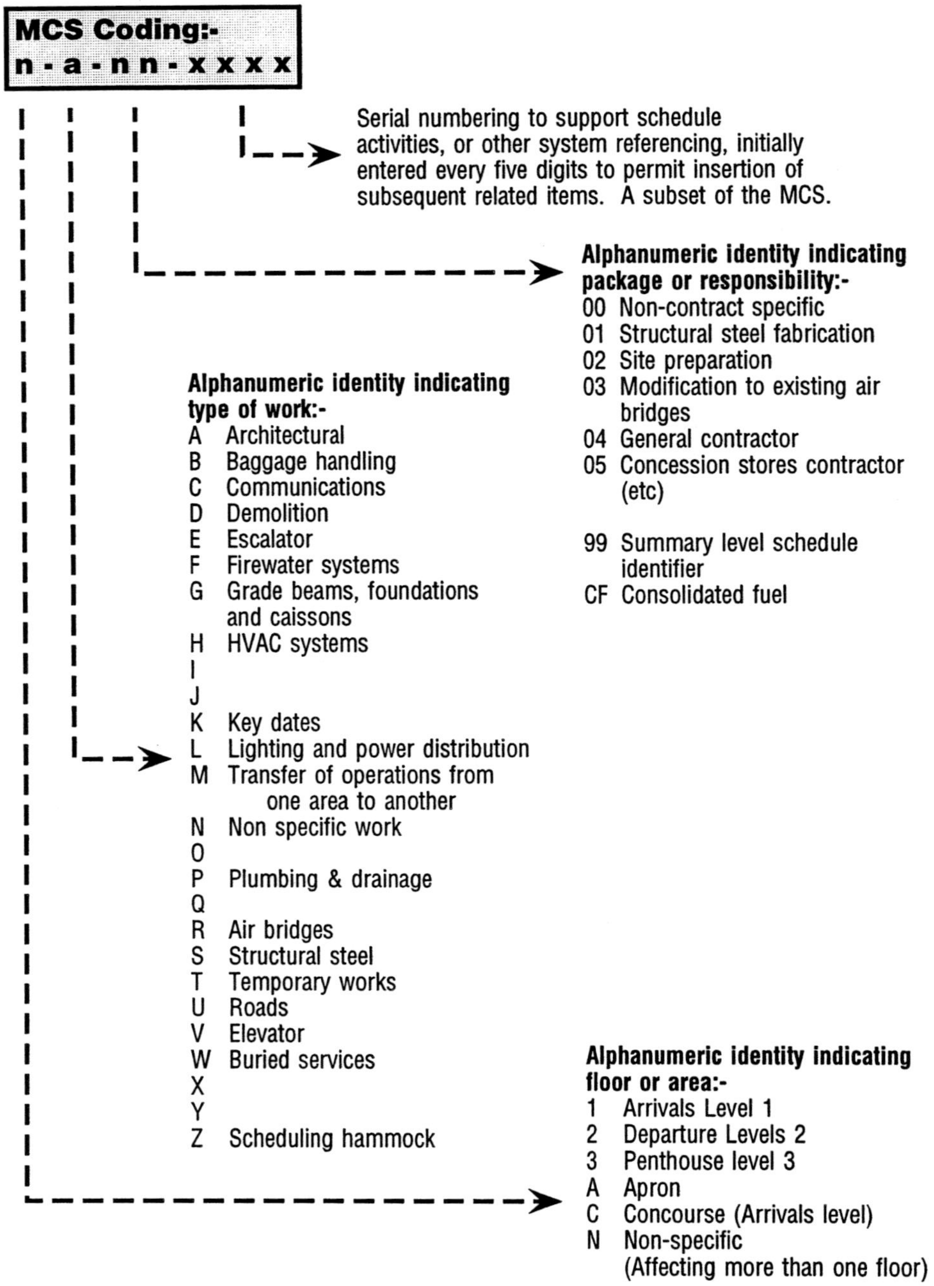

Figure 11-3. Three-level MCS as used on a large Airport Reconstruction Project

mechanical work. A contract with a single subtrade for a simple deliverable would probably be let at level 4.

11.3 Derivative Codes and Identifiers

The optional level 5, shown in Figure 11-1, is not strictly part of the cost code structure. Yet it is important because it can play a valuable role in unifying management information processing and reporting for the project

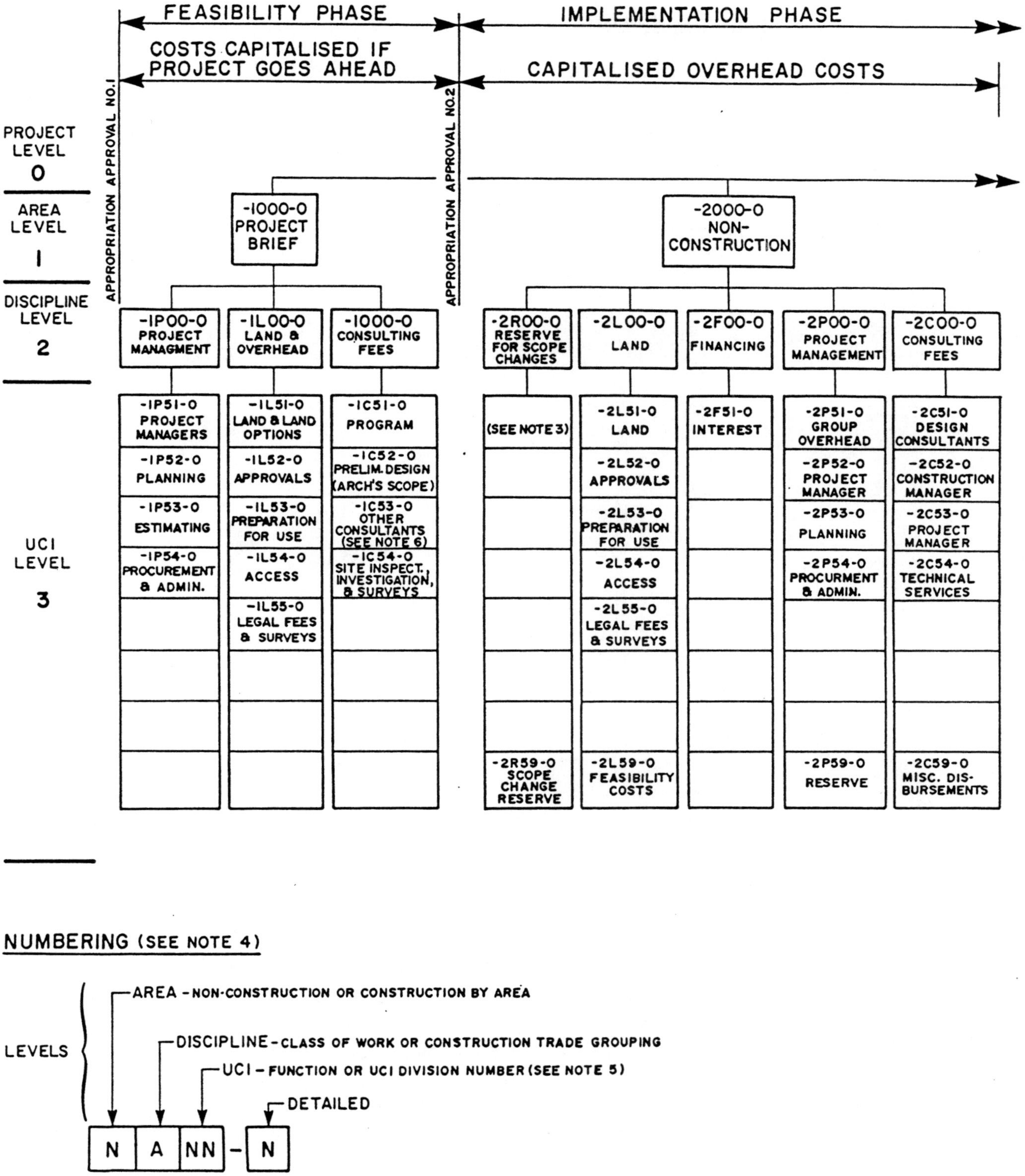

Figure 11-4a. Example of a WBS as used on Multiple Building Projects

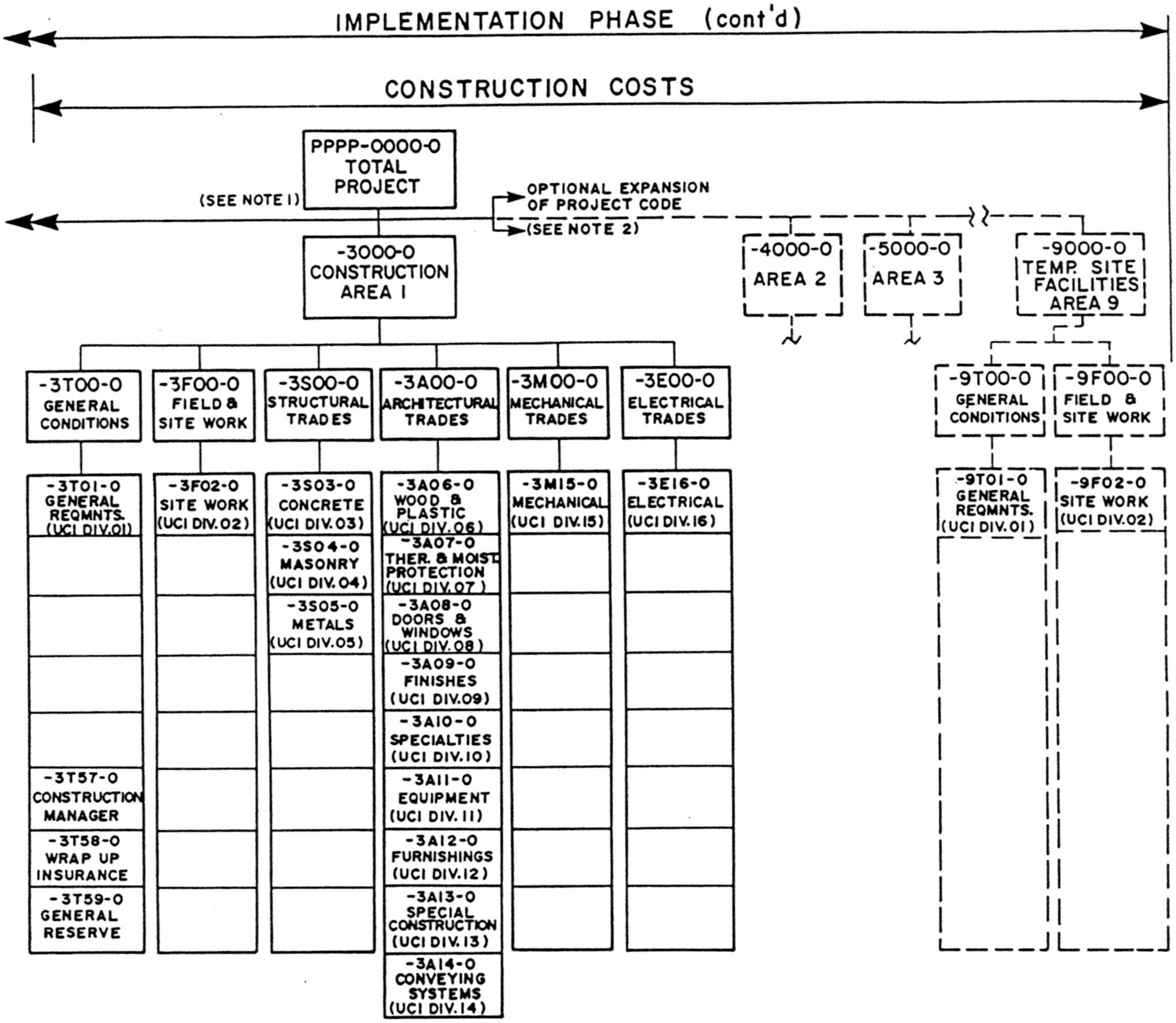

NOTES

1. ALWAYS USE 5 CHARACTER PROJECT CODE IN CONJUNCTION WITH 4 DIGIT PROJECT IDENTIFIER (PPPP).
2. USE DOTTED LINE PORTION OF STRUCTURE TO SEGREGATE PROJECTS INTO CONSTRUCTION AREAS OR GEOGRAPHIC AREAS. OPTIONAL CATEGORIES 4000-0 THROUGH 8000-0 ARE FOR THIS PURPOSE.
3. SUBDIVIDE RESERVE FOR SCOPE CHANGES (2R00-0) DOWN TO THE WORK PACKAGE LEVEL IN ACCORD WITH THE SPECIFIC RESERVE PROVISIONS, IF ANY, ON PROJECT.
4. FILL CODE LEVEL WITH A ZERO, OR ZEROES, TO INDICATE THE LEVEL HAS BEEN SUMMARIZED INTO NEXT HIGHER LEVEL.
5. TO ESTABLISH OVER 9 WORK PACKAGES IN 3RD-LEVEL UCI CATEGORY, ADD '20' TO NUMERIC VALUE OF 2 DIGIT CODE SEGMENT TO CREATE OVERFLOW CATEGORY.
6. OTHER CONSULTANTS eg. MECHANICAL, ELECTRICAL (IF USED INDEPENDENTLY)

Figure 11-4b. Example of a WBS as used on Multiple Building Projects (cont.)

team. Level 5 can also be used to code and sort different resources, and different sources of labor and materials. For example, a particular project group or department may be required to provide skills or parts for many different work packages, on different areas of the project, or even for different projects. By calling for a data sort by department across all work packages, departmental information will be abstracted that will enable the group to project their work loads and assess their priorities.

Other characters can be attached to the Master Code to identify specific items of information or documents associated with the project. Figure 11-5 shows just how flexible the coding system can be. In any case, the MCS is the central key to the adoption of a uniform and universal information classification and retrieval system on the project.

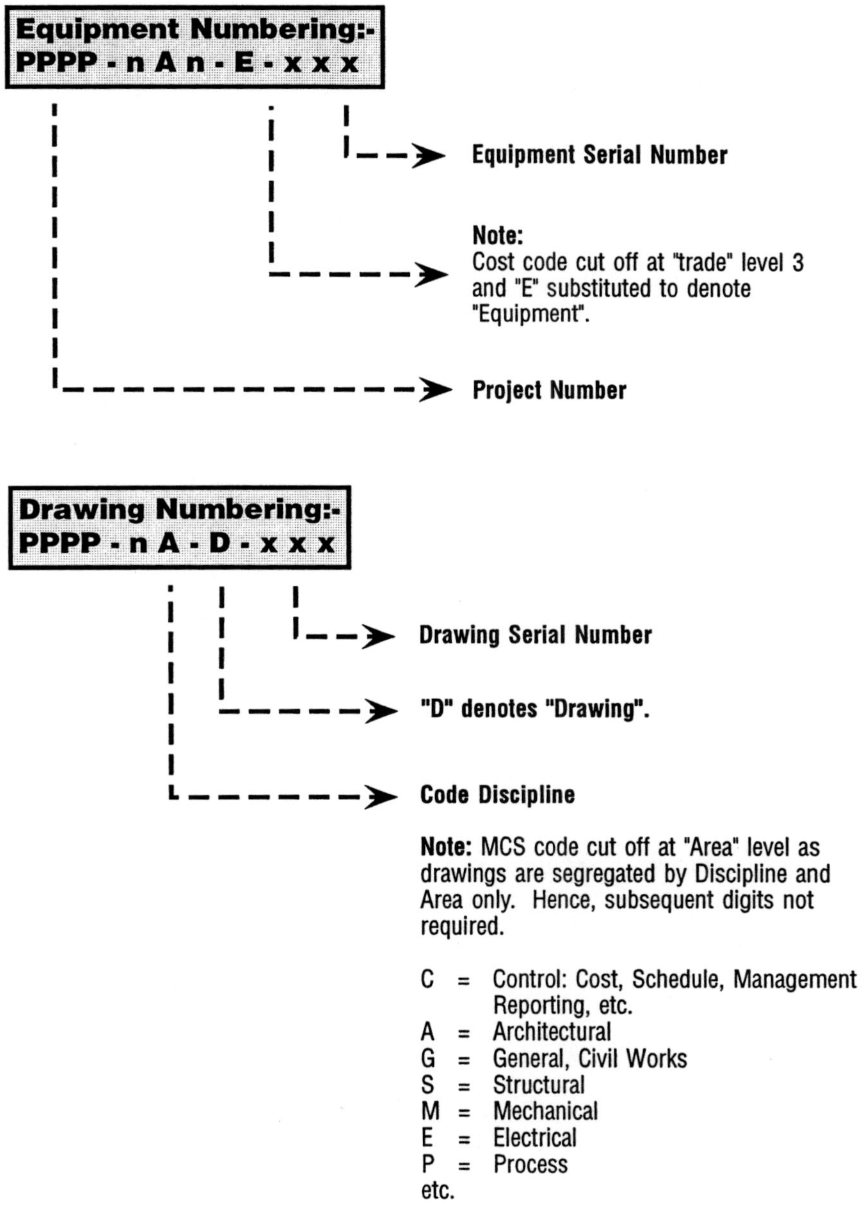

Figure 11-5. Examples of MCS Referencing Flexibility

Suggested applications for the derivative coding are summarized for reference as follows:

- Subcoding of labor and materials to obtain reports by different classifications
- Identification of subtasks for scheduling purposes
- Equipment and part numbering
- Contract numbering
- Drawing numbering
- Filing of documents and correspondence

11.4 Entry of Actual Cost Data

The FIS is the first to capture project expenditures (actual costs) which should be posted simultaneously to the Capital Works in Progress (CWIP) account and to the project. However, reporting dates may not be coincident. Also, cost data input to the PCMS may be on-going and subject to different policies, compared to the expenditure data accumulated for batch input to the FIS. Therefore, reconciliation will be required periodically and both systems must have the capacity to produce a transaction audit trail. This is so that the vouchers supporting the most recent entries in both the project and financial records can be readily identified upon demand.

Audit trails will be needed by the project team — make them responsible for coding PCMS data.

This audit trail is particularly valuable to the project team. They will need it for preparing regular forecast updates of outstanding commitments and expenditures that are required to complete the project.

The simultaneous entry of expenditures into the FIS and the PCMS constitutes the data transmission interface between the two systems. The data has to be coded with identifiers for both the appropriate FIS category and the WBS cost class. Contractor and supplier billings should come to the FIS from the project after careful checking and formal approval. They should be coded by the project team at the time of approval.

A set of well established procedures and processing methods within the FIS should be used to code and vouch for other charges to the project. Typically, these are internal charges incurred by other departments in providing services to the project. Examples of "direct" costs include corporate employee payroll and expenses, materials and supplies, equipment use and rental (including computer time), and any internal interest-during-construction at the prevailing average or special corporate rate. In addition, the sponsoring organization may wish to add "indirect" or overhead costs. These would be computed on some pro rata basis such as total project value or value of corporate services provided.

These internal charges are really "soft" costs because they do not arise from contractual commitments established at "arms length" and presumably could be modified. Instead, they depend on some element of subjective judgment or internal policy. Some vigilance is necessary to ensure that the project budget is not being used as a convenient dumping ground for costs unwanted elsewhere.

Genuine internal charges to the project should only be those that the organization has incurred because of project activities. In other words, the project should only be charged with those costs that would not otherwise have been incurred but for the project. The point is, the project should not be charged with any part of the organization's normal cost of doing business.

Accept only corporate "but for..." charges against the project budget.

Whatever arrangement is established to capture and code such internal charges, it is the project manager who is ultimately responsible for the total project budget. Therefore, the following requirements should be met:

- Every charge to the project should be covered by a formal documented commitment.
- The project manager must have the opportunity to examine and accept all charges made against the project.

All project expenditures should be routinely checked against commitments by the project's project accountant. It follows that every external expense should be covered by a purchase order or contract at the time of commitment. Similarly, internal charges should also be formally preauthorized by some suitable internal document. Payroll distribution is particularly troublesome to deal with in this respect because it requires an intermediate source document, such as individual time sheets, or a Journal Voucher distribution sheet.

The project accountant should be required to examine all supplier invoices, holdback release authorizations, progress claims and similar source documents for goods and services obtained directly by the project. He or she should check that the project team has properly vouched for, audited and coded all invoices before sending them to the Controller's department. It then only remains for these documents to be processed for payment and entered in the FIS.

11.5 Benefits and Characteristics

The principle behind the Project Cost Management System is the subdivision of the total project scope into a systematic hierarchy. A unique label from the Master Code Structure identifies each element in the PCMS hierarchy. If properly constructed, the MCS has the following characteristics.

- Satisfies the work package rules described in Chapter 5
- Has a flexible, modular format capable of expansion
- Is alpha-numerical

- Uses mnemonics making it easier to remember and use and therefore reduces coding errors
- Has a consistent and compatible structure at all levels
- Uniquely references firm blocks of work
- Follows sequence of work
- Standardizes similar items
- Creates a disciplined environment
- Reflects contracting strategy
- Reflects responsibilities
- Facilitates coordination
- Ties in estimates, scheduling and cash flow
- Enables control over
  - Cost estimates
  - Contracts
  - Changes
  - Commitments and expenditures
- Ties in with financial records
- Creates an audit trail
- Given an element number, any element can be quickly traced and its relationship to the rest of the structure can be clearly seen.
- Elements can be added or removed without disrupting the numbering system. (Note, deleted numbers should never be reused in order to preserve an accurate history of the project.)

Such a Master Code Structure is highly suited to electronic data processing.

CHAPTER 12

Cost Control Reporting

12.1 Accounting Difficulties in Estimating Cost to Complete

(a) Steps in the flow of funds

As noted in Chapter 4, Section 4.2 (d), the reason for setting up a project cost management system (PCMS) is because the corporate financial control system does not provide the kind of information needed for managing a project. However, the financial accounting system does capture all of the organization's expenditures, and this information is required to operate the PCMS. A frequent difficulty arises in reconciling the two for purposes of preparing an estimated cost to complete.

Moving funds through the accounting system parallels moving the facility from concept to reality.

Figure 12-1 shows the flow of funds through an organization's financial and accounting system. Note how the idea of a new facility moving from concept to reality is paralleled by moving funds through the accounting process. The steps in this accounting process can be described as follows.

Proposal estimates — no funds committed at this point.

Capital Appropriation Request (CAR) — funding characterized, but no corporate funds actually encumbered.

CAR approved — corporate funding encumbered, i.e. must be set aside for future expenditures.

Contracts awarded — funding committed for the extent of the work contained in the contract. Any residual, positive or negative, would flow back to contingencies or allowances.

Work done — costs are incurred as a result of contracts activities.

Invoice submitted — Contractor sends invoice for agreed value of work done. This forms part of the total committed.

Invoice entered — the invoice amount, less any holdback, is entered for payment. At this point, the gross amount is usually considered disbursed, although only the net amount will be paid. The difference, the holdback, is transferred to a suspense account for payment later according to contractual or regulatory terms.

Check issued — money is drawn on the organization's corporate account in favor of the contractor.

Check cleared — funds are transferred from one bank to another. At some point, often at financial year end, the value received for the expenditures is recognized as a fixed asset. However, the amount recognized is not usually the cumulative total of expenditures but some percentage of completion of the final value of the facility.

The diagram shown is somewhat simplistic. In some organizations there may be additional sub-routines associated with the budget approval process or the disbursement process. For example, a check requisition may have to be prepared and approved before a check can be made out and delivered to the recipient.

(b) The problem with forecasting

The problem with forecasting comes in preparing a PCMS estimated cost to complete. Figure 4-5, Chapter 4, showed that the jumping off point is the information provided by the corporate accounting system. But is this interface at the "invoiced", the "incurred costs" or the "contracted commitments"? Or is it some of each depending on the particular item?

To be able to forecast, you must know where the accounting entries are to date.

In practice the choice usually lies somewhere between Committed and Disbursed. Obviously it is important to know, and to know exactly. It is very important to recognize that the estimated cost to complete must be calculated according to whichever is selected.

If most of the work is in fixed price contracts, then the simplest course is to forecast based on commitments plus any changes or adjustments "in the pipe line". If work is being done under a remeasurement contract, that is, a unit price contract, then it will be necessary to assess outstanding quantities at the time of the last progress measurement. This means going to another level of detail.

If the work is under some form of cost plus contracts, then although there is a commitment to contract and payment, there is no commitment to any fixed final cost. So a commitment value is simply not available. The same is true for work by direct labor, which is the situation most contrac-

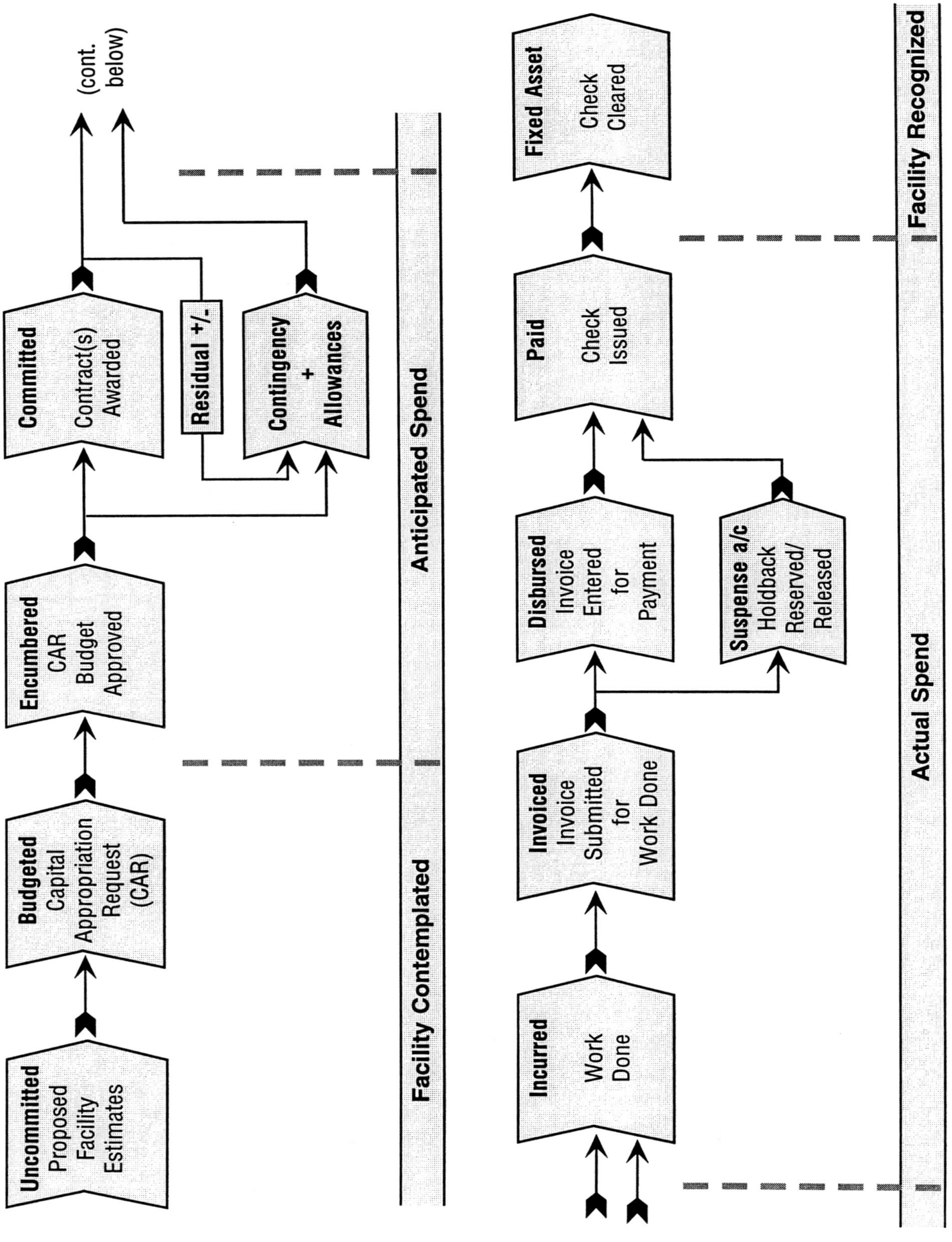

Figure 12-1. Flow of Funds through the Accounting Process

tors are in. Here, it is necessary to know the actual disbursements right up to the cut-off date for the forecast.

This is the approach taken in the Earned Value and Performance Analysis Technique discussed in Chapter 14, Section 14.1, but the collection of costs is very detailed and sometimes difficult. As an example, it is known that a major delivery of materials or piece of equipment was made before the cut-off date. The question then arises, is the corresponding amount included in the expenditures currently reported by the financial system? Even if it is, does the amount include charges for taxes, freight, customs, handling and clearance charges, frequently beyond the contracted commitment because some of these may be due to a third party. These amounts could make quite a difference to the estimated total cost of the project at completion.

Or consider a delivery made by a contractor at the beginning of its invoice period. The invoice may not be assembled and delivered to project control until some four or five weeks later. It may be several weeks more before the invoice is approved and entered into the financial accounting system. If the financial accounting only records items that have been disbursed, there may be a lag of several more weeks between the delivery and the value showing up in the records. A few organizations even reconcile only to their bank statement, which means indebtedness does not show until the payment is cleared, which is even later.

To know the status of the financial accounting, it may be necessary to have a complete listing of the last period's accounting entries.

It is not uncommon that the only way to know what is included in the current financial accounting report is to review a complete listing of entries over the last couple of months. This can be a very tedious task. However, failure to do so frequently results in overlooking items that are known but do not appear either in the accounts or the forecast because they were "in process". Even large amounts can "fall between the cracks" resulting in a favorable but untrue Estimated Cost at Completion.

On most construction projects, because they are usually mixtures of the different types of expenditure, the estimated-cost-to-complete is based on a mixture of commitments and actual disbursements. For this reason, and because of the work involved, it is probably unreasonable to undertake a rigorous estimate of cost-to-complete every month. Instead, it should be at some longer interval to suit the duration of the project and its current stage.

(c) Cash flow projection

The focus of the corporate finance department is the cash requirements for the project, the projected cash flow. Because of the high cost of money, significant savings can be gained by careful timing of payments. However, this requires a careful cash balancing act. If there are unnecessarily high draw downs, excessive interest penalties will be incurred because of funds sitting idle in the project bank account. If the draw downs are too low, the result will be disgruntled contractors and suppliers, supplier interest penalties or lost discounts.

Realistic projections require a team input.

The springboard for projections of cash flow is the amount currently disbursed. Realistic projections will require the combined project management inputs of contract administration, purchasing, scheduling, and cost estimating. The result should be a cash flow "S" curve that simulates anticipated project progress and the applicable invoice policy and procedure payment timing.

Be careful in generating this report. Issues which must be considered include:

- Recognition of prior payments to date
- Actual assessed progress compared to invoiced progress, if different
- Anticipated rate of future progress
- Inflation, contingency and allowance transfers
- The relevant contractual payment modes, e.g. progress invoice, prearranged progress payment sums, or payment on completion
- Regular or accelerated invoice processing time to capture discounts
- Retention and subsequent pay out of contractual holdbacks

12.2 PCMS Reports and Reconciliation

(a) Preparing reports that are useful

Cost control is about numbers — but they also require explanation.

Many project managers, and project accountants too, miss the point when it comes to reporting numbers. The information is presented in one way or another but the trends, the implications for the future, and how the recipients of the report will react, are overlooked. Cost control reporting is about numbers, so avoid the common mistake of trying to present them in narrative form. On the other hand, do not just list them either. A report that does not point out the problems and how they can be solved serves no real purpose.

Present PCMS reports in a standard summary format and then explain what they mean. Presenting summary data in a self-evident graphical format is even better. Remember, all project people are busy people so keep the following points in mind.

- Few people take the time to read an entire report. So it must be assembled so that the most important information appears at the top and supporting information follows later.
- Just telling readers what the numbers are, is of little value. The whole reporting process is only useful when it shows actions that must be taken to correct problems. Focus on the variances between actual and planned. Better still, focus on the changes in variance

since the last reporting period. Explain what they mean in terms of the project's objectives.

- Items constituting major problems requiring urgent action or solutions need special high-lighting. Even this information is only constructive when planned solutions, such as a work-around, are proposed or specific action, such as a budget adjustment, is requested.
- On the first page, make sure that the scope and purpose of the report and the report's effective date are all clearly stated in the title. Then list the major conclusions, recommendations and action requests.

(b) Outputs from the system

The output from the Project Cost Management System (PCMS) is a set of reports for the project or, in the case of multiple projects, for each active project. These reports are designed to aid project decision making by providing the most effective and rapid information necessary for project management to achieve project objectives.

During the planning phases, the project needs to be reported on two levels. The upper, long term level, charts the estimated final cost of the completed project. It will contain only forecasts and may be subject to substantial variations until a viable economic scope is established. The lower, short term level, reports on the status of the project's development. In effect, it represents a mini project, whose end objective is to produce an acceptable Project Brief.

During planning, report the project on two levels — the status of the current phase, and the estimated final project cost.

On the upper level, the preparation of each successive project cost estimate, i.e. order-of-magnitude, concept, and appropriation, should all be structured according to a progressively developing and consistent break-down structure. This will be made much easier if a Master Code Structure (MCS) as described in the previous chapter is introduced at the outset. It will provide a sense of direction, particularly for a more orderly sequence of decision making and the "level of detail" required at each stage. Following appropriation approval, the upper level becomes the single active level for the project. All cost classes and types displayed on the reports should be updated accordingly.

It should be noted that items of a certain level of detail for one project are not necessarily the same for another. This may be because of a change in emphasis. For example, a "flagship" project, compared to a strictly commercial one, may pay particular attention on external public appearance. It may call for a different layout, higher standards and different siting requirements etc. Incidentally, as a business decision, the associated higher costs will be factored into the economics of attracting business and delivering product.

There are four principal sets of information produced by the PCMS of which the single most important is probably the summary with its information on variances. The four sets are:

1. **Summary Level Variance** — a comparison of forecast final cost with authorized appropriation

Three other principal sets of information support the Summary Variance as follows:

2. **Appropriation Reconciliation** — a reconciliation of the present authorized capital appropriation with the original one

3. **Commitment/Expenditure** — a comparison of expenditures to date with total commitments

4. **Current Estimate** — a current re assessment of the Estimated Cost at Completion

Section 12.3 describes the details of these four essential elements.

(c) **Reconciliation to a cut-off date**

The PCMS must have an "audit trail" to enable reconciliation with the FIS.

Many construction contracts require that a progress measurement cut-off date is established on the 25th day of each month. This allows time for the contractor to submit its formal agreed invoice by the end of the month. To the FIS, this becomes the month end expenditure to date. It is good strategy for the PCMS to adopt the same cut-off date so that corresponding PCMS reports are consistent and available by the end of the month. This strategy helps periodic reconciliation and frequently makes the more detailed PCMS reports available before the FIS reports.

The implication is that the higher management reports and the one-line project summary reports may not have the same print dates. Even so, they will carry the same "as-of" dates and most of the data should be the same. Because the emphasis in the PCMS reports is on forecast future costs, instead of actuals or period costs, this lack of cut-off uniformity is not a serious deficiency.

In any case, an audit entry trail, as described in Chapter 8, is necessary to reconcile differences between corresponding sums reported in the PCMS and the FIS. This is to ensure a satisfactory "level of comfort" with the reports from both systems. The audit entry trail is also essential for reliably forecasting outstanding commitments and future costs. For example, it can answer the question "What is the latest change order included in the reported commitment against a particular contract?"

12.3 Report Format Details

In the illustrations of the formats that follow, the columns are numbered and column entries that are computed from previous columns, or brought forward from other reports, are shown accordingly. It should be noted that each report always shows the total of all the cost classes in the project. Each report may be longer or shorter according to the required level of detail in the cost classes. As described in Chapter 10, shorter reports with the same essential information but less detail can be generated for progressively higher levels of management.

(a) Summary Variance Report (SVR)

The SVR is the primary cost control report of the PCMS.

This report is the primary cost control report for the project produced by the PCMS. Essentially, it compares the project team's best current forecast of final project cost, with the currently authorized capital appropriation. Figure 10-4, Chapter 10, showed schematically the process for arriving at the project variance.

Figure 12-2 displays the report format. Column (1) shows the project code number that identifies the cost class at the level of detail being reported. Column (2) gives a short form description of the work package. Column (3) shows the latest Authorized (Capital) Appropriation.

Column (4) shows amounts committed by formal documentation, such as purchase orders, contracts and other agreements. It should be borne in mind that not all legal commitments are firm in terms of end cost. Obvious examples are cost plus forms of agreement and unit price contracts. These depend on remeasurement and final agreement on quantities before the contract value becomes firmly established. In these cases, additional backup reports are required that show original and latest estimates of quantities or resources to be consumed to arrive at the latest forecast of final cost.

Columns (5) and (6) show anticipated commitments and revised total costs respectively. In a rigorous periodic reassessment of final project cost, column (5) will be derived from the difference between a reestimated total for column (6) and updated column (4). At other times it may be admissible to revise column (5) based on the latest information, and arrive at column (6) by adding column (5) to column (4). It is not acceptable to arrive at column (5) simply by subtracting column (4) from column (3).

Variance column (7) shows the amount of difference between the latest forecast of final cost and the Authorized Appropriation.

The most useful column in the report is column (8). This is the column that project management looks at first! It shows the change in the variance since the last reporting period, which is a measure of how well the project team is performing. It enables the team to identify quickly any significant changes that have taken place since the previous report. These

••••• Summary Level Variance Report ••••• (page #)

Distribution:
1
2
3

Project: (name)
Owner: (name)
Phase: (Planning/Implementation)

Project No. ####
As of: (date)
Issued: (date)

•••••• Reference ••••••		••••Estimated at Completion••••				••••Variance•••• Better or (Worse)		
Code # (1)	Cost Class Description (2)	Authorized Appr'n (3)	Committed to Date (4)	Anticipated Commitmnts (5)	Revised Total (6)	Total (7)	Period (8)	Reference (9)
From Report Type 2 Col 1	From Report Type 2 Col 2	From Report Type 2 Col 7	From Report Type 3 Col 5	(Calculated) =(6)-(4)	From Report Type 4 Col 10	(Calculated) =(3)-(6)	Calculated from change in (6) since last Report	Cross Refs to explanatory notes
Sample Summary Entry								
2F1-00	Field Preparation	936,500	920,150	10,000	930,150	6,350	(32,650)	See Notes 1, 2, & 3

Explanatory Notes

1. In the previous month a diverted gas line was discovered during excavation. Contingency Transfer (AC#1) from the Corporate Project Contingency Account has been approved to cover the Utility's price of $24,000
2. The newly exposed rock face has been remeasured. Rock volume has increased by 950 CY and Bulk Excavation reduced (CO#5).
3. The Excavation Contractor has indicated a claim for delay waiting for the gas main relocation.

Figure 12-2. Summary Variance Report (SVR) **Report Type #1** may be due to changes in either the current estimate or the authorized appropriation. Therefore, a rapid scan of this column shows immediately where attention should be focused on the project if the indicated trends are to be avoided, corrected or accommodated.

(b) Appropriation Reconciliation Report (ARR)

The ARR tracks any changes to the project's baseline budget.

Figure 12-3 shows the format of the Appropriation Reconciliation Report. This report, the first of three supporting the Summary Variance Report, provides the reference standard for the control of costs and the evaluation of cost performance. It retains the original Capital Appropriation as its essential baseline, and provides an "audit trail" of any approved changes that have resulted in the currently Authorized Appropriation. Initially, with no changes, the two are the same. As the project progresses, changes to the current appropriation may be justified as follows:

1. **The Project Team reassembles work packages into new contract packages** to arrive at a more cost effective procurement strategy. There is then no change in total appropriation or project scope.

2. **The Owner approves scope changes** recommended by the Project Team.

3. **The Owner requests and approves scope changes.**

4. **When a project takes several years**, a policy to adjust the appropriation automatically to allow for past inflationary impact on future expenditures may be adopted as discussed in Chapter 8, Section 8.5. In this way the Summary Variance Report always makes its comparison in current dollars. This is an alternative and more rigorous approach compared to simply providing for inflation through an inflation allowance.

By managing the Authorized Appropriation in this pro-active way, a realistic reference standard can be maintained. By keeping it up-to-date, active cost control on the project is possible.

In Figure 12-3 Columns (1) and (2) are the same as for the Summary Variance Report (Report Type 1). Column (3) shows the original Appropriation as authorized by the issue of some formal corporate document. For a management company, or contractor under contract, it may be the amount(s) stipulated in the contract documents. In this case, the amounts in this column do not change throughout the producing phases of the project.

Frequently, the breakdown of the original Appropriation is only to some higher level and does not correspond to the Work Package levels

••••• Appropriation Reconciliation Report ••••• (page #)

Distribution:
1
2
3

Project:	(name)	Project No.	####
Owner:	(name)	As of:	(date)
Phase:	(Planning/Implementation)	Issued:	(date)

•••••• Reference ••••••			•••• Authorized Changes ••••				
Code # (1)	Cost Class Description (2)	Original Appr'n (3)	This Period (4)	Previous Total (5)	Total to Date (6)	Authorized Appr'n (7)	This Period Change Refs (8)
To Report Type 1 Col 1	To Report Type 1 Col 2				(Calculated) =(4)+(5)	(Calculated) =(3)+(6) To Report Type 1 Col 3	
Sample Entries - Field Preparation							
2F1-01	Clear site	27,500			0	27,500	
2F1-02	Dewatering	145,000			0	145,000	
2F1-03	Temp. shoring	270,000			0	270,000	
2F1-04	Excavation	470,000			0	470,000	
2F1-07	Relocate Gas line	0	24,000		24,000	24,000	AC #1
2F1-00	Totals	912,500	24,000	0	24,000	936,500	

Figure 12-3. Appropriation Reconciliation Report (ARR) **Report Type #2**

required to manage the project. In such cases, the reconciliation between columns is shown by a subtotal corresponding to that higher level. This makes managing contract packages easier as an approval for a reallocation of the Authorized Appropriation is not necessary.

Columns (4), (5) and (6) provide for adding or subtracting approved changes from cost classes existing under the original Appropriation, or for adding new cost classes to the description list. Some contractors prefer to keep all approved contract changes separate from their original contract for billing purposes. This is particularly true if they maintain only simple records of account.

Contract changes should be invoiced with their associated contract — not as separate invoices.

Sometimes, many small changes are issued that cover only one or two cost classes. This often occurs in commercial building projects. If changes are invoiced separately, progress measurements become unnecessarily difficult, and progress payments and hold back calculations become tedious and contentious. This is because, in effect, every change is being handled like a separate contract. Therefore, this arrangement can only be described as highly unsatisfactory and should be discouraged. All such changes should be allocated to appropriate contract cost classes.

On the other hand, a single large change may be issued to cover many cost classes, such as an additional wing to the new facility. Here it makes eminent good sense to account for it completely separately, possibly as separate project.

Column (7) records the new Authorized Appropriation amount to be reflected in column (3) of Report Type 1. All changes to the original Appropriation should be documented by a Capital Appropriation Change Order (CACO). This includes reallocations referred to in (a) above which result in no net change to the total. For those changes occurring "this period" as shown in column (4), column (8) gives the cross references to the full description of the CACO. This information is particularly important for planning, scheduling and forecasting purposes. If it is known that changes are being considered, or are "in the pipe-line", then it is vital to know whether or not the authorized total includes them.

(c) Commitment/Expenditure Progress Report (CEPR)

The CEPR shows status of commitments, and work done.

Figure 12-4 illustrates this report. It shows progress first in terms of contract awards and other commitments. Secondly, it shows progress in terms of work done on design or construction as reflected by the gross amounts approved on invoices for payment.

Column (1) is the same as for Report Type 1. Column (2) is first headed with the contractor or supplier's name and contract or order number, followed by the established coded cost classes. Column (3) shows the amount committed in the original purchase order or contract or, if the contract is awaiting formal signature, the "letter of award".

•••• Commitment/Expenditure Progress Report •••• (page #)

Distribution:
1
2
3

Project: (name)
Owner: (name)
Phase: (Planning/Implementation)

Project No. ####
As of: (date)
Issued: (date)

●●●●●● Reference	●●●●●●	●●●●●● Commitments	●●●●●		●● Expenditures	●●	Holdback	Expended	CO#
Code #	Contractor/Supplier and/or Cost Class	Original Amount	Approved Changes	Total to Date	This Period	Total to Date	To Date	Percent	This Period
(1)	(2)	(3)	(4)	(5)	(6)	(7)	(8)	(9)	(10)
				(Calculated) =(3)+(4) To Report Type 1 Col 4				(Calc'd) =(7)/(5)%	
Sample Entries - Field Preparation									
2F1-01	Clearall Co	27,500		27,500	0	27,500	2,750	100	
2F1-02	Unwatering Inc.	135,000		135,000	16,250	47,250	4,725	35	
2F1-03	Shore Up Ltd.	265,000		265,000	24,500	79,500	7,950	30	
2F1-04	Jack's Excavating	455,588	13,062	468,650	53,076	136,741	13,674	29	CO#5
2F1-07	Gas Utility	24,000		24,000	24,000	24,000	2,400	100	
2F1-00	Totals	907,088	13,062	920,150	117,826	314,991	31,499	34	

Figure 12-4. Commitment/Expenditure Progress Report (CEPR) **Report Type #3**

Column (4) shows approved changes. If the changes are many, it may be more convenient to show in this column the total changes to end of last period, with this-period changes listed below it. The corresponding change order reference number(s) can either be shown in the description column or a remarks column. Where the organization lacks internal arrangement for formally "committing" soft costs such as salaries and expenses, it is usual to leave column (3) blank and just enter actual amounts paid to date in column (4).

Column (5) is the total that is transferred to Report Type 1. Columns (6) and (7) show amounts approved for payment or, for internal soft costs such as employees salaries and expenses, the amounts paid to date.

As a gross check on the coding accuracy of posted invoices and payment vouchers, column (7) should be scanned to ensure that no entry exceeds the corresponding entry in column (5). If an expenditure exceeds a commitment, either one of the entries is incorrect, or the voucher should not have been processed for payment. Column (8) shows the amounts held back from (or released to) contractors, according to statutory or other requirements. Therefore, it shows the status of net cash flow.

Column (9) provides a useful guide to progress, particularly when compared to an overview of progress in the field.

(d) Current Forecast Worksheet (CFW)

The CFW provides a way to arrive at forecast figures.

This page, though part report, is more in the nature of a worksheet required to justify the Summary Variance Report. That is, its purpose is to arrive at a revised total forecast of the cost of the project, for entry into column (6) of Report Type 1. Figure 12-5 shows the Current Forecast Worksheet.

Information for this report is perhaps the most difficult to generate. It requires a careful and objective reassessment of all the work that remains to be done to complete the project, and the uncommitted costs relating to this work. Having completed this process, it also requires a careful look at the resulting total picture.

It deals in estimates and "soft" figures. It requires the collection of subjective information in the regular course of other work, an examination of trends and indicators, and the application of experience and prudent judgment. Some information may be highly sensitive and there may be strong pressures to temper the figures according to the audience they serve. If the results are likely to become public, it may be necessary to strike a "political" balance between information sought by project sponsors on the one hand, and the expectations of the practitioners involved in the project on the other.

Whatever the circumstances, a regular disciplined effort should be established for every project. It should be part of top management policy to call for such reviews, because a review of this type is not normally a

•••••• Current Forecast Worksheet •••••• (page #)

Distribution:
1
2
3

Project: (name)
Owner: (name)
Phase: (Planning/Implementation)

Project No. ####
As of: (date)
Issued: (date)

•••••• Reference	••••••			•••••••• Prudent Commitment Allowances ••••••••					
Code #	Contractor/Supplier and/or Cost Class	Anticipated Award or Actual Commitment	Last CO#s included	COs Issued but still outstanding	Defined Changes not yet issued	Allowances for un-identified changes	Anticipated claims from contractors	Total Allowance	Revised Estimated at Completion
(1)	(2)	(3)	(4)	(5)	(6)	(7)	(8)	(9)	(10)
		From Report Type 3 Col 5						(Calc'd) =(5) +(6) +(7)+(8)	(Calc'd) =(3)+(9) To Report Type 1 Col 6
Sample Entries - Field Preparation									
2F1-01	Clearall Co	27,500						0	27,500
2F1-02	Unwatering Inc.	135,000						0	135,000
2F1-03	Shore Up Ltd.	265,000						0	265,000
2F1-04	Jack's Excavating	468,650	CO #5				10,000	10,000	478,650
2F1-07	Gas Utility	24,000						0	24,000
2F1-00	Totals	920,150		0	0	0	10,000	10,000	930,150

Figure 12-5. Current Forecast Worksheet (CFW)

Report Type #4

statutory or accounting requirement. Only in this way will the necessary time be set aside from the usual busy daily routine to conduct this important project management task.

On larger projects, a more rigorous forecast review should be conducted at less frequent intervals.

On larger and longer projects it is better to take a different policy approach. This approach encourages updating of the report by the project team on a regular reporting basis, say monthly, but insists on a rigorous review at less frequent intervals. The rigorous review might be conducted, say, quarterly or half-yearly and cover all outstanding cost classes. A somewhat larger group of key players should be involved in these reviews, to improve both the balance of the input and the "confidence level" in the results. Such larger group might well include a representative from the controller's or audit departments.

In the format shown in Figure 12-5, columns (1) and (2) are the same as for Report Type 3. Column (3) shows actual commitment to date from column (5) of Report Type 3, with the last change order number included in the amount inserted in column (4). This ensures that all concerned are aware of the cut-off point on firm commitments.

If an anticipated commitment amount for a cost class is somewhat firm, like a submitted tender not yet formally awarded as a contract, this too can be entered in column (3). As a consequence, it should be noted that the total of column (3) will not be the same as the total of column (5) in Report Type 3. This is because the purpose of this format is to separate the entries according to the degree of certainty.

Column (10) of this Report Type 4 arrives at the revised total estimated final cost for entering in the anticipated commitments in column (5) of Report Type 1. To be sure that these amounts reflect the best current information and judgment, it is necessary to review four cost types regularly. These four cost types make up the total "prudent commitment allowance" in column (9). They are as follows:

1. **Changes issued but outstanding (Column 5)** — These entries will be changes that have been defined and estimated or priced, but are still in process of approval and have not yet been recorded as commitments.

2. **Defined Changes, not yet issued (Column 6)** — These entries will be planned changes for which documentation has not yet been completed.

3. **Allowances for unidentified changes (Column 7)** — This column is for allowances for future changes that are not included elsewhere and that have not yet been identified. Generally, figures entered here represent a true residual contingency according to the risk associated with the remaining work to be completed.

4. **Anticipated claims for extra payment (Column 8)** — The value of entries in this column is probably the most variable and the most difficult

to predict. Even when a claim for extra has been documented by a contractor, often only well on into the project, the level of final settlement is usually most uncertain. Therefore, entries in this column should only be for claims for which notice has been received from the contractor, or for expected claims for difficulties beyond the contractor's contractual responsibility and control. Such claims might include items such as delayed access to the work area or similar major schedule delays.

Always keep notes of the make-up of forecast figures — for next time!

Information for the allowances section will be collected by the project team, and will come from design, purchasing and construction staff. Notes and calculations should be kept and carefully filed for follow-up. These notes will simplify and speed the same process at the time of the next review.

(e) Consolidation of the Four Principal Reports

For ease of reference, the four types of principal reports described in the previous section are sometimes consolidated into fewer more comprehensive reports. This also avoids lengthy repetition of cost class descriptions. Unfortunately, the number of possible characters on a standard printout line usually limits the information that can be presented. So some preselection is necessary. This inevitably leads to a reduction in usefulness and clarity but may be acceptable as a trade-off simply to reduce the sheer volume of paper. Figures 12-6 and 12-7 show a two-part report that presents most of the essential information contained in the four principal reports.

In the examples shown it should be noted that the following information is missing. Part one of the two-part PCMS report omits the previous total of authorized changes, which may be acceptable. However, it is not clear whether the references in column (10) refer to authorized changes to the appropriation, or to approved changes to the commitment. Also omitted are last CO numbers included, holdback to date, and percent expended information.

In part two of this two-part PCMS report, the changes-issued-but-outstanding column has been omitted, and there is less distinction between fact and speculation under commitment allowances.

Figure 12-8 shows an attempt to consolidate selected key information on to one report only for a large engineering project. The format is particularly interesting because of the introduction of column (2) which shows the amounts transferred from the approved Appropriation to the working project budget. It reflects the owner's evident policy to exercise some direct control over the cost management of the project. The owner does this through progressive releases of the corporate Appropriation by approving only specific budget application amounts.

••••••• Project Cost Management Report - Part A ••••••• (page #)

Distribution:
1
2
3

Project: (name)
Owner: (name)
Phase: (Planning/Implementation)

Project No. ####
As of: (date)
Issued: (date)

••••• Reference	•••••		•Authorized Changes•			••••• Commitments	•••••		•• Expenditures (Gross)	••	
Code # (1)	Cost Class Description (2)	Original Appr'n (3)	This Period (4)	Total to Date (5)	Latest Appr'n (6)	Original Commit's (7)	Approved Changes (8)	Total to Date (9) (Calc'd) =(7)+(8)	This Period (10)	Total to Date (11)	Reference (12)
Sample Entries - Field Preparation											
2F1-01	Clear site	27,500			27,500	27,500		27,500		27,500	
2F1-02	Dewatering	145,000			145,000	135,000		135,000	16,250	47,250	
2F1-03	Temp. shoring	270,000			270,000	265,000		265,000	24,500	79,500	
2F1-04	Excavation	470,000			470,000	455,588	13,062	468,650	53,076	136,741	CO#5
2F1-07	Relocate Gas line	0	24,000	24,000	24,000	24,000		24,000	24,000	24,000	AC#1
2F1-00	Totals	912,500	24,000	24,000	936,500	907,088	13,062	920,150	117,826	314,991	

Figure 12-6. Project Cost Management Report -Part A (PCMR-A)

Report Type #5A

••••••• Project Cost Management Report - Part B ••••••• (page #)

Distribution:
1
2
3

Project: (name)
Owner: (name)
Phase: (Planning/Implementation)

Project No. ####
As of: (date)
Issued: (date)

••••• Reference •••••		•••••• Prudent Commitment Allowances ••••••						••• Variance ••• Better or (Worse)		
Code #	Cost Class Description	Anticipated Awards	Defined Changes not yet included	Allowance for un-identified changes	Anticipated claims from contractors	Total not yet committed	Revised Estimated at Completion	Total to Date	This Period	Remarks
		(13)	(14)	(15)	(16)	(17)	(18)	(19)	(20)	(21)
						(Calc'd) =(13)+(14) +(15)+(16)	(Calc'd) =(9)+(17)	(Calc'd) =(6)-(18)	Calculated from change in (18) since last Report	
Sample Entries - Field Preparation										
2F1-01	Clear site					0	27,500	0	0	
2F1-02	Dewatering					0	135,000	10,000	0	
2F1-03	Temp. shoring					0	265,000	5,000	0	
2F1-04	Excavation				10,000	10,000	478,650	(8,650)	(8,650)	See Note 1
2F1-07	Relocate Gas line					0	24,000	0	(24,000)	
2F1-00	Totals	0	0	0	10,000	10,000	930,150	6,350	(32,650)	

Explanatory Notes
1. The Excavation Contractor has indicated a claim for delay waiting for the gas main relocation.

Figure 12-7. Project Cost Management Report - Part B (PCMR-B) **Report Type #5B**

This inhibits any commitments and expenditures on cost classes until a satisfactory design and estimate is presented for each particular contract package. If delay claims by other affected contractors are to be avoided the procurement strategy must be carefully managed. Since the variance column (9) compares forecast-final-cost to appropriated-budget, entries in this column also highlight budget items not yet released. Chapter 16, Section 16.5 - Basic Control Procedures, discusses a similar approach.

Where the contract is based on remeasuring actual quantities at agreed unit prices, a supplementary report is required to support the forecast final cost. Figure 12-9 shows a Quantity/Forecast Report. In such cases, the contracted amount remains an estimate only until final quantities are determined and agreed at the end of the contract. Such contracts are common in civil engineering works and add an additional element of uncertainty to the forecast. The sum totals of columns (8) through (13) on report Figure 12-9, are transferred to columns (3) through (8) respectively on report Figure 12-8.

12.4 Other Informative Reports

(a) **PCMS related reports**

Other reports that can be generated by the PCMS serve several different purposes particularly where multiple projects are involved. For example:

1. **Errant Entries Report** — for the capture of costs incorrectly coded, and charges to projects that have been closed after final billings have been settled etc.

2. **Audit Trail Reports** — for tracing commitment and expenditure entries to PCMS and FIS, as well as expense distributions such as overheads, IDC, etc.

3. **Journal Voucher Listings** — for approved transfers due to policy changes, etc.

4. **Projects Summary Report** — an executive summary one-line-entry listing of all projects in progress.

5. **Vendor Report** - a listing of purchases by vendor.

6. **Contractor Report** — a listing of contracts by contractor.

7. **Project Fiscal Expenditures** — expenditures on projects reported by fiscal period.

•••••• Contract Status Report •••••• (page #)

Distribution:
1
2
3

Project: (name)
Owner: (name)
Phase: (Planning/Implementation)

Project No. ####
Report No. (date)
Period Ending: (date)

•••••• Reference	••••••				•• Incurred Cost ••		••• Estimated •••			Variance in
Code #	Contractor/Supplier and/or Cost Class	Capital Cost Estimate	Approp'td Budget	Contr'td Amount	This Period	Total to Date	To Complete	At Completion	Change This Period	Approp'td Budget B or (W)
(1)	(2)	(3)	(4)	(5)	(6)	(7)	(8)	(9)	(10)	(11)
							(Calc'd) =(9)-(7)	From Report Type 4 Col (10)	Calculated from change in (9) since last Report	(Calc'd) =(4)-(9)
Sample Entries - Field Preparation										
2F1-01	Clearall Co	27,500	27,500	27,500		27,500		27,500		0
2F1-02	Unwatering Inc.	145,000	145,000	135,000	16,250	47,250	87,750	135,000		10,000
2F1-03	Shore Up Ltd.	270,000	270,000	265,000	24,500	79,500	185,500	265,000		5,000
2F1-04	Jack's Excavating	470,000	470,000	455,588	53,076	136,741	348,434	478,650	(13,062)	(8,650)
2F1-07	Gas Utility		24,000	24,000	24,000	24,000		24,000	(24,000)	0
2F1-00	Totals	912,500		907,088	117,826	314,991	621,684	930,150	(37,062)	6,350

Figure 12-8. Contract Status Report (CSR)

Report Type #6

8. **Capital Expenditure Forecast** — monthly cash flow summary of all projects over required period for capital budgeting. Also shows holdbacks and releases for cash planning.

9. **Asset Valuation for Construction Insurance** — pulls out progressive work in place for all projects, up to time of capitalization, but only for those costs representing insurable assets. This gives the summarized information required to establish proper construction insurance.

10. **Asset Valuation for Capitalization and Capital Cost Allowance** — pulls out costs appropriate to both classes and converts remainder to current expense. Supports transfer of data to corporate books of account, property records, market leasing proforma, etc.

11. **Historical Costs to Estimating Base** — conveys data to estimating system unit cost library. This is particularly valuable for higher level estimates such as "order of magnitude" and "concept" estimates.

12. **History of Project Schedules and Timetables** — captures data on leading activities for scheduling future projects, particularly at the feasibility stage.

(b) General Descriptive reports

Project management also produces several narrative type reports. While these do not bear directly on project costing, they are useful in describing the status of the project and therefore giving meaning to current and future cost figures. These reports will also be useful in any post audit of the project.

- Project Summary Report — a description of the current status of the project and covering major contracts and purchase orders in particular
- Master Schedule and Short Term Plan Progress Reports — reports covering major or critical activities which show management's intent about the project's master plan
- Awarded and Unawarded Work Reports — a narrative description of the status of commitments
- Variance Analysis report — a narrative description and explanation of variances including planned responses
- Delays and Early Warnings Report — a summary of delays and their causes with possible difficulties that lie ahead
- Progress Photographs — pictorial representation of the project's progress. Personal photography is particularly useful to provide specifics when opportunity to capture details is limited. Profes-

•••••• Unit Price Contract Status Report •••••• (page #)

Distribution:
1
2
3

Project: (name)
Owner: (name)
Phase: (Planning/Implementation)

Project: ####
Contract: ###
Description: (work)
Period Ending: (date)

Pay Item # (1)	Pay item Description (2)	Unit (3)	Quantities: Orig'l Award (4)	This Month (5)	To Date (6)	To Complete (7)	Final Total (8)	Unit Price (9)	Costs: Orig'l Award (10)	This Month (11)	To Date (12)	Final Total (13)	Period Change (14)
						(Calc'd) =(8)-(6)			(Calc'd) =(4)x(9)	(Calc'd) =(5)x(9)	(Calc'd) =(6)x(9)	(Calc'd) =(8)x(9)	Calculated from change in (13) since last Report
Sample Entries - Excavation													
Jack's Excavating													
1	Bulk	CY	39,450	3,845	15,385	23,115	38,500	7.25	286,013	27,876	111,541	279,125	6,888
2	Rock	CY	6,050	1,200	1,200	5,800	7,000	21.00	127,050	25,200	25,200	147,000	(19,950)
3	Final Grade	SY	24,300			24,300	24,300	1.75	42,525	0	0	42,525	
									455,588	53,076	136,741	468,650	(13,062)

Figure 12-9. Unit Price Contract Status Report (UPCSR)

Report Type #7

sional photography should be used for general information and public relations purposes.

CHAPTER 13

Managing Cost Changes

13.1 Preparing for the Unexpected

Avoiding "scope drift" requires strict discipline.

Uncontrolled increases in the project's scope of work compared to the original plan is a primary cause of delay and cost overrun. This "scope drift" often goes unnoticed until it shows up in the cost and schedule reports. Ensuring that the project remains within the approved scope requires strict discipline in monitoring and comparing to plan. If some redesign and reestimating is necessary, so be it. The integrity of the project will be better safeguarded as a result. Alternatively, if changes are necessary, then they must be properly documented and provided for.

Unexpected problems surface even with the best of planning and monitoring. Some may be truly "unforeseeable", though most probably should have been, which simply reflects weaknesses in the original planning assumptions. Such planning weaknesses may include:

- Predictions that prove to be false or understated
- Lack of timely information for construction performance
- Loss of control during detail design or construction
- People or services not available when required
- Lack of competence in key individuals or workforce
- Misunderstandings, burn-out and sickness.

Don't be afraid to stop a project, or part of a project, while a serious situation gets sorted out!

Weaknesses such as these should be carefully examined as soon as they are identified and suitable mitigating steps, contingency plans or work-arounds started, drawing on appropriate allowances if necessary. If these steps are not sufficient, then the project manager may have to negotiate changes in the work, take more time, or call on more money to complete the project successfully. If a situation develops that is beyond recall, then perhaps the project should be halted until a new project strategy can be properly developed and agreed. This could prove cheaper than a continuing effort at "fire fighting".

A good project manager does not relish requesting a revision of the project's constraints, nor an owner accommodating them, once they have been agreed. So wise project managers ensure that, from the beginning, they have some contingent cost and schedule management flexibility. Sometimes, this flexibility can be effectively built in by identifying some peripheral or minor scope component that is not mandatory. Such flexibility greatly improves the project manager's ability to exercise influence in managing the project. This approach may be more acceptable to the owner of the facility because the sum is no longer an "unidentified" item, but will realize something tangible — if possible.

Good management requires some built-in flexibility.

If time and cost reserves are set aside, should they be under the control of the project's owner/sponsor, the project/construction manager, or the discipline/design managers? Should the reserves be global like big pots to be dipped into by anyone? Or should they be allocated on some logical basis? Finally, having regard to the propensity for any spare time and money to be used up long before all the work is completed, should these allowances be made public or kept secret?

A prudent owner will hold some schedule and financial reserves for its own needs, and the project manager may or may not be aware of their existence. An "unsophisticated" owner, on the other hand, may not know enough to have them, so the project manager should not count on access to any "secret" reserves.

13.2 Contingency Allowances for Project Implementation

As discussed in earlier chapters, effective cost control in the producing phases depends on having an approved and realistic project budget as a reference baseline. This approval normally depends on the budget estimate contained in the Capital Authorization Request (CAR) that is submitted at the conclusion of the development phase, as described in Chapter 6, Section 6.1(b). Included in the CAR should be a Contingency Allowance that is different, separate, and in addition to the schedule and financial resources arrived at by good estimating techniques. Planning assumptions may not be true for several reasons so contingencies are needed for:

Effective cost control depends on having an approved and realistic budget to work with.

- Shortcomings in the information on which the project plan was based
- Shortcomings in predictions, and
- Shortcomings in the control of the project

Good estimating requires stating the estimating strategy and assumptions associated with all the items included. For example, if a probabilistic estimating technique is used in developing the estimate of cost, then a "range" of cost will be associated with each cost class. This range is really like a "basic contingency" allowance, both positive and negative, for that item. Basic contingency covers inherent variability in the cost of the particular element. The values carried forward from a probabilistic estimate to a project budget may be such that the probability of overrun is limited to some pre-determined level. In that case, no additional "basic contingency" should be added at the end. That would be accounting for it twice.

Avoid any double counting of contingency that has already been factored into estimate figures.

For purposes of arriving at a suitable allowance, the execution phase can be viewed as having three stages. These stages may be described as follows:

1. **Pre contract Award** — In this stage, detailed design, working drawings, specifications and other contract documents are produced as the prerequisites to placing an order or contract. As described in Chapter 4, design progress reviews should be conducted by estimators at, say 30%, 60% and 100% of working drawings. These reviews may result in an updated forecast that will vary from the required project budget.

2. **Contract Award** — This is the contract tendering and award stage. When placing an order or contract, especially if firm price bids are being sought, a variance will inevitably exist between the estimates developed pre-tender and the schedules and prices received. This is due to market pressures at the time of bidding. These may include service and material price fluctuations, impending labor agreements or disputes, differences in productivity assessments, and whether contractors and suppliers are busy or slack and their consequent attitude to risk.

3. **Post Contract Award** — It is in this stage of supply and construction that the various problem items surface. This will be apparent from the need to issue Change Orders and Field Orders. In many ways, the number of changes that are issued after contract award is a reflection of the quality of planning or the quality of detailing. Change Orders and Field Orders are discussed in the next section.

"Fast-track" projects are more risky. They require more allowances and contingency.

If the owner of the new facility has deliberately adopted a "fast-track" approach, then all the information required will not be available at the outset. The consequences to be managed include correspondingly higher risks, an increased number of changes, and a need for a larger contingency or other specific allowances. Variations from the awarded price also result from cost overruns/underruns on unit price and cost plus contracts. Significant variations in the final cost also arise from the settlement of contractors' claims.

Typical approaches to setting the "right" value for the contingency sum vary from applying standard allowances, to percentages based on experience, to a careful statistical analysis of the project estimate. If Range Estimating has not been used, this assessment may be based on the total of the most probable variances of each cost class contained in the WBS structure.

The fixed-percentage option has been characterized as the "big pot" approach. When anything goes wrong, everyone dips into the big pot. Unfortunately, the pot always seems to empty long before the project is completed. The perception exacerbates the reality because people are tempted to raid the pot before it is too late!

A "big pot" contingency quickly gets emptied — long before the project is finished!

In the statistical approach, no single contingency entry is adequate in the actual event because the amounts are based on statistical swings and round-abouts. Either way, what is most important is how the contingency allowance is managed. How ever the amount is arrived at, it is recommended that it should be distributed between the three project execution stages described above. This will place responsibility for a specific amount in the hands of the major functional areas associated with each stage. Figure 13-1 shows a matrix chart that relates functional responsibilities to these three stages.

Suppose an overall allowance, including contingencies, has been set at, say, 10%. Then a suggested distribution might be a 5% allowance assigned to the award stage, and 1% each assigned to the owner, the manager and the designer for a total of 3% in the pre-award stage. This leaves 2% for the post-award stage, plus whatever can be carried forward from the two earlier stages. This carry-forward can be justified as follows.

If firm price tenders have been called for and market conditions are depressed, then very competitive bids may be received. This could mean that little, if any, of the award stage allowance is used. Indeed, it might even be enhanced. If the lowest tender is accepted, as a result of which there are apparent savings, then it is appropriate to increase the post-award contingency allowance. This is because the probability of contract administration difficulties and/or claims have been increased by market conditions.

Don't spend savings from highly competitive bidding too soon — the savings may not be realized.

Of the three stages described, contract award is probably the most uncertain. Even under good bidding conditions on a "good set of documents", core bids (i.e. excluding those containing errors or extremes) are likely to vary between 5% and 10%. If the bids are scattered well outside this range, the documents should be reexamined for possible ambiguity or lack of clarity and precision.

If cost management of the project execution phase is to be effective, a positive and systematic approach to contingency management must be taken in each of the three stages described. By doing so, changes in the status of the contingency allowance and therefore the trend in the final project cost can be made evident. More importantly, adverse trends can be reported to those who can affect the future course of events on the project.

13.3 Post-award Changes: Classification and Handling

Procedures are required to evaluate and control changes in project scope, quality, time and cost when they arise. Decisions to make any such changes should rest with the project manager and the project's owner and

Responsibility	Stage		
	Pre-Award	**Award**	**Post-Award**
Owner	Minor:- Policy Changes Scope Changes **1 %** Enhancements		Policy Changes Scope Changes Enhancements **1/2 %** Budget & Cash Flow Difficulties
Manager	Schedule Delays **1 %**	Tendering Variances Market Conditions **5 %**	Other Contractors Equipment Dleivery **1/2 %**
Designer	Re-evaluation of Design **1 %** Design Changes		Coordination "Making it work" **1/2 %**
Contractor			Changed Conditions Claims for Delays **1/2 %** Inflation Legal Interpretation
			Total Contingency 10 %

Note: The Table shows a suggested distribution of an implementation allowance of 10%, including contingency, for a fixed price contract project. Any unused contingency from the Pre- and Award stages should be carried forward to the Post Award stage. Total allowance remains at 10%.

Figure 13-1. Possible "Contingency" Allocation for a Fixed Price Construction Project sponsor, although authority to manage project allowances and contingency may be delegated to the project manager within agreed limits. These procedures are usually documented in the project's project management manual. Project changes usually surface in the PCMS as changes documented under one or more of the implementation phase contracts. These contracts include the consulting agreements and the construction contracts.

Changes can be classified in different ways. Classification by source is the most useful for control purposes.

The changes themselves may be classified in several different ways for different purposes. For example, they may be classified in value ranges, so that different degrees of supervision and control may be applied as the change is carried out. They may be classified according to the method of assessment such as lump sum by prior agreement, collection of actual time and material costs during performance, or post evaluation by negotiation or litigation. They may be classified by the party affected most by the change, such as extra work to be carried out by the owner, the consultant, the general contractor or subtrade contractor.

For management control, the most useful method of classification is simply to differentiate according to the primary source of the change. That is, a change could be triggered by the owner, the designer, or the contractor. These may be defined as follows.

Owner's change

- Changes in scope required by the owner or his user representative to enhance or simplify the facility, or to take advantage of new materials or technology
- Changes required by Statutory Authorities to meet new regulations imposed on the owner since contract signing

Designer's change

- Modifications necessary to cover design omissions because of gaps in the scope description
- Modifications necessary to make the system work because of design errors or conflicts

Contractor's change

- Changes due to unforeseen field conditions beyond the contractor's contractual responsibility
- Changes because of other contractor's work or lack of
- Changes in price only (not in scope) due to other considerations such as schedule delay or acceleration caused by the owner, or by labor disputes outside the contractor's control and responsibility

The justification for this classification is that it places responsibility where it belongs — with the originators. The different groups may also require somewhat different analysis and evaluation criteria for management approval and authorization to proceed. It is strongly recommended that all potential changes are recorded at the time of discovery and classified as suggested for control purposes.

The nature of most changes is such that they are unhappily "discovered" during project execution. Perhaps this is not surprising. The ramifications of the many and often complex decisions taken during the planning and design stages become better understood by more and more people as the project unfolds into reality. The discoveries may be made by any of the parties to the project whether or not they are the prime cause.

The later a change is made — the more costly it will be.

One thing is certain, however. The further along in the organizational structure from the owner to the ultimate installer, that the need for change is discovered, the shorter will be the time available for dealing with it. Also the more costly it will be.

Changes and potential changes should be identified as early as possible. Each should be assigned an MCS number and a separate change file. This file can then be used to track and expedite the progress of the change in an effort to minimize its impact. For example, it may be necessary to chase the designers for design details, or it may be necessary to chase trade contractors for quotations to enable costing and approval. The review and approval process can be greatly speeded up by such an organized approach.

It is normal on larger and more complex projects to use several administrative vehicles, or procedures, for carrying out the changes noted above. Such procedures include:

- Notice of a contemplated change
- Formal Change Order
- Field Order
- Field Clarification Instruction or Field Instruction
- Backcharging
- Processing claims for extra payment

These procedures are described in the Sections that follow. The contractor is advised not to commence any changed work without proper authorization. Without such confirmation, the contractor may well find himself totally responsible and unable to collect compensation.

13.4 Documenting Changes

(a) Contemplated Change Notice (CCN)

Before making a change in the work of a contract, it is desirable to know the implications on the project's cost and schedule. This is typically done by issuing to the contractor a Contemplated Change Notice (CCN) or Request for Quotation (RFQ). The CCN or RFQ gives best the opportunity for careful evaluation and documentation. It should be mandatory for costly changes, especially where options are available and can be considered. However, depending on the organizational structure and approvals required, this procedure can be time consuming and counter productive if subsequent delays to the project follow.

(b) The Change Order (CO)

This procedure is the formal vehicle for making a change in the work of the contract. It is issued to a construction contractor to change the scope of work and the contract price. Once formalized it becomes a commitment document. Therefore, it should contain an explicit Scope Statement of the change required.

(c) The Field Order (FO)

The Field Order, as its name implies, is for use on site. It is sometimes more appropriately called an Emergency Field Order, and it is generally a much more expeditious procedure than (a) and (b) above. But it lacks an opportunity for careful evaluation and so restraints should be imposed on its use. The following specifics should be mandatory:

- **Maximum Value**
- **Specified Duration, and**
- **Method for Agreeing The Cost.**

FOs are faster and expedite the work — but they are more difficult to control. Avoid them if possible!

With such controls in place, the FO process will be expedited by delegating responsibility to authorized representatives in the field. Because adequate time is needed for proper verification, Field Orders should only be issued with the written proviso:

- **Subject to final verification against the terms, conditions and technical requirements contained in the contract documents**

Use of the FO helps to ensure that work in the field is not delayed. In the event that further examination shows the work to be already included under the contract, it becomes merely a confirmatory order and not a contract change. Whether to use a CO or an FO is usually a question of maximum value and urgency.

A useful administrative step is to finalize groups of FO's by issuing a summary under a confirmatory Change Order. This applies especially to FO's carried out on "cost plus".

(d) The Field Clarification (FC)

The need for an FC often leads to the need for a CO.

The Field Clarification or Field Instruction is not strictly a change control procedure. It is intended only to clarify details provided in the drawings and specifications already issued. Indeed, the FC should be issued on the clear understanding that:

- **The following information is for clarification only and is not intended to alter the scope, cost, or schedule of the contract in any way.**

In practice, the need to provide clarification may itself lead to the discovery of a need for change. A wary and cost conscious contractor will usually be on the look out to ensure that such instructions are not really changes in disguise. He may promptly contest the no cost, no schedule change implications. If he is right, a CO or FO should be substituted for the FC as soon as possible.

Each of these procedures should be formally documented and provided for in the contract documents.

13.5 Factors to be considered in Pricing Changes

The cost of changes are much more than just the direct costs.

In pricing changes, or evaluating submitted quotes for changes, several factors should be considered. These factors are besides the "normally" estimated direct costs for the work covering labor and payroll burden, materials, equipment rental and operating costs, and indirect overhead costs. The factors may be associated with production, material costs, overheads or impacts as listed below.

Special factors associated with production include:

- Size and complexity of the change
- Size and capability of the contractor(s) relative to the added work
- Relative state of associated site work
- Additional planning and supervision required
- Extent of mechanization possible if access is now limited
- Retraveling the learning curve
- Labor agreements and trade practices relative to the status of existing work
- Climatic conditions relative to the original work

Special factors associated with material costs include:

- Potentially higher prices for proprietary items
- Odd lot sizes that add to cost of supply
- Any storage costs that may be necessary

- Special delivery costs
- Salvage of job materials
- Escalation of costs since the original job began
- Taxes

Special factors associated with overheads:

- Special equipment required to perform the change
- Added premiums for payment and performance bonds
- Additional premiums for insurance coverage because of new exposure
- Additional inspection and testing costs

Impact costs that may be incurred:

- Added mobilization and demobilization
- Changes in the method or manner planned for associated work
- Changes in the sequence or timing of associated subsequent work
- Discontinuity
- Congestion of the work area
- Premium time incurred to overcome delays
- Rework by other trades damaged because this change is done out-of-sequence

13.6 Backcharges

Backcharges taker care of changes in scope between contractors — provided they do not change the overall project scope.

Even on smaller projects, it is not unusual for construction to be executed by two or more contractors, both under contract to the owner. A typical example might be the landscaping and planting of a site after the general building contractor has left it clean and leveled. Assuming no gaps in scope description between the contracts, there may still be differences on site due to the first contractor not completing its work to a standard acceptable to the second. If the first contractor is no longer on site, or no longer has suitable equipment available, it may be necessary to have the second contractor complete the unsatisfactory work. This should be at the expense of the first contractor.

This means changes in scope to the two contracts, one a subtraction and the other an addition, but no change to the total project scope. The result should be a no-net-change in cost to the owner. Contract documentation is still necessary, but with the added need to ensure that there is no additional charge against the owner's budget when all accounts have been settled.

This could be done by two self balancing Change Orders or Field Orders. For audit purposes, the documentation is much more readily traced if a formal Backcharge procedure is adopted. Contracts usually provide for the issuance of Change Orders and Field Orders and negotiation of their dollar value. In a similar way, provision should also be included in the contract for legitimate Backcharges.

Adjustments in scope between subcontractors to the same general contractor are often adjusted in kind rather than in cash.

If a contentious issue, such as the situation described above, arises between two trade contractors subcontracting to the same general contractor, then the general contractor should resolve the issue without involving the owner. Often the general contractor does this by trade-off in kind. To their mutual benefit, the parties simply agree to exchange services instead of cash, and so avoid the need for documentation. Some record may still be required by the owner's representative, to satisfy interim progress assessments and statutory evidence of payment requirements.

The complex nature of most projects involves many different trade contractors and the requirement for backcharges between them is common. A good example is backcharging for central clean up and disposal of refuse that is generated by, and the contractual responsibility of, individual trades. The owner who chooses to supplant the general contractor by adopting construction management will find an urgent need to formalize backcharging procedures.

13.7 Contractor's Claims for Extra Payment

(a) The meaning of "claim"

Don't confuse "claim" with "invoice"— Reserve the word "claim" to mean requests for additional payment.

The term "claim" should not be confused with a contractor's legitimate progress invoice. Only use it to mean a request by a contractor for payment additional to its contract. The request should specify some basis for the claim, typically work allegedly not already covered by the contract. If admitted, such claims change the final cost of the project and procedures are necessary to take such claims into account. This should be done as early as possible to avoid surprises on the final day of reckoning. On the other hand, no prudent owner wishes to do anything to encourage claims.

Contractor's claims can arise for a variety of reasons. They may have varying degrees of validity depending on the type of contract and interpretation of its specific terms. The cost of labor disputes, for example, may or may not be permitted under the contract. Either way, a settlement may ultimately be reached by negotiation, simply on grounds of equity and reasonable good will. Project circumstances that are conducive to generating claims are as follows.

- Uncertainty in contract scope definition
- Inexperienced contractor
- Inexperienced project team
- Uncertain timing
- Problems associated with state-of-the-art technology
- Inadequacies in items supplied by owner

- Dependence by contractor on work of other contractors working for the owner
- Long contract duration

Perhaps the most common cause for claims results from the owner failing to meet contractual obligations in good time. As a result, the contractor's work is delayed with consequent extra cost for an unproductive workforce and for the disruption of out-of-sequence work. Appendix D gives brief descriptions of different types of construction delay claims.

Financial consequences of a delay rarely surface until later.

The prime focus of a contractor is to get the work done and get paid. The issue of claims often surfaces only when the contractor concludes that costs are out of line with earnings. The contractor often does not reach this conclusion until well on into the contract and the result is a scramble to find out where the money went! This may be long after a legitimate cause, such as an earlier delay, which results in the contractor's later adverse financial situation. By this time, records and memories of the occurrence may have become blurred to say nothing of being biased.

Analysis of many claims suggests that both parties often contribute to the problem situation with subsequent efforts at schedule recovery tending to make things worse. From a records standpoint, leaving claims to the end of the contract may be to the contractor's ultimate advantage because all the circumstances can be examined with hindsight. Unfortunately, this often happens in court only to the lawyers' advantage!

(b) A simple early warning system

Require a "Statement of Claims" with each invoice — and make it part of the contract.

Simple early warning procedures can be established that help to avoid legitimate claims deteriorating into dog fights. The following approach requires the contractor to declare his position by submitting a STATEMENT OF CLAIMS form with each monthly invoice. This form requires the contractor to state that there are either:

1. **No outstanding claims for costs beyond the terms of the contract,** or

2. **There are outstanding claims for which documentation has commenced** (e.g. resulting from the issue of a Field Clarification, or an unpriced Change Order) **But for which the final value has not yet been agreed,** or

3. **There are anticipated claims for extra payment but for which documentation has not yet been submitted.** (The contractor should be required to provide some further details within a specified time.)

The precise values under (3) may still not be known until both parties have been able to document their positions. Minimum documentation usually includes:

- Summary narrative describing the claim and its causes
- The amount claimed justified by appropriate costing
- Schedules, Actual and As-planned
- Daily diaries or similar supporting authentic documentation

Agreement may or may not be reached by negotiation. Indeed, final settlement may not be achieved until after reconciliation of all other contract matters. If the issue is highly contentious, one or other of the parties may take the matter to court. Even so, the procedure suggested does help to reduce the uncertainty in the estimated final project cost of most items. Therefore, it forms an important part of project cost management.

For this procedure to be effective:

The submission of a statement of claims form with each monthly progress invoice must be made a requirement of the original contract.

An owner is wise to settle if the chances of winning in court are less than 60%.

Should the owner settle? The owner should settle or deny with reasonable promptness. The owner's decision could well be determined by answering the question: "If the contractor took the matter to court, would we have a better than 60% chance of winning?" This question is stacked in favor of the contractor because in litigation the benefit of any doubt usually goes to the contractor. This is because the owner had original responsibility for preparing the contract document.

Any of the changes discussed earlier in Section 13.3 — Post-award Changes: Classification and Handling, may be handled by the CO or FO procedures. A Backcharge procedure can be used in cases of scope transfer resulting in a no-net-change to the total project cost. The essential point is that pro-active and prompt administration of these matters during construction will greatly help to maintain good project relations and reduce friction on site. In doing so, the effort, aggravation and paperwork associated with many otherwise unnecessary claims can be avoided.

CHAPTER 14

Resource Loading and Production Curves

14.1 Earned Value and Performance Analysis Technique

The Earned Value and Performance Analysis technique, also known as Cost/Schedule Performance Management, is useful because it relates both actual cost and schedule performance to the planned budget and schedule. Properly conducted, the technique not only tells us where we are today, but how well we have been doing so far. This can provide the basis for a good assessment of where we shall be at the end of the project, or at least indicate whether corrective action is required. Figure 14-1 shows the Earned Value concept.

"Earned Value" is a good way to know how you're doing — but it requires a lot of measuring.

(a) Description of technique

The technique begins with plotting a Baseline Budget against a Baseline Schedule so that the value of work that should be done, i.e. value earned at any time during the project, is shown graphically. The resulting plot should generally take the shape of a letter "S". This first curve is called the Budgeted Cost of Work Scheduled, or BCWS. The BCWS is fixed throughout the project as the project's Earned Value reference baseline.

During the project, measurements of physical progress are measured at regular intervals and, when plotted against time, represent Progress S-curves. But schedules and activities inevitably change so the earned value, i.e. credit for completed work expressed in budgeted units of measure, departs from the planned baseline curve. This earned value is called the Budgeted Cost of Work Performed (BCWP). Simultaneously, the Actual Cost of Work Performed (ACWP) is also determined. This ACWP, is obtained from the incurred costs to Time Now. The BCWP and ACWP and their projections to the end of the project are consistently updated as successive data is collected.

Both these actual curves are compared to the baseline plan, the BCWS. Since the results are presented graphically, the effects of cost and schedule variances at "Time Now" can readily be seen. By analyzing the results, estimates can also be made of anticipated variations at completion. For example, comparison of what has been earned (BCWP) with what should have been earned (BCWS) gives a measure of Schedule Variance (SV). The vertical scale measures this in terms of cost. The same comparison on the horizontal scale shows the Time Now variance. If the BCWP is less than the BCWS then the Schedule Variance is negative and the work is currently behind schedule.

Comparison of the BCWP with the ACWP gives a measure of Cost Variance (CV). Again, if the BCWP is less than the ACWP, then the CV is negative suggesting a cost overrun on the work done to date.

By projecting the cost performance to date to the end of the project, it is possible to assess the cost Estimated at Completion (EAC) and the Variance at Completion (VAC). Comparison of repeated determinations of these values and their projections to completion over successive periods, gives period changes in the variances. Comparison of these period variances will show whether the total position is improving or deteriorating or, alternatively, the extent to which management intervention has been successful.

When projecting existing trends, make due allowance for "initial learning" and "final wind down".

It should be born in mind when assessing progress on uncompleted tasks that the actual cost of work performed depends on productivity and productive efficiency to date. This varies significantly throughout the task due to the effects of "initial learning" and "final wind down" discussed in earlier sections.

The technique is conceptually attractive and is useful in tracking total progress on sizable complex projects involving many significant activities by different trades and/or under conditions that change during the work.

In reality, this form of comprehensive tracking requires considerable effort to maintain, and possibly qualified dedicated staff to collect reliable data. Cost data must be collected that reflects the actual progress of the work which means that work-in-progress must be measurable and it must be measured. Data collection is relatively easy for civil works trades, but for systems such as mechanical and electrical much more detailed progress surveys are required to assess the true Time Now status. In addition, special treatment may be necessary to deal with such issues as staged payments for large purchases of off-site equipment. Either that, or subjective judgments are made that may defeat the purpose of the exercise.

Smaller jobs may not justify the added work involved in the EV technique.

In any case, the surveys are at best estimates of work-in-hand and the completion totals are estimated projections. So on most projects the technique is not usually considered worth the effort. The exceptions are large complex projects, projects with significance risks, or projects with contracts that require this approach. It is appropriate on high-risk projects where the Owner and Contractor share the risk of cost growth. When the technique is adopted, an essential element in its successful use is a realistically shaped Earned Value baseline plan S-curve.

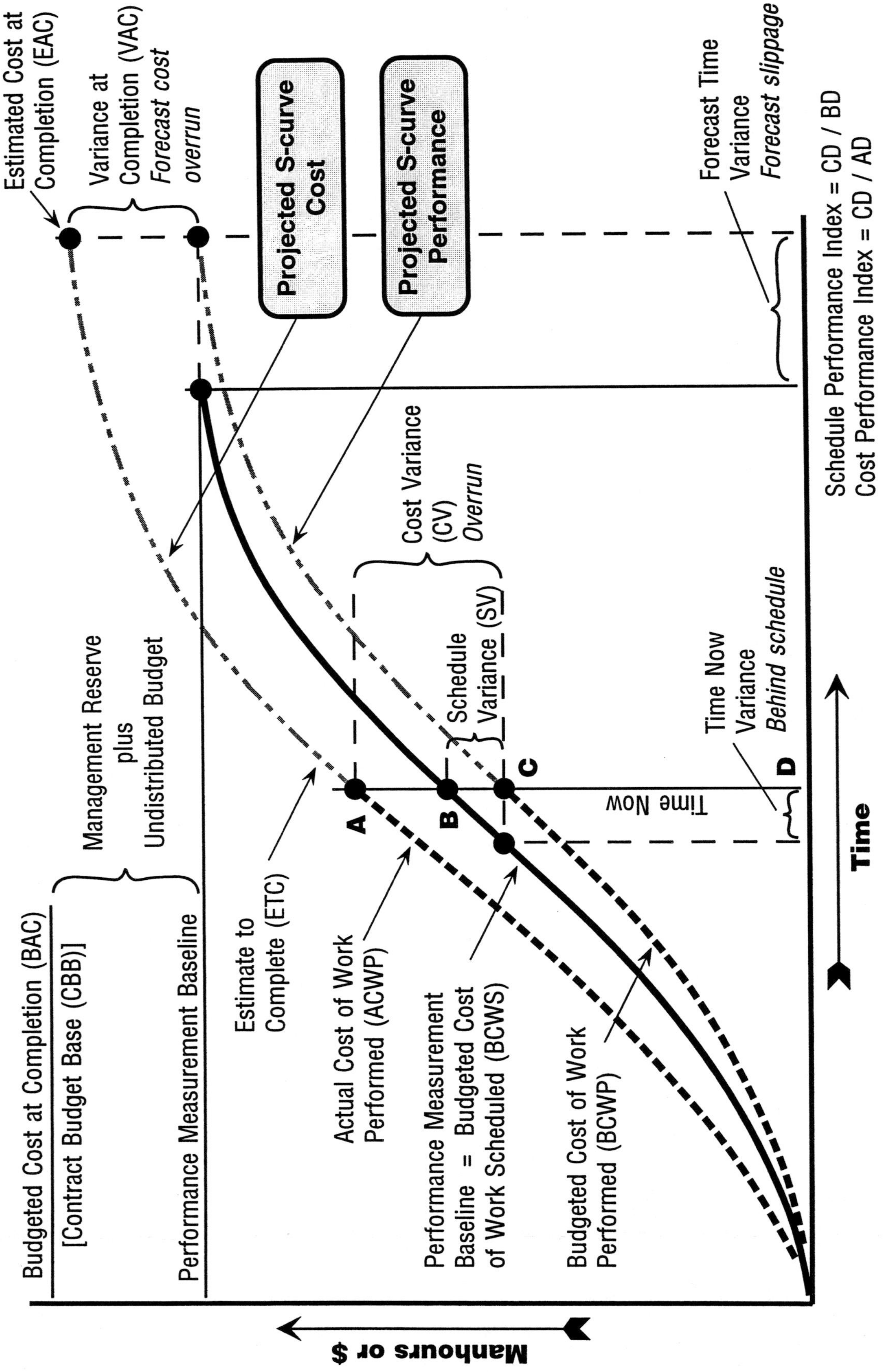

Figure 14-1. Earned Value and Performance Measurement

On other projects, a better strategy is to identify and track major critical site activities that are measurable and plot those S-curves as surrogates for the whole job. This is much more cost-effective for tracking the progress of the project.

(b) Summary of principle terms

Some of the principle terms used in the Earned Value technique are as follows.

ACWP: Actual Cost of Work Performed — is the actual cost incurred and recorded of the work done up to Time Now. ACWP includes Actual Direct Costs, Applied Direct Costs and Apportioned Costs.

Actual Direct Costs — are those identified specifically and directly with the work in question.

Applied Direct Costs — are those recognized in the requisite time period and associated with the consumption of labor, material, and other direct resources, irrespective of the date of commitment or the date of payment. These costs are charged to work-in-progress when:

- Labor, material or other direct resources are actually consumed.
- Materials are withdrawn from inventory and used.
- Materials or other resources directly associated with the work are received, accepted or recorded as accounts payable, and
- Planned payments for milestone accomplishments are recognized and recorded as costs incurred.

Apportioned Costs — are those which are not readily identifiable with the work directly, but are apportioned to it on a regular, consistent and agreed basis such as by measurement, time or cost. An example might be the allocation of plant servicing costs calculated on the time based costs of plant engaged on a variety of work, including the work in question.

BAC: Budget at Completion — is the sum of BCWS and the Management Reserve plus any Undistributed Contingency Budget. Yet, depending on the strategy adopted for handling the management reserve the manner of calculating the VAC associated with it may differ on different projects.

BCWP: Budgeted Cost of Work Performed — is the planned cost of work done up to Time Now.

BCWS: Budgeted Cost of Work Scheduled — is the planned budget.

CV: Cost Variance — is the BCWP less the ACWP. A negative result means that there is a cost overrun on the work done to date.

EAC: Estimate at Completion — is the estimated cost to complete all work including the cost of the work up to Time Now. This is sometimes called the Forecast Final Cost (FFC)

SV: Schedule Variance — is the BCWP less the BCWS. The Earned Value Schedule Variance is measured in dollars and a negative result means that work is currently behind schedule (schedule overrun.)

The most useful output from "EV" is the current trend in Period Variance of the final project cost.

VAC: Variance at Completion — is the BAC less the EAC. A negative result indicates an expected overrun at the end of the project. The final step is to calculate Period Variances which are the differences in the VAC between successive sets of data collection. Period variances in VAC show the trends on the project from reporting period to reporting period. These trends are examined to determine whether the position is improving or deteriorating relative to current projections.

This final step in Earned Value calculations probably provides the most useful indicator of project health, from the perspective of management's project cost control.

14.2 Production, Progress, and Productivity

Once the design details are known and work is ready to start, the cost of most materials for construction can generally be estimated with a reasonable degree of confidence. While the prices negotiated and the quantities required may vary from the budget, the costs remain relatively stable. Much more uncertain are the costs of the labor or equipment intensive activities. Important variables in this respect include:

Human variables affect project costs the most.

Production (Rate) — The rate at which units are produced over a given period, independent of the number of man-hours consumed.

Progress — The quantity or value of work done up to the time of measurement compared to the planned expectation, and

Productivity — In its broadest form, productivity is how well the resources of an organization are brought together and used to accomplish a set of results. It is the efficiency of doing the work, that is, the ratio of output to input. When measurements are taken over a period of time, the period productive efficiency is the number of units produced in that period divided by the number of man-hours to do so.

The following sections provide a better understanding of these variables, and how they affect the tracking and control of costs.

14.3 Production and Resource Loading (input)

The amount of work produced is clearly related to the resources applied as input, though not directly on a one-to-one relationship. Many factors affect the relationship such as availability of the work, availability of equipment and materials, familiarity with site conditions, and how well the work on the site is organized and managed. For purposes of the following discussion, it is assumed that the job site is "well-run" as described in Chapter 1, Section 1.2.

On a well-run construction site, the input of resources, including people, materials, equipment, etc. is varied according to the planned timing and availability of the work. This also applies on all but the smallest construction jobs where small crew size may limit flexibility. Even on small maintenance "projects", this flexibility may be improved by managing the labor levels over several concurrent assignments. Consequently, the resource loading over the whole of the job, and the resulting output, follows a distinctive pattern within surprisingly narrow limits.

On a well-run job, resource input follows a familiar pattern.

Figure 14-2 shows an example of labor loading for a profitable civil contract that was predominantly formwork and concrete placing.[1] The histogram displays the make up and total numbers in the production work force, week by week over a 38 week period. Resident Engineers, Construction Managers and others on construction sites responsible for tracking and supervising construction activities will readily recognize the general profile of this histogram. As may be expected, labor builds up to a peak level in the early stages and remains somewhat stable over a period of peak production. Towards the end of the work, it steadily declines to zero as the work is completed. In practice, this general profile is typical[2] whether the work in question is a whole construction project, a sub-contract, an individual trade or a construction activity of significant duration.

When the cumulative total of on-going work, the histogram data, is plotted against time, the resulting curve follows the shape of the letter "S" as shown in Figure 14-2. If the histogram data is typical, then it follows that the shape of the resulting S-curve is also typical. The important points to note are that:

- The initial part of the curve represents "build-up" and can hardly be any other shape
- The central part of the curve is "steady-state", or effectively a straight line slope, and
- The latter part of the curve represents "run-down" and closely mirror-images the early part of the S-curve.

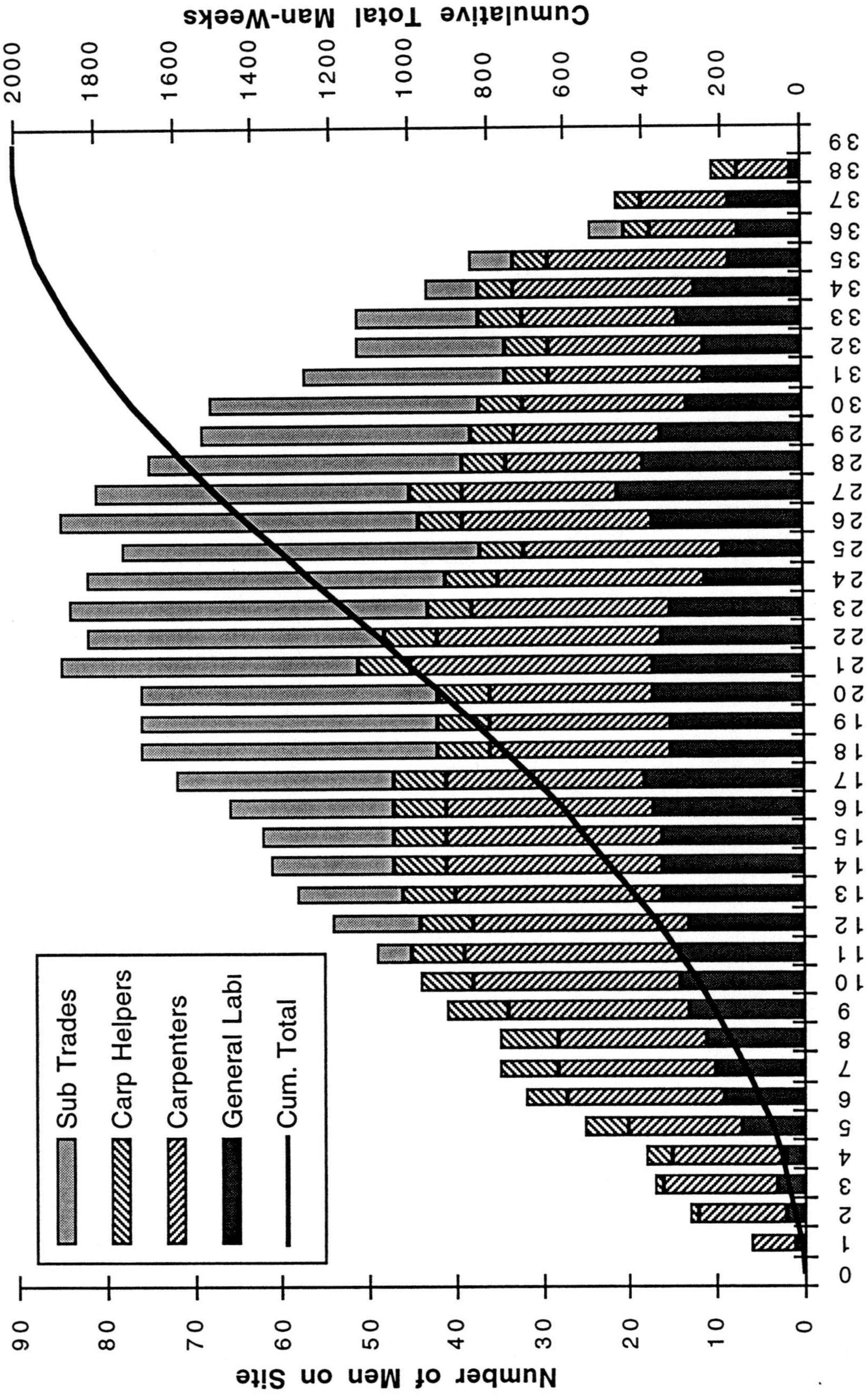

Figure 14-2. Site Labor Loading - Civil Work (Predominantly Concrete)

For convenience, these components will be called Stages 1, 2 and 3 respectively. There are many practical reasons for the shape of each of these stages.

Stage 1 — **In this stage there is an accelerating build up of the work force because:**

Here is why the resource input pattern on a project is familiar.

- Access to the work has to be opened up from a zero start, so that the work becomes progressively more available.
- Necessary preliminary preparatory activities, including planning and understanding local conditions, ordering of materials, etc., often require fewer people but more intensive supervision (Start right to go right!).
- Key people may be brought in to start the work, but supporting labor is recruited locally. The recruiting and selection of local labor take time.
- With productive efficiency in mind, crews are added only as experience builds and the work becomes available.
- Further crews are added only as pressure builds to get the job done within the required time frame.

Stage 2 — **reaches a steady state because:**

- The working environment has reached optimum conditions for balanced performance and repetition.
- The job reaches the physical limitations and capabilities of the people and equipment provided.
- Adding more labor or separate crews would over-crowd the working area and reduce productivity.
- Adding crews reduces the number of repetitions available to each for deriving the benefits of "productivity improvement".
- In either case the costs would be higher.
- Alternatively, if the work force is held to a lower level, the elapsed time to do the work will be prolonged, with consequent higher overheads and, possibly, contract penalties to be faced.

These obvious trade-offs require careful management and balance.

Stage 3 — **In this stage almost the reverse of Stage 1 is true. Labor is progressively reduced because:**

- The work begins to run out.
- The remaining work space not occupied by following trades, or owner occupation, runs the danger of becoming over crowded.

- Morale sometimes deteriorates as the end of the work is in sight and people leave to join more active sites.
- The less productive crews or individuals are let go first.
- The more difficult work may have been left to the end, may be more congested, or otherwise require only the skills of those brought in at the beginning.
- Pressure to complete "the last few percent" dies down as management attention turns to more critical work.
- Latent defects may surface upon final inspection requiring rework with no added measurable product to show for the effort.

Application of S-curve theory to construction work includes comparative estimating, forecasting, and quantifying the effects of delays on performance. In any application of S-curves to practical work, the natural loss of productivity in the last 25% of the production must not be over looked.

14.4 A First Approximation to Project Resource Loading

Figure 14-3 shows the data from Figure 14-2 replotted to a horizontal time scale of 100% and a vertical scale such that the total average labor loading is also at 100%. Superimposed is a smooth envelope curve representing the same data. This curve is the shape of an asymmetrical dome and, since it is directly related to the shape of the labor loading curve discussed earlier, also is typical. The typical fit is not perfect, of course, but it is sufficiently close to draw some conclusions regarding planning and management of similar type jobs.

However, the mathematics of this curve is complex and not particularly useful for the purpose. A simple profile made up of straight lines would be easier to work with. Such a first approximation to project resource loading has been suggested[3] according to the following simple empirical relationship. On a well-run project expect:

How to plot a Standard Resource Input curve

- 40% of the effort to occur in the first 50% of the total time
- Another 40% in the next 25% of the time, and
- The last 20% of effort in the last 25% of the time
  Where "effort" is the input measured in man-hours or dollars

The resulting figure is a trapezoid. For convenience, this will be called "Standard Resource Input" (SRI) envelope, albeit an empirical but practical one. This envelope is also shown plotted on Figure 14-3. It should be noted that because the period of peak loading is 25% of the total, the peak level is 160% of the overall average. This is a valuable indicator. If the duration of the work and total labor-days are known, the level of site support services required for the workforce during the period of peak production can be determined.

When the SRI envelope is plotted cumulatively it results in an SRI S-curve as shown by Curve (a) in Figure 14-4.

In 1983, the National Electrical Contractors Association (NECA) issued a report on the "Rate of Manpower Consumption in Electrical Construction" in the US.[4] NECA collected data from 40 different contractors on 54 building projects in 32 cities. The projects represented four broad types of buildings competitively bid that contractors felt were typical of their business. Figure 14-5 shows the SRI envelope compared to the NECA typical labor loading. The profiles are very similar, but the peak electrical labor loading occurs some 10-12% later than in the SRI. This is not surprising since electrical work typically includes a high volume of work in the finishing stages. Even so, it does show that the extent of deviation is quite narrow as noted earlier.

14.5 Production S-curves in Practice

As described earlier, the typical S-curve is made up of three stages namely, Build-up, Steady-state and Run-down. Stage 1 is the most critical because the unique conditions of the site are experienced for the first time. This sets the stage for what should be a steady, productive, and profitable run at the main body of the work. Stage 2 is significant because peak productivity and efficiency must be attained and maintained without interruption for actual profit to be generated. Stage 3 is significant for ensuring that the work is brought to an effective and satisfactory conclusion without wasting time and money. For example, if the labor is cut too early the work gets extended. If it is cut too late unnecessary cost is incurred in paying for unproductive man-hours.

Since Stage 1 is the most critical to the subsequent successful conduct and completion of the work, it is worth examining it more closely. The shape of this part of the S-curve is made up of two components:

Stage 1 of the S-curve is made up of two components.

1. **The build-up of resources**
2. **Added production through productivity improvement**

Build-up of resources has been discussed at length with examples in earlier sections. Added production through productivity improvement implies that the rate of output will exceed that which might be inferred simply from examining the resource loading. This is a normal and key management expectation, which will be reflected in the shape and timing of the progress S-curve for the job. Again, it can be expressed in a second simple empirical relationship as described in the next section.

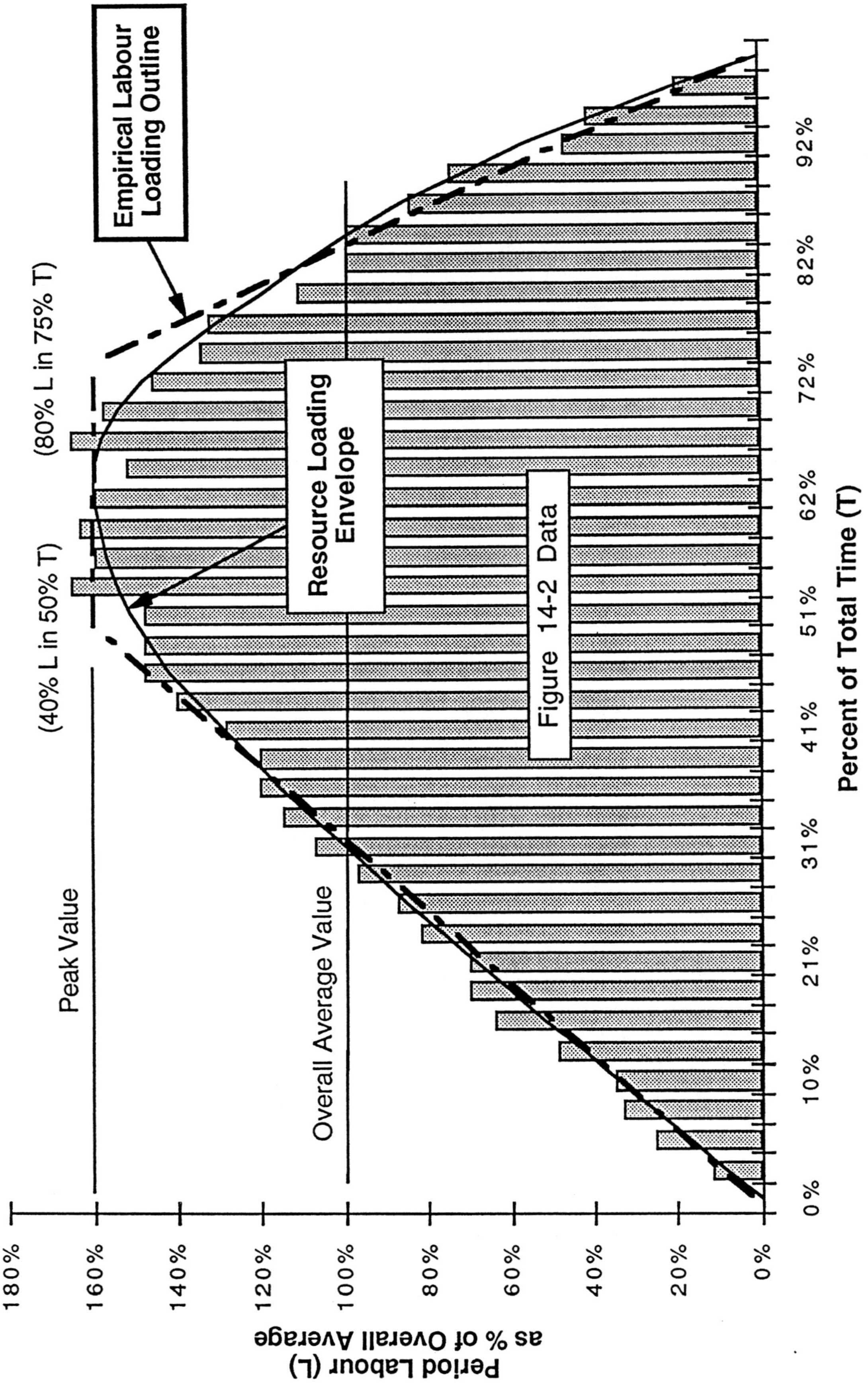

Figure 14-3. Site Labor - Civil Work: Histogram,

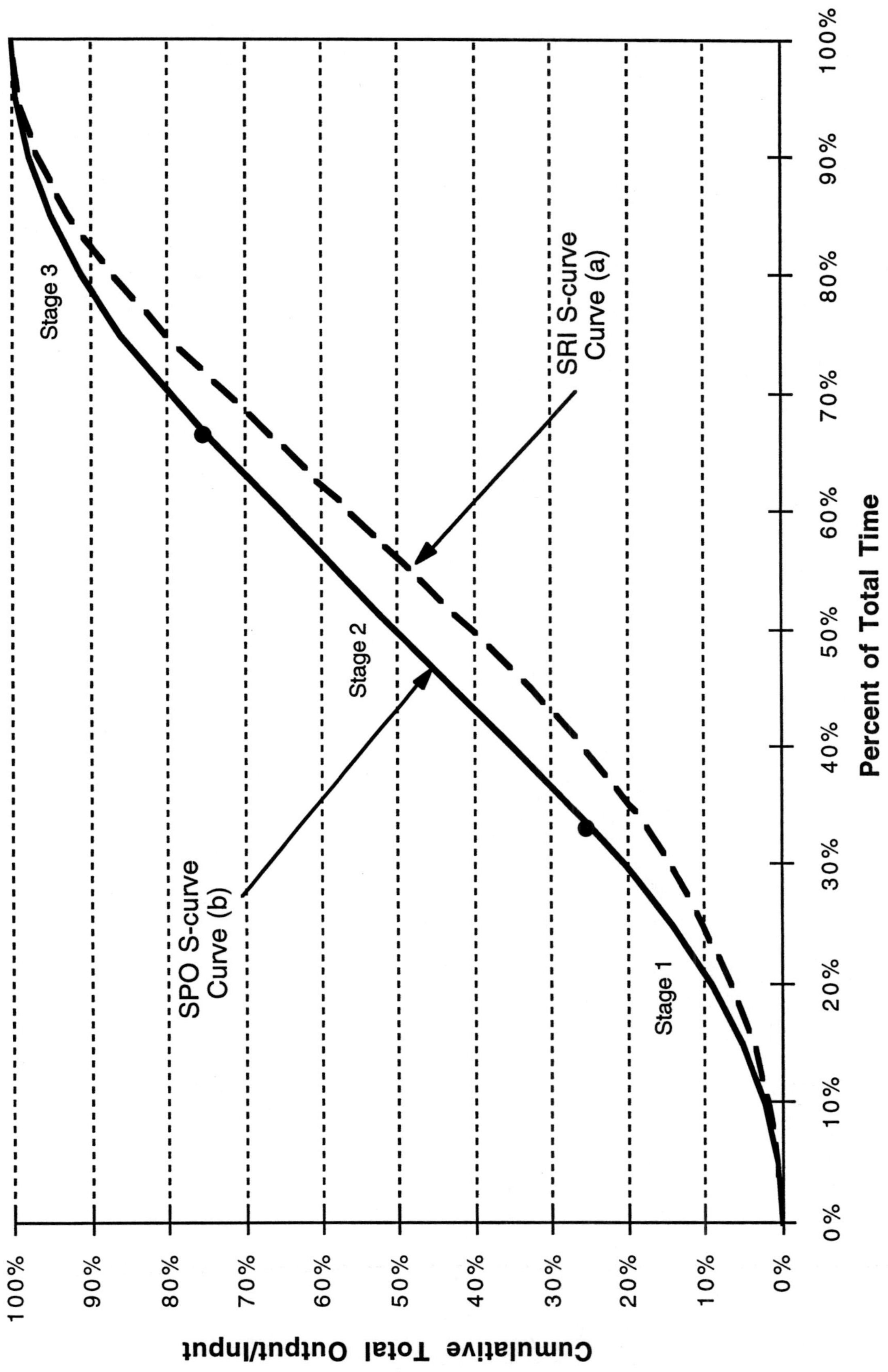

Figure 14-4. S-curves: Standard Production Output (SPO) vs. Standard Resource Input (SRI)

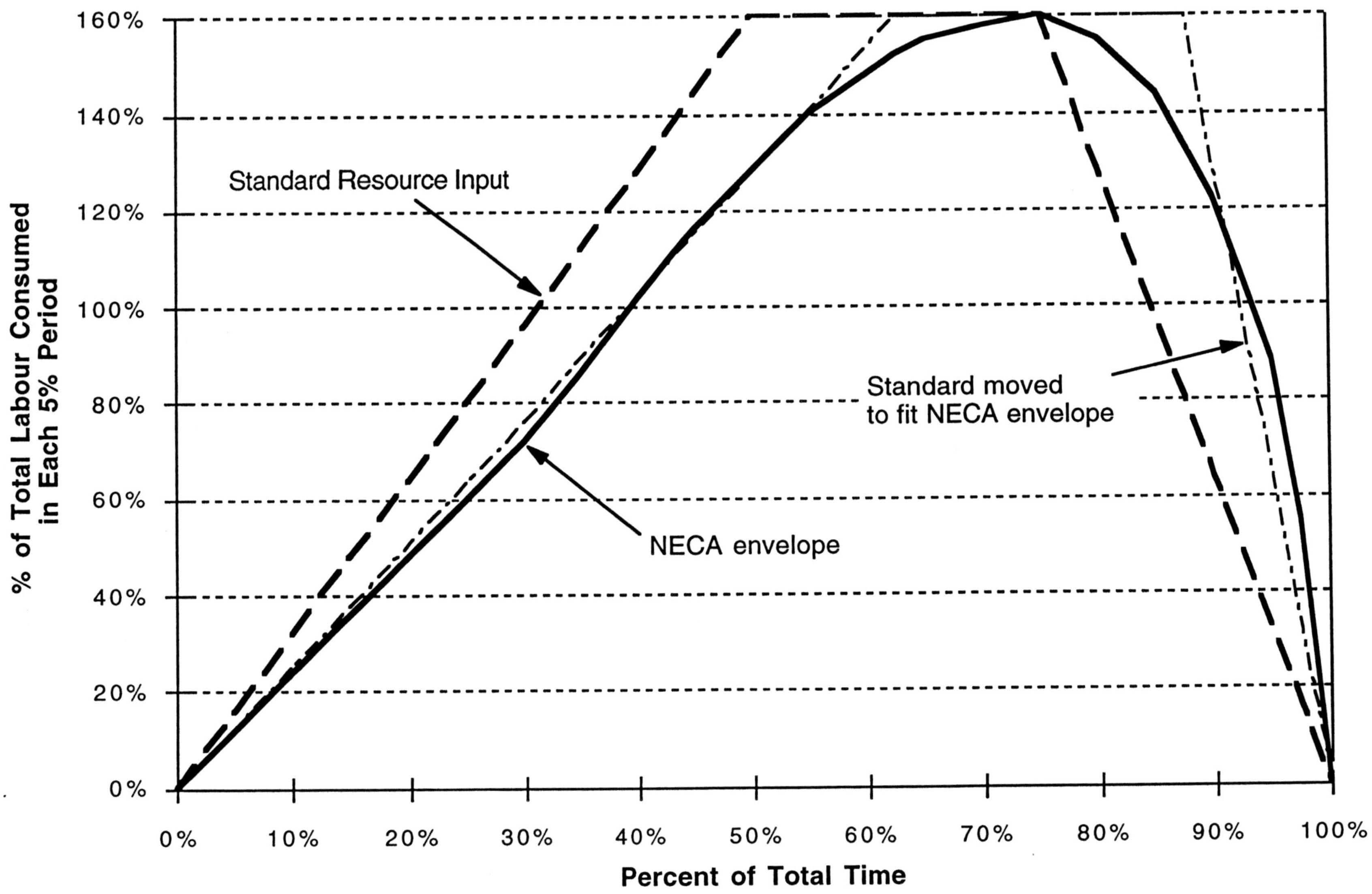

Figure 14-5. Electrical Work in New Buildings: Labor Loading compared to Standard Resource Input

14.6 A First Approximation to a Progress S-curve

The following empirical relationship has been suggested as a first approximation to project progress or output.[5] On a well-run project expect:

How to plot a Production Output curve.

- 25% of measured progress to be done in the first third of the total time,
- Another 50% in the next third, and
- The remaining 25% in the last third of the time.
- A curve representing an accelerating rate of progress will be exhibited in the first 25% of the time, while a similar but opposite curve will occur in the last third.

For convenience this will be called "Standard Production Output" (SPO) S-curve. Note that if this profile is used for planning or forecasting, the 100% Total Time base must be given a realistic planned duration. If the profile is used for post completion analysis, the Actual Total Time may be substituted.

SRI and SPO curves are useful for initial project planning.

Figure 14-4 shows the SRI and SPO S-curves plotted together. The differences between the two curves are essentially developed during Stage 1 of the S-curves, i.e. the first 33% of the Total Time. A realistic productivity improvement ratio (see Chapter 15) of 86% in Stage 1 would account for the difference between the output and the input S-curves.

Obviously, the best source of information for planning and estimating is derived from experience of similar previous work. In the absence of specific experience these "standard models" can be used as a first approximation, particularly for initial planning.

14.7 Watch for the Rollout Effect

Careful management of a well-run project avoids the "Rollout Effect".

The final cost of a project can be significantly increased because of the Rollout effect.[6] Figure 14-3 showed a typical site labor resource loading envelope. Suppose this represents the planned resource loading shown by curve A in Figure 14-6. Now suppose the initial planning is too optimistic, or the front end of the schedule slips due to initial delays for one reason or another such as waiting for working details or shop drawing approvals from the designers. Common sense and cost consciousness dictate that labor will only be recruited for tangible work that can be planned and immediately undertaken. Site management is naturally reluctant to load up with unproductive labor.

This results in a delayed build-up of resources shown by the beginning of curve B. But if schedule pressure is brought to bear, the result may be an attempt to catch-up once the information is available. This means that an even more rapid build-up of resources will be attempted. Other circum-

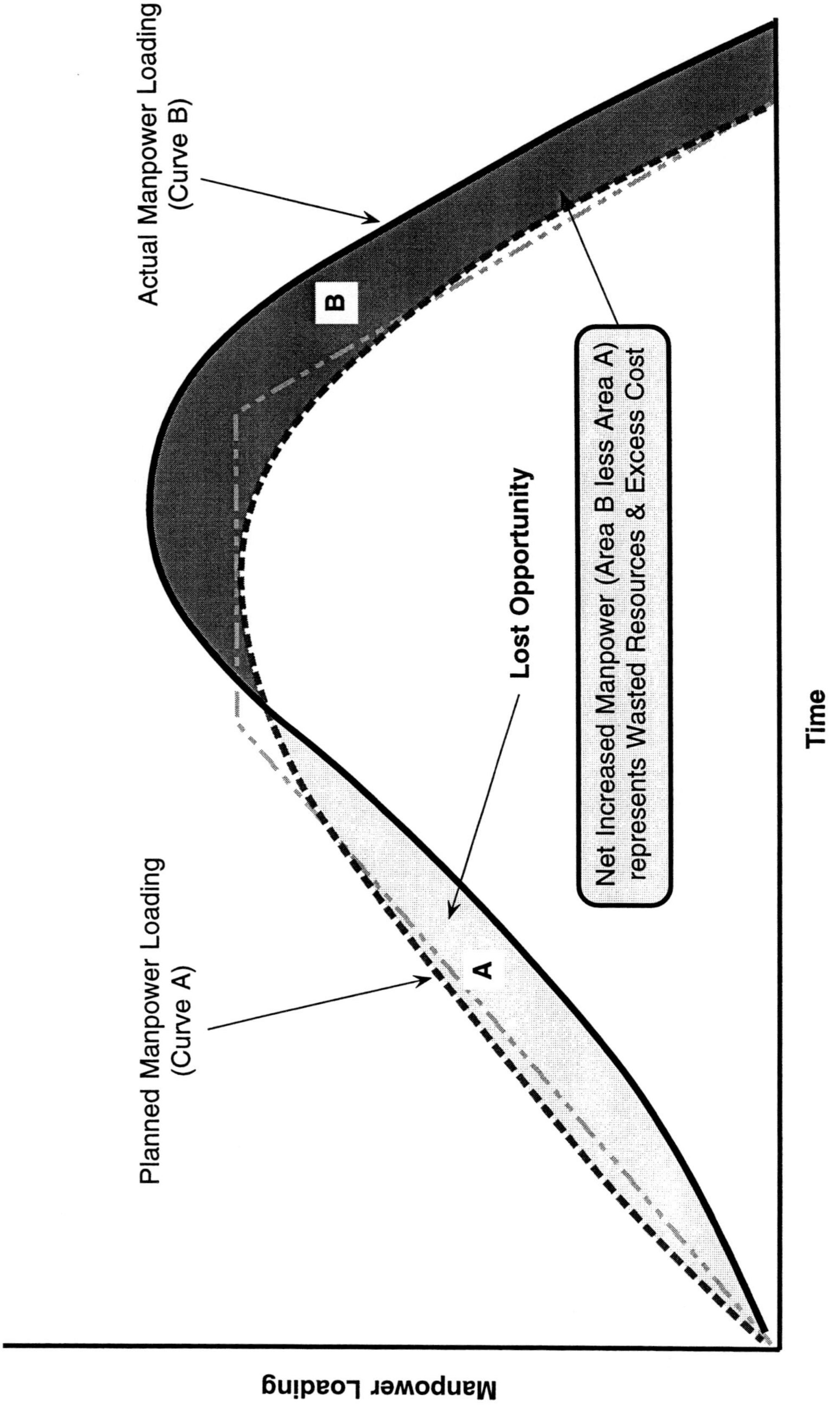

Figure 14-6. The Rollout Effect

stances, such as the physical limitations of the site, could lead to productivity lower than planned so that still more catch up is needed and applied.

Total labor then peaks much higher than planned. The result is a labor loading as shown by the rest of curve B, with or without a delay in completion. Typically, the initial savings in delayed cost as represented by area A, are more than over taken by the increased cost of the subsequent loading shown by area B.

The "Rollout Effect" can cascade through a project. Fast-track projects are particularly prone to this problem.

The situation described above was attributed to delayed information from the designers. Yet, a similar situation can develop in the designers' office if the owner is tardy in providing the designers with their detailed requirements or approvals. The designers could suffer a similar Rollout Effect with increased design costs and late shipment of drawings to the site. If the project is large and proprietary process design is being developed directly by the owner, then the same could happen in the owner's office. So Rollout can have a trickle down effect on the project.

Fast-tracked projects are particularly prone to this condition. Rollout can be substantial and has accounted for cost increases between 10% and 20% on some projects.

References

[1] Wideman, R. M. 1970-93. From the author's personal notes and records of progress tracking. AEW Services, Vancouver, B.C.

[2] Christian, J., and Kallouris, G. 1991. An expert system for predicting the cost - time profiles of building activities. Canadian Journal of Civil Engineering. Ottawa, Ontario. Vol. 18.

[3] Allen, W. 1979. Developing the Project Plan. Notes prepared for the Engineering Institute of Canada Annual Congress Workshop on Project Management. Toronto. pp3-9.

[4] National Electrical Contractors Association (NECA), 1983. Rate of Manpower Consumption in Electrical Construction. Bethesda, Maryland

[5] Wideman, R. M. 1970-93. From the author's personal notes and records of progress tracking. AEW Services, Vancouver, B.C. (This empirical progress curve has been used on the job by the author for many years and has been offered to students in cost management and cost control project management workshops.)

[6] Dozzi, P. 1991. Estimating and Controlling the Cost of Capital Projects, University of Alberta, Alberta, (Adapted from a paper presented to an International Seminar on Project Management for Developing Countries in New Delhi, India, Proceedings, p 219)

CHAPTER 15

Productivity and Learning

15.1 Learning Curves

Even on construction where repetition is limited, considerable productivity improvement is possible.

Many construction projects offer various opportunities for repetitive work, though the total number of repetitions may be somewhat small compared to manufacturing processes. But when carefully managed and tracked such work provides distinct opportunities for productivity improvement.

Common experience tells us that skill and productivity in performing tasks improve with experience and practice through repetition. This experience is particularly relevant to construction where every task "starts afresh". Studies of this phenomena have shown that this improvement has a characteristic curve that can be estimated with reasonable accuracy in many situations. This curve represents the change in unit cost associated with a change in productivity as a result of repetition. This is known as the "learning curve" or "experience curve".

"Experience" of the job is not the same as "learning" skills — but we'll call it "learning" anyway.

Some authors differentiate between "learning" and "experience". Generally, "learning" is the acquisition of basic skills for the work, and "experience" is the knowledge acquired about the particular work activity and its time and place. Unfortunately, there is confusion in the construction industry since focus is on the latter while referring to it as the former.

In the following sections it is assumed that all labor has already got the skills for the work, and the term "learning" will be treated as synonymous with "experience". There are several different ways of plotting this relationship that help analysis.

15.2 Productivity Improvement Through Learning

The theory behind productivity improvement through learning is worth examining because there are somewhat different, though similar, approaches to the mathematics involved. In addition, the methodology can make a useful contribution:

- In showing the importance of consistent management direction and effectiveness
- In showing the benefits of establishing on a job the highest possible degree of repetition
- In ensuring sufficient and continuous availability of work before commencement
- In underpinning work crew motivation and attitude
- Conversely, in showing the adverse affects of interference to the flow of work
- In forecasting output, and therefore time and cost to completion
- In estimating work that is comparable, but may be significantly different in the amount to be done.

15.3 Original Theory

Costs per unit decrease with repetition — in a predictable way.

The phenomenon of "learning" was first expressed mathematically in 1936 by T. P. Wright. He observed in the aircraft industry that certain costs per unit tend to decrease in a predictable pattern as the workers and their supervisors become more familiar with the work. These decreasing costs are a function of a learning process in which a unit of work requires fewer man-hours to produce as more units are produced. The key elements of the theory may be summarized as follows.[1]

- The repetition of any task leads to an improvement in productivity because of the experience gained.
- This phenomenon is well established in the mass production industry as well as in the construction industry, under appropriate circumstances.
- The application of the theory (in the construction industry) assumes that operatives start with the necessary basic skills and the

Number of Units in Sequence	Cumulative Average Time per Unit	
	90% Ratio	80% Ratio
1	100.0	100.0
2	90.0	80.0
4	81.0	64.0
8	72.9	51.2
16	65.6	40.9
32	59.1	32.8

Figure 15-1. Examples of Cumulative Average Time per Unit

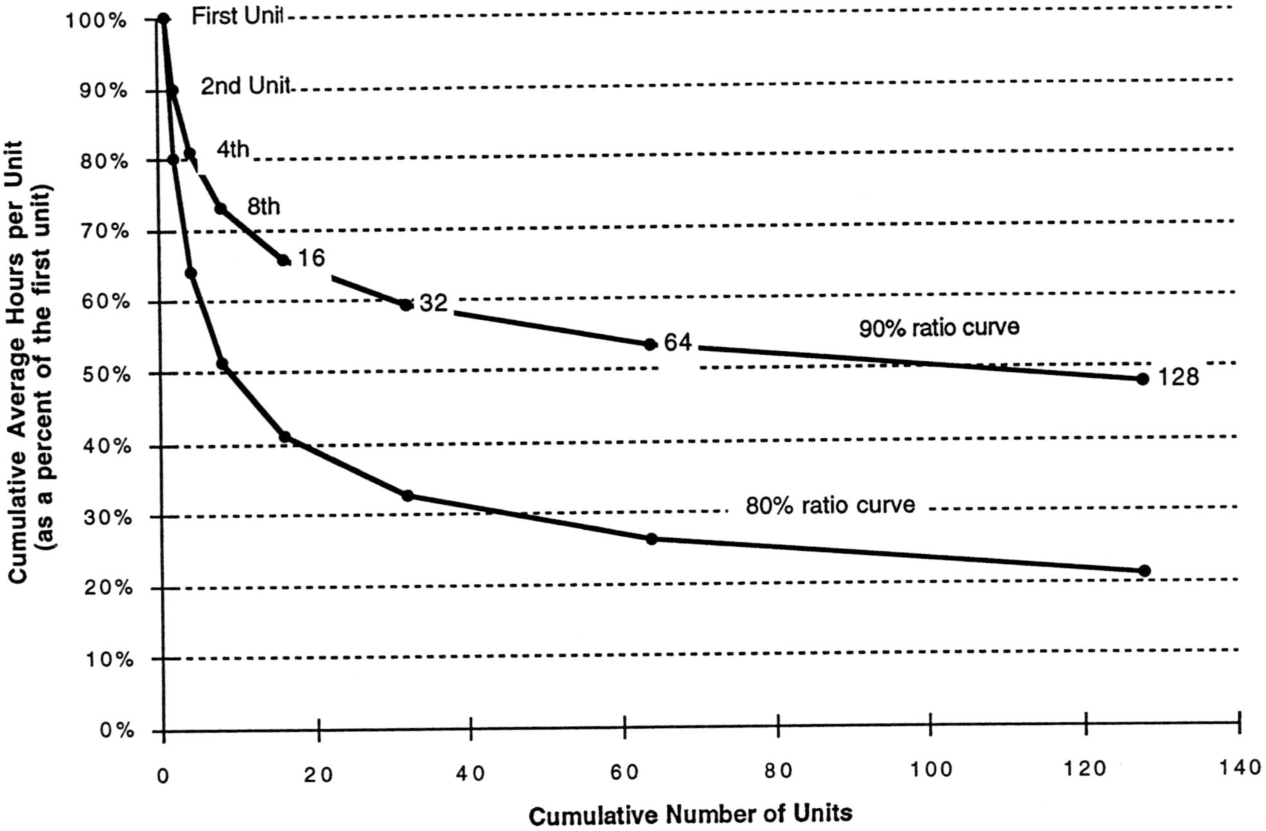

Figure 15-2. Theoretical Learning Curves: 90% and 80% Ratios

required support for the work to be done.

- Productivity improvement then typically follows a constant ratio relationship that is expressed as follows.

For every doubling of units, the cumulative average time per unit is reduced by a constant ratio.

The table shown in Figure 15-1 illustrates this relationship by showing examples of cumulative Average Time per Unit.[2]

In the Table, the time taken for the first unit is 100%. At a 90% ratio, the average time taken for the first and second unit is 90%, that is, the actual time taken for the second unit is 80%. When the fourth unit is reached the average time taken for all four units is 90%x90% = 81% and so on.

Figure 15-2 shows these values plotted as curves. If the same data is plotted on log-log paper, the results are straight lines as shown in Figure 15-3. This form of presentation is more useful for manual analysis or mathematical illustration.

15.4 Two Approaches

Two approaches to productivity improvement calculations have been put forward. The first focuses on the Cumulative Average Time for 'n' units. The second, a modification of the first but focusing on the time taken for the 'n'th unit, is more useful in most construction applications. In the first approach, the log-log relationship shown in Figure 15-3 can be expressed mathematically as follows.

The cumulative average time (or cost) for each of 'n' units up to the 'n'th unit, when plotted against the number of units on log-log paper, produces a straight line.

This may be called the "Log Linear - Cumulative Average Approach" (The LL-CA Model). This relationship is useful in forecasting or comparing similar operations but with significantly different numbers of units involved. It is also useful in analyzing large amounts of data as, for example, the records of many units produced from a precasting yard. This is because the cumulative average curve has considerable power to smooth out the unit data. It can also be deceptive because this power increases as the quantity increases.[3] It is, therefore, less useful for examining the expectations for individual units or the latest unit as would be useful in tracking actual progress on a construction site.

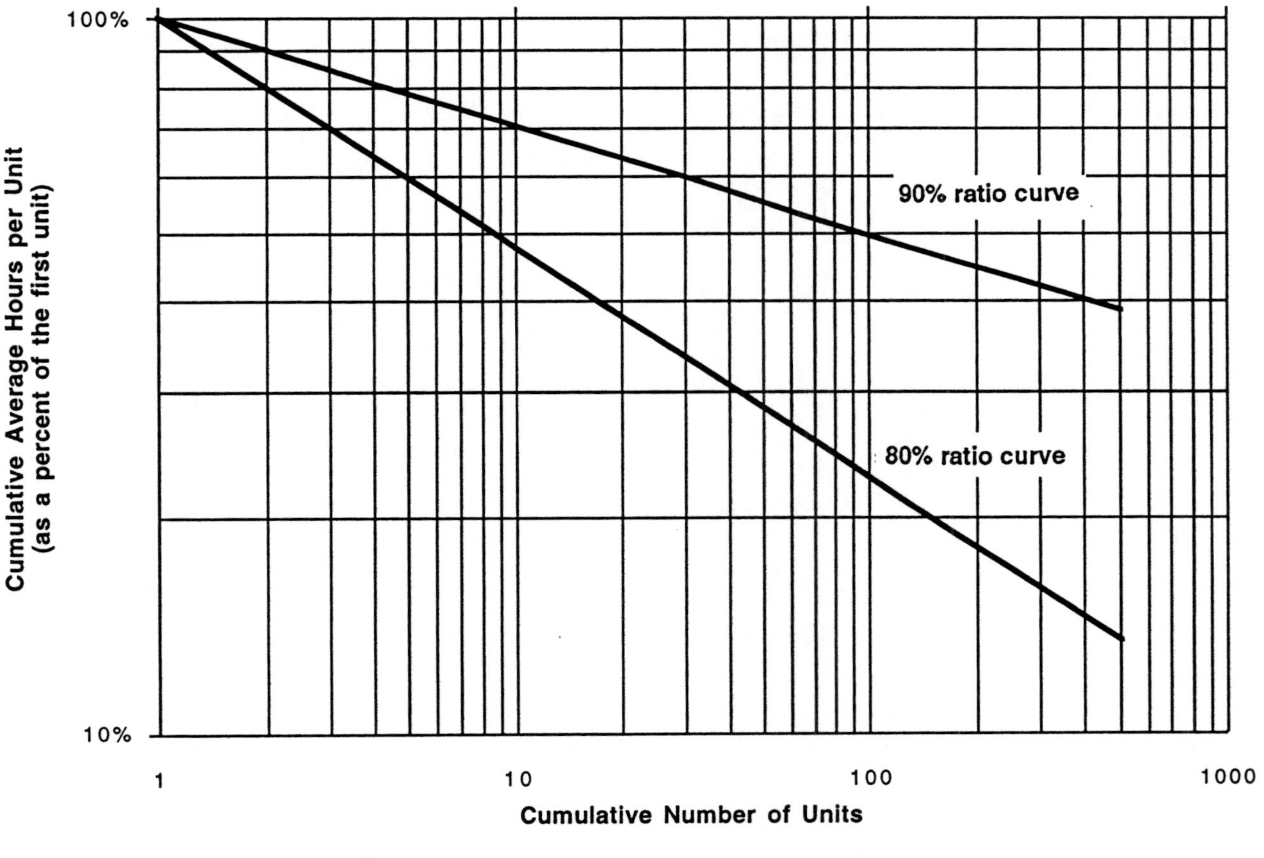

Figure 15-3. Theoretical Learning Curves: Plotted to Log-Log Scales

This has led to the second approach, a variation of the first relationship, that states as follows:

> *The time (or cost) of the 'n'th unit, when plotted against the number of units on log-log paper, produces a straight line.*

The results of LL-CA and LL-U calculations are similar — but far from identical.

This may similarly be called the "Log Linear - Unit Approach" (The LL-U Model)[45]. Appendix B develops and compares the mathematics of both models. The table in Figure 15-4 shows calculations of the time *to* the nth unit and the time *of* the nth unit over a range from one to fifty for ratios ranging from 70% to 95% as calculated by each approach. The Cumulative Average figures are shown on white background, while the corresponding Cumulative Unit figures are shaded. As might be expected, the results of the two approaches are similar but not identical. The differences in results obtained from the two approaches vary from about 7% for a repetition of only five units at a 95% productivity ratio to over 100% for 50 units at a ratio of 70%.

In practice, one would select one approach or the other, and use a different set of ratios. It does mean that when comparing the learning ratios on different jobs or of different crews on similar work, the method of calculation must be the same and it must be specified.

15.5 Practical Example of Learning Curve Application

Consider the construction of a 25 storey concrete high-rise building. From the second floor up, all floors are virtually the same, so that the second floor is the first of a uniform series. Construction data is collected as follows.

A hypothetical but practical example.

Time sheets are carefully marked up with job allocations, and hours are abstracted for forming and pouring concrete on each standard floor. The man-hours for the first in the series is noted as 1175 man-hours. The second, third and fourth in the series take 855, 905, and 735 respectively. Figure 15-5 shows this data plotted on log-log paper using the LL-U Model. At this stage the data suggests a line whose slope is -.152 (approx. 90% learning ratio) and that future floors would be expected to take the times shown in Column 1b of the table shown in Figure 15-6.

But actual records for the next two floors, five and six, produce results of 700 and 690 respectively. The addition of the latest data suggests a new line whose slope is -.234 (approx. 85%) also shown in Figure 15-5, and the new times taken to complete are shown in Column 2b of Figure 15-6. The new result shows a reduction in total hours of approx. 2200 hours (12%), or the equivalent of four extra floors!

Unfortunately, the practical reality does not follow either of the two projections. When record keeping is continued until all floors are completed, the results are as shown in Column 3 of Figure 15-6. For purposes

Lp = r s=logr/log2	0.950 -0.074				0.900 -0.152				0.850 -0.234			
n	Cum-Av Tn/U1	Un/U1	Cum-Unit Tn/U1	U'n/U1	Cum-Av Tn/U1	Un/U1	Cum-Unit Tn/U1	U'n/U1	Cum-Av Tn/U1	Un/U1	Cum-Unit Tn/U1	U'n/U1
1	1.0	1.000	1.0	1.000	1.0	1.000	1.0	1.000	1.0	1.000	1.0	1.000
5	4.4	0.829	4.7	0.888	3.9	0.675	4.4	0.783	3.4	0.538	4.2	0.686
10	8.4	0.784	9.0	0.843	7.0	0.602	8.1	0.705	5.8	0.452	7.3	0.583
15	12.3	0.760	13.2	0.818	9.9	0.565	11.5	0.663	7.9	0.409	10.1	0.530
20	16.0	0.743	17.2	0.801	12.7	0.540	14.8	0.634	9.9	0.382	12.6	0.495
25	19.7	0.731	21.2	0.788	15.3	0.521	17.9	0.613	11.8	0.362	15.0	0.470
30	23.3	0.721	25.1	0.777	17.9	0.507	20.9	0.596	13.5	0.346	17.3	0.450
35	26.9	0.713	29.0	0.769	20.4	0.495	23.9	0.583	15.2	0.334	19.6	0.434
40	30.4	0.705	32.8	0.761	22.8	0.485	26.7	0.571	16.8	0.323	21.7	0.421
45	34.0	0.699	36.6	0.755	25.2	0.476	29.6	0.561	18.4	0.314	23.8	0.410
50	37.4	0.694	40.3	0.749	27.6	0.469	32.4	0.552	20.0	0.307	25.8	0.400

Lp = r s=logr/log2	0.800 -0.322				0.750 -0.415				0.700 -0.515			
n	Cum-Av Tn/U1	Un/U1	Cum-Unit Tn/U1	U'n/U1	Cum-Av Tn/U1	Un/U1	Cum-Unit Tn/U1	U'n/U1	Cum-Av Tn/U1	Un/U1	Cum-Unit Tn/U1	U'n/U1
1	1.0	1.000	1.0	1.000	1.0	1.000	1.0	1.000	1.0	1.000	1.0	1.000
5	3.0	0.418	3.9	0.596	2.6	0.314	3.7	0.513	2.2	0.224	3.4	0.437
10	4.8	0.329	6.6	0.477	3.8	0.230	5.9	0.385	3.1	0.152	5.2	0.306
15	6.3	0.287	8.8	0.418	4.9	0.193	7.6	0.325	3.7	0.123	6.6	0.248
20	7.6	0.261	10.8	0.381	5.8	0.171	9.2	0.288	4.3	0.105	7.8	0.214
25	8.9	0.242	12.6	0.355	6.6	0.155	10.5	0.263	4.8	0.094	8.8	0.191
30	10.0	0.228	14.3	0.335	7.3	0.144	11.8	0.244	5.2	0.085	9.7	0.174
35	11.1	0.217	16.0	0.318	8.0	0.135	13.0	0.229	5.6	0.078	10.5	0.160
40	12.2	0.208	17.5	0.305	8.7	0.127	14.1	0.216	6.0	0.073	11.3	0.150
45	13.2	0.200	19.0	0.294	9.3	0.121	15.1	0.206	6.3	0.069	12.0	0.141
50	14.2	0.193	20.5	0.284	9.9	0.116	16.1	0.197	6.7	0.065	12.7	0.134

[white box] = Cum-Av Approach   [shaded box] = Cum-Unit Approach

Figure 15-4. Table comparing Cumulative Average and Cumulative Unit productivity from 95% to 70% Ratios

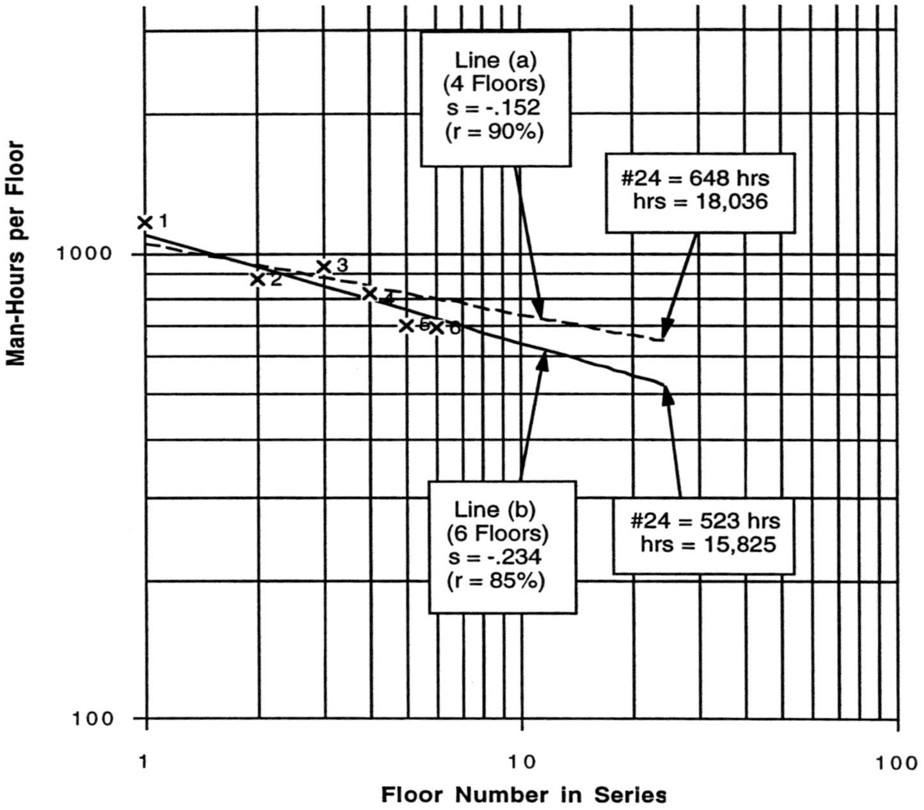

Figure 15-5. High-Rise Construction: Labor Hours per Floor Observed and Projected

Floor#	Col 1a Observed 4 floors	Col 1b Projected 90% learning	Col 2a Observed 6 floors	Col 2b Projected 85% learning	Col 3 Final All floors
1	1175		1175		1175
2	880		880		880
3	940		940		940
4	820		820		820
5		822	700		700
6		800	690		690
7		781		698	620
8		765		676	700
9		752		658	695
10		740		642	720
11		729		628	650
12		720		615	620
13		711		604	680
14		703		593	670
15		696		584	710
16		689		575	660
17		683		567	640
18		677		559	670
19		671		552	750
20		666		546	710
21		661		540	850
22		656		534	790
23		652		528	935
24		648		523	1060
Projected Totals:-		**18036**		**15825**	***18335***

Figure 15-6. High-Rise Construction: Table of Labor Hours Observed, Projected and Final

of comparison, the two sets of projections and the final actual results are shown plotted in Figure 15-7. It will be seen that the "tail end" of the actual results departs significantly from the ends of the original projection. So does the final total of man-hours shown in Column 3 of Figure 15-6 (16% higher than the second projection).

In construction, productivity improvement does not go on for ever — in fact, it reverses after about two third done.

When the final actual results are plotted at normal scales, as shown in Figure 15-8, the plot displays a distinctive shape sometimes called the "Bath Tub" effect. In fact, this profile is simply a reflection of the S-curves discussed in Chapter 14. In other words, productivity stabilizes (improvement falls to zero) and then decreases towards the end of the run of work.[6]

It should be noted that when the data shown plotted according to the LL-U Model is plotted according to the LL-CA Model the results are much more difficult to interpret. Figure 15-9 illustrates this point. The ratio values are also different. More importantly, for purposes of practical application, the effect of accumulating the results to averages for plotting purposes, mostly conceals the significant changes in trends associated with the "Bath Tub" effect. Thus, the LL-U Model, although not as consistent with

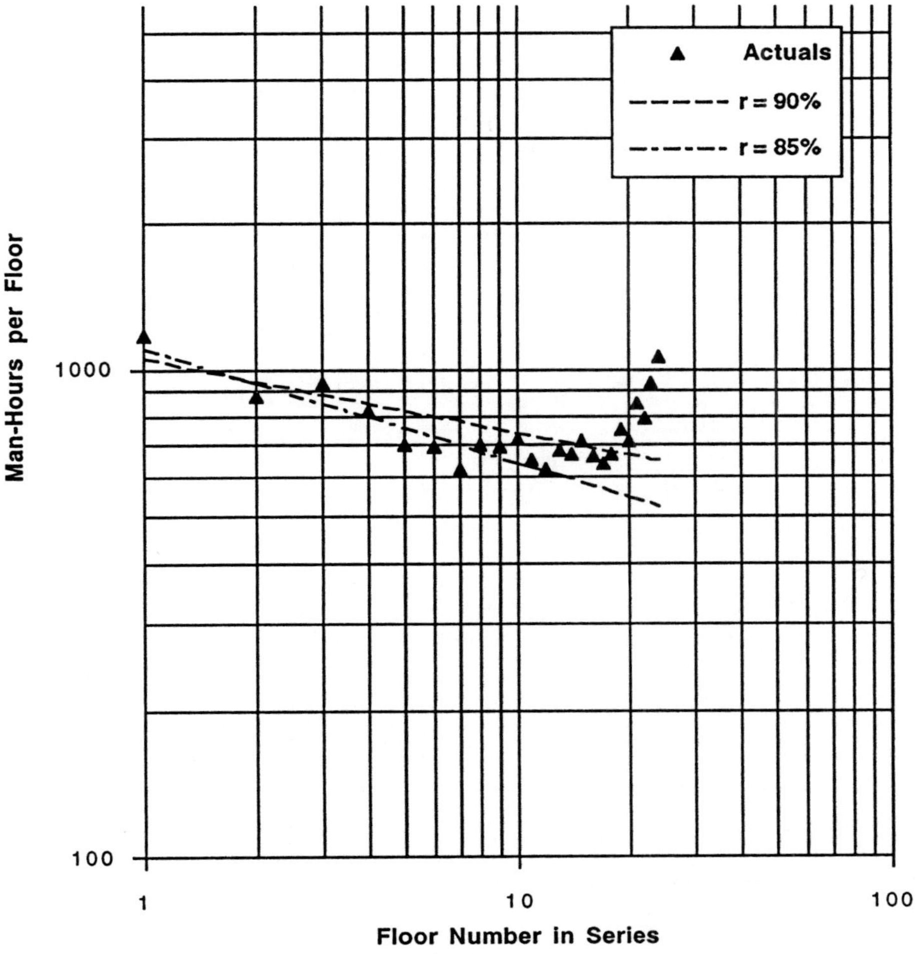

Figure 15-7. High-Rise Construction: Cumulative Unit Projected and Observed, LL-U Model

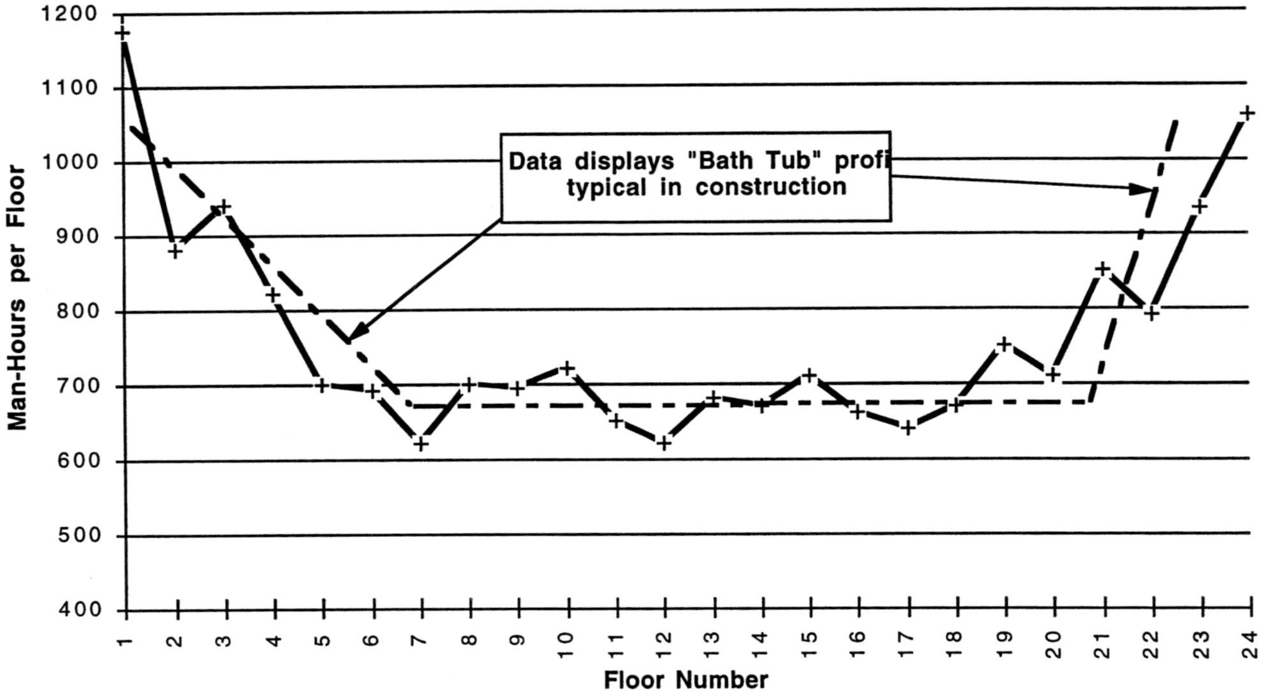

Figure 15-9. High-Rise Construction: The Bath Tub Effect

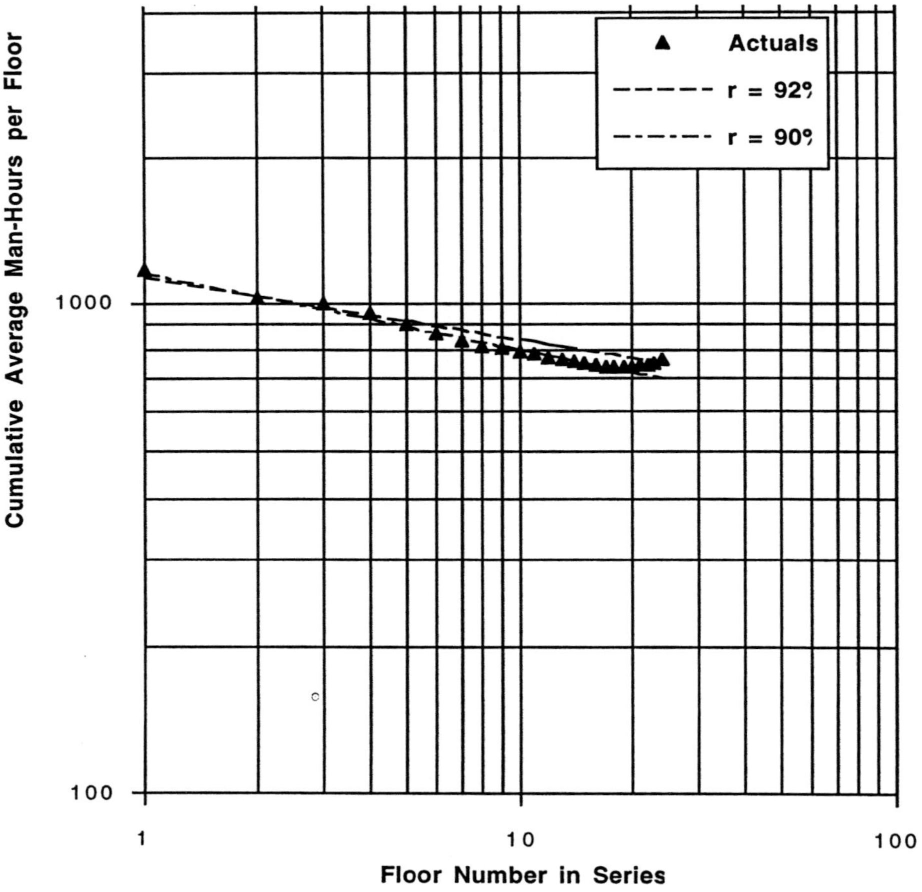

Figure 15-9. High-Rise Construction: Cumulative Average Projected and Observed, LL-CA Model

the original theory, is a more useful tool in many practical applications and for project management observation and control.

Application of the theory is limited.

The underlying message is that "Learning Curve Theory" should not be applied beyond the first 25% or so of the complete construction site activity under consideration. That is, for no more than one-third of the planned total time. In our high-rise construction example, the target for reaching optimum performance must be the 6th or 7th floor.

15.6 Issues Regarding Total Time and Stage 1 Time

A reasonable question to ask is how can the planner be assured of choosing the right total time (i.e. equivalent to 100%) and why should the learning always take 30-35% of that value? Should it not be possible to contemplate a 36-storey high-rise, instead of the 24, and still get the Stage 2 efficiency of the 24 storey high-rise in the first six floors?

You can't apply a 24-storey theory to a 36-storey project!

The practical reality is that if the building is that much larger the whole scale of the project is correspondingly larger and will be organized accordingly. This includes increased use of temporary materials, plant, equipment and site organization all optimized to suit the larger project.

In any case, the planned time must still be realistic and achievable even if it is being compressed. Having chosen this time, it is essential that all the supporting logistics of the site, including management, supervision, equipment, supplies etc., must all be present to support this plan. Failing this, in the author's experience, the job simply "takes on a will of its own" and charts its own track record. It is the determination reflected in the site's organizational culture that ultimately determines the outcome.

As an example, Figure 15-10 compares actual production of rock excavation with planned production on a not-so-well-managed site preparation project. Final quantities were significantly higher than originally anticipated, the planned peak level of production was never reached, and Stage 1 of the S-curve took more time. Not surprisingly, the whole project took a lot longer to complete — and ended in litigation.

15.7 Other Applications: Impact Studies Associated with Claims and Litigation

Learning Curve theory has been used in the analysis of claims arising from interference with a normal flow of repetitive work in construction, such as the introduction of late changes in requirements. In order for the methodology to be applied, it is necessary to identify suitable units of work carried out without interruption, or that should have been carried out without interruption. It is also necessary to identify the corresponding resource inputs over an observable period. Often, to establish a valid calculation, some "normalizing" of the units of work is necessary, since construction is rarely exactly consistent.

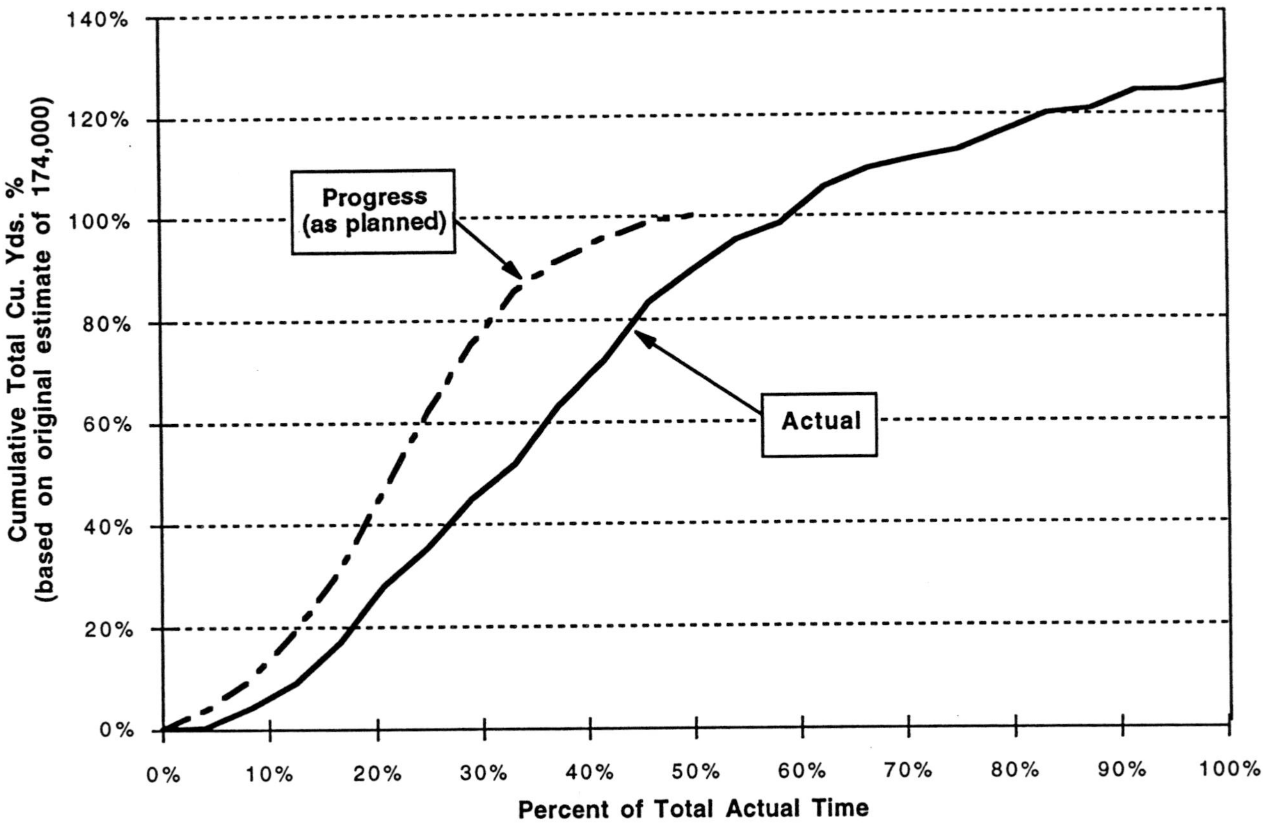

Figure 15-10. Bulk Rock Excavation: Actual vs. Planned (with significant quantity overrun)

A better way of calculating production losses due to interference — even if production units are dissimilar.

Figure 15-11 shows this applied to one area of the project shown in Figure 15-10. Individual rock blasts varied significantly, but these have been collected into sets of 2000 cu. yds. In effect, this means calculating a short-term rolling average, and choosing an appropriate set size, in this case an average daily production. In this way, it is possible to plot the results and draw inferences regarding performance.

Figure 15-10 shows the manhours per set. The level of "Normal" productivity is chosen as a line through levels of steady production in the middle stage of the work. The learning curve calculation then determines the initial legitimate learning to arrive at this level. Hence, "Normal" is based on actual values and represents the level of productivity that could have been maintained under normal unaffected conditions. Two periods of delays and obstructions stand out clearly and the extent of lost productivity can be estimated from the data. This is known as the Differential Method of calculation and can be useful in assessing the value of a claim, once responsibility has been established.

Such results are developed from actual data recorded on the job at the time. This approach eliminates objections of theory and estimating accuracy because it is based on actual field conditions, with the actual equipment used, and the particular crews operating it. In short, it represents

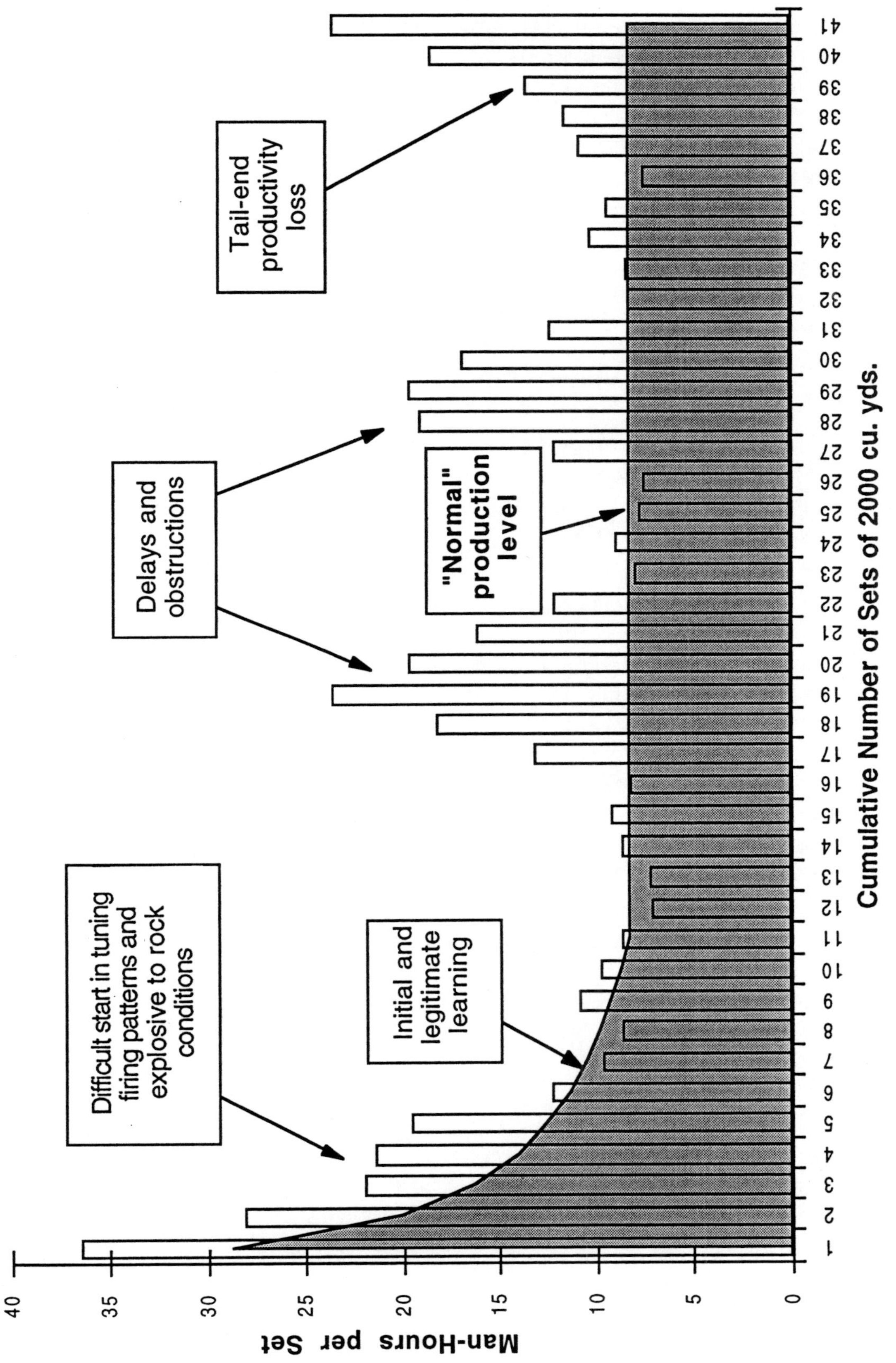

Figure 15-11. Bulk Rock Excavation: Productivity Losses Compared to a 70% Learning Curve

actual jobsite performance. It is therefore independent of any inherent short-comings of the contractor's original estimate, site supervision, crew or equipment, or of comparisons of results achieved by others on other sites under different conditions. On the other hand, it does depend on sufficient reliable observations being taken at the time, to provide a reasonable comparison that generates confidence in the results.

Keeping good time and activity records on the jobsite is essential!

The importance of keeping good time and activity records as the work proceeds for purposes of management and control cannot be over emphasized.

References

[1] Adrian, J. J. 1987. Construction Productivity Improvement. Elsevier Science Publishing Co., Inc., New York, N.Y. p154.

[2] Chellew, J. H., 1974. The use of the learning curve. Proceedings PMI Seminar/Symposium, Drexel Hill, Pennsylvania. p163.

[3] Thomas H. R. 1986. Learning Curve Models of Construction Productivity. Journal of Construction Engineering and Management, ASCE, New York, N.Y. p250.

[4] Defense Systems Management College, 1989. Applying Learning Curve Theory to Actual Data. PMI Seminar/Symposium Education Workshop, Drexel Hill, Pennsylvania. p1.

[5] Drewin, F. J. 1982. Construction Productivity - Measurement and Improvement through Work Study. Elsevier Science Publishing Co., Inc., New York, N.Y. p102.

[6] Barrie, D. S. and Paulson, Jr. B. C. 1978. Professional Construction Management. McGraw-Hill, New York, N.Y. p224.

Part 4: Practical Application to a Large Construction Project

CHAPTER 16

Control in the Planning Phases

16.1 Introduction

Larger projects attract larger problems.

As the size and complexity of projects increase, so do the number of problems involved. To bring large diverse projects to successful completion there needs to be total cooperation and smooth interactions between all the parties involved. This chapter suggests how the principles discussed in earlier chapters may be applied to a large construction project of long duration. Projects that might fall into this description include:

- Energy projects such as thermal and hydroelectric schemes
- Distribution networks such as power, pipelines or communication systems
- Infra structure such as road, rail, sea and air connections; or
- Very large building programs such as a university campus.

It is probably true to say that no project will succeed unless its management has the will, determination, and commitment both to project results and a satisfying conclusion. Equally important is a knowledge and understanding of the principles, policies and procedures required to reach traditional success goals expressed by scope, quality, time and cost constraints.

This chapter and the next are based on practical organizational strategies and control philosophies adopted from the management, engineering, design and construction of various large projects. The outline presented contemplates a Project Cost Management System (PCMS) as described in previous chapters. On some large projects, the PCMS is sometimes called Project Information and Control System. Which ever term is preferred, we envisage its operation within the corporate environment and framework which typically prevails in an owner's organization.

The PCMS must be tailored to the organization it serves.

In practice, a PCMS must be tailored to the particular project organization it serves. The various components can be readily modified to suit smaller projects and multiple projects. Therefore, the description should be of interest to anyone involved in a construction project, especially those working in a matrix style of organization.

16.2 Practical Project Control Principles

A large project requires a Strategic Plan — the forerunner of a Project Brief.

The first step in a large, long duration construction project is to establish and document a Strategic Plan for the project. A typical check list for the narrative content of such a plan, the forerunner of the Project Brief discussed in Chapter 7, is as follows. (See also Appendix C, pC-3)

- General Project Scope Description, Rationale and Justification
- Scope of Work
- Technical Basis and Quality Standards
- Regulatory and Certification Requirements
- Operating and Maintenance Requirements
- Cost and schedule constraints
- Procurement Strategy
- Construction Strategy
- Temporary Project Facility Requirements
- High Level Project Organization
- High Level Project Procedures
- Computer and Communications Support
- Owner/Sponsor Standards and Procedures
- Project Control Procedures

Certain general tactical principles can be stated for establishing the controls for a larger project. For example:

Start with a set of tactical principles.

1. Set up a central control group responsible to top management for the complete cost and scheduling philosophy and system application.
2. Ensure that this group understands the project goals and objectives, including any subsequent changes.
3. Identify the various cost and schedule responsibility centers as early as possible.
4. Have the various responsibility centers participate in developing their respective goals and objectives and ensure that these are consistent with the general project goals and objectives.
5. Keep the controls as simple as possible and automate data processing as much as possible.
6. Design "checks and balances" into the control system but not to the extent that they seriously impede progress.
7. Ensure awareness of cost, schedule and quality requirements, and their actual status, at all levels of the project organization through an effective and regular communications strategy.

8. Ensure that exception reports (i.e. actual at variance with the plan) reach the appropriate responsibility centers promptly. Serious differences of position should be agreed with the responsibility center concerned. If agreement cannot be reached, allow the responsibility center to publish its own opinion, in cooperation with the control group.

Satellite control groups are required for large responsibility centers or remote locations.

On very large projects, some responsibility centers may be large, or at remote locations. For these centers, it may be necessary to establish sub control groups. These sub-groups would help the center with its day to day cost and schedule control but would be functionally responsible to the central control group for integrated information.

16.3 Owner and Project Manager Organizations

The owner and its investors considering a proposed construction project will recognize the associated financial risk and their responsibility in setting realistic financial objectives. Not always so clear to the owner are the project risks relating to capital cost, schedule, cash flow, quality and consequent operating costs. These also translate into financial risk, and call for direct involvement in the project at an executive level. Therefore, the owner requires to have effective and appropriate management in place to arrive at a successful result. The upper part of Figure 16-1 shows a typical corporate organizational structure.

The Owner's management must be involved — and stay involved.

Now, the essential elements of a construction project in which the owner's management must be involved, include:

- Establishing and maintaining the project scope, criteria and clarification information
- Ensuring availability of owner's staff when required
- Overall project planning including required end dates or tie-in dates
- Financing and cash flow
- Selection of preferred project organizational structure and terms of reference
- Selection of equipment and materials to satisfy operating requirements
- Owner's reviews and approvals and ensuring regulatory approvals are obtained
- Contract administration
- Commissioning, start up and operation

To meet these requirements, the owner should direct or assign specialist staff from the respective corporate divisions. These representatives must handle, or be satisfied with, the various aspects of the project as noted below.

Financial Division

- Financial Planning
- Treasury
- Project accounting

Legal and Administrative Division

- Contracts
- Insurance
- Corporate secretary

Marketing and Public Relations Divisions

- Market forecast variations and economics
- External public
- Internal public
- Governments

Project Division

- Site selection, property acquisition and access
- Design parameters
- Services and construction contract strategy
- Project control interface
- Project management audit

Operating Division

- User requirements in operating, maintenance, safety and performance
- Input to design, materials and systems selection, environmental and regulatory requirements
- Specify and approve operating and maintenance manuals
- Provide staff for operator training, commissioning, start-up and running
- Establish selection and quantities of spares and consumables
- Coordinate phase in and any concurrent outages required

A project needs a sponsor.

Each of these divisions probably already reports to the President and Chief Executive Officer of the company. If not, they should certainly do so on a large project. The project will also require a "sponsor". The purpose of having a sponsor is to have an individual identified who, for project purposes, represents the owner and its responsibilities.

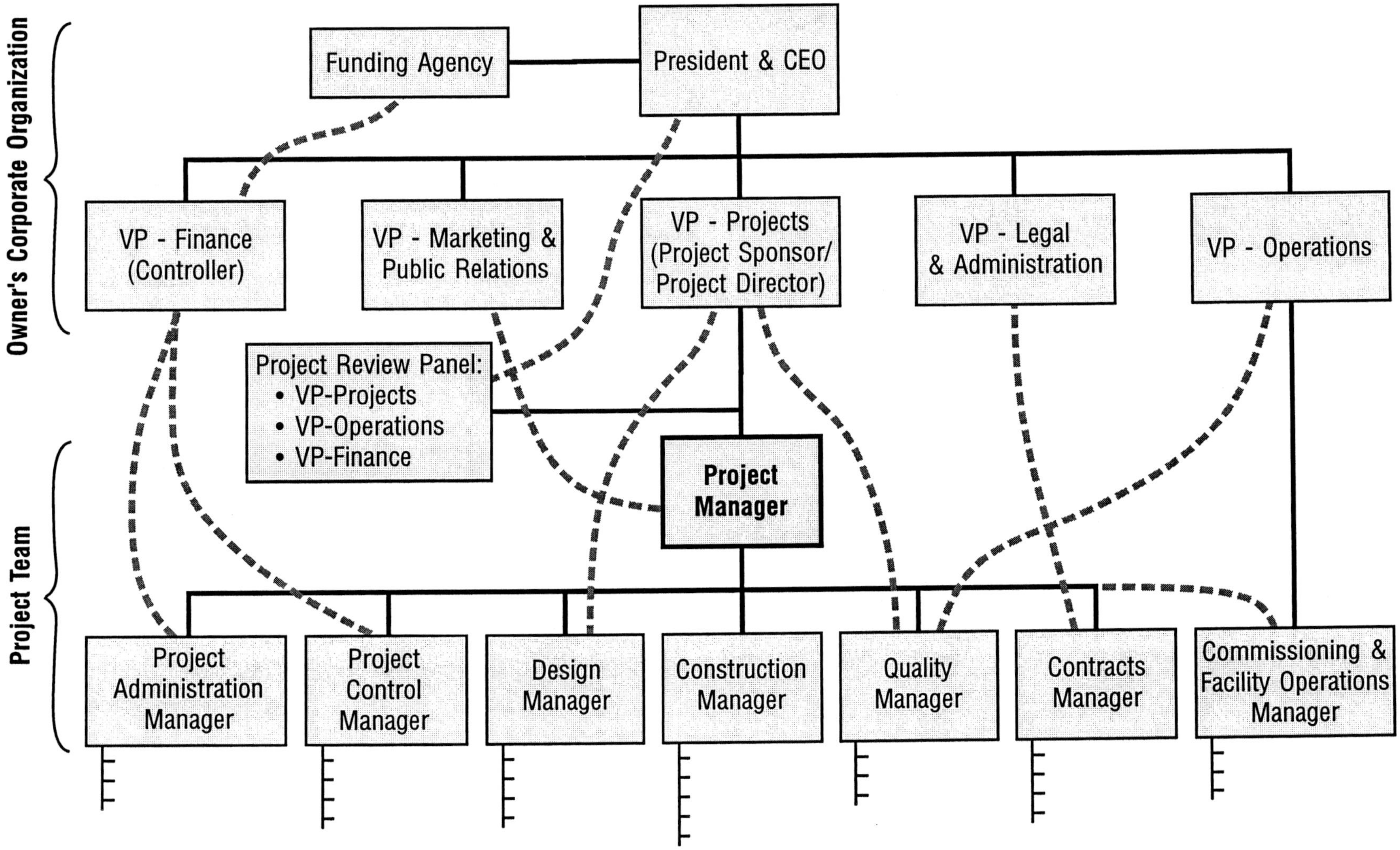

Notes: The Project Review Panel acts as an Advisory Board
For details of the Project Management Team, see text
——— = Lines of Formal Communication and Responsibility
- - - - = Working Contact and Communication

Figure 16-1. Owner's Senior Staff Relationships for a Large Project

The VP-Projects Division may either act as the project's sponsor or delegate this responsibility to a Project Director who then acts as the "Owner's Representative" in all matters. The VP-Projects will also be responsible for appointing the Project Manager for the project. This project manager may either be an individual on the owner's staff, drawing on in-house resources to manage the project, or a completely independent firm appointed to fill that role.

On a large project, the "Project Manager" may be an individual or an independent company. A large project also needs a "Project Review Panel".

In addition, the owner will be well advised to establish a Project Review Panel. This panel would be charged with overseeing the project and any project management audits required, and resolving technical issues and conflicts. It would draw on the resources of both the owner-organization and those of the project manager. It may also draw on outside independent resources for advice when needed.

The project manager and supporting organization should be made responsible for all the work involved in the project. That is to say, the planning, organizing, execution and control of design, procurement, construction, administration, quality commissioning and final audit.

Under the arrangements outlined, and shown in the lower part of Figure 16-1, the project manager's organization will include the following main divisions and their responsibilities:

Design

- Design development planning, sequence and administration
- Execution by discipline or specialty
- Design development dependencies and coordination
- Quality assurance and value management of design work
- Technical documentation for work packages or contracts
- Process design changes
- Technical field support.

Procurement

- Assemble general and trade contract documentation
- Preparation of commercial terms
- Prequalification, tendering and bid evaluation
- Submittals and reviews
- Permanent equipment and materials purchasing and expediting
- Transportation, warehousing, customs and duties
- Documentation and settlement of final payments

Construction

- Managing construction methods, safety, scheduling, and costing
- Processing construction permitting

- Field personnel, organization and labor relations
- Temporary facilities
- Construction plant hire and temporary materials ordering
- Field supervision and progress measurement
- Operator training, and plant testing, commissioning and start up

Project Control

- Work breakdown planning and scheduling
- Estimating and budgeting
- Cost collection and forecasting
- Progress analysis and reporting
- Analysis of claims for additional payments

Quality Control

- Input to quality standards, specifications and contractor prequalification
- Inspection and testing
- Off site quality control and expediting

Administration and Finance

- Project financial accounting, progress billing approvals and payments
- Financial analysis and cash flow projections
- Systems and procedures development and maintenance

If the "Project Manager" is an outside company, it should act as an extension of the Owner's organization.

Where an independent organization is hired to act as project manager, formal lines of communication must be established to document instructions and approvals for contractual purposes. The project will be immeasurably better served if the Project Management company is retained to act as a direct extension of the owner's own organization. In this way the total integration of both groups is possible and contact can be maintained both laterally and vertically between the combined organizations. This arrangement ensures the continuous functioning of the project within the bounds of the respective delegated authorities.

This approach also serves to maintain the owner's "comfort level" It ensures early reaction to changing conditions affecting the project as a whole and significantly improves the probability of project success.

16.4 Basic Control System

The purpose of the basic control system is to provide the project team with a management control tool. This is done by breaking down the project's scope into manageable units, as described in earlier chapters, and measuring status and performance compared to a master plan. This should high-light adverse trends so that management can take corrective action such as applying additional resources. This enables control to be maintained over the scope, quality, time or cost of each unit.

The WBS and its Work Packages provide the required control over all aspects of the project.

The universal "manageable unit" is the Work Package. This applies to management and administration, planning, design, and all the elements of the construction work. Each work package must meet the criteria described in Chapter 5, and satisfy the hierarchical project work breakdown structure. Each work package must have a decimal or other systematic alpha numeric coding for classification and data processing purposes.

Original project budget figures, subsequent changes or transfers, escalation and interest during construction, must all be separately identified as cost classes, and tracked through cost types, as outlined in Chapter 4.

Control of all costs should be on a cost-as-incurred basis. This is particularly important on a long duration project where the escalation provision for inflation has a significant impact on the figures. This permits cost comparisons on a current basis at any time. It also reflects actual physical progress with a minimum amount of "interpretation" required by the various responsibility centers.

All cost-to-budget comparisons should be on a cost-as-incurred basis.

Central to the planning process, though frequently overlooked until later, is a carefully considered procurement strategy. This strategy should be developed at the earliest possible time in the planning phases. This will determine the extent to which project administrative services, and the work of design and construction are handled internally or externally. The various elements of the project can then be assembled and handled accordingly.

The early development of the procurement strategy is vital because it will have a significant impact on the work breakdown structure (WBS) and therefore the quality of subsequent control. It starts with identifying the geographic areas and their technical relationships, and ends with identifying trade work packages. The contents of these work packages should be grouped into preliminary contract packages that best satisfy the project's goals of cost and schedule. Flexibility should be built into the WBS to permit rearrangement to suit construction market conditions at the time of tendering.

The WBS must be consistent with the procurement strategy.

Similarly, the time schedule is broken down and handled at several levels. Having established the general project schedule goals, a master schedule with milestone dates is developed. Detailed schedule planning may be dealt with on a shorter term basis. Chapter 17, Section 17.1 describes the process of developing a Short Term Plan.

16.5 Basic Control Procedures

The process for controlling work-in-progress consists of:

- Setting objectives in terms of progress, cost and time
- Monitoring project activity in the same terms
- Comparing actual with plan
- Forecasting the results and alerting management to deviations.

Control means acting — not just observing.

Unless this sequence results in appropriate redirection of the project when needed, the process is not effective and the project is not being satisfactorily controlled.

To be effective, the control reporting function must

- Be as simple as possible
- Be as up-to-date as possible
- Be tailored to suit the various responsibility centers and supervisory levels
- Avoid duplication
- Use common project wide terminology.

The Work Breakdown Structure and its cost class coding provide the common project reference and information vehicle for this reporting function. It covers technical scope, quality, schedule, cost and records management.

As discussed in Chapter 4, the owner's Financial Information System and chart of accounts will not serve the needs of the project. The chart of accounts is designed to serve the organization's requirements in terms of assets and expense accounting for tax and insurance classification purposes. The project WBS must be designed to facilitate project control. Although the two are not directly compatible, they do have to be reconciled at least annually for purposes of fiscal accountability.

The WBS is designed to serve the project — but it must also be reconcilable with the fiscal accounts.

As explained in Chapter 7, every project should have well established major Executive Control Points. These control points represent key milestone events in the project's Master Schedule. Undoubtedly, the most important of these occurs at the transition of the project from feasibility to implementation. Presentation of the Project Brief and its executive approval marks this transition.

The Project Brief includes the Capital Appropriation Request based on the project estimate. Chapter 6 discussed the conversion of this estimate into a realistic working project implementation budget, for purposes of effective cost management. The project budget will reflect the WBS cost classes and coding, including design, construction, management, escalation and contingency. The project budget will not be as detailed as the ultimate WBS but must match it at some higher level.

For major long duration construction projects, it has been found effective to add a further step in the capital control system. As well as providing greater executive control, this extra step permits more effective accounting for escalation and contingency. The amounts corresponding to the various cost classes are first recorded in unappropriated accounts and become the approved control budget for the life of the project.

An optional extra control step for large projects helps in handling escalation and contingency.

As appropriations and commitments are made, funds are transferred from the unappropriated accounts, including escalation and contingency, to appropriated and commitment accounts. When procurement strategy is changed and work is repackaged, corresponding transfers between accounts may be made, with explanatory justification. In this way the original Project Brief estimate can be tracked through the life of the project to completion, in spite of escalation, policy or procurement changes and similar factors.

Thus all transactions are entered and compared on a current value basis. Approved appropriations, commitments for major contracts and purchases, and expenditure-to-date can all be recorded promptly. The WBS coding ensures that account activities are identified with their respective responsibility centers, and control reports can be issued accordingly.

On long duration projects, annual budgeting by responsibility center is advisable to establish further budgetary control. This provides a current frame of reference for comparison with actual results, that can be integrated with the short term planning. Significant variations are highlighted and analyzed to establish the cause whenever they develop. These are then reported to project management for corrective action and influence on future forecasts.

On long duration projects an extra fiscal control step helps in fiscal accounting and cash flow management.

The system also enables the development and maintenance of a financing plan to provide the funds required to undertake the project. By including the timing of expenditures, cash flow requirements can be projected and some control over future Interest During Construction (IDC) charges exercised.

With the system described, it will be seen that:

- Control is sufficiently flexible to allow scope transfers between responsibility centers or between work packages.
- All cost commitment decisions are strictly controlled and justification fully documented
- Escalation and IDC, important items of cost, and changes in rates can be monitored
- Major scheduling revisions can take account of escalation and IDC
- Cash flow is forecast and monitored.

The following section and Chapter 17 provide more specific descriptions of management control during the progressive stages of the project. It will be noted that budget figures updated to current dollars are constantly required for control reference. Therefore, transfers from the escalation budget to the unappropriated accounts should be made regularly. This could be monthly, quarterly or half yearly according to corporate policy.

16.6 Cost Control in the Planning Stage

The estimate to design and construct the proposed facility presented in the Project Brief should include:

- Sunk costs to date including pre-design feasibility studies, planning and the preparation of the Project Brief
- Studies still outstanding, detailed design, working drawings and specifications
- Procurement, including legal support, contract documentation, tendering and award
- Estimated construction cost based on the preliminary designs and scope definition
- Management of construction, including inspection, testing and quality control
- Project management
- Owner's project related management
- Escalation allowance
- Interest on borrowed money (IDC)
- Contingency

The construction cost estimate will have been based on appropriate contract packages reflecting the complete scope of the project, using prices current at the time of preparation. Construction will be the largest collective item in the estimate. Even so, the remaining items form a significant part of the total project cost. These added items should all bear some definable relationship to the components of the construction cost.

On a long term project, estimates of escalation and IDC may need to be supported by a long term economic forecast.

The escalation allowance should be determined from a review of the project's scope and schedule. Also included should be projections of changes in corresponding future labor and material costs for the balance of the project, calculated from the time of the last estimate. A project of many years may require an analysis of broader long term economic conditions including future competition between contractors and suppliers.

The IDC will require a similar economic review.

The contingency will be a reflection of the risks associated with the various elements contained in the scope. As described in Chapter 8, Section 8.6, it will be a reasonable allowance based on experience and the particular project. It should have regard to the status of design at the time of the estimate, specific uncertainties of site conditions and so on. For purposes of control it should be managed by area of responsibility.

The first step after project approval to proceed is to develop a more detailed project schedule.

When the project is approved for construction to commence, a comprehensive plan of activities must be developed. This will result in more detailed schedules that reflect the Master Project Schedule and show the sequence and inter-relationships of all major activities. The major activities include design, regulatory approvals, tender documents, procurement, construction and commissioning for each geographic area of the project. In this way inter-related target dates can be established, each of which must be met if the project is to be completed on schedule. The comprehensive plan should also include contingency planning in the event that any key date is not met.

Typically, the scheduling described is computerized using software that is compatible, workable and enables "what if" inquiries, how to take advantage of time saved, recording of actuals, updating, and forecasting of final time and cost. Appendix A provides a check list for a comprehensive PCMS system.

CHAPTER 17

Control in the Producing Phases

17.1 The Short Term Plan

The Short Term Plan can be an excellent schedule control tool.

With the approval of the Capital Appropriation Request for construction funding, the project has successfully passed a major hurdle and moves from a planning mode to a producing mode. The goals and objectives have been set as a crystallized project scope, and a Work Breakdown Structure and Master Schedule have been established with critical milestone dates to mark the way. As the detailed working drawings and construction each commence and accelerate towards peak production, schedule direction and control is required at a much more detailed level. This can be done through a rolling Short Term Plan (STP). A good STP presented in bar chart or similar graphical form will be:

- Logical
- Simple and easy to work with
- Easy to monitor
- Flexible, easy to revise
- Accurate and timely

It must also:

- Anticipate problems
- Promote effective communication, and
- Be useful!

(a) Mechanistic Guidelines

Mechanistic Guidelines provide the methodology.

Some mechanistic guidelines for devising an STP are as follows:

1. The Short Term Plan should be approximately one eighth of the total project schedule (but not exceeding one year to satisfy fiscal

requirements). Thus, detailed planning of an eight month project would be conducted at intervals of one month. A two to three year project would be planned in detail at intervals of four months, and so on.

2. Updating and development of the next period short term plan should commence when the present short term plan is not more than 50 % expired.
3. Current schedule status should be regularly monitored, recorded and reported against the STP and the master schedule. This approach ensures continuity, currency, relevance, visibility and awareness of the scheduling process. It also avoids wasting effort on too much detail too soon, or before sufficient information is available.
4. A separate STP should be prepared for each geographical area or responsibility center.
5. The method of presentation of the STP is most important and should be standard throughout the project.
6. The activities in the last 25% of the previous STP period should be shown in the ensuing STP period. This ensures continuity in the presentation of the plan. It also establishes confidence in the mind of the reader that the information contained in the new planning period is relevant and consistent with on-going work.
7. Each activity in the plan should provide a brief description of the scope, a measure of quantity, methodology, level of effort and output assumed and (therefore) estimated activity duration. Quantity, methodology and output includes measurement in terms of dollar value and rate of expenditure. Too often this information is overlooked so that the reader has little understanding of the activity durations shown and how they were arrived at. Without this essential information, there is no indication of the resources to be called upon to get the required results. Nor is there the information to verify whether actual trends will meet cost and schedule targets.
8. Master Schedule information should be shown on the STP as a frame of reference. Ideally, the objectives contained in the STP should reflect those of the Master Schedule. This will provide the justification and encouragement to support any special efforts shown on the STP to bring the project back on target.
9. The STP itself should be reviewed at regular intervals, weekly or two-weekly depending on the length of the project. If a simple bar chart format is used, status at time now for each period review can be shown by drawing a "contour line" through the activity bars. Successive contours provide a very visible way of showing whether trends are improving or deteriorating.
10. At the end of each STP period, a rigorous analysis of the project budget and schedule should be undertaken to establish current trends, actual progress to date and latest forecasts. This information

should be used to establish an up-to-date cost and schedule forecast for the whole project, including escalation and remaining contingency, for the information of senior management and the project team.

(b) Humanistic Guidelines

Humanistic Guidelines are designed to satisfy the customer — though that may involve more work.

Some humanistic STP guidelines for consideration are as follows.

1. The degree and range of information shown on the STP should reflect the needs of the recipients that it serves.
2. The STP should reflect the degree of uncertainty involved in the planning of the activities involved.
3. The development of the STP should be an iterative process involving as much listening as telling. In other words it should encompass the knowledge, experience and commitment of those who will be directly responsible for doing the work.
4. The focus of STP preparation should be on process more than product. That is, priority should be given to, and agreement reached on, work methods, production means and logistics for attaining the STP objectives.
5. The STP will be the better for being prepared at the location of the work where others can be involved, instead of through structured meetings at some remote location.
6. Participation and encouragement resulting in motivation and challenge are better forms of control than exhortation.

These humanistic guidelines may involve more work and make otherwise simplistic planning more difficult, but experience has shown that they do result in better performance.

17.2 Detailed Design Stage Control

The type and level of control effort vary with the stage of the project. As illustrated in Chapter 3, the control of the preparation of the working drawings and specifications is a vital part of cost and schedule control.

During detailed design control must be at two levels.

In this stage, as in the planning phases, project costs must be controlled at two levels. The lower level is the cost of the design effort itself while the upper level is the future cost of facility constructing.

At the lower level, the cost of design work should be monitored on a frequent and regular basis. Design status reports should show the current disposition of all working drawings completed, under way and anticipated by each responsibility center involved.

The reports will also show the cost to date, the forecast cost to complete and compare this to the authorized budget. The "cost" to date and forecast may be expressed in man-hours, as this information is often more readily available. The reports must be reviewed for potential overruns in both effort expended and schedule delay. Prompt response is necessary to find out causes and implement corrective action.

At the upper level, experience suggests that commitment to the construction cost estimate by the designers only takes hold as the design concepts are crystallized into working drawings and specifications. Therefore, effective control must be exercised over scope and quality during the design process. This is done through a set of "Design Transmittals". The Design Transmittal describes the scope of work to be designed by each discipline, studies and recommendations conducted to date (or to be conducted), general arrangement and any other relevant information. It also includes technical and quality standards, construction budget allowance in current dollars, budget allowance for the design effort, and the schedule for design reviews up to final approved tender documents. In effect, it is the engineers response to the owner's scope requirements. A similar response by an architect is usually called a "Functional Design Report".

A Design Transmittal, or Functional Design Report, is the technical equivalent of a Project Brief.

The design reviews are check points as detailed design and working drawings progress. The information available is examined for conformity with the design intent contained in the Design Transmittal and objectives of the component or system. The information is also used to reestimate the construction cost and compare it to the budgeted allowance.

In general, three design reviews and check estimates are recommended. These should be conducted when the design work is 30-35%, 60-70% and 100% complete respectively. The purpose is to verify technical content and standards and the current construction cost position. If the trend is excessive, redesign may be necessary to reduce total cost. Redesign can be done more easily in the earlier stages of the working drawings and at less additional cost.

The 100% review includes the complete set of bid documents. The corresponding pre-tender estimate is therefore equivalent to an "internal bid" directly comparable to contractors' submissions in response to the tender invitation. This estimate is essential for assessing the quality of the bids and helps in any negotiations. It is also useful in the administration of the contract.

The design reviews and check estimates should be conducted with the assistance of independent consultants as required.

17.3 Procurement Stage Control

Before release, or concurrent with the 100% review, the contract tender documents are normally sent to the owner for final approval. When they are released by the owner, they become the responsibility of the Procurement Division.

The responsibility of the Procurement Division is to secure firm contract commitments. Special attention is given to establishing competitive bidding, careful tender analysis and potential schedule impacts. Encouraging competitive bidding is an important aspect of procurement. This can be done by setting the size and content of contract packages in line with the construction industry's capability, particularly the local construction industry. Odd combinations of trades or unbalanced work content inevitably increase tender prices. Therefore, the procurement strategy must be carefully thought through at an early stage in the project planning, as discussed in Chapter 9.

Competitive bidding on do-able contract packages is one of the best ways to control costs.

Competitive bidding is an important element of cost control but a reasonable period must be allowed for the contractors to prepare their tenders. For contracts valued at under $100,000, the bidding period may be 2 to 3 weeks. Above this, the period should not be less than 4 weeks and for large contracts, not less than 6 weeks. Contractors require this longer time to notify and circulate contract documents to their subcontractors and for them in turn, to submit competitive subtrade bids.

During the tender period, contact should be maintained with the construction industry to ensure that all contractors have a proper understanding of the tender documents. This will help to secure reliable bids. The issue of addenda, other than for clarification in response to contractors' questions, should be carefully avoided.

To ensure that only reliable bids are obtained from qualified contractors, it may be necessary to prequalify contractors before tendering. This can be done by having contractors submit evidence of their bonding capacity, financial strength, staff availability, their experience and current work load. Tenders are then solicited only from those who are interested and capable of performing the work.

Bonding capacity is a good way to ascertain a contractor's financial viability.

Soon after tender closing, bids are analyzed and compared to the 100% check estimate, the budget allowance in current dollars, each other, and their respective schedules and completion dates. For long contract durations, it may be necessary to use discounted cash flow techniques to establish the least cost on a present worth basis. The flow diagram shown in Figure 17-1 shows a simplified sequence in maintaining cost and commitment control through the procurement process.

Prior to award of a large or long contract, a capital appropriation transfer may be necessary as described in Chapter 16, Section 16.5. This is done by submitting a Request for Transfer (RFT). Approval of the RFT triggers the transfer of funds from the unappropriated project budget accounts to the appropriated and commitment project fiscal accounts. The RFT will include a brief description of the work to be performed, the recommended contractor, its bid, and the amount provided for it in the unappropriated budget after the required escalation transfers. The request will also be accompanied by the tender analysis, list of other bidders and

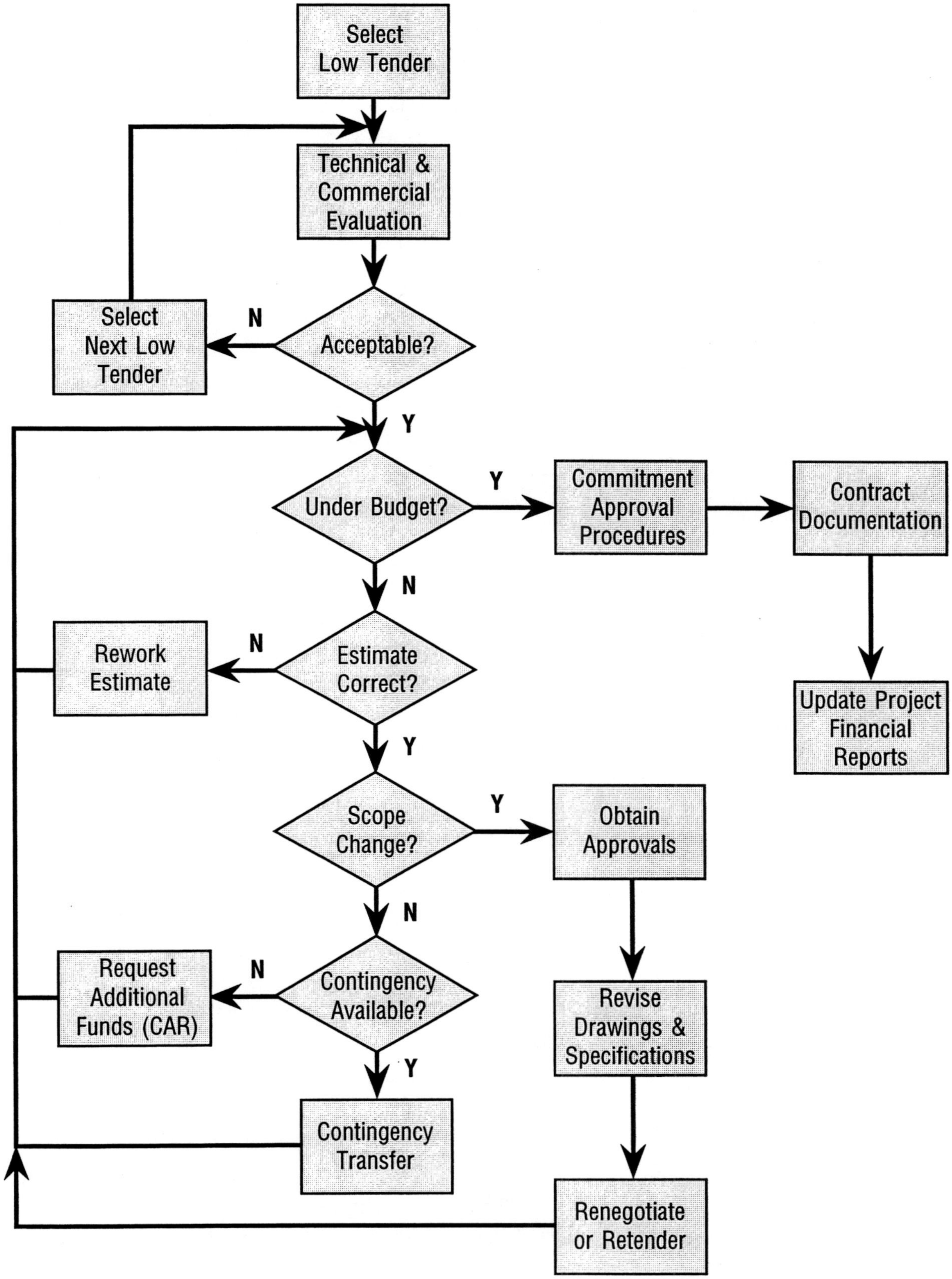

Figure 17-1. Cost and Commitment Control (Procurement Stage)

any necessary explanations of significant variations between the recommended bid and the 100% check estimate or the unappropriated budget.

The amount to be transferred will be based on the tender amount. Note that it may be necessary to add additional allowances to cover associated cost plus work such as testing and sampling normally associated with the type of contract.

Thus the RFT becomes a key financial and cost control instrument. Its approval authorizes a particular scope of work to be awarded to a specific contractor for a specific amount. It also confirms the various transfers from the unappropriated accounts to the commitment accounts.

Tender award dates make good visible milestone dates.

The tender issue and contract awards of the major contracts are very visible dates. They provide excellent key milestone dates in the Master Project Schedule. They are therefore recorded and reported accordingly, as they represent a good "fix" on the state of project progress.

17.4 Construction Stage Control

In terms of the total effort required on a construction project, the labor expended in the construction stages is by far the largest. Chapter 1 illustrated this point.

The effort required to exercise control in these stages is similarly and correspondingly greater. But by this time the form and content of the project have been largely crystallized, so the thrust of the control effort is on containing costs by emphasizing schedule adherence. However, inspection and testing to ensure quality adherence will also require considerable control effort.

As the project moves from design to construction, the focus of control moves from content to time

Before the contractor starts construction work on site, various paper work must be in place. Indeed, a contractor should not be permitted to commence any permanent work on the site until the signed contract agreement has been exchanged. This ensures that the owner of the site will be protected by the contract conditions on the one hand, and the contractor will get paid on the other. The flow diagram in Figure 17-2 shows a simplified sequence of paper work activity from award of contract to the start of work. In particular, it shows who is responsible for initiating the activity, i.e. the owner, project team, or contractor.

A lot of paperwork is necessary before work can start.

As part of construction initiation, the contractor will be required to submit his detailed schedule for doing the work. This schedule should show the expected rate of progress and, if satisfactory, should be approved as soon as possible. Regular, prompt and accurate reporting of progress compared to this approved construction schedule is then essential so that the completion of critical activities can be accurately forecast. Similar to Figure 17-2, the flow diagram in Figure 17-3 shows a simplified sequence in approving and maintaining schedule control.

The status of construction progress should be reviewed and agreed by both the contractors and members of the project team at regular monthly

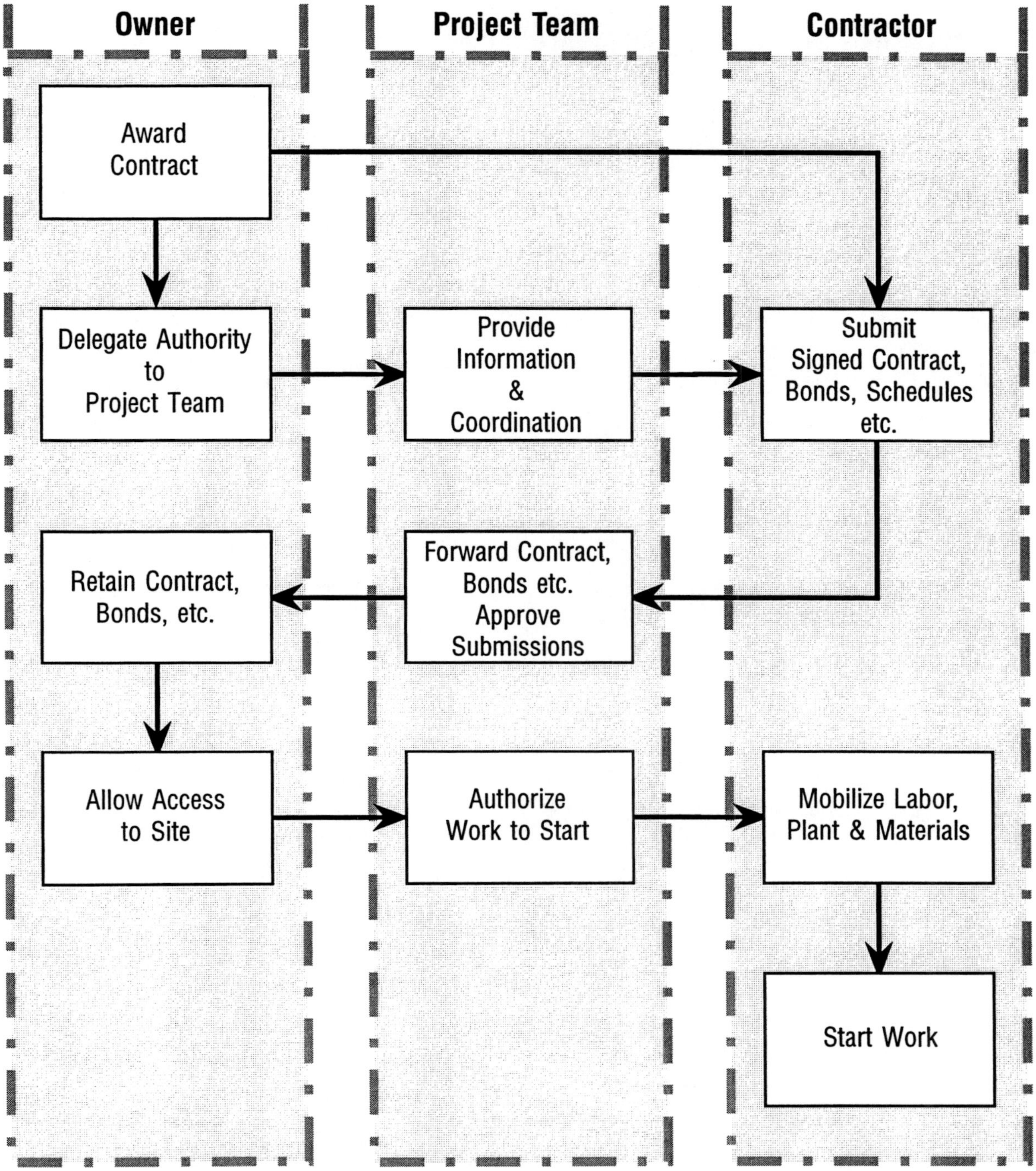

Figure 17-2. Contract Administration: Construction Initiation

intervals. This will enable contractors to prepare their progress invoices for work done on a firm basis. This not only speeds approval and processing, but helps the contractor to make a better assessment of his progress and financial position. The flow diagram in Figure 7-4 shows the sequence and respective responsibilities in processing progress invoices and consequent payments.

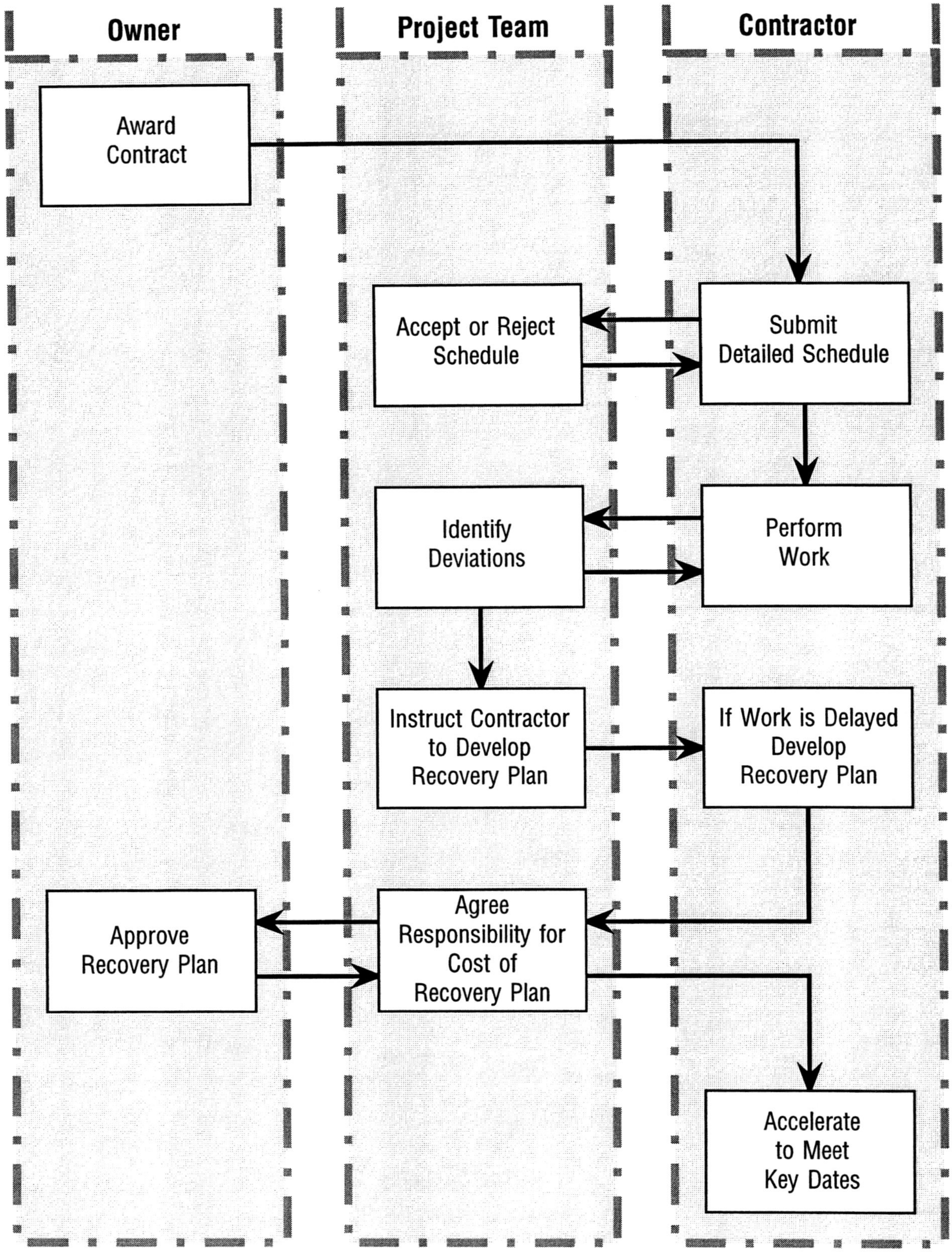

Figure 17-3. Contract Administration: Maintaining the Schedule

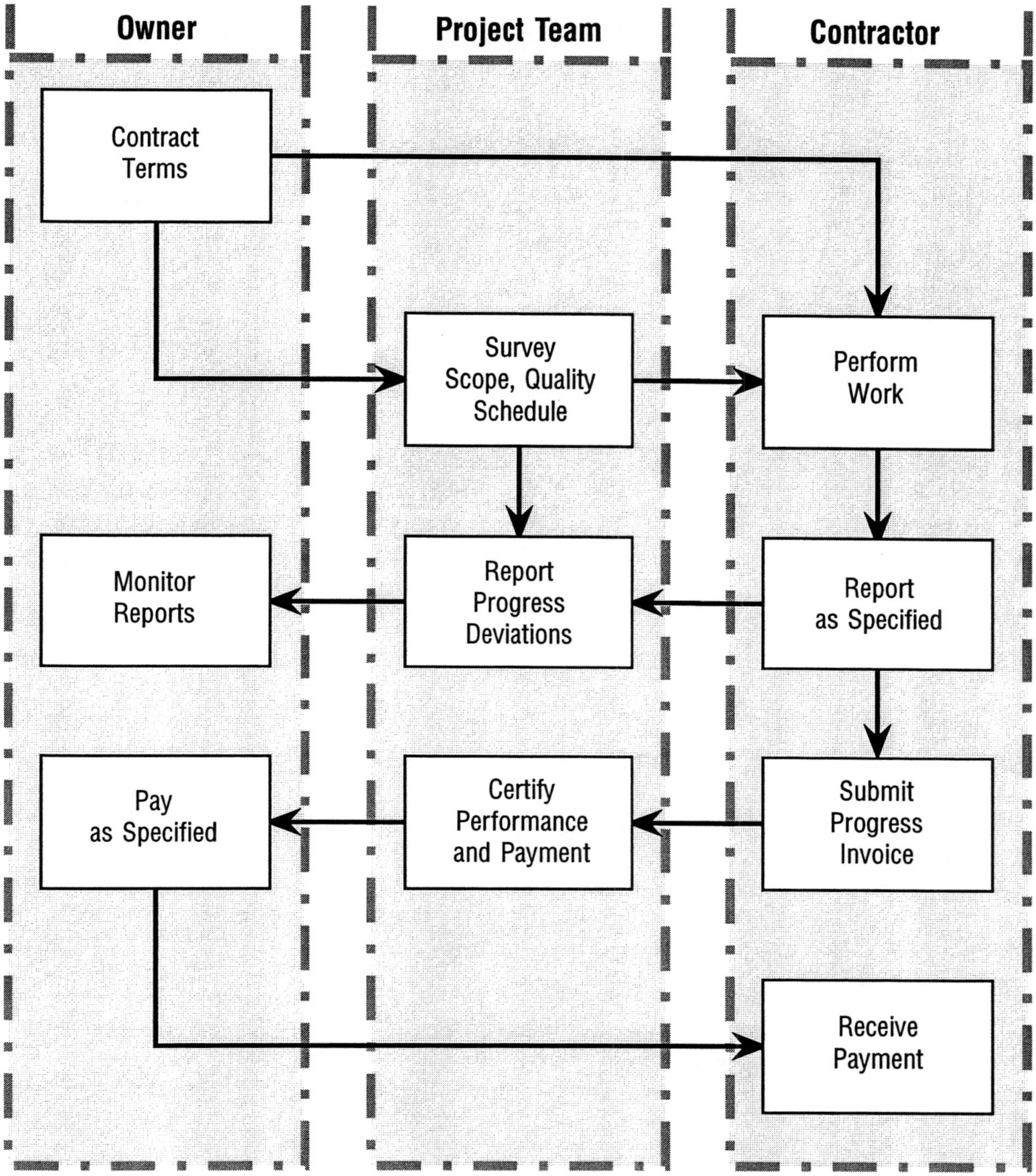

Figure 17-4. Contract Administration: Progress Invoicing and Payment

Contract status and progress forecasts should be reviewed and confirmed with the contractor at frequent site meetings held at regular intervals for this purpose. Where slippage is critical and clearly the responsibility of the contractor, the contractor should be required to describe his plan for recovery and, if satisfactory, should be instructed to carry it out.

Changes in the work during a firm-price contract are particular sources of aggravation and potential contractor claims. This is because the delay following reorganizing the labor, materials and equipment frequently results in the work not being done in the right sequence, by the right people, in the right detail and at the right cost. Therefore, every effort should be

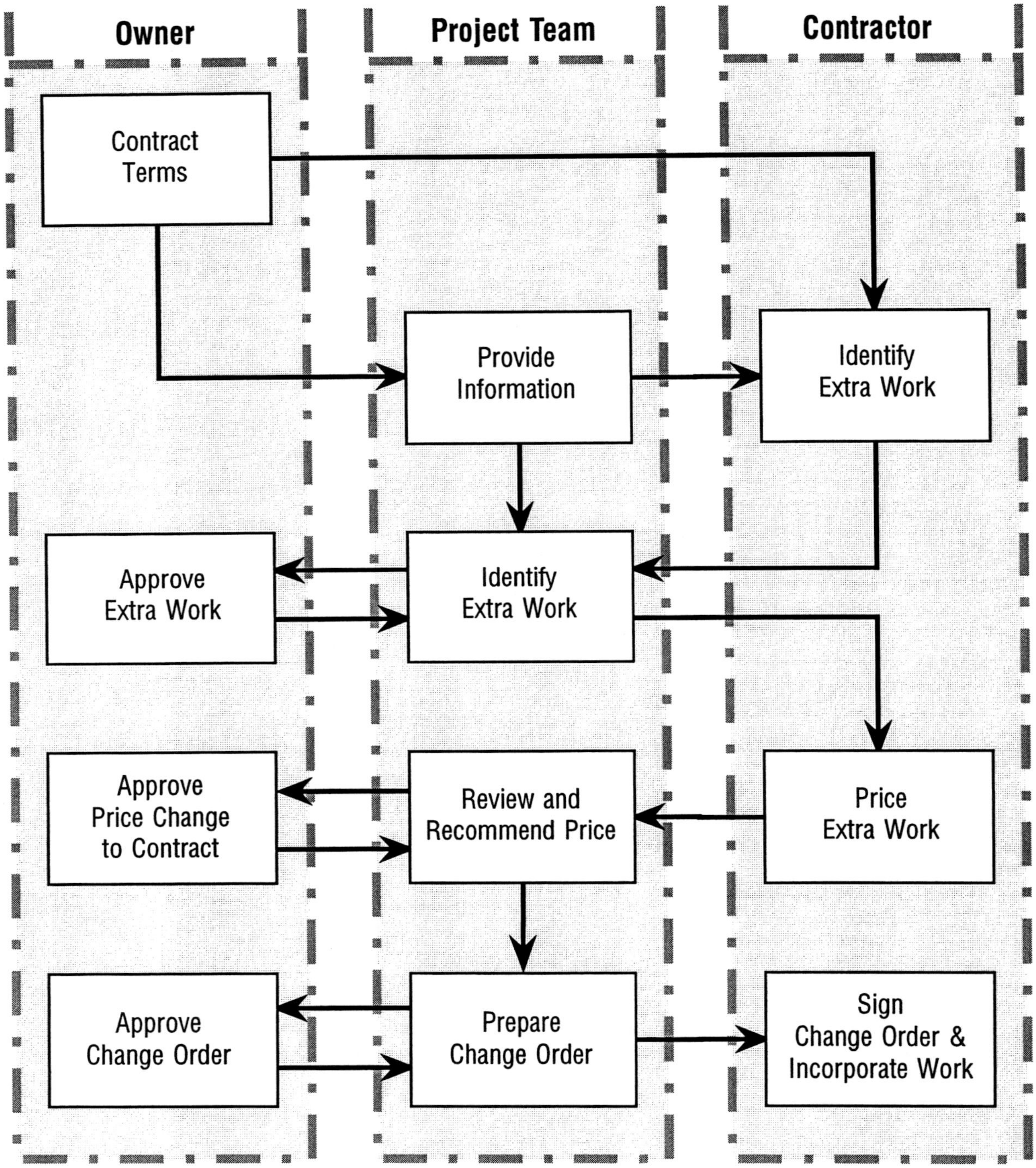

Figure 17-5. Contract Administration: Processing Scope Changes

made to avoid changes by good, timely planning and design. Where a change is unavoidable, its impact should be carefully assessed against the contractor's schedule. Either proper schedule allowance must be made for the impact of the change, or costs for acceleration approved as part of the cost of the change. The flow diagram in Figure 17-5 shows the sequence in processing contract changes.

Constructing buildings seem particularly prone to changes — which are very disruptive.

Building construction projects seem particularly prone to large numbers of changes. Complex analysis is often necessary to assess the collective effect on the schedule, since the effects are not necessarily cumulative. Large numbers of changes can be highly disruptive. They have a demoralizing effect on the work force as the flow of work is interrupted and productivity sags further while awaiting deliveries of unscheduled materials. Probably more contractor claims and settlements for extra contract payments arise from this cause than any other.

For discussions of construction risks, and methods for handling changes and contractors' claims, see Chapters 8 and 13 respectively.

17.5 Project Control Reports: General Descriptions

Good progress reports answer the following questions:

- What is the plan or target?
- What is the current status?
- What end results are now projected?
- What is the thrust of activities in the immediate future?
- What is the explanation or justification?

Chapter 12 details key project control reports from the PCMS, most of which apply to any size of project. Chapter 16, Section 16.5 detailed an additional capital expenditure control step suitable for large long duration projects. This results in certain additional key reports. The following are a typical set of reports and their respective contents on a large project.

Project Summary Report — provides in one or two pages a consolidated presentation of actual progress performance compared to plan for all key areas. Essentially, it covers management and supervision, design, unappropriated and appropriated funds, total cost-to-date, escalation, contingency, IDC, forecast final cost (in current and future values) and work force status. This report is best presented in a series of "thumb nail" but legible trend charts.

Management Information Reports — provide financial information such as balance sheet, operating statement and similar data as required by shareholders, tax and regulatory authorities.

Cash Flow and Commitment Reports — forecast the funds required to meet expenditures through the up-coming STP period. For senior management the reports give the source and application of funds and show the current progress of expenditure against appropriations. Future STP period projections are summarized into the long-term project financial plan. On very large projects, where large sums of money are involved during construction, it will be necessary to prepare forecasts of weekly or even daily cash requirements, to improve IDC performance.

Master Schedule and STP Progress Reports — are issued at regular intervals with updated progress-to-date and planned progress. The STP reports are segregated by Responsibility Center and provide the information described in Section 17.1. Exceptions to the Master Schedule are highlighted as are also the activities interfacing between design, procurement and construction.

Unawarded Work Reports — are used during the design stage to confirm the need for design check estimates. This is part of the process for arriving at the estimated total cost at completion.

Awarded Work Reports — follow those described in detail in Chapter 12. As suggested in Section 17.7, rigorous reestimates of outstanding work are carried out in each STP period to update the estimated cost at completion.

Escalation Report — As recommended in Chapter 8, Section 8.5, on long duration projects regular transfers are made from the escalation account to all unappropriated accounts. This is done according to the amounts remaining in those accounts and the actual inflation experience. Therefore the Escalation Report shows the current period transfer and cumulative transfers to date. It also shows past escalation trends and latest projection of future trends against those assumed in the original project plan. These values are used to update the impact on future expenditures and therefore the estimated future draw down on the escalation budget. Comparison of the amount remaining and the projected draw gives a measure of the quality of the original escalation forecasts.

Contingency Report — records approved transfers to appropriated accounts. If a contract work package is projecting with some certainty a final surplus in its appropriated budget item, the difference is credited back to the contingency account. The report therefore reflects variances in the project's appropriated accounts. The report may also provide information on provisional contingency commitments. This may result from the design check estimates noted in the Unawarded Work Reports, or from policy changes not yet reflected in the design check estimates. Always be careful to ensure that there is no duplication of allowances carried into the project's estimated final cost at completion.

Variance Analysis — All significant variances whether originating with management, in design, procurement or construction, are analyzed and recorded as part of the final project record. They are usually generated on request by the responsibility center concerned and presented in a standard format.

17.6 Project Control Reports: Distribution

The hierarchical design of the WBS and corresponding Master Code Structure described in Chapter 11 enables reports to be issued in detail or in summary. This helps to ensure that the reports suit the different levels of management in the organization. In addition, the different levels of the organization will likely be interested in different selections of the reports available. The style and structure of the organization will determine the correct distribution of appropriate information to the various managers. The distribution of information can also be a touchy issue.

Designing information reports for different levels of management can be a touchy issue.

Striking a balance between too little and too much, what a manager would like to know compared to what he needs to know (based on responsibility) can be a matter of delicate judgment. Three main levels of cost and schedule reporting are recommended Each should be structured as closely as possible to serve that management level. Each report must be carefully constructed to support management control over the responsibility area concerned.

Top Management should receive general cost, progress, and appropriation status reports at a summary level. The breakdown on these reports is limited to the responsibility center level only. They therefore highlight the status of the project generally but also flag significant exceptions or trends contrary to the plan. These reports also include the status of the escalation and contingency accounts. An STP report, although more detailed in terms of immediate activities, is similarly summarized.

Middle Management, that is to say Division Managers in charge of responsibility centers, should receive Division Managers' Reports. These provide data down to the contract work package level. STP information should include packages completed in the previous STP, those to be awarded in the next STP, and all current STP activities.

The information contained in these reports and their distribution is segregated according to responsibility center. Collectively, the reports provide backup information to the Top Management summary level reports. Top Management may also use them, but only on request.

At the third level, Supervisors and Coordinators should receive "Detailed Reports" that cover individual pay items in the larger contracts, major purchase orders and corresponding schedule activity. As well as cost figures, these reports include units of measurement and/or percentage completion as indications of progress. The design work packages are usually reported in man hours. Like the Division Managers' reports, these reports are segregated according to Supervisors' responsibility areas. Like the middle level reports, this third level can provide supporting back up information to middle managers but again only on request.

A separate report that may be generated at this level provides information on contractors' claims for extra payment. Such reports cover the period from the time claims are first formally noted to the time they are settled, paid for, and recorded in the PCMS. Obviously, the Division Manager concerned and Top Management only should hold these reports in strict confidence.

Claim status reports should be separate and confidential to upper management.

During periods of intensive or changing activity in any area of the project, it may be necessary to plan and report on a weekly or two-weekly basis. This would be dealt with as necessary entirely locally.

The field inspection reports are also handled locally. In terms of control, field reports provide information on:

- Progress of major or critical activities preferably in a uniform diagrammatic format
- Progress status of the major contracts and purchase orders
- Estimated site population
- Delays and their causes
- Early warning of possible difficulties ahead
- Progress photographs. Personal photography is quite adequate providing prints are always titled and dated. The Public Relations Division should take care of professional photography.

Field reports must be reviewed by Supervisors for action as necessary and retained as a matter of historic record.

17.7 Policies and Procedures

Written policies and procedures form an essential part of project control. They ensure uniformity of approach throughout the project organization, and consistency of application in spite of staff changes over the life of the project. While policies generally flow from top management, the managers responsible prepare the procedural sections. Procedures can become very controversial as various responsibility centers identify their respective interfaces and seek "to protect their territory".

Policies and procedures are necessary for consistent control — but they, too, can be a touchy issue.

Unfortunately, even minor changes in organizational structure, responsibilities, company or position titles, frequently have ramifications throughout large sections of the written material. This is an unfortunate but necessary part of good housekeeping. If this house keeping is not carefully maintained, discipline may become somewhat sloppy. In any case, flow charts and diagrams often provide a much better substitute for these wordy descriptions.

In designing policies and procedures, it should always be born in mind that stating good general objectives and firm policies are much more important than detailing the procedures and guidelines that follow. Interestingly, many manuals seem to overlook the need for a clear statement of policy before embarking upon the procedural details.

Clear statements of policy are essential prerequisites to procedural details that follow.

A good standard policy-and-procedure outline should include the following headings:

- Objectives
- Policy
- Definitions
- Approach (i.e. methodology, if required)
- Related forms
- Related procedures
- Flow diagram
- Procedure details
- Responsibility (for performance)
- Supporting contractual references

For purposes of project control, the following functional areas require appropriate policies and procedures:

- Management information
- Finance, accounting
- Project accounting
- Administration
- Planning, scheduling, estimating and costing
- Engineering
- Procurement
- Construction
- Insurance
- Personnel

CHAPTER 18

Looking Beyond Project Controls

18.1 Introduction

In the last analysis, the test of project management's success is the degree to which the project objectives have been reached on time and within budget to the satisfaction of the customers and/or users. Note particularly the reference to "customer satisfaction"! The "customers" are all the stakeholders involved in the project, together with the constituents who are in any way affected by its outcome. "Satisfaction", an elusive notion at best, is the perception of these people and how they feel about the project when it is operational. In turn, this perception is likely to be strongly influenced by the prevailing "environment".

In the last analysis, it is the "customer satisfaction" that counts.

The term "stakeholder" is used here to refer to all those who have a "stake" in the project or who otherwise participate in it directly. "Constituents" are those who are affected by it indirectly or even remotely. Collectively their attitudes, understandings or particular vested interests all contribute to the project's "environment". This environment can and needs to be "managed" just as surely as every other aspect of the project can be managed towards success.

What does this mean for the project manager in practical terms? Meeting a construction project's constraints of scope, quality, time and cost are undoubtedly critical factors. Yet, if the real objective is to finish with a successful project, then important though these criteria are, they are not the ultimate determinants of success. To some, this may sound like heresy, but with today's increasing concern for the physical and cultural environments, those who ignore this environment do so at their peril.

Stakeholders are those who participate in the project directly. Constituents are those who are affected by the project. These are the people whose expectations and concerns have to be reckoned with.

The combined degree of satisfaction of all the participants, customers or stakeholders will be a measure of project success. Construction project stakeholders are typically many and various, often with opposing interests. Indeed, the cynic might say that the most successful project is one in which all the stakeholders are about equally dissatisfied!

For simplicity, the project environment may be thought of as having two components. Working outwards from the center, the first is the internal project culture and its immediately surrounding corporate culture. The second is the external social, economic and physical surroundings.

18.2 Inside the Project

(a) The internal project culture[1]

A positive project climate makes for better project performance.

The culture that develops within a project is often a reflection of the project's leadership style and organizational structure. This can vary considerably according to the size and nature of the project. Therefore, the project manager should recognize the need to spend some positive effort in influencing this culture for the benefit of those working on the project. It means creating a project management environment in which every decision and action is designed to make individual experience better than it would have been had the project not been launched. It requires a focus on the quality of this experience and not just an overriding preoccupation with computer printouts and weekly progress reports.

It is clear where the process must begin. It is only through good team relationships that good project management practices can flourish. By attending to what the team members need to perform their respective contributions, the project manager can establish effective relationships with each participant. This positive environment seldom goes unnoticed. In time, it will be passed on beyond the project's boundaries.

(b) Effective internal strategies[2]

The organization's Executive must play its part.

Projects fail for many internal reasons, some of them technical, some of them managerial. Yet even the technical failures can often be traced back to a communication failure within the project team when a positive environment is lacking. As a matter of project experience, several prerequisites have been identified with successful projects. While these prerequisites do not necessarily guarantee success for future projects, their absence may well lead to sub-optimal success, if not outright failure. Thus, the Executive responsible for the project has a vital role to play and should insist on the following:

Senior Management Support — Senior management must clearly show support for the project management idea by active sponsorship and control.

External Authority — The project manager must be seen as the authoritative agent in dealing with all parties, and be the responsible and single formal contact with them.

Internal Authority — The project manager must have the necessary managerial authority within the project organization to ensure response and cooperation.

Commitment Authority — The project manager must have the responsibility and authority to control the commitment of resources, including funds, within prescribed limits. The results of these decisions must be both accountable and visible.

Project Manager Involved in All Major Decisions — No major technical, cost, schedule, or performance decisions should be made without the project manager's participation.

Competence — The project manager and his team members must be competent. Other functional personnel assigned to the project must also be competent.

Project Team — The project manager should have a say in the assembly of the project team. This helps considerably in obtaining their personal commitment, support and required quality of service.

Management Information Systems — Effective project management information and control systems must be in place.

18.3 Outside the Project

Turn upsets into opportunities.

On some projects, adverse external events come as a surprise to the project manager or the team and these surprises are treated as obstacles to progress instead of possible opportunities. Because projects generally only exists due to external circumstances, the project team should recognize that they must be responsive to the external environment.

(a) A positive approach

Short and long term impacts are important.

Today, there is a growing awareness and concern for the impact of infrastructure and facility construction on the physical environment. Fortunately, today's design disciplines are well aware of the need to mitigate adverse affects. Equally, the project manager must be similarly concerned about the project's technology, and manage the project accordingly. This applies to both the implementation and shorter term practical construction impacts of the project as well as it's long term operating impacts.

It is essential that external events do not obstruct progress by coming as a surprise to the project team. The project team must be attuned to, sympathetic and comfortable with the cultural, organizational and social environments of the project. This means working with many different people to get the best results. Most modern construction projects are highly technical and complex so that this added dimension of project management is very demanding.

This suggests the possibility of influencing the project environment in a positive way, for the better reception of the change that the project will introduce. For example, peoples' typical resistance to change will no doubt be evident amongst some stakeholders. Others may have vested interests or personal or group agendas that are only indirectly related to the project. This requires identifying the project's stakeholders and constituents and their ability to affect its successful outcome. If these can be determined in good time, they can be faced proactively. This way risks that are likely to undermine the success of the project can be identified and significantly reduced.

Positive influence helps people overcome resistance to change.

Failure to take such a positive approach will inevitably lead to a less than optimum project outcome.

(b) The nature of the external environment[3]

What is the nature of this larger environment? Clearly, it includes the project's customers, users, competitors, supporters and detractors who are all its stakeholders and constituents. It also includes the project's geographic, climatic, social, economic and political settings, as well as the latest technology that it incorporates and the resulting environmental impacts. In short, it includes almost everything that can impact the success of the project.

The external stakeholders and constituents are obviously more difficult to identify than those internally. Many people may be involved, especially now that there is a growing awareness and concern for the affects of projects on the physical environment. This is particularly true of commercial, industrial and infra-structure projects. The problem is that people are understandably resistant to change because the known is always more comfortable than the unknown.

External stakeholders and constituents are more difficult to identify — but the effort is worth it.

For example, when an area has remained stable for a significant period, individuals develop all sorts of habits and impressions with which they are comfortable. Change threatens to destroy this comfort base, forcing them to start over, so that they have a self interest in blocking the change. A perception that there will inevitably be winners and losers, and an initial lack of understanding of the project all too often represents a serious obstacle to progress. Any of the actors or factors shown can affect the planning, organizing, staffing and directing of the project, which are the project manager's main responsibilities.

This external environment represents a complex set of interdependent relationships that constantly react with the project as it becomes reality. Even more important, the factors listed have a habit of changing during the life of the project, especially if the project takes many years to complete and comes on stream in successive phases. Because of its external environment, this translates into a high degree of uncertainty and risk surrounding the project. The greater the degree of interdependence, the greater the degree of uncertainty and the greater the challenge for the project manager and project team to manage them wisely. It also shows how important it is to make due allowance in the project's budget.

(c) Not the same for every project

The environment is affected by every project — it is therefore different for every project.

The external environment is different for every project. It is likely to be determined by four primary considerations:

- The product or service provided by the facility when in operation
- The technology and the manner of its application
- The location of the facility, and
- The political and cultural attitudes of the local people at the time of construction.

Potential difficulties in these areas and their probability of occurrence should be identified and attempts made to solve them in advance. This can be done if the project team learns to interact with those institution and interest group representatives and influential individuals who make up the project's constituents. To do this effectively, it is essential to develop a sound strategy.

If the project is particularly large and politically vulnerable, it may be desirable to conduct a constituency analysis at an early stage of planning. Such an analysis would be designed to identify all those constituents who might have an impact on the project, their potential concerns and their relative ability to influence the course of events. This would be followed by developing promotional material and project alternatives designed either to assuage or to mitigate these concerns.

(d) Effective external strategies[4]

The "right attitude" serves well both the internal as well as the external environment.

Developing the right attitude is the way to have a positive influence on a project's internal culture. Similarly, the right attitude is essential for developing a sound external stakeholder environment. Perhaps this attitude is best reflected by adopting a mind set that reverses the traditional organization pyramid. That is, place the project stakeholders at the top of the chart followed by the front-line project supervisors and on down to the project manager at the bottom. This graphic inversion helps the project team to visualize their role as a truly service organization designed to serve the best interests of a successful project outcome, both perceived and real.

Suggested steps in this process include:

1. Learn how to understand the role of the various stakeholders.
2. Learn how this information can be used in developing the project scope definition and therefore improve both the perception and reception of the project.
3. Identify the real nature of each stakeholder group's business and their consequent interest in the project
4. Understand the stakeholders' and constituents' behavior and motivation
5. Assess how they may react to various approaches
6. Pinpoint the characteristics of their own environments and design responses that develop a good relationship
7. Learn project management's role in responding to the stakeholders drive behind the project
8. Find the key areas that will have the most impact on the successful reception of the project.
9. Develop a Project Public Relations Plan aimed at dealing with the issues identified

Watch out for the "fatal flaw" — though minor, it could bring the project to a standstill.

Always remember that even a minor stakeholder group may discover that "fatal flaw" in the project's concept that could bring the project to a standstill! Failure to deal with these issues will inevitably lead to a less than optimum project outcome.

(e) Identifying the stakeholders' groupings and categories[5]

One technique for dealing effectively with the project's external environment is to rank the required stakeholder linkages by conducting a stakeholder analysis. Such an analysis would be designed first to identify all the potential stakeholders who might have an impact on the project, and then to find their relative ability to influence it.

A "political" project may require a "stakeholder analysis".

Project stakeholders and constituents may be recognized in any of the following groupings:

- Those who are directly related to the project by having a stake in its process such as suppliers of inputs, consumers of outputs, and those involved in the project process itself
- Those who have influence over the physical, infra-structural, technological, commercial/financial/ socioeconomic, or political/legal conditions
- Those who have a hierarchical relationship to the project such as government authorities at local, regional and national levels, and
- Those individuals, groups and associations, who have vested interests, sometimes unrelated to the project, but who see it as an oppor-

tunity to pursue their own ends.

Having identified the various stakeholders and constituents, each may be assigned to a category according to their relative ability to influence the project. Three categories are suggested:

1. Those whose requirements can be moderated or constrained
2. Those whose requirements can be influenced, and
3. Those who need to be appreciated

If concerns are intense, the project may require a Public Relations officer.

Within each category, each may then be further rated by order of importance in influencing the project. Members of the project team can then set their priorities accordingly to maintain stakeholder information linkages that create the best conditions for project success. If the project is large enough, or the stakeholder linkages are sufficiently intense, these efforts may be assigned to a "Public Relations" group within the project team.

18.4 Introducing Project Public Relations

Good honest information works wonders.

Traditional management has long since recognized the classic input-process-output model with its management information feedback loop for controlling output as shown in Figure 18-1. Dynamic managers also recognize that opening communication channels in both directions, such that modified management strategies result, can be a powerful force. The key is quality information. Whether this is presented in verbal, written or graphical form, improvement in performance can be quite remarkable. Indeed, most "knowledge" workers demand this type of feedback and the Japanese have built their industrial reputation on the "quality circle" that uses this principle.

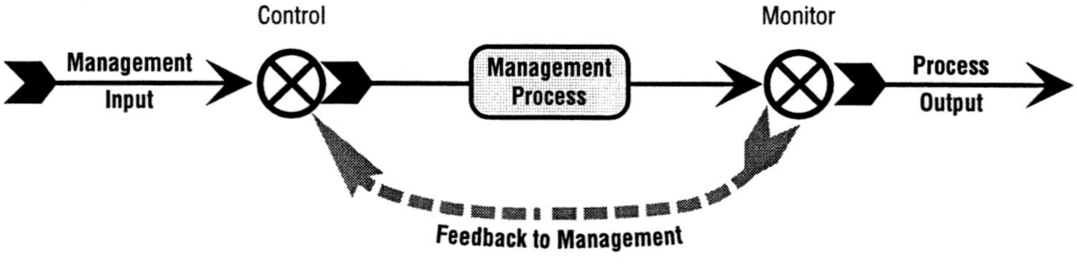

Figure 18-1. Managing the Environment: Traditional Management Feedback

The same principle is true in project work though regretfully less evident on construction projects. On a major project, especially if it is publicly funded, a Public Relations general information function is normal. This more proactive stance, or positive feed forward, is usually known as Project Public Relations (PPR) and becomes a vital part of control on a complex project. Often, this takes the form of a general information and progress center. This center should exhibit pictures, diagrams and models of the planned facility. It should also show up-to-date charts of general progress information that will be of genuine interest to the work force and the public at large.

To a surprising extent, the project team's ability to exercise this positive feed forward will help them control the project in terms of final cost, schedule and satisfaction. Figure 18-2 shows the idea of this public relations feed forward. A favorable perception means successful reception!

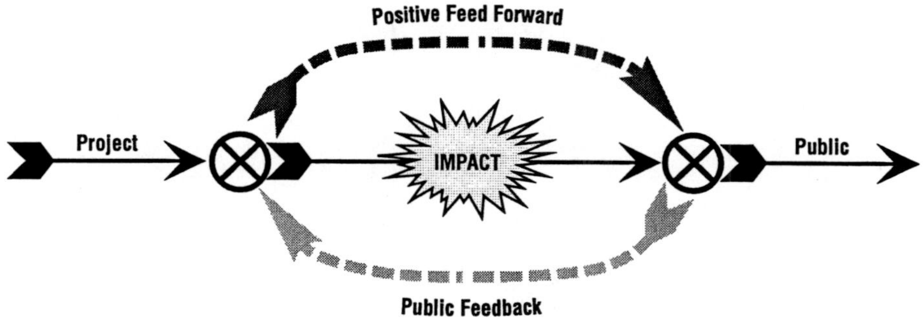

Figure 18-2. Managing the Environment: Public Relations Concept

(a) The Project Public Relations Plan[6]

Conduct a PPR Plan like a project.

Good public relations requires a strong identity and a planned program with clear goals. It commences with appointing someone to be responsible who is outgoing and positive, yet able and willing to listen. He or she must be able to prepare carefully constructed text and presentations, and to work through a program thoroughly and systematically. The PPR function should be conducted to the same standards as the rest of the project process.

The following eight steps are recommended for developing a PPR plan.

1. Know the project organization and its objectives thoroughly
2. Find out who the interested publics will be and the characteristics of each
3. Establish the relative importance of each to the project and, in particular, identify the "high risk" areas
4. Assess the current reputation of the sponsoring organization as perceived by each interest group
5. Decide appropriate action in each case
6. Develop strategy, resource requirements, priorities and schedule that are in sympathy with the project itself
7. Implement the PR program
8. Continuously monitor the effectiveness of the program during its execution, and adjust as necessary for optimum results

(b) Ensuring the effectiveness of the PPR Plan

What are the hallmarks of successful PR? Here is a top ten check list:

- Honesty and sincerity about the purpose and benefits of the project are plainly evident
- Participation in those decisions that have some degree of flexibility, or are viable alternatives, which could result in enhanced project value
- Stakeholder-friendly information facilities available both during the project and after completion
- Care and concern genuinely expressed for the project stakeholders' interests
- Information requirements anticipated and provided ahead of time
- Timely (rapid) response provided to information requests
- Enthusiasm and genuinely sincere appreciation expressed in response to inquirers
- Flexible personal responses provided, where special issues dictate
- Project team members empowered to make decisions to solve urgent and obvious local problems
- Recovery from inevitable lapses of existing services during construction activities, in ways that impress

(c) Consultants in Constructive Citizen Participation[7]

Dire are the consequences of poor or inadequate information. Just listening is a great palliative.

In the last few decades the public's values, goals and assumptions have changed considerably. With emerging concerns for the environment, this trend is likely to accelerate. So project sponsors and administrators are finding themselves spending more and more of their time and resources simply reacting to conflict and crisis, much of it coming from the community around them. The result has been project postponements and schedule delays.

Many project delays, postponements and cancellations might have been avoided had a more trustworthy project environment been created. Mistrust stems from uncertainty, poor communication, inadequate information exchange, basic philosophical differences, and general lack of credibility. Mistrust leads to confrontation, polarized positions, inflexibility, and entrenched adversarial roles. For resolution, each party needs to understand, if not entirely accept, the legitimate and differing interests, roles and expectations of the other.

Very often, the issue in the public's mind is not so much how to stop the project altogether, but how to have their concerns integrated into its strategic planning. Unfortunately, once conflict has developed, special dedication and skill are required in its resolution. Constructive participation of the local citizenry and other project constituents from the outset can help to avoid this situation.

This has now become a field of consulting expertise. Such consultants have developed various techniques for working constructively on stakeholder conflict, or they specialize in acting as independent mediators through communication, education, analysis and soliciting other courses of action. Any such approach that smoothes the path of a major project and avoids costly delays makes an inestimable contribution to pro-active cost control.

18.5 Linkages, Part of the Project Manager's Job

Successful project management is more than just cost and schedule — it runs the whole gamut of human relations.

Clearly, the project manager's job is no longer confined to controlling events within the project organization. It is no longer sufficient to think of project management as simply the monitoring of time and cost by planning, scheduling and resource leveling, as many software programs might have us believe. Nor even is it sufficient to include the many other organizational tasks of the project manager, as leader of the project team.

Vitally important as these things are, these are not sufficient for effective and successful project management in today's dynamic world. What is equally important - often more so to finish with a successful project - is the need to communicate through linkages to the external environment. This is especially true of infra-structure projects that place emphasis on development and innovation and must respond to increasingly rapid change.

The reason is simple. Every construction project exists for a purpose relating to, and within, its surrounding environment. Therefore, its creation and implementation must be responsive to its environment by maximizing the benefits, as far as possible, to all the stakeholders, and minimizing the adverse impacts by deliberate mitigation. Clearly, how the project is structured and how the project manager works within the total project environment can make all the difference between failure and success.

References

[1] Wideman, R. M. 1990. Managing the Project Environment. Dimensions of Project Management, Springer-Verlag, New York. p55-57.

[2] Ibid. p59

[3] Wideman, R. M. 1991. Total Project Management of Complex Projects: Improving Performance with Modern Techniques, International Seminar on Project Management for Developing Countries. Oxford & IBH Publishing Co. Pvt. Ltd., New Delhi, India. p112.

[4] Wideman, R. M. 1990. Managing the Project Environment. Dimensions of Project Management, Springer-Verlag, New York. p61.

[5] Youker, R. 1987. Analyzing the Project Environment, 13th Asian Development Bank Seminar MS, Manilla, Philippines.

[6] Wideman, R. M. 1985. Good Public Relations, an Essential Part of Successful Project Management, Seminar/Symposium Proceedings, Project Management Institute, Upper Darby, PA. Track 1, pp1-16

[7] Connor, D. M. 1989. Promotional Literature, Connor Development Services, Victoria, B.C.

Postscript

One more time: Plan your work — Work your Plan!

Throughout this book the emphasis has been on management strategies that enable effective and proper project control. But control is only possible by preparing a carefully thought-through plan, exposing it for criticism and comment, pursuing its execution with commitment and vigor, tracking performance and then making any necessary adjustments. Just as this process provides a powerful tool for management, it also provides powerful motivation for improved performance by all those directly involved. This is because working as a team towards a project's goals can provide great experience, involvement, achievement, recognition and satisfaction.

A somewhat similar strategy is necessary and effective in dealing with other stakeholders and constituents in the environment into which the project is being launched. This is especially true if the project is being publicly funded. In today's world of concern for the physical and cultural environment, such a process is essential. These days, the word "control" with its dictatorial overtones may be too strong. Perhaps "chaperoning" the project through the process is a more apt description.

But what kind of person is the project manager that can do all this? That is a tough question because successful leadership styles vary considerably. It is also vitally important because choosing the right project manager can make or break the success of the project. Still, it is not difficult to draw up a list of some of the things to look for, such as:

The ideal paragon of virtue!

- Articulate
- Bold
- Creative
- Decisive
- Energetic
- Flexible
- Genuine
- Humane
- Imaginative
- Jack-of-all-trades
- Keen
- Logical
- Methodical
- Negotiation capable

Still more virtues.

- Objective-driven
- Persuasive
- Quick
- Receptive
- Steadfast
- Tolerant
- Upright
- Visionary
- Warm

Having selected the right person, what are the project manager's own deliverables? Here are some of the things that you should expect:

The Project Manager's personal products.

- Project Terms of Reference
- Descriptions of scope deliverables
- Quality definition
- Project planning assumptions
- Project cost estimating assumptions
- Procurement strategy
- Work Breakdown Structure
- Milestone plan and network bar chart
- Budget breakdown
- Summary of potential risks
- Project organization chart
- Responsibility chart
- Task definitions
- Progress reporting standards
- Project control standards
- Problem resolution mechanisms
- Change control standards
- Other policies and procedures
- Progress reports
- Short Term Plans
- Mid-term project brief
- Post project summary report

So once it is all over, it is reasonable to ask: "Did we get what we paid for?" And "Is it what we wanted?" Indeed, the test of project management's effectiveness is how well project objectives have been met:

Assessing the results.

- In producing the required deliverables
- To the required quality and performance
- On time
- Within budget, and
- To the satisfaction of the "customers"

The final step for the project team is to assemble, summarize and archive the project records while still fresh in people's minds. This measure provides vital background information that will be needed during the operation of the facility and should not be overlooked. It will also provide useful information for future projects. The project's archive should include answers to the following issues:

Finally, the project record.

- What was the project all about, exactly what was delivered?
- How satisfactory were the deliverables?
- How long did the project take?

- How much did it cost?
- Who did the work?
- What were their strengths and weaknesses?
- What were the pitfalls?
- What changes were made after the original Project Brief?
- What recommendations can be made for next time?

Communication is the name of the game!

APPENDIX A

PCMS Computer Check List

A Project Cost Management System is required to handle cost and schedule planning, reporting, forecasting and control of most aspects of a capital project. The following is a conceptual definition check list for a comprehensive system. It is intended to be used either for developing a particular project need, or for comparing the capability and suitability of available systems.

A. Hardware

- Networked computer based.
- High speed computer response.
- Handles communications between sites fast and efficiently.
- Distributed information storage at sites accessible from other sites (subject to access privileges)
- Requires minimal operator support, apart from ensuring that hardware receives normal regular maintenance.

B. Software

B.1 General Requirements

- Can support single or multi projects.
- Meets cost and schedule management requirements through all stages of a project, from concept through to commissioning.
- Meets requirements of multiple functional users, e.g. project, engineering, construction and finance.
- Multi information requirements fully integrated.
- Cost and schedule components can be uncoupled and run separately if input information is not compatible, or not available.
- Accepts data entry by users on a real time basis, as data becomes available.
- Security of entry protects data and ensures access appropriate only to functional responsibility of particular user.
- Automatically collects statistics on user access and extent of computer operation.

- Can produce hardcopy reports corresponding to different levels of detail in a hierarchical project breakdown (cost coding) structure.
- Can report all data at the lowest data-available level, even though that data is not broken down to the lowest level existing in the system.
- Can suppress all levels of subtotals that simply repeat the line above.
- Can suppress all lines containing zero information.

B.2 Cost Modeling from Historical Records

System can produce:

- Standard model profile: Where typical projects are repeated, system should provide a standard Project Breakdown Structure with typical capitalization, commitment, and schedule profiles, as an aid to project planning.
- Model variation: Has ability to modify model data base to input various scenarios, and what-if analyses such as variations in contracting and scheduling strategies, escalation and IDC.
- Historical Records: Transfers key project data covering cost and schedule results to system archives. Also retrieves same in a usable project format.

B.3 Project Scheduling

- Has multi project capability
- Can couple and uncouple scheduling system at the cost control system interface. Therefore has ability to tabulate or plot cash flow, IDC, fiscal budgeting and escalation distribution.
- Can handle several different calendars for the same project, which are assignable to different levels of detail.
- Schedules engineering design activities and handles data for man-hour control.
- Can update interactively.
- Identifies critical activities and resource constraints.
- Project and multi project resource leveling analysis, for engineering man-hours or construction resources, from demand or availability sides.
- Has easy-to-read graphics capability in a variety of report formats.

B.4 Feasibility Phase Control

- Can handle projects at two levels:

  a) Hard and soft costs to perform project feasibility/concept design studies, as a mini project with its own planning phase constraints.

  b) Systematic development of the total Project Breakdown Structure, Master Planning Schedule, Capital Cost Estimate and Cash Flow Forecasts, for purposes of feasibility and financial analysis.

- Capability in feasibility analysis covering:
  - project scope definition
  - estimating and master scheduling
  - escalation
  - contingency
  - Interest During Construction (IDC)

- Can simulate or model:
  - alternative schedule approaches
  - alternative procurement approaches
  - varying escalation index rates

- Provides escalation/IDC cost trade off and index sensitivity analysis.

B.5 Engineering Man-hour Control

System can handle:

- Engineering, procurement and overhead man-hours from time sheets, according to designated work packages.
- Man-hours budgeted, incurred and forecast reports.
- Man-hour scope changes.
- Forecasts of multiple resource requirements for each activity.
- Production of resource and demand histograms, bar charts, and man-hour trend curves.
- Identification of critical activities and resources, and overall schedule restraints.

B.6 Implementation Phase: Pre Award

Once a project receives approval to proceed, project data will expand rapidly. Estimate updates at progressive design reviews and schedule refinements must reflect procurement strategy. Therefore system must be able to handle:

- Budget scope changes.
- Estimates during design and pre-contract award.
- Escalation distribution.
- Commitment package planning and definition of contract price schedules.
- Procurement scheduling and resource analysis.
- Bid evaluation.
- Estimated Cost at Completion and budget and period variance calculations so that corrective action can be taken.

B.7 Implementation Phase: Post Award

As each commitment package is awarded, either as a contract or purchase order, contract administration records are required covering expediting, progress measurement, change orders and contractors' claims for extras. So system must be able to handle:

- Award and contract commitment details to pay item level.
- Control of commitment levels.
- Record of all incurred costs.
- Estimated Cost to Complete including changes in process, outstanding and contemplated, also contingency and contractors' claims for extra.
- Estimated Cost at Completion and budget and period variances to pay item level.
- Schedule refinement and update.
- Calculation and presentation of cash-flow-to-date and update of cash flow forecasting.
- Calculation of IDC to date and update of IDC forecast.

B.8 Project Accounting and Financial Management

System is able to handle:

- Information in support of contractors' work-in-progress and verification of suppliers' invoices.
- Payment processing.
- Holdback, retentions and releases.
- Debit memos and approvals.
- Vendor status.
- Short and long range fiscal budgeting and cash flow.
- Cumulative cost curve and trend reports.

APPENDIX B

The Mathematics of Learning Curves

Learning Curve Mathematics is based on the observation that when a particular task or sequence of work is repeated without interruption certain costs per unit tend to decrease in a predictable pattern. This is attributed to the experienced gained as the workers and their supervisors become more familiar with the work being repeated. There are, however, two approaches or mathematical models for purposes of practical application.

Model A: Log Linear - Cumulative Average (LL-CA)

This model was first stated mathematically in 1936 by T. P. Wright who observed that productivity improvement typically follows a constant ratio relationship in the form

For every doubling of units, the cumulative average time per unit is reduced by a constant ratio.

When plotted to log-log scale, the result is a straight line. Expressed more fully

The cumulative average time (or cost) for each of 'n' units up to the 'n^{th}' unit, when plotted against the number of units on log-log paper, produces a straight line.

This is called the Log Linear - Cumulative Average (LL-CA) Model.

Suppose the time for the first unit is taken as 100% and the ratio 'r' is 80%. Then the average time for the first and second units is 80%. That is the second unit took 60% of the time of the first unit. When the fourth unit is reached, the average time taken for all four units is 64% and so on.

Consider Figure B-1 and the following relationships.

Let C_n = y ordinate = Cumulative Average Time over 'n' units (CAT_n)

n = x ordinate = number of units

N = n^{th} unit

U_1 = Time to produce first unit (constant) = T_1

U_n = Time to produce n^{th} unit

s = Slope of CAT line on log-log plot

r = the constant ratio (by definition), known as the Learning Curve Ratio; Learning Rate; Decremental Rate of Experience; Learning percent; or Percent Learning. Usually expressed as 80%, 90% etc.

(s', r', = corresponding symbols for Model B.)

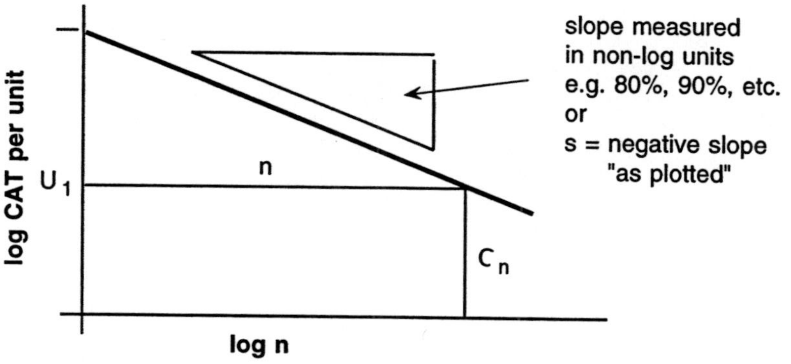

Figure B-1. Typical Learning Curve Plotted on Log-log Scale

From Figure B–1:

$$\log C_n = \log U_1 + s \log n$$

or $C_n = U_1 n^s$ (Note the form $y = a x^b$) .... (1)

By definition

$$r = \frac{C_{2n}}{C_n} = \frac{U_1 (2n)^s}{U_1 (n)^s} = 2^s$$

(Where 'r' = % Learning Curve)

$$\therefore \quad s = \frac{\log r}{\log 2} \quad \text{.......... (2)}$$

T_n = Time up to the nth unit (i.e. time to complete n units)

$$= nC_n = nU_1 n^s = U_1 n^{(s+1)} \quad \text{.......... (3)}$$

Time for the nth unit $= U_n = U_1 \{n^{(s+1)} - (n-1)^{(s+1)}\}$ .... (4)

For purposes of plotting n against T_n (Learning Curve):

1) Select any value of r (ratio)

2) Calculate $s = \frac{\log r}{\log 2}$

3) From $T_n = U_1 n^{s+1}$, calculate $\frac{T_n}{U_1} = n^{s+1}$ for values of n

4) If required to "fit" a particular point:

calculate $T_N \times T_n$

Model B: Log Linear - Unit (LL-U)

Model A is useful in forecasting or comparing similar operations but with significantly different numbers of units involved. It is less useful for examining results for individual units as in tracking progress on a construction site. This has led to a variation that is expressed as follows.

The time (or cost) of the 'n'th unit, when plotted against the number of units on log-log paper, produces a straight line.

This is called the Log Linear - Unit (LL-U) Model.

Again, assume that the time for the first unit is taken as 100% and the ratio 'r' is 80%. In this model, the reduction of time between the first and second unit will be 20%. Between the 2nd and 4th units it will be a further 20% and so on. That is to say, the fourth unit will take 64% of the time of the first unit. This is very different from Model A in which the fourth unit must take about 48% of the first unit.

In Figure B-1 the 'y' ordinate is now 'time per unit' (instead of Cumulative Average Time per Unit). Using the symbols previously listed, the new relationship is expressed by

$$U'_n = U'_1\, n^{s'} \qquad \text{.......... (5)}$$

By definition

$$r = \frac{U'_{2n}}{U'_n} = \frac{U'(2n)^{s'}}{U'(n)^{s'}} = 2^{s'}$$

$$\text{or} \qquad s' = \frac{\log r'}{\log 2} \qquad \text{.......... (6)}$$

and

$$T_n = \text{Time up to end of the } n^{th} \text{ unit} = U'_1 + \int_1^n U'_1\, n^{s'}\, dn$$

Integrating:

$$= U'_1 + \left[\frac{U'_1\, n^{s'+1}}{s'+1} + k\right] - \left[\frac{U'_1}{s'+1} + k\right]$$

or

$$T_n = U'_1\left[1 + \frac{n^{s'+1}}{s'+1} - \frac{1}{s'+1}\right] \qquad \text{.......... (7)}$$

and

$$\frac{T_n}{U'_1} = 1 + \left[\frac{n^{s'+1}}{s'+1} - \frac{1}{s'+1}\right] \qquad \text{.......... (8)}$$

In the special case where T_1 is equated to 100%, then U'_1 equals 1

$$T_n = 1 + \left[\frac{n^{s'+1}}{s'+1} - \frac{1}{s'+1}\right] \qquad \text{.......... (9)}$$

Plotting Stage 1 of the Standard Progress Output (SPO) S-curve

Here Model A is easier to use and the difference from Model B is small. By definition of the SPO S-curve, the learning curve must "force fit" to the start of Stage

2. That is to say, one quarter of the units at one third of the time and at the same slope of Stage 2 which, between points N and N+1, is two thirds.

Let T_N and N = the point at which the S-curve joins the start of Stage 2
Let T_n = the point to be plotted but where $n < N$
Then from equation (3) above

$$\frac{T_n}{T_N} = \frac{U_1\, n^{(s+1)}}{U_1\, N^{(s+1)}}$$

or

$$T_n = T_N \left(\frac{n}{N}\right)^{s+1} \qquad (10)$$

In the special case where 100% of the units are being plotted against 100% of the time, the learning curve ratio can be calculated by trial and error to 71%, or $s \cong -0.5$.
Thus,

$$T_n = 33.3\% \left(\frac{n^{-.5+1}}{25\%^{-.5+1}}\right) = 0.333 \left(\frac{n^{0.5}}{0.25^{0.5}}\right)$$

or

$$T_n = 0.67\sqrt{n} \qquad (11)$$

Stage 1 of the SPO S-curve shown in Figure 14-4, Chapter 14, is plotted according to equation (11).

APPENDIX C

Construction Project Management: Summary of Major Responsibilities[1]

The following briefly describes the major functional responsibilities of Project Management on a construction project.

A. Strategic Planning

If the project is large and complex, it may be necessary to prepare a strategy for the project management planning - in short, planning the plan. A logical approach to preparing a project plan commences with a general project description and a clear statement of project objectives. Next follows a high level project Work Breakdown structure (WBS) with a corresponding project organization and functional responsibility chart.

Then comes the assignment of responsibilities, the development of a high level schedule network and consequent resource loading. It should then be possible to develop an optimized Master Schedule. The results of this planning effort should be assembled into a document with a title such as Strategic (or Conceptual) Project Plan. It should be a major deliverables of the project's Concept Phase.

Part A of Figure C-1, Project Planning Documentation, shows the contents of a suggested Strategic Project Plan established by the end of the Concept Phase. Part B of the figure shows how the Strategic Plan is elaborated into a much more detailed Project Brief by the end of the Development Phase. The Table of Contents shown was developed for a large public infrastructure project.

The following sections describe the functional responsibilites in support of the planning and execution of the project.

B. Planning and Scheduling

Scheduling is a key function in managing a project. Failure to establish and reach key milestone dates inevitably affects project costs unfavorably. There are four steps:

- Planning: establishing the required activities, their logical sequence, restraints and interfaces
- Scheduling: adding durations and resources, adjusting for optimum results and identifying resulting key milestone dates
- Control: exercising positive corrective action over unacceptable variances

C. Budgeting and Estimating

At the earliest possible time an acceptable project budget breakdown must be established that properly reflects the best estimate of the cost of the work. This will form the basis for regular cost monitoring and reporting.

From time to time, updated cost estimates and detailed estimates of individual work packages will also be required. The quality and accuracy of these estimates will improve as the project proceeds and information becomes available in greater detail. To obtain "best value for money", major cost components may be subject to comparative "value analysis" where suitable alternatives exist.

D. Cost Control and Accounting

Control of costs is achieved through monitoring, analyzing, reporting and exercising control over commitments and expenditures with due regard to schedule. A key element is maintaining visibility of the Forecast Final Cost of the Project and exercising corrective action in good time by regular progress assessment and determination of future commitments and expenditures.

Project accounting deals with the control and historic recording of actual cash payments to consultants, contractors, suppliers and others for services provided to the project. The project budget and the manner of collecting this data must be compatible in order to make the required comparisons.

Definitive and detailed procedures are essential in this function to ensure the financial integrity of the project.

E. Regular Status Reporting

Regular reporting of timely current information is essential for keeping the client and others up-to-date on the status of the project so that all necessary decisions and actions can be taken promptly. Typical reports include:

- General project status
- Progress compared to schedule
- Cost compared to budget
- Activity status of consultants, contractors and management
- Procurement status
- Permits, agreements and contract negotiations
- Construction status

Project Planning — Table of Contents

Part A - Strategic Project Plan (Result of Concept Phase)

1 Business Aims and Objectives
2 Background to Project
3 Project Scope Description
4 Justification and Alternatives Considered
5 Schedule and Cost Summary

Part B - Project Brief (Result of Development Phase)

1 Scope of Work
2 Technical Standards:-
- Environment
- Performance Criteria
- Design Approach
- Location and Layout
- Quality and Safety
- Evaluation Studies
- Technical Specifications*

3 Applicable Government and Regulatory Agency Requirements
4 Applicable Owner Standards and Procedures
5 Procurement and Contracting Strategy
6 Construction Approach
7 Operating and Maintenance Requirements
8 Certification and Commissioning Requirements
9 Master Schedule
10 Capital Appropriation Budget and Cash Flow Projection
11 Project Organization:-
- Organization charts
- Responsibilities and Authorities

12 Project Team Facilities
13 Computer Support Requirements
14 Project Procedures and Standards:-
- Approach
- Project Procedure Manual
- Planning and Progress Monitoring
- Budget and Cost Monitoring
- Engineering and Design
- Procurement and Contracts
- Material Control
- Construction
- Quality Assurance/Quality Control
- Certification
- Accounting/Financial
- Documentation Control
- Administration and Personnel
- Project Reporting
- Union Interfaces
- Publicity
- Training
- Safety
- Project Auditing

* **Note:** The Technical Specification section is more often enlarged to a separate companion document providing the "Technical Basis" for the project.

Figure C-1. Project Planning Documentation

F. Management of Design Consultants

This function ensures that the design work is proceeding promptly and that the output of this work will be within the constraints of the project's scope and budget. It may include:

- Working with the owner to prepare a design brief outlining the project requirements to form the basis of consultant selection, including pre-qualification based on capability and staffing
- Selection recommendations
- Negotiating fee structures, terms of reference and responsibilities with the respect to the project team
- Award recommendations
- Briefing, expediting and ensuring regulatory and user input coordination
- Verifying the consultant's performance and conformance to the project's scope

G. Procurement and Contract Administration

The extent of special expertise and the level of effort required in this function is substantial as shown in the following sub-sections.

G.1 Procurement

Procurement involves the systematic execution of procedures for purchasing all materials, equipment and services needed for the project, in good time and in a way that is cost effective. This process includes:

- Establishing procurement criteria and procedures consistent with the owner's requirements and good commercial practice
- Interaction with the project scheduling and budgeting activities
- Agreement with the owner regarding signing and requisitioning authorities
- Prequalification of suppliers of goods and services, including sourcing, availability and market conditions
- Establishing suitable standard documents for proposals, tender calls, contract general and special conditions, and purchase orders
- The issue, receipt, assessment and recommendations for award of proposals/bids/quotes
- Establishing a material management and control system, including verification of materials and equipment received
- Administration of contracts

G.2 Expediting

Expediting is essential to ensure scheduled deliveries will be met or, alternatively, to decide corrective action for late deliveries. This applies to all materials, equipment and services needed for the project whether procured externally or provided internally by the owner.

G.3 Quality Assurance and Control

Quality itself is the composite of material attributes, including performance features and characteristics, of the product or service required to satisfy the need reflected in the project's scope statement.

A quality assurance program identifies these objectives and establishes a strategy of client interfacing for organizing and coordinating planned and systematic controls for maintaining established standards right from early design work through to commissioning.

Following identification of specific system requirements, a quality control program is necessary to exercise direct influence on results by the collection of specific technical data for analysis and decision on acceptance or rejection.

G.4 Payment Certification

Payment certification involves verifying interim and final payment entitlement for every consultant, supplier and contractor engaged on the project according to the terms of the respective contracts. In the case of suppliers and contractors, much of this work is delegated to the respective consultants who have a professional responsibility to ensure that the work conforms to their technical requirements. The volume of paper work can be substantial and records must be closely integrated with Project Accounting and record keeping.

H. Management of Construction and Commissioning

H.1 Construction Management

Construction management includes the setting of a strategy for procurement and implementation of contracted services for constructed work. Where a construction management approach is used, it is important that the project manager ensures that the construction manager oversees the following, to the extent that they are not incorporated into individual contract documents:

- Provides input to the design, and reviews contract documents for constructability and cost
- Provides input to the project schedule with respect to construction activities and logic

- Recommends tendering strategies and procedures for the selection of tenderers, including tenders for pre-purchased equipment
- Has responsibility for calling, receiving, evaluating and comparing tenders and recommending contract awards
- Mobilizing and managing the construction site, including temporary facilities, site logistics, storage on and off site for pre-purchased materials and equipment and general site conduct
- Mobilizing contractors, reviewing their schedules, labor and methodology
- General day-to-day scheduling, coordination and supervision
- Expediting submission and review of shop drawings and samples
- Field contract administration, distribution of field clarifications, special work authorizations, and distribution of any change orders
- Claim avoidance measures
- Harmonious trade contractor and labor relations
- Monitors construction progress and cost
- Calls for inspection and reinspection of defective work
- Certification of contractors' physical progress
- Submission of required as-built drawings, operating manuals and instructions and similar contract completion documentation
- Administers the correction of faults during the warranty period

H.2 Commissioning

Typically, commissioning and startup is carried out by the owner's users or operational staff who will run the facility. Prior to startup, every system and every part of the project must be brought into operational mode ready for formal handover. The whole project team is therefore required to help by organizing and managing the transition from construction/installation to operation. A carefully developed set of commissioning procedures is necessary to ensure orderly and successful project completion, including:

- Responsibilities and organization
- Detailed equipment and systems commissioning and startup sequence, including check-out, static tests, "dry and wet" operational tests, performance tests, etc.
- Client acceptance, including equipment and systems tagging, opportunities for training and general familiarization, designation of temporary working and storage areas for operations staff, etc.
- Deficiency lists, and their progressive correction
- Building occupancy permits
- Ensuring completion of all final contract documentation

References

[1] Wideman, R. M. 1991. Total Project Management of Complex Projects: Improving Performance with Modern Techniques, International Seminar on Project Management for Developing Countries. Oxford & IBH Publishing Co. Pvt. Ltd., New Delhi, India. p118-121.

APPENDIX D

Types of Construction Delays

"Time is money" is a popular phrase and is probably no truer than in the construction industry. Delays are a common cause for claims from contractors for additional payment. Determining whether the work was in fact delayed is one thing, but determining who was responsible for the delay may be quite another.

Because of the complexity of construction work, more than one delay can occur, they may be the responsibility of different parties and may also overlap. So, the allocation of responsibility can be difficult and is frequently the subject of construction litigation under a construction contract by either party on the other. Because of this litigation aspect, delay in a contractual sense has come to mean a time overrun beyond the required completion date of the project.

Delays can be costly to both parties and may be the result of delayed access, late delivery of materials, equipment failure, poor organization, rework, strikes, change orders, and so on. Besides, they may be interconnected making the situation even more complex. In recent years, considerable attention has been given to the nature of delays in construction and attempts have been made to relate cause and effect. The objective of this effort has been to resolve disputes by assessing schedule impacts of the delays and so arrive at damages and entitlements.

For this purpose, delays have generally been classified according to liability, falling into two major types: Excusable and Non-excusable Delays. Excusable Delays are further subdivided into Excusable Compensable and Excusable Non-compensable Delays. Delays that apparently overlap in an analysis of the circumstances are called Concurrent Delays. Each type of construction delay may be defined as follows.[1]

Excusable Delays — delays that are not attributable to the contractor's action or inactions. Excusable delays when founded, entitle the contractor to a time extension if the completion date is affected.

Excusable Compensable Delays — delays that are caused by the owner's actions or inactions. Also, the contractor is entitled to a time extension and damage compensation for extra costs associated with the delay.

Excusable Non-compensable Delays — delays that are neither the contractor's nor the owner's fault. The contractor is entitled to a time extension but not to damage compensation.

Non-excusable Delays — delays that are caused by the contractor's or its subcontractor's actions or inactions. Consequently, the contractor is not entitled to a time extension or delay damages. On the other hand the owner may be entitled to liquidated or other damages.

Concurrent Delays — two or more delays that take place or overlap during the same period, either of which occurring alone would have affected the ultimate completion date. In practice it can be difficult to apportion damages when the concurrent delays are due to the owner and contractor respectively.

It is probably in the best interests of all parties to a contract that delay definitions and the manner of compensation is spelled out in the contract language.

Many delay claims are resolved using scheduling techniques such as the critical path method based on network analysis or simple pictorial bar charts which address specific impacts. The general methodology is to establish the schedule that was both intended and feasible at the time of the contract. This schedule is expressed in terms of both logical activity sequence and achievable production rates. This is known as the "As-planned" schedule.

A similar schedule, known as the "As-built" schedule, is then reconstructed from the historical data of the project to reflect what actually occurred. The "As-planned" and the "As-built" are then compared to highlight differences that should lead to cause and effect and presumably to responsibility. The time component of added costs can then be calculated based on the schedule differences.

To quantify damages in difficult cases, or to cover other aspects of the delay impacts, various analysis techniques have been developed some of them quite sophisticated. However, discussion of such techniques is beyond the scope of this book.

References

[1] Battika, M. and Alkass, S. 1994. A Computer Integrated System for Construction Delays Analysis and Their Impact on the Project Costs. CSCE Annual Conference Proceedings, Winnipeg, Manitoba, p 451.

APPENDIX E

Glossary of Project Cost Management Techniques

The following is an alphabetical listing of techniques and methodologies with outline descriptions that are available or commonly used in Project Cost Management. Words in all upper case within a description are terms also defined in Appendix F: Glossary of Project Cost Management Terms. "See also" refers to other Techniques in this Glossary.

Arrow Diagramming — A technique that may be used in both CPM and PERT to display the NETWORK sequence and timing of ACTIVITIES. The technique is EVENT oriented in that the connecting arrows represent the ACTIVITIES. It is simple to understand and display straight forward NETWORKS. Its flexibility is limited in comparison with PRECEDENCE DIAGRAMMING. See also CPM and PERT.

Brainstorming — A group of people, selected for their creativity and knowledge, are brought together to seek solutions to particular problems or simply to find better ways of meeting objectives. Suggestions, however outlandish, are encouraged and pursued during a creativity session. From this, many ideas, some entirely new, are brought forward for analysis and ranking. Brainstorming is an essential part of the Value Management technique.

Break-Even Charts — Often it is possible to draw a graph showing the relation between the increased cost of accelerating PROJECT progress and the cost benefit of reduced PROJECT OVERHEAD and earlier cash flow from product sales. When IDC is factored in near the end of a commercial PROJECT, almost any cost that results in greater progress can be justified, provided that the benefit is actually realized. This is why many PROJECTS end up working heavy overtime close to completion. The charts can be used to show how the cost of better planning can be justified to produce the same result at less total cost.

Computerized Information Retrieval — The larger and more complex a PROJECT, the more difficult it is for managers to find the information they require from the mounting volume of documents, studies, reports, contracts, specifications, drawings, changes, and proposed changes. Even simplified computerized cross referencing of these documents can help considerably. It should be part of the PROJECT's Records Management Program, which see also.

Computer Modeling — A technique for establishing past PROJECT results as an interactive mathematical computer program. By selectively modifying data on models of similar PROJECTS, it is possible to anticipate the affects on related dependencies in PROJECTS proposed or in progress. This technique is useful for determining the optimum choice, e.g. where a complex series of options, each with their own interdependent cost and schedule impacts, are available for achieving almost the same objective. When programmed, a SCHEDULE NETWORK containing Network Branching becomes such a Computer Model.

Contribution Analysis — An analysis to show how much an effort, system, material or component is contributing to PROJECT objectives and its consequent success. It is particularly useful in simplifying a PROJECT MANAGEMENT organization or system. See also Systems Analysis and Value Management.

Corporate Planning — PLANNING by top-level management to establish:

a) What exactly are its overall objectives, and
b) The long range PLANNING required in every part of the organization to achieve those objectives. Generally a highly systematized approach to the forecasting of need for and selection of future PROJECTS.

Costing Systems — Systems established to determine current costs and their trends up or down so that appropriate management action can be taken. Usually requires the setting of reference standards, often the first point of controversy.

Cpm Critical Path Method — An ACTIVITY oriented time control technique used for planning complex PROJECTS. Used mostly but not necessarily in the IMPLEMENTATION PHASE. It requires breaking down the PROJECT into ACTIVITIES, arranging them into a logical sequence, estimating the duration of each and so arrive at that series of ACTIVITIES that determines the minimum possible duration of the PROJECT. These are the CRITICAL PATH ACTIVITIES. See also Arrow and Precedence Diagramming.

Cybernetics — The study of man machine relationships to optimize output performance. Generally given inadequate attention on PROJECTS. See also Method Study.

Data Processing — The conversion, sorting, allocation or otherwise systematic and standard manipulation of PROJECT data by computer programming. It speeds results and reduces the staff that would otherwise be required for manual effort. Great care is required to ensure useful output and avoid the counter productive overloading of managers with unnecessary information. See also Systems Analysis.

Decision Theory — A technique for helping to reach decisions under uncertainty and risk. All decisions are based to some extent on uncertain forecasts. Given the criteria selected by the decision maker, Decision Theory points to the best possible course whether or not the forecasts are accurate. (For example, used to determine the best product capacity level for a PROJECT).

Decision Trees — A method of displaying a whole network of decisions in a logical sequence. Consequent decisions appear like the branches of a tree. When the probability of a given outcome of each decision is also shown, it becomes possible to select the best course of action. See Network Branching.

Discounted Cash Flow — A method for comparing the relative merits of PROJECT investments taking into account the value of money, taxation, varying operating costs, earlier cash returns for reinvestment etc. Also known as Internal Rate of Return. Although theoretically not as sound as Net Present Value, it is easier to present and relate to interest rates on borrowed money. Neither DCF nor NPV takes into account PROJECT RISKS.

High Level Forecasting Techniques — These include trending, "S" curve modeling, moving averages, exponential smoothing etc. These are used to obtain rapid indications of current PROJECT status, especially where the processing of a large volume of data would otherwise be required. One or more leading indicators may be used such as man-hour totals, concrete placed, payments-to-date, etc. An indispensable part of an effective PROJECT MANAGER'S CONTROL information. See also Regression Analysis.

Incentive or **Bonus Schemes** — A scheme by which the work force will receive extra pay or other rewards if certain targets or objectives are achieved. The targets are usually expressed as a certain quantity in a certain time, including completing a PROJECT by a fixed date. The scheme must be carefully thought out if it is to benefit both OWNER and work force. The work force must perceive that the extra reward is worth the extra effort. The approach has limited application because frequent use can become a normal expectation or even abused or hence counter productive. It does, however, have particular application near the end of a PROJECT to gain earlier completion. See also Break-even Charts.

Information Theory — The mathematical modeling and analysis of information processing for the benefit of PROJECT organization and communication.

Job Description — A carefully thought out structured but concise written description of a person's job. It will cover authority, responsibility, work content, reporting and working relationships, duties and skills required. Used primarily for MANAGEMENT and supervisory positions. Most useful in developing PROJECT organization structures and selecting or recruiting candidates most suited to the work required. Unfortunately, every minor reorganization required to respond to successive STAGES of the PROJECT tends to render them in need of updating.

Job Evaluation — A systematic assessment of job content. (See also Job Description). It establishes the worth of a job in terms of salary or wage compared to other jobs. Many elaborate schemes have been developed and applied with varying degrees of success. While some structure is necessary on a PROJECT, pay is more likely to be governed by market conditions, scarcity, individual knowledge, performance or trade agreements. These factors generally also recognize such PROJECT aspects as higher stress, cyclical work loading and potential for termination upon completion.

Management By Exception — The issue of management reports to responsible managers only when action is called for. This helps the manager to avoid wading through voluminous reports where progress is going according to plan. However, the system may require subjective judgment by someone who is not as well placed to do so as the manager himself. Exception reports tend to be harbingers of bad news without the good news.

Manpower Planning — Knowledge of a PROJECT's WBS, SCHEDULE and other objectives, and a general understanding of the PROJECT life-cycle is required to develop a Manpower PLAN. The PLAN should show what types of positions have to be filled, in what numbers and when. This helps to establish qualification requirements, alternate ways of staffing, and realistic lead times for recruiting. See also Organization and Methods and Job Description. It may also point up a resource restraint. See also Resource Leveling.

Marginal Costing — Determination of incremental cost and hence trade-off value of additional material for performance or safety, additional labor for faster progress, and so on. It is used where unit costs are not appropriate because some costs such as rental or overheads are already in place. Some adjustment must be made for reduction in productivity due to work transfer or for divided responsibility following introduction of a second shift on the same ACTIVITY.

Market Research — By researching published data on the construction industry, it may be possible to schedule the construction of a PROJECT at a time when tenders will be more competitive. Market Research may also reveal new or more economic materials, systems and methods for incorporation in the SCOPE of work.

Mathematical Programming — See Computer Modeling.

Merit Rating — Another way of providing INCENTIVE but on an individual basis. A systematic assessment of a person's worth compared to others. Factors should include productivity and quality of work, time keeping, loyalty, and general contribution to the team effort. Impact is often only marginal because large differences between people, when known by others, can be counter productive. See also Job Evaluation.

Method Study or **Work Study** — By systematically studying a repetitive TASK, it is often possible to identify parts that do not contribute usefully, or can be improved to reduce the labor, material and/or time required for their performance. Can be applied to almost any type of work. Has particular application to improving cost and SCHEDULE performance on long duration PROJECT ACTIVITIES containing highly cyclical TASKS. Examples are continuous sliding formwork, tunneling, track laying and so on. Time study is usually necessary to measure the increment of time required for each individual movement making up the total TASK.

Net Present Value — When a Rate of Return is applied to the stream of annual cash flows resulting from a PROJECT investment, it is possible to calculate whether the discounted value is greater than the cost of the investment. In times of high interest and inflation especially, the method gives more accurate results than simple pay back periods and average return.

Network Branching — There may be more than one way for undertaking a part of a PROJECT, but the choice may not be clear until the PROJECT has progressed to a certain point. This form of graphical display enables the various options to be represented. See also Network Planning and Decision Trees.

Network Planning — A technique for graphically displaying the logical sequence, timing and inter-relationships of the ACTIVITIES that comprise the PROJECT. Used for PLANNING and SCHEDULING a PROJECT and is the basis for MONITORING and CONTROLLING the time required to reach specific goals. Two popular drawing conventions or notations used, are Arrow and Precedence, which see also.

Organization and Methods — Study of the best form of organization, systems and procedures to accomplish the PROJECT. It includes line and staff relationships, communication and coordination interfaces between disciplines and responsibility areas and so on. Setting down the framework establishes working relationships recognized by the whole team. This improves necessary information transfer and reduces unnecessary communication, work load and stress on the PROJECT organization.

Pert (Program Evaluation And Review Technique) — An event oriented system. Generally used in research and development field where activities and durations between events are difficult to define at the planning stage, yet completion of these activities by specific dates is essential to the success of the PROJECT. Typically, these projects involve massive programs, many large organizations, and extensive operation in many different locations. See also Arrow and Precedence Diagramming.

Pert-Cost — See also Program Evaluation and Review Technique. In this cost approach, costs and time are estimated for each task so that the cost of making schedule changes can be evaluated.

Precedence Diagramming — An ACTIVITY oriented system in which ACTIVITIES are displayed in uniform boxes complete with ACTIVITY number, start duration and finish dates. The logical relation between ACTIVITY boxes is shown by logic connector lines. Lead and lag times can also be shown. The display is more effective than Arrow Diagramming and is also easier to revise, update, and program on computer. See also CPM and PERT.

Random Observation — A technique for building up a picture of an ACTIVITY by taking sufficient random observations. The alternative is to observe the ACTIVITY continuously, which may itself influence performance of the ACTIVITY. Particularly useful on a site, for example, to establish the extent and effect of (unproductive) walking, waiting, communication, break time etc. associated with several concurrent and possibly interrelated ACTIVITIES.

Records Management — Every PROJECT large and small is involved in Records Management to a greater or lesser degree whether recognized or not. A conscious effort in this area can greatly reduce the time and effort required to trace information or to avoid duplication of work in the field due to oversight or misplaced information. A good Records Management program should:

- Encompass all records having a bearing on the PROJECT's CONTRACTS
- Establish policies for standardizing required forms, reports, procedures and manuals
- Ensure smooth and consistent distribution of information throughout the PROJECT organization on a need-to-know basis
- Expedite all required or outstanding information
- Ensure security of vital records
- Provide necessary retention for historical purposes
- Meet legal retention requirements
- Withdraw and destroy obsolete duplicates. See also Systems Analysis.

Regression Analysis — Where past data is insufficient for direct forecasting of future levels of ACTIVITY it may still be possible to make assumptions based on relationships with other ACTIVITIES that can be forecast. This applies particularly to Apportioned-Effort tasks and to a lesser extent to Level-of -Effort tasks. See Work Packages, Chapter 5.

Replacement Theory — A statistical methodology for arriving at the optimum life of replaceable elements in a PROJECT. It considers replacement cost, maintenance and down time costs, tax implications and scrap value.

Reporting by Responsibility — The separation of management action reports by Responsibility Areas or Cost Centers so that managers only get information on that element over which they have control. See also Management by Exception.

Resource Allocation or **Leveling** — Progress on certain types of PROJECT can be constrained more by limitations of resources (people, machines, materials and money) than by logical sequence dictated by technical considerations. Generally such PROJECTS are "horizontal" e.g. highway construction, rather than "vertical" e.g. high rise construction, although the latter may be constrained by both considerations. The resource loading required can only be determined after a SCHEDULE of ACTIVITIES has been developed. The SCHEDULE may then be modified, possibly prolonged, either to reduce the total resources required to complete the project or to "level" out peak demands. This avoids congestion at some times and inefficient resource usage at others. It is an iterative process of computing the schedule considering the limited availability of resources. In this way both time and cost may be minimized.

Risk Management or **Analysis** — Risk is the likelihood of an event occurring that is detrimental to PROJECT success. Identification of all PROJECT RISK categories and assessing their probability and impact is an important aspect of PROJECT MANAGEMENT. Therefore, sufficient time and resources should be devoted to risk assessment as an integral part of the PROJECT PLAN. Managing and CONTROLLING risk involves assigning responsibility to those in the PROJECT TEAM who can best control the consequence of each risk category. The objective is to mitigate risk/cost on the project. Unpredictable PROJECT RISKS should be assumed by the OWNER since they cannot be costed, see Chapter 8.

Simulation — See Computer Modeling

Statistical Quality Control — Various statistical methods and relationships are available for determining performance quality and the adjustment necessary to achieve specified results. Used particularly in the sampling of high volume materials such as steel and concrete strengths, earthwork compaction and so on. Indirectly, tests and helps to maintain quality of workmanship as in weld testing. The aim is to balance the cost of inspection against the penalty of allowing faulty materials and workmanship to escape detection. It is particularly useful for concrete control on large heavy engineering projects such as hydro electric schemes.

Statistical Project Stock Control — Where significant stocks are held to meet demands, or intermittent peak demands, this technique seeks to minimize total cost, while considering a variety factors. These factors include the cost of placing an order;, discounts available on bulk order and delivery; cost of holding stock including capital tied up; deterioration, higher usage and wastage if freely available; over ordering; obsolescence; cost of warehousing; demand variability; and lost productivity when out of stock. The technique has limited application unless the PROJECT is large with few WORK PACKAGES or many similar PROJECTS are supplied from a central store. Beware of solutions provided by computer programs that may not recognize specific PROJECT conditions. See also Computer Modeling.

Systems Analysis — The study of the management systems required to be put in place to accomplish the PROJECT. Before establishing any system, especially those to be computerized, it is essential to establish who needs and who wants the information output, why, when and at what level. Only then can the best system for the purpose be established. More often than not on a PROJECT, systems "happen" ad-hoc because of some urgent need and without the knowledge or participation of others who may be affected. Systems Analysis often provides the opportunity both to improve performance on the PROJECT and to eliminate wasted or marginal effort. See also Contribution Analysis.

Value Management, Engineering or **Analysis** — This technique is a creative, organized approach designed to optimize the total cost and/or performance of the PROJECT. Usually applied only to the most significant elements of a PROJECT by analyzing their contribution and identifying functionally acceptable substitution. VM often results in improved performance and/or appearance and simplification at a payoff many times the cost of the VM program. It is best applied in the earliest stages of a PROJECT. VM is not popular because of its "real" front end cost compared to "notional" downstream savings. Also because it is seen by designers as a threat to their credibility. See also Brainstorming in this Glossary and VM in Chapter 3.

Work Breakdown — A technique for representing all the components, software, services and data contained in the PROJECT SCOPE STATEMENT. It establishes a hierarchical structure or product oriented "family tree" of elements. It is used to organize, define and graphically display all the WORK ITEMS or WORK PACKAGES to be done to accomplish the PROJECT's objectives. See Chapter 5.

Work Study — See Method Study.

APPENDIX F

Glossary of Project Cost Management Terms

An alphabetical listing of terms and their definitions commonly used in Project Cost Management. Words in all upper case within a definition are terms that are defined elsewhere in the glossary.

Accountability — Being answerable to one's superior in an organization for the exercise of one's AUTHORITY and the performance of one's duties. See also RESPONSIBILITY

Activity — A TASK or series of TASKS that is performed over a period of time.

Activity Oriented Schedules — Schedules which present information in terms of ACTIVITIES (i.e. periods of time, as opposed to points in time, e.g. MILESTONE dates). See Precedence Diagramming, Appendix E.

Administrative Management — Management that operates in the public trust, such as national, regional or local government administrations. Designed to survive indefinitely, the intended goal is to provide an environment acceptable to its constituents for their survival, prosperity and comfort.

Agreement — A term often used to refer to CONTRACTS between an OWNER and his professional consultants.

Anticipated Award Cost — The most probable CONTRACT price at time of TENDER AND AWARD. It forms part of the FORECAST TO COMPLETE. See COST TYPES.

Appropriation — An allocation of funds to a PROJECT by the owner or sponsor in response to a CAPITAL APPROPRIATION REQUEST (CAR) or a REQUEST FOR APPROPRIATION (RFA). In a structured organization, a COMMITMENT cannot be made until an appropriation has been obtained. However, a lower threshold value may be set below which a formal appropriation is not required. Prefeasibility and similar studies are such examples.

Arrow representation of an **Activity** — Activity duration usually shown next to the arrow (above or below). Used in both CPM and PERT scheduling systems.

Arrow Diagramming — A technique used in CPM or PERT. See Appendix E.

Authority — The sum of rights and powers assigned to a position or vested in a person, often specified in his or her job description. The Authority to make financial COMMITMENTS is an important aspect of managing projects.

Award Letter — A letter sent in response to an offer that accepts that offer.

Backward Pass — Calculation of latest finish and start dates. Used in CPM scheduling.

Bottom Up Cost Estimating — The preparation of detailed estimates for every task in the WORK BREAKDOWN STRUCTURE and summing them up to provide a total project cost ESTIMATE or COST PLAN

Budget — If unqualified, it is better to reserve the term "budget" for annual or fiscal financial allocations of the Organization. This should include a capital budget for on-going and proposed construction projects. The acceptance or approval of a capital budget is not necessarily AUTHORITY to proceed. An APPROPRIATION must be obtained before COMMITMENTS can be made. See also FEASIBILITY BUDGET and PROJECT BUDGET.

Capital Appropriation Request — A submission that must be prepared to obtain an APPROPRIATION of funds for FEASIBILITY or IMPLEMENTATION PHASE costs. Once granted, the appropriation becomes the FEASIBILITY BUDGET or PROJECT BUDGET, and COMMITMENTS may be made by designated persons associated with the PROJECT, within the limits of their AUTHORITY.

Change Order — A form issued to a CONSTRUCTION CONTRACTOR to change the SCOPE of work and CONTRACT price, and hence a COMMITMENT DOCUMENT.

Claim — The term "claim" should be reserved for extra payment sought by a CONSTRUCTION CONTRACTOR for work allegedly not included in the SCOPE of its CONTRACT, or otherwise for damages or loss suffered because of actions or omissions by the OWNER. Thus a claim is a legitimate request for additional compensation (cost and/or time) due to a change in the terms of the contract. The term Claim would also apply to demands arising from a contractual dispute.

Commitment Document — A CONTRACT, CHANGE ORDER or PURCHASE ORDER issued for the supply of goods and services. The document legally binds the Organization and commits it to financial and other obligations. A LETTER OF INTENT is also a Commitment Document.

Commitment Or Committed Cost — A COST TYPE. The value of COMMITMENT DOCUMENTS issued for the SCOPE of the work within a COST CLASS as of a reporting date. A cost class may be partially or completely committed at any particular time.

Concept, Concept Phase — The first PHASE of a project in which the need is examined, alternatives are assessed, the goals and objectives of the project are established and a sponsor is identified.

Conceptual Design — An early STAGE in the life of a PROJECT that should result in the preparation of a document containing a FUNCTIONAL PROGRAM, sketches and outline drawings, a concept ESTIMATE and a set of design standards.

Construction Cost — Any of the COST TYPES (APPROPRIATIONS, COMMITMENT, EXPENDITURE or ESTIMATE TO COMPLETE) associated with the SCOPE of the construction work. See also PROJECT COST.

Construction Contractor — A corporation or individual who has entered into a CONTRACT with the Organization to perform construction work.

Construction Management — A company that performs the duties of the CONSTRUCTION MANAGER and his staff. Especially on large construction projects, such firms may take over the role of a general contractor, by providing day-to-day supervision and direction of activities by general and subtrade CONSTRUCTION CONTRACTORS.

Construction Manager — The title of a position on the project team. This person is responsible to the PROJECT MANAGER for directing the construction of a project within AUTHORITY and RESPONSIBILITY limits, usually established by the CONTRACT. On smaller projects, a CONSTRUCTION CONTRACTOR may assign this role to a superintendent.

Construction Stage — That part of a PROJECT life cycle during which the construction work is carried out. See also IMPLEMENTATION PHASE.

Contemplated Change Notice — A form issued to a CONSTRUCTION CONTRACTOR requesting its quotation for a proposed change in the SCOPE of work that would be included in its CONTRACT.

Contingency — A component of the Authorized APPROPRIATION or ESTIMATED COST AT COMPLETION for the PROJECT's SCOPE of work or a particular COST CLASS. Contingency is an ESTIMATOR'S ALLOWANCE for the cost of unknowns, changes to make things work or estimating error. The anticipated award price of a COST CLASS may also contain allowance for ESCALATION. However, a Reserve for Scope Changes is not a contingency in the same sense. A Scope Change Reserve is an allowance from which transfers can be made into specific COST CLASSES when the SCOPE of work in the class is amended by the OWNER. The APPROPRIATION for that class should be amended accordingly following the transfer.

Contract — An agreement in law between the Organization as OWNER, and a Consultant (See AGREEMENT) or a CONSTRUCTION CONTRACTOR. It is a COMMITMENT DOCUMENT. The term contract is used to refer to the document itself. Construction contracts are often classified and described by the terms of payment they contain: Stipulated Price or Lump Sum, Unit Price, COST PLUS, etc.

Control, Controlling, or Project Control — A PROJECT MANAGEMENT function that involves comparing actual performance with planned performance and taking corrective action (or directing or motivating others to do so) to yield the desired outcome when significant differences exist. See also COMMITMENT.

Coordination — The bringing together, or integration, of separate work efforts of the project, to form a complete, harmonious and workable deliverable. It includes ensuring that all contributors, management, consultants and contractors, understand the common goals, priorities and scheduled activity sequence. A coordinator does not have the same authority as a PROJECT MANAGER, but nonetheless may still be responsible for the results. Persuasive power is usually exercised through tenure, recognition of expertise, or experience.

Corporate Management — Management in the private sector intended to survive profitably and indefinitely based on providing a product or service. It recognizes that its products will not live forever but will be superseded by other products having the advantage of superior quality, cost, timeliness or acceptability. This recognition requires corporate management to set aside funds for technological development to maintain market advantage. The overall corporate activity must maintain a satisfactory return on investment for its share holders.

Cost — See PROJECT COST

Cost Check — A periodic estimate to give an up-to-date analysis of cost compared to progress on a design or construction WORK ITEM.

Cost Classes — Subdivisions of the total SCOPE of work in a PROJECT forming the PROJECT BREAKDOWN STRUCTURE and to which costs are assigned.

Cost Model — Subdivides the total construction cost into costs for functional facility elements and systems, for example: Building Exterior Envelope. This leads to fewer sub-divisions than the UCI trade subdivisions, since several trades make up the typical enclosure. Useful in VALUE MANAGEMENT since it enables complete systems of various types to be compared in linear, square or cubic units of measure.

Cost Plan — Sub divides the total PROJECT BUDGET into meaningful COST CLASSES each with its own related outline specification or SCOPE. It provides the first principal frame of reference required for a valid cost control system.

Cost-Plus — A form of CONTRACT for construction work in which the CONSTRUCTION CONTRACTOR is reimbursed for the costs it incurs in performing the work plus a lump sum or percentage fee; hence, cost-plus. This type of contract is favored where the SCOPE of the work is indeterminate or highly uncertain and the kinds of labor, material and equipment needed are also uncertain. Under this arrangement complete records of all time and materials spent by the contractor on the work must be maintained.

Cost Reviews — Planned, systematic and rigorous reassessments of the ESTIMATED COST AT COMPLETION of the SCOPE of work in a COST

CLASS. Each Design Review is accompanied by a reforecast of cost. See also ESTIMATE TO COMPLETE.

Cost Types — Four different cost types are typically associated with the SCOPE of work in a COST CLASS. They reflect whether a cost is authorized, contractually committed, spent or forecast for spending. These types are:

1. Authorized **Appropriation**
2. **Committed Cost**
3. **Expenditure** (or Actual)
4. **Estimate To Complete,** or Forecast to Complete, or Uncommitte

Types 1 and 4 contain CONTINGENCIES. The sum of type 2 and type 4 is the ESTIMATED COST AT COMPLETION. Before any commitments are made within a cost class, the type 4 cost contains a component called the ANTICIPATED AWARD COST, which in turn may contain an allowance for ESCALATION. Type 3 costs are further sub-divided into payments and retentions (HOLDBACKS).

CPM — A technique for PLANNING a PROJECT. See Appendix E.

Critical Activities or Work Items — ACTIVITIES or WORK ITEMS that, if not completed by the indicated time allowed, will increase the total PROJECT duration by the corresponding extent of the delay in completion of that ACTIVITY or WORK ITEM. (I.e. ACTIVITIES or WORK ITEMS with ZERO FLOAT).

Critical Path — The route through the NETWORK that has only CRITICAL ACTIVITIES.

Day Work Account — A method of payment for work not included in the SCOPE of the CONTRACT that the CONSTRUCTION CONTRACTOR is obliged to perform at the request or direction of the OWNER or its agent. Generally, such day-work-account is paid for on unit-price or COST-PLUS terms.

Deliverables — Physical items or measurable outputs that are identified as part of the PROJECT's product or objectives. Deliverables include intermediate products or services that are necessary for achieving the project's final results. Deliverables are always measurable because they can be counted or observed in some way.

Design Alternatives — During FEASIBILITY and the DESIGN STAGE (concept, development, and working drawings), the designer will identify several technical solutions that all satisfy the functional requirements and the standards that constrain the choices. The alternate designs are compared in terms of cost effectiveness, often using an analysis of TRADE-OFFS to arrive at an optimum solution. Ideally, the one that is finally chosen and implemented is the most economic combination of design alternatives. Used extensively in VALUE MANAGEMENT.

Design Contingency — The estimated allowance for the cost of changes to the design that are required during construction to make the PROJECT SCOPE work in practice.

Detailed Design Stage — That part of a PROJECT life-cycle during which working drawings, standards, specifications and tender documents are prepared. See also IMPLEMENTATION PHASE.

Development Phase — Also called the FEASIBILITY PHASE. That part of a PROJECT LIFE-CYCLE comprising feasibility studies, if required, PLANNING, engineering or development, after which a CAPITAL APPROPRIATION REQUEST is made, supported by a PROJECT BRIEF. See also IMPLEMENTATION PHASE.

Earliest Finish — The earliest day that the WORK ITEM can finish if it starts on its EARLIEST START and is completed in its expected time.

Earliest Start — The earliest day that the WORK ITEM can start provided every preceding work item starts at its earliest start day and is completed in its expected time.

Escalated Base Price — The base price estimate adjusted for inflation up to the time of tender

Escalation — An anticipated rise in uncommitted costs of resources (labor, material, equipment) over time, due to reduced purchasing power of money. A component of a COST TYPE. The allowance for escalation is a component within the ANTICIPATED AWARD COST of a COST CLASS.

Estimate (of cost) — Prediction or forecast of costs that will occur in the future, but are not yet committed; a COST TYPE. Estimates are described or qualified based on the supporting design information available at the time the estimate is prepared. In ascending order of precision and certainty, the following descriptions are used for estimates of the final project cost, the names being a reflection of the stage in which they are prepared:

1. Order of Magnitude
2. Feasibility
3. Capital Appropriation
4. Design Review
5. Pre-tender
6. Post-tender

Estimate to Complete — A COST TYPE. An estimate of the value that remains to be committed within a COST CLASS as of a specified date. The Estimate to Complete, when added to the COMMITMENT to date yields the ESTIMATED COST AT COMPLETION of the SCOPE of work in the class. This information should be updated monthly. A rigorous review of the Estimate to Complete for each COST CLASS should be implemented by the PROJECT MANAGER at regular specified intervals. See Chapter 12.

Estimated Cost at Completion — See FORECAST FINAL COST

Estimator's Allowance — An allowance included in a concept estimate because the estimator cannot predict the method the Consultant will use to satisfy the SCOPE requirements for the PROJECT.

Event — A point in time when certain conditions have been fulfilled, such as the start or completion of one or more ACTIVITIES.

Event Oriented Schedules — Systems which present information in terms of events (i.e. points in time). See Arrow Diagramming, Appendix E.

Executive Control Point — A point between project STAGES when top management has the opportunity to review the project status, the PLAN for the ensuing stage, verify its consistency with their latest business objectives and give, or withhold, approval to proceed.

Expenditure or **Project Expenditure** — A sum of money paid out for work relating to the PROJECT as evidenced by an invoice, receipt or similar payment voucher. For CONTROL purposes expenditures should be recognized when payment vouchers are approved by the PROJECT MANAGER, i.e. long before accounts payable disburses funds or cheques are cleared at the bank.

Extra Work Order — See FIELD ORDER

Feasibility Phase — See DEVELOPMENT PHASE

Feasibility Budget — The authorized APPROPRIATION of funds to cover the cost of work in the FEASIBILITY PHASE only.

Feasibility Report — A document that sets out all solutions considered to meet a particular set of PROJECT requirements, evaluates the ability of each to meet PROJECT objectives, gives an outline description of the recommended solution, and explains the reasons for selection.

Field Clarification — A Site Instruction issued to a CONSTRUCTION CONTRACTOR. A written pro-forma document intended to clarify or interpret the CONTRACT drawings or specifications at no change to the contract price.

Field Order Or Emergency Field Order, or Emergency Work Order. An unplanned authorization for a CONSTRUCTION CONTRACTOR to perform work beyond the SCOPE of its CONTRACT and hence a COMMITMENT DOCUMENT. A field order is generally issued in response to an urgent situation encountered during construction. It constitutes an extension to the CONTRACT.

Float — The additional time available to complete NON-CRITICAL ACTIVITIES or WORK ITEMS without affecting the CRITICAL PATH (i.e. the total project duration).

Force Account — See DAY WORK ACCOUNT

Forecast Final Cost — The sum of COMMITTED COST and ESTIMATED TO COMPLETE. See COST TYPES.

Forecast To Complete — See ESTIMATE TO COMPLETE

Forward Pass — Calculation of the EARLIEST START and EARLIEST FINISH dates on a precedence NETWORK.

Functional Program — A written description of the OWNER or USER NEEDS that must be fulfilled by a proposed facility. The description generally has a statement of the functions, production capacity and similar criteria. It is a component of the CONCEPTUAL DESIGN.

Holdback — Or retention. A sum of money withheld from a CONSTRUCTION CONTRACTOR's payment according to the terms of its CONTRACT, and/or statutory obligation to ensure protection against valid third party claims.

Implementation Phase — That part of the PROJECT life-cycle during which working drawings, specifications and CONTRACT documents are prepared, CONTRACTS are tendered and awarded, and the construction work undertaken. See also FEASIBILITY PHASE.

Inflation — See ESCALATION

Instruction or **Site Instruction** — See FIELD CLARIFICATION

Interest-During-Construction (IDC) — The cost of borrowing money to meet project construction expenditures

Invoice — A document issued by a CONTRACTOR as a request for payment for work performed in accordance with the terms of its CONTRACT. The invoice should be checked and coded by the project accountant before being sent to the PROJECT MANAGER for approval. An invoice is the document initiating a PROGRESS PAYMENT.

Latest Finish — The latest day a WORK ITEM can finish without affecting the PROJECT duration assuming that all subsequent work items start as soon as they are able and are completed in their expected times.

Latest Start — The latest day that a WORK ITEM can start without affecting the final PROJECT duration. This assumes that it is completed in its expected time and all subsequent work items start as soon as they are able and are completed in their expected times.

Letter Of Intent — A type of letter sometimes issued to a contractor to confirm the award of a CONTRACT and pending the signing of formal contract documents. It is a COMMITMENT DOCUMENT. It allows the contractor to prepare for mobilization. Permitting work to start on site before the contract is signed is not recommended as the OWNER is without full protection at that point until the CONSTRUCTION CONTRACT is signed.

Management — A process in the PROJECT MANAGEMENT system that consists of direction and CONTROL to gets results according to established performance standards for SCOPE, quality, time and cost. The process includes participation in setting the performance standards and in MONITORING performance.

Master Schedule — A SCHEDULE containing ACTIVITIES and MILESTONES corresponding to a high level of project CONTROL. It is the master reference base for time CONTROL and should only be revised under the conditions described in Chapter 17.

Milestone — A key or important intermediate goal in the NETWORK. A major milestone typically requires senior management approval before proceeding further.

Monitoring — The capture, organization and reporting of measures of performance against standards for PROJECT SCOPE, quality, time and cost; a SYSTEM process in PROJECT MANAGEMENT.

Needs or **User Needs** — Also REQUIREMENTS, the OWNER's or USER's requirements to be satisfied by a proposed facility. In the CONCEPTUAL DESIGN stage the needs are analyzed and formulated into a FUNCTIONAL PROGRAM. In the PLANNING and development phase the needs are translated into a PROJECT BRIEF.

Network, Network Diagram — A schematic display of the sequential and logical relationships of the ACTIVITIES that comprise the PROJECT. Two popular drawing conventions or notations for scheduling are ARROW and PRECEDENCE DIAGRAMMING.

Network Planning — A tool used for planning and scheduling a PROJECT. See Appendix E.

Node — In CPM networks, a point when all activities leading up to an EVENT have been completed and when all activities leaving the EVENT may start. Nodes are junction points in the network.

Non-Critical Activities or **Work Items** — Those ACTIVITIES or WORK ITEMS that have positive FLOAT (i.e. within defined limits, can take longer to complete than is planned without affecting the total project duration.)

Notice Of Change — See CHANGE ORDER

Overhead — Costs arising from management and supervision, office expenses, INTEREST-DURING-CONSTRUCTION, and any other general costs associated with the PROJECT not directly attributable to design or construction.

Overrun — An increase in the time or COST compared to the PLAN. A reduced SCOPE without a corresponding reduction in the time or COST would be considered an overrun.

Owner or **Sponsor** — The party legally responsible under the terms of a CONTRACT for financing the PROJECT.

Package — See WORK PACKAGE

Pert — A technique for PLANNING a PROJECT. See Appendix E.

Phase — A larger part of the life of a PROJECT. See FEASIBILITY PHASE and IMPLEMENTATION PHASE. A Phase may encompass several STAGES.

Physical Restraint — A situation in which a physical ACTIVITY or WORK ITEM must be completed before the next ACTIVITY or WORK ITEMS in the sequence can begin (e.g. concrete must harden before removing formwork).

Plan — A future course of action.

Planning — The process of preparing a PLAN. It involves answering the questions what must be done in the future to reach the PROJECT objective, how it will be done and when it will be done.

Policy Restraint — Someone in AUTHORITY dictates the sequence in which all or some part of the work is carried out on the PROJECT.

Positive Float — The amount of time available to complete NON-CRITICAL ACTIVITIES or WORK ITEMS without affecting the total PROJECT duration.

Precedence Diagramming — A technique used in CPM and PERT, see Appendix E.

Predecessor Work Item — A WORK ITEM that directly precedes one or more WORK ITEMS in the logic sequence of a precedence NETWORK.

Preliminary Design — The design prepared in the PLANNING stage of a PROJECT and submitted as part of the PROJECT BRIEF. The drawings and specifications that comprise the Preliminary Design should be clearly specified as a matter of policy and provide the basis for the Appropriation estimate.

Process — An orderly and progressive sequence of activities that may be represented by a network and that, on completion, results in the creation of a PRODUCT.

Procurement — A process for establishing contractual relationships to accomplish project objectives. The assembly, tendering and award of CONTRACTS or COMMITMENT DOCUMENTS. Specific procedures should be established for the Procurement Process.

Product — The output from a PROCESS in tangible or intangible form. Examples include the PROJECT BRIEF as an output from the planning phases, or the completed facility as an output from the producing phases. See also called DELIVERABLES.

Program Management — A management style very different from ADMINISTRATIVE or CORPORATE or enterprise MANAGEMENT. The objective of program management is to complete a set of projects usually related in some way by a common goal. The life of a program management organization may be quite extended. However, it is characterized by the completion of the projects or tasks under its responsibility, each of which has a clear and finite termination.

Program management is terminated when all its projects are completed. See also PROJECT MANAGEMENT.

Progress Payment or **Progress Draw** — A payment in response to an INVOICE submitted by a CONSTRUCTION CONTRACTOR, requesting payment for work completed, or otherwise progress to a specific date. The invoice should be supported by the supervising Consultant's Progress Payment Certificate. The term CLAIM should not be used to refer to regular billings for work carried out as part of the SCOPE of a CONTRACT.

Project — A process or undertaking that encompasses an entire set of ACTIVITIES having a definable starting point and well defined objectives the delivery of which signal the completion of the project. Projects are usually required to be accomplished within limited resources.

Project Break-Down Structure — See WORK BREAKDOWN STRUCTURE

Project Brief — Also called a Project Charter. A document submitted with a CAPITAL APPROPRIATION REQUEST for the IMPLEMENTATION of a PROJECT. See Chapter 7. A good project brief should include at a minimum:

- An introduction or executive summary
- A general statement of business aims and objectives associated with the project
- A statement of project scope
- The economic and technical approach adopted
- Justification, alternatives, areas of uncertainty and risk
- Regulatory approvals and requirements
- Preliminary design sketches, block diagrams, standards
- Project Master Schedule
- Procurement Plan
- Project estimate and proposed capital appropriation request
- Other resources required from the sponsoring organization e.g. land, space, staff, etc.
- Financial statement and economic projections
- Cash flow projection
- Quality, schedule and cost controls
- Project team organization

Project Budget — The authorized CAPITAL APPROPRIATION of funds generally based on the ESTIMATE contained in the accepted PROJECT BRIEF released for the IMPLEMENTATION phase of the PROJECT.

Project Close Out — The full completion of a PROJECT signed off by all responsible parties and the finalization of all paperwork. Contractually concluded by a consultant's TOTAL PERFORMANCE Certificate.

Project Code — A set of symbols assigned to a set of COST CLASSES or subdivisions of the SCOPE of work in a PROJECT. The Project Code reflects a systematic (or hierarchic) sub-division of SCOPE i.e. its WORK BREAKDOWN STRUCTURE.

Project Cost — Any of the COST TYPES (APPROPRIATION, COMMITMENT, EXPENDITURE or ESTIMATE TO COMPLETE) associated with the total SCOPE of work in a PROJECT, i.e. the sum of all COST CLASSES forming the PROJECT. The Project Cost should comprise all of:

1. The cost of all work in the PLANNING PHASES of the Project
2. The cost of all work in the IMPLEMENTATION PHASES of the Project
3. OWNER's management and overhead costs during the IMPLEMENTATION PHASE (e.g. Consultant Services, Corporate Overheads, Reserve for SCOPE Changes, Land, Financing, etc.)

See also CONSTRUCTION COST.

Project Director — The owner's representative who has responsibility for overseeing the project or projects; the manager of a very large project that demands senior level responsibility; or the person at the board level in an organization who has the overall responsibility for project management.

Project Hand Over — The acceptance of the facility by the facility operators for occupancy and training even though construction may not be fully completed.

Project Management — May be informally defined as "The art of directing and coordinating human and material resources to achieve stated objectives within limits of time, budget, and stakeholder's satisfaction." Or more formally defined as "The application of modern MANAGEMENT techniques and systems to the execution of a PROJECT from start to finish, to achieve predetermined objectives of SCOPE, QUALITY, time and COST, to the equal satisfaction of those involved. See also MANAGEMENT.

Project Manager — The person who heads up the PROJECT TEAM and is assigned the authority and responsibility for conducting the project and meeting project objectives through PROJECT MANAGEMENT.

Project Risks — A term used to refer to a broad complex of sometimes interrelated project EVENTS detrimental to PROJECT success. The likelihood of such EVENTS is difficult if not impossible to forecast with any degree of certainty. See Chapter 6.

Project Sponsor — See Project Director.

Project Team — The central management group headed by the PROJECT MANAGER and responsible for the direction, conduct and successful outcome of a PROJECT.

Purchase Order — A COMMITMENT DOCUMENT generally used only for the procurement of materials and equipment by the organization. Its use may be limited to a maximum value. The document is addressed to a supplier and commits the Organization to the purchase according to the terms and conditions of the order. A Purchase Order is different from a CHANGE ORDER, although it may be modified to double as such.

Quality or **Quality Standards** — Stipulations of measurable physical properties or characteristics, which materials, equipment or constructed items must have as a minimum. Basic design criteria and standards should be defined and signed off by the OWNER in the CONCEPTUAL DESIGN. In a CONTRACT document, quality standards are generally expressed in the specifications by reference to published Codes and Standards.

Request For Appropriation — See CAPITAL APPROPRIATION REQUEST.

Requirements — See NEEDS.

Reserve For Scope Changes — A sum of money set aside for changes in the OWNER'S REQUIREMENTS and to be used only at the direction of the OWNER.

Resource Leveling — See Resource Allocation in Appendix E.

Responsibility — The duties, assignments, and ACCOUNTABILITY for results associated with a designated position in the organization. The responsibilities of individual persons on specific projects during the IMPLEMENTATION PHASE should be made known through formal, precise statements, in the PROJECT BRIEF and in CONTRACTS for Consultants and CONSTRUCTION CONTRACTORS. Both sets of statements should be made known to other members of the Organization's staff.

Schedule — A time sequence of ACTIVITIES and EVENTS that represent an operating timetable. The schedule specifies the relative beginning and ending times of ACTIVITIES and the occurrence times of events. A schedule may be presented on a calendar framework or on an elapsed time scale.

Scheduling — The process of converting a general or outline PLAN for a project into a time-based SCHEDULE based on available resources and time constraints.

Scope, Project Scope — The set of verifiable end products, or outputs, which the PROJECT TEAM undertakes to provide to the project sponsor. The required set of end results or products with specified physical or functional characteristics.

Scope of Work — The work content of a PROJECT or any component of a PROJECT, such as a WORK PACKAGE or a COST CLASS, i.e. a summary description of the work involved in constructing a PROJECT. Note: Scope of Work is different from a Scope Statement.

Scope Statement — A summary description of the PROJECT's measurable products, intermediate or end-items, or DELIVERABLES.

Sign-Off — The formal acceptance of a planned or proposed course of action, constituting AUTHORITY for the planner or proposer to proceed with the action. Key sign-offs in the PROJECT life-cycle, by OWNER and USER, occur at the conclusion of the CONCEPT and PLANNING PHASES.

Slack — See FLOAT

Stage — A smaller portion of the project life-cycle. Stages may be identifiable by milestone EVENTS that are SIGN-OFFS or approvals by authorities outside the Project Team. Stages in the life-cycle of a construction PROJECT may be identified as

0. Pre project studies of needs and opportunities
1. Project concepts and economic studies
2. Feasibility or functional design
3. Engineering, project planning and project brief
4. Working drawings and specifications
5. Tendering and contract award
7. Construction
8. Facility commissioning, start up or hand-over

Note: Operation of the resulting facility is part of the Facility Life-Cycle, not the Project Life-Cycle

Substantial Performance — Is considered to be reached when:

a) The work or a substantial part of it is ready for use or is being used for the purpose intended
b) The work to be done under the CONTRACT can be completed or corrected at a cost of not more than (say) 1% to 3% of the contract price depending on the size of the CONTRACT, and
c) Is so certified by a Certificate of Substantial Performance issued by the supervising consultant.

Successor Work Item — A WORK ITEM that directly follows one or more WORK ITEMS in the logic sequence of a precedence NETWORK.

System — A methodical arrangement of ACTIVITIES or parts designed to achieve repetitive or reproducible results.

Task — The term usually used to refer to a piece of work contained within a WORK PACKAGE. While it is an identifiable piece of work, its extent is less than that which qualifies it as a WORK PACKAGE. See also ACTIVITY.

Tender and Award Stage — That part of the PROJECT life-cycle during which CONSTRUCTION CONTRACTORS are invited to prepare and submit bids, a selection is made and CONTRACTS are awarded. See also IMPLEMENTATION PHASE.

Top Down Cost Estimating — The preparation of a cost ESTIMATE by using judgment and experience to arrive at an overall total amount, usually done by an experienced estimator or manager making a subjective comparison of the PROJECT with similar previous projects.

Total Float — The amount that an ACTIVITY can be lengthened without delaying the PROJECT completion, assuming that all other activities are done in their normal time.

Total Performance — Is achieved when all work, including all deficiencies listed at the time of the SUBSTANTIAL PERFORMANCE inspection is complete, accepted, and a Certificate of Total Performance is issued by the supervising consultant.

Trade-Off — In an economic analysis or assessment of DESIGN ALTERNATIVES, certain products or certain input resources are interrelated so that increasing one reduces the others. Between such products or resources there is a "trade-off" cost or revenue as one is substituted for another. In preparing a building design, for example, there is a relationship between heating capacity and amount of thermal insulation installed. This can be translated into a set of "trade-off" costs that vary over the range of feasible heating capacity values for any given temperature range. See also VALUE MANAGEMENT.

Updating, Schedule Updating — Revision of a SCHEDULE or NETWORK to reflect progress to date. Fully completed items are eliminated and the date of the update becomes the new reference date for the PROJECT.

User — The intended occupant or operator of the constructed facility.

Value Management — A technique for optimizing cost and/or performance. See Appendix E.

Variance — The difference between an actual or estimated cost and an authorized appropriation for the SCOPE of work in a COST CLASS. Variances can be negative (under-run) or positive (over-run).

Work Breakdown Structure — A product-oriented family tree of elements that completely organizes, defines and graphically displays the components, software, services and data to be produced, as well as the work to be done, to achieve the specified PROJECT outcome. See Work Breakdown, Appendix E.

Work Breakdown Structure Dictionary — A publication that describes in detailed narrative form each element of a WORK BREAKDOWN STRUCTURE, the element's products, work content, unique MASTER CODE identifier and other pertinent information.

Work Item — A portion of the PROJECT that can be clearly identified and isolated.

Work Package — A generic term for units of work as a sub-division of the total SCOPE of a PROJECT. As a PROJECT progresses through the various STAGES, work packages will be identified at progressively lower (greater) levels of detail. At any given level the content of the work packages will be entirely contained within any given CODE item definition. While an agreement or CONTRACT will contain one or more work packages, such work packages should be the responsibility of only one department, consultant, sub-consultant, contractor or trade contractor. The smallest work package should still be large enough to be a scope of work that could be competitively bid and awarded as a CONTRACT by itself. A Work Package may be further sub-divided into TASKS and resources (labor and materials etc.).

Zero Float — Describes a WORK ITEM or ACTIVITY on the CRITICAL PATH (i.e. a delay in its completion would cause a corresponding delay in the project completion date).

Index

D

E